DEACONESSES

This book is a remarkable achievement: scrupulously attentive to both history and theology; inclusive of Orthodox traditions and experience of the broadest purview; concrete, practical, and informative; inspiring in presentation, and visionary in scope. Required reading for all who care about the health and future of Orthodoxy as a living presence in our world.

> Dr. Susan Ashbrook Harvey
> William Prescott and Annie McClelland Smith Professor of History and Religion, Brown University

As I write these words, an Orthodox parish dear to me is grieving. Our long-serving deacon passed away a few days ago. His funeral and burial are tomorrow. As I look back on his ministry in the parish and beyond, my appreciation grows for the deacons—both women and men—who over the centuries have regarded ordination to the diaconate not as a stepping stone to a more exalted position in the ecclesiastical hierarchy, but as dedication to *martyria* and *diakonia*, to witness and service.

The scholarly articles gathered in *Deaconesses* draw on multiple disciplines to argue for restoration of this venerable order. Equally compelling are the shorter reflections, which present contexts for diaconal ministry that we may not often think of, whether in the past or today in the Far East, sub-Saharan Africa and other lands of mission or in ancient homelands in the Near East that are now wracked by war and civil strife. Characterizing these contexts are the real needs to which diaconal ministry tries to respond—and very often these are the needs of women. In antiquity, before the baptism of infants became common, an obvious task for female deacons involved catechesis and maintenance of decorum at baptisms. An obvious task for female deacons today—a need as yet largely unmet—includes advocacy and care in cases of molestation, spousal abuse, and other situations in which the marginalized and "invisible" of society need to be given voice and agency. As we face the challenges of a rapidly changing world, may the ministry of deacons both male and female flourish once again!

> V. Rev. John H. Erickson
> Professor Emeritus and former Dean
> St. Vladimir's Orthodox Theological Seminary

DEACONESSES:

A Tradition for Today and Tomorrow

Edited by

John Chryssavgis • Niki Papageorgiou

Marilyn Rouvelas • Petros Vassiliadis

Holy Cross Orthodox Press

Brookline, Massachusetts

© Holy Cross Orthodox Press, 2023
Published by Holy Cross Orthodox Press
Hellenic College, Inc.
50 Goddard Avenue
Brookline, MA 02445

All rights reserved. No part of this publication may be reproduced stored in a retrieval system, or transmitted, in any form or by any means, electronic, mechanical, photocopying, recording or otherwise with the prior permission of Holy Cross Orthodox Press.

ISBN 978-1-935317-82-1
ISBN 1-935317-82-2

Library of Congress Cataloging-in-Publication Data

Names: Chryssavgis, John, editor. | Papageorgiou, Niki, editor. | Rouvelas, Marilyn, editor. | Vassiliadis, Petros, editor. | Holy Cross Orthodox Press, issuing body.
Title: Deaconesses : a tradition for today and tomorrow / edited by John Chryssavgis, Niki Papageorgiou, Marilyn Rouvelas, Petros Vassiliadis.
Description: Brookline, Massachusetts : Holy Cross Orthodox Press, [2022] | Includes bibliographical references.
Identifiers: ISBN: 978-1-935317-82-1
Subjects: LCSH: Deaconesses—Orthodox Eastern Church. | Deaconesses—Christianity—History. | Women in Christianity—History. | Women in church work. | Ordination of women—Orthodox Eastern Church. | Ordination of women—Christianity. Women clergy—Orthodox Eastern Church. | Women clergy—Christianity.
Classification: LCC: BX341.52 .D43 2022 | DDC: 262.1419082—dc23

*Dedicated to all laity, theologians, and hierarchs
who courageously and patiently contribute
to the restoration of the Order of Deaconesses*

*On the occasion of the 35th anniversary of the
1988 Rhodes Consultation*

CONTENTS

Foreword	xi
Message by His All-Holiness Ecumenical Patriarch Bartholomew	
Introduction	xv
The Editors	

I. GENERAL PERSPECTIVES

Chapter 1	3
"The Diaconate in Christ": A Fresh Look at the Role of Deacons *John Chryssavgis*	
Chapter 2	11
The Role of Women in the Church, the Ordination of Women, and the Order of Deaconesses: An Orthodox Theological Approach *Petros Vassiliadis*	
Chapter 3	39
Female Deacons in the Byzantine Church *Valerie Karras*	
Chapter 4	97
Orthodox Responses to the Possibility of a Rejuvenated Female Diaconate: The United States Context *Teva Regule*	

II. SCRIPTURAL PERSPECTIVES

Chapter 5   113
Christian Women at the Altar Table:
Ancient Precedent for the Reinstitution of the
Order of Deaconesses
Ally Kateusz

Chapter 6   135
A Sociological Approach to the
Invisibility of Deaconesses
Niki Papageorgiou

Chapter 7   141
The Gospel References to Women:
A Sociological Reminder
Dimitrios Passakos

Chapter 8   155
The New Theories about Mary Magdalene
Aikaterini Drosia

III. HISTORICAL PERSPECTIVES

Chapter 9   165
The Person of Deaconess Phoebe
in the Work of Church Fathers
and Ecclesiastical Writers in Early Christianity
Eirini Artemi

Chapter 10   177
St. Nino and Ordination of Women Deacons
in Georgian Tradition
Leonide Beka Ebralidze

Chapter 11   189
Female Diaconia in the Context of Ecclesiologies
Zoya Dashevskaya

Chapter 12   209
The Order of Deaconesses according
to the 1917–18 Sobor Discussion
Alexander Mramornov

IV. ECUMENICAL PERSPECTIVES

Chapter 13   219
Women Deacons in the Roman Catholic Church
Phyllis Zagano

CONTENTS

Chapter 14   229
Female Diaconal Service in the
Coptic Orthodox Church: Past and Present
Christine Chaillot

Chapter 15   251
A Nearly Forgotten History:
Women Deacons in the Armenian Church
Knarik O. Meneshian

Chapter 16   269
The Distinctive Diaconate Case in the Anglican Church:
An Orthodox Approach
Spyridoula-Eleni Mantziou

V. SPIRITUAL PERSPECTIVES

Chapter 17   281
The Institution of Deaconesses in the
Light of the Modern Mission of the Orthodox Church
Evi Voulgaraki-Pissina

Chapter 18   293
The School of Deaconesses and the
Opposition in the Church of Greece
Vassiliki Stathokosta

Chapter 19   305
St. Nektarios and the Deaconesses
Evanthia Adamtziloglou

Chapter 20   317
The Role of Women in the Life of the Church
according to St. Amphilochius of Patmos
Nikolaos G. Tsirevelos

Appendix   329
  (i) In Memoriam of Deaconess Maria   329
  (ii) The Statement of Support by Orthodox Liturgists   339
  (iii) Resources   343

Contributors   345

FOREWORD

It is with special joy that we welcome this important collection of essays on the historical and theological sources related to the fundamental role of women in the early and Byzantine Church, as well as the significance of the order of deaconesses throughout the centuries to our day.

The Church has never ceased to encourage and promote women to participate in various areas of its multidimensional ministry, while always seeking and creating new opportunities for their effective contribution to the life of the Church. In the same spirit, therefore, we believe that the effort to rekindle the order of deaconesses must continue, especially given that since the time of the apostles, deaconesses have proved a vital and invaluable part of the edification of the faithful, who always honored and respected them. Moreover, despite the fact that the practice of ordaining deaconesses periodically dwindled, it was never formally abolished by the Church.

The late Professor Evangelos Theodorou, an Archon of the Ecumenical Throne, tirelessly championed the argument that deaconesses were established in their ministry not simply by a laying-on-of-hands (*cheirothesia*), but by sacramental ordination performed within the altar space and before the Holy Table during Divine Liturgy, exactly like the ordination of the male deacon. Deacons and deaconesses have, according to Professor Theodorou, a "sacramental diaconal priesthood," with the only difference being that the deacon can later also obtain the "sacramental hierurgical priesthood."

We wish to take this opportunity to praise the priceless and diverse ministries of Orthodox women throughout the history of the people of God. We would like, instead of providing any personal comment, to reiterate what the ever-memorable Professor Ioannis Foundoulis once remarked about the importance of women's contributions to Church life:

> A simple but wise and devout man said some years ago: "If there were no women, then there would be no religion." He was of course referring to Divine Worship, which for him was identical with "religion." And within Divine Worship, from the depth of his simple heart, he included all those little things that constitute the paramount issue of Divine Worship: the chanting at the supplicatory and salutations services, the steadfast attendance at the liturgical services in the temple, the lighting of vigil oil lamps and candles, the incensing of icons, the baking and offering of *prosfora*, the preparation of *kollyva,* the adornment of churches and the cleaning of chapels, the familiarity with festive, holiday, and fasting periods for the proper arrangement of family life, the teaching of their children and grandchildren—and, why not, of their husbands—about the appropriate way of prayer and participation in Divine Worship, in the liturgical gatherings on Sundays and feast days, as well as the preparation for and the partaking of Holy Communion. I have a feeling that he was right!

Therefore, we honor the hosts of Holy Women for their total dedication to Christ and the Church, while praising the diaconal spirit and sacrificial love of all Orthodox women who continue to sustain the truth in love.

Finally, we extend our wholehearted paternal and patriarchal blessings to the editors and contributors, as well as to the readers of this volume, which we believe should be received and read with great interest for the edification of the Church. May the life-giving grace and great mercy of our God of love be with you all.

At the Ecumenical Patriarchate, Spring 2022

Prayerfully yours,

Bartholomew
*Archbishop of Constantinople – New Rome
and Ecumenical Patriarch*

INTRODUCTION

The diaconal ministry and witness have for centuries been marginalized at the expense and peril of the image and fullness of the church. We are quite fortunate to live at the dawn of a blessed era that is characterized by optimistic signs on both the institutional and scholarly levels. One powerful and paramount example of this is His All-Holiness Ecumenical Patriarch Bartholomew's bold conviction and determination to convene the Holy and Great Council in June 2016, which declared that "the Church does not live for herself but . . . for the whole world" (Preamble).

At the same time, the future of the Orthodox Church's witness to the world depends on a clear and unconditional affirmation of the entire Body of Christ, both men and women. The dignity and responsibility of women must be affirmed not simply at a soteriological level, but also at a liturgical and administrative one. Indeed, the discussion about the role of women in the church, along with their access to the "sacramental" diaconal ministry, are issues that preoccupy the current theological discourse. More details, both archeological and biblical, as well as historical and theological, are increasingly coming to the surface. This book raises much of this evidence, focusing on the diaconal nature of the Christian vocation and priesthood, which has been overlooked by centuries of patriarchal bias and institutional clericalism. The church should always be a sacrament of Eucharist, not reflect a pyramid of authority.

Many of the contributors to this volume presented their papers and reflections at the second international symposium, "Deaconesses: Past–Present–Future," (January 31–February 2, 2020) organized by the Center for Ecumenical, Missiological and Environmental Studies (CEMES) and the International Hellenic University at the University of Thessaloniki in Greece.[1] They explore the diaconal ministry of women on the basis of recent theological and academic developments, primarily in biblical, archeological, and patristic scholarship—adding to the foundational work already done by many scholars. This book is meant to showcase the great diversity of perspectives from both within the Orthodox Church as well as in other religious communities regarding the order of deaconesses. It features pieces that range in approach from the highest levels of academic scholarship to the most fundamental, practical applications based on personal knowledge, first-hand experience, with occasional polemics. This broad approach is taken for two main reasons: first, the latest developments for the order of deaconesses affect all levels of God's Holy Church and cross ecumenical and regional lines; second, it is important to showcase the overwhelming support for this institution among not merely some random minority of isolated individuals, but rather among many respected Christians of good conscience across the globe.

The overall conclusion and general recommendation of this symposium and comprising the foundation for this publication, was that "there is no biblical or theological, canonical or liturgical, patristic or pastoral reason for the contemporary church to delay or obstruct the full restoration of the historical institution of deaconesses."

The seminal symposium opened with official messages from the Ecumenical Patriarchate (which organized the historical meeting on women and deaconesses in 1988 on the island of Rhodes, Greece), the Patriarchate of Alexandria (which recently tried to reestablish the order of deaconesses in parts of its African missions), and the Church of Greece (which hosted the event in light of its own practical experience with deaconesses during the twentieth century). This ensuing

---

1. The first CEMES conference was entitled "Deaconesses: The Ordination of Women and Orthodox Theology" (January 22–24, 2015).

book from the symposium has benefited from the editorial skills of Fr. Gregory Edwards, who carefully translated or amended texts submitted in Greek.

Some authors of this collective effort also issued an appeal through a "Letter to the Churches" on the importance of restoring deaconesses, stressing:

1. The urgent need to revive the diaconate, male and female, in response to growing pastoral demands and missionary challenges facing parishes and faithful throughout the world.
2. That the Orthodox Church has always retained the order of the deaconess, even when this fell into disuse in times of turmoil or persecution.
3. The great importance of restoring the order of deaconess as distinct from ordination to the priesthood and not merely as a reflection of and in response to modern developments or expectations.
4. That the appropriate moment (kairos) to implement the decisions of the Inter-Orthodox Consultation in Rhodes (1988) is the present, when the church is called to address unprecedented challenges.
5. That the initiative of the Patriarchate of Alexandria in appointing deaconesses is prophetic and deserving of support and emulation by other Orthodox Churches throughout the world.
6. That the scholarly evidence in support of the male and female diaconate should be pursued in order to define the principles and parameters for restoring the order of deaconesses.

A creative revival of the diaconate for men and women in our age can arguably become a source of resurrection for the ordained ministry as a whole, thereby playing a crucial role in the broader mission of the church. In this respect, the restoration of the diaconate in general, and of deaconesses in particular, may well prove both timely and vital.

The Editors

I

GENERAL PERSPECTIVES

Chapter One

"THE DIACONATE IN CHRIST"
A FRESH LOOK AT THE ROLE OF DEACONS

John Chryssavgis

Reimagining the Diaconate in the Church

Let me begin with two personal remarks: the first is an anecdote, the second a personal confession:

I recall a striking image of the important role that deacons have in our church from an experience not too long ago in Constantinople. Following a Lenten supper, the Ecumenical Patriarch entered the small chapel where some of the clergy were waiting to commence the nightly compline service. As His All-Holiness looked around, he was amazed to find seven deacons and not a single priest; all of the priests were on assignment elsewhere. Sensing his surprise, I cheekily said: "Your All-Holiness, this is exactly what the church should look like. Lots of deacons, only some priests, and even fewer bishops!" Let's not forget that, while providing a useful and helpful analogy for us today, Justinian's paradigm of sixty priests, one hundred deacons, forty deaconesses, and ninety subdeacons reflected cutbacks in sixth-century Constantinople!

Yet as I looked around, it occurred to me that each deacon had a special and specific ministry: one served in the private patriarchal office, another as his archdeacon in liturgy and administration, while I served in the United States; another was deputy secretary of the holy synod, while another was an office scribe; the remaining two worked in the library and the English office. Moreover, what was evident was that these clergy had served as deacons for many years; there is a long tradition of diaconal ministry at the Phanar. My point here is twofold: These clergymen did not have to be priests in order to be ordained; and they did not have to be priests in order to carry out their ministries. It was extraordinary, even inspiring to watch as the patriarch moved to the front and vested the priestly stole—an unassuming but compelling sign that he too had a precise and distinct role at that moment, beyond any official title or institutional office. As St. John Chrysostom reminds us, "even bishops are called deacons."

And here is my confession, in fact an act of thanksgiving, in the definition of "confession" in the Psalms: I did not intend to become a deacon. Perhaps unlike most ordained clergymen, I became a deacon by serendipity, not selection; coincidentally, not conscientiously. Although I cringe when people tell me they were "called to become priests," I believe that I was called to become a deacon—a conviction I embraced in 1984, when my bishop asked if I would be ordained and remain a deacon in order to serve the church expressly in the ministries of education and administration.

This is why, several years ago, in a meeting of Orthodox bishops held in Chicago, I felt that one hierarch touched on the heart of ordination as vocation, when he asked me, "Is someone even called to the diaconate? Do we not normally say that people are called to the priesthood?" I remain convinced today—as I replied then—that one is not called to the diaconate any more than one is not called to the priesthood or episcopate. We are called primarily to the royal priesthood, to the priestly ministry of all believers and to serve (*diakonia*—the very word means "service").

That may surprise you because you may be wondering why on earth so many people feel that they are called to the priesthood, enter seminary, and are then ordained. What I am saying is that this is not the proper starting-point; these are not the right questions when it comes to vocation.

You see, I learned from a young age from my presbyter-father that our noblest task is to become followers of Christ, who came not to be served but to serve (Mark 10:45). This implies that our noblest goal is to be Christians—not deacons, not priests, and certainly not bishops. And the journey to become disciples of Christ begins at the moment of baptism. St. Ignatius of Antioch prayed "not only to be called a Christian, but also to be found one" (Rom 3). I would argue that the sacrament of ordination is actually much easier to reach than the sacrament of baptism is to undergo.

There is something else that I also learned over many years in church administration, parish ministry, and theological education, namely, that the priesthood has become the cause of much confusion and suffering, much abuse and anxiety, resulting from a misunderstanding of authority in the church—and this is a problem encountered by both clergy and laity. This is why I believe that understanding the diaconate allows us to better understand all three orders of the priesthood.

Unfortunately, tradition and convention have an uncanny ability to obscure the original and theological reasons for which the early church defined the threefold ministry and perceived the diaconate. Yet, toward the end of the first century, Ignatius of Antioch asserts that the church realizes its unity most completely and most comprehensively only when the community is "with the bishop and the presbyters and the deacons." St. Ignatius adds that "without these, [the community] cannot even be called a church."

As the early church expanded and extended into the fourth century, the golden age of the diaconate, deacons played more meaningful and multiple roles. However, deacons were never considered novices or apprentices. There was never an indication or implication that deacons were a condition or obligation for elevation to priesthood. And so in the seventh century, Isidore of Seville would state, "Without the ministry of deacons, the priest has the name but not the office. The priest consecrates and sanctifies, but the deacon dispenses and shares."

An Alternative Concept of Priesthood in the Church

Unfortunately, over the centuries, we have misconceived and even distorted the ministry, focusing more on the aspect of authority and grace rather than on the practice of service and sacrifice. Deacons became transitional and dispensable, in many cases almost symbolic and invisible. And while this phenomenon was never restricted to a particular region or period, the Church of Russia even sought (on several occasions during the nineteenth century) to eliminate the diaconate entirely, while no more credible a theologian than Fr. Georges Florovsky saw little if any purpose or prospect for the restoration of the diaconate.

Thus, seminarians are ordained to the priesthood after serving only briefly as deacons, as if they are somehow expected to "move on" or "move up." The diaconate has been reduced to a stepping-stone for the priesthood, just as the celibate priesthood is for the episcopate—the latter two stages somehow considered more significant for the ordained ministry; whereas the diaconate is reduced to a sub-priesthood, rarely perceived as a lifelong or permanent office.

I would argue that there is something seriously missing from the ordained ministry if deacons are undervalued or omitted in the overall picture. A fuller vision of ministry should equally recognize the role of the bishop as the bond of unity, the role of the presbyter as the celebrant of sacraments, and the role of the deacon as completing this circle of community. We really need an alternative vision of the priesthood understood from the following three perspectives:

First, the image of the church that we should have in our mind and conversation is that of a dinner table, and not of a corporate ladder. The church is not a pyramid, where all attention and authority are focused on the summit. We should imagine the church as a sacrament, where the focus is on the Eucharist, where "the least is greatest" (Matt 23:12), "the last is first" (Matt 20:16), and "the leader is servant" (Matt 20:26). If this is our "icon" of the church, then we can well imagine deacons as waiting at tables or serving community needs, rather than as pawns at the bottom of some institution.

Second, I propose a circular approach to ordination and ministry. Try to recall the movements of a deacon in liturgy—constantly moving inside and outside the altar, between the Gospel or chalice and the congregation or communicants. Deacons are mediators between clergy and laity, striving to hold together and reconcile the church and the world.

This constant motion of the deacon defines the "go-between" dimension of the diaconate. Think of servants/deacons moving between the master and the guests at the feast in Cana of Galilee (John 2); think of the angels ministering as deacons after Christ's temptation in the desert (Matt 4), or the deacons described as ambassadors of the church to the world by Ignatius of Antioch (*Philad.* 10). This "between-ness" also explains the ambiguity of the deacon's status as clergy and laity while at the same time neither clergy nor laity—an ambiguity that I believe reflects the fundamental and essential nature of a church "in the world" but "not of the world" (John 17:11–16).

Third, let me draw your attention to another perspective. When we adopt a linear approach to the church, we tend to think of the apostolic succession of bishops as an unbroken line of continuity with the early disciples. However, we should not only reflect on the church's historical dimension; we should also remember its horizontal dimension, which includes all its members and all its concerns. The church is always at its best when it embraces the whole world, and the church is clearly at its worst when it isolates itself from the world.

Widening Our Concept of the Diaconate

Now by breadth, I mean the fullness or "plenitude" of the church, which implies the diversity of gifts expressed in the "royal priesthood of believers" that I referred to above. Such gifts include talents and skills of baptized believers (men and women), who should be enlisted sacramentally by the church. That is what "calling" signifies; it is not some presumption—arrogant at worst and ignorant at best—of an otherworldly enlightenment, but the church's discernment of particular abilities and aptitudes in the community. It is a "chrismation" of these "charismata" in the church. This is how I understand Paul's Letter to the Corinthians (1 Cor 12) about the variety of gifts and multitude of services within the Body of Christ.

Thus, for example, matters of pastoral care, practical administration, financial concern, and even theological education could easily be delegated to male and female deacons. Here is my vision: Someone whose administrative gifts are welcomed for the organization of a parish could be "ordained" to perform this task in the community, serving as a deacon either part-time or full-time in that capacity. The same would occur with someone proficient in youth ministry or fundraising, in catechism or chaplaincy, in pastoral care or social work, and so on. Deacons may also be "called" and "commissioned" to preach, counsel, and perform parish or community services.

In this way, ministerial dignity would be "conferred" on these individuals, while their particular strengths would be formally incorporated and solemnly integrated within the community. They would be empowered through an imposition of hands and by the grace of the Spirit, their various charismata sacramentally bound to the holy altar.

The fundamental and essential question in our minds should be: does someone have to be a priest in order to do what he is doing? "Ordained" is one thing; "ordained a priest" is another! Restoring and reviving the diaconate could thus have profound significance and consequence for our parishes and their ministries, complementing—not competing with—the priesthood. Let me flesh this out a little more:

- The work of the Orthodox Christian Mission Center executive director is a diakonia, not the ministry of a priest; the CEO of International Orthodox Christian Charities could be a deacon, not a layman.
- Teaching at a theological faculty or Orthodox seminary (like Holy Cross and St. Vladimir's) may be a deacon's calling—neither a priest's nor a layperson's. Otherwise, it actually complicates and confounds matters.
- Facilitating a youth office or camp program of a diocese is a diakonia, not the training or waiting ground for candidates to the priesthood?

- Chaplains and counselors on campuses, military bases, hospitals, or prisons should be ordained deacons.

Choir directors, parish outreach leaders, young adult ministers, adult educators, and stewardship officers—these are specific services optimally suited for deacons, including women who are both involved in and leading these types of ministries and more, even as chaplains recognized and blessed by a number of Orthodox Churches. Therefore, women should be sacramentally ordained deacons in the same way they were in the early church. I am not saying that all of these ministries are reasons for ordination to the diaconate, but they are certainly not reasons for exclusion from the diaconate.

All of these vital ministries may sometimes seem like they are on the margins of the church, but we should remember that history is often written on the margins of the world, not behind the closed doors of a synod.

Turning the Church Upside-Down

I have argued that our understanding of the priesthood should be turned upside-down, flowing not from the top down, but springing up from the fundamental or foundational notion of diakonia and the grassroots level of ecclesia. That is how the faithful will appreciate what matters most in the church's ministry. A revival of the diaconate could also generate a revitalization of our parishes, which would become more global and less insular. Because the diaconate would not just be rooted in the apostolic experience; it would reflect a very modern expression and may awaken fresh ministries, unrestricted by traditional reproductions.

You see, beyond authority and bureaucracy in the church, beyond leadership and management in the parish, there is the priceless dimension of service and serving. Beyond celebrating liturgy and sacraments in the holy altar, there is attending to human beings as the living altar of the Body of Christ. And deacons symbolize—actually, they realize—the evangelical precept of service. When the disciples asked Jesus about priorities and privileges, he reminded them that they were not to seek positions of power in order to dominate others. Nor were they given any assurance of entitlement or authority on earth or in heaven. They were asked whether they were prepared to share Christ's suffering and death: "Whoever wants to be great among you must be your servant; whoever wants to be first must be servant of all" (Mark 10:43).

Deacons were always closer to the humble laity than the other clergy. Being familiar with the wider community, they were the bishop's "eyes and ears." Understanding the daily struggles of parishioners, they could prepare the *prothesis* and recite the intercessions. And in dismissing the congregation after the Eucharist, they were sending them back into the world as witnesses to the kingdom and its righteousness.

In a word, the deacon's role was administrative—serving alongside, supporting and sustaining the ministry—reinforcing the church as collegial, communal, and collaborative. Their task was to discern and facilitate the ministry of all people, assisting and providing for them in their challenges, enhancing and enriching community and unity in the church. This is precisely why, whereas bishop saints are normally recognized as such by virtue of being bishops, deacon saints are always acknowledged for their specific service—as martyrs or confessors, evangelizers or philanthropists. Their unique charisma or office is their distinctive diakonia in the church's ministry.

And so deacons were especially responsible for organizing and administering charitable programs for the suffering. After all, the church is expected to be fully present where people are vulnerable, to stand among those who are marginalized, to relieve the hungry and thirsty, to welcome the homeless and the foreigner. Deacons established social and financial structures where outcasts are accepted and the needy fed. This is what gives heart and hope to the church. And, ultimately, this community becomes a visible sign and tangible icon of the alternative justice of the heavenly kingdom that we all seek.

Chapter Two

THE ROLE OF WOMEN IN THE CHURCH, THE ORDINATION OF WOMEN, AND THE ORDER OF DEACONESSES: AN ORTHODOX THEOLOGICAL APPROACH[1]

Petros Vassiliadis

The role of women in the church, their access to the "sacramental" priesthood, and the order of deaconesses are three different though interrelated issues that occupy our current theological discourse. Within the Orthodox Christian world, the ordination of women was by and large vehemently rejected as an issue of non-Orthodox pastoral concern and a Western phenomenon, mainly influenced by the ideals of modernity.

Having been engaged during my tenure as an academic theologian with other more debated issues in Orthodox theology, I was reluctant—as so many other theologians in our time—to engage in thorough scholarly research on such a non-issue for my church. However, recently, I was for more than two years actively involved with a seminar and an international conference on "Deaconesses, the Ordination of Women, and Orthodox Theology" and especially

---

1. Most of what follows came from my article dedicated to His Beatitude Theodore II, the Pope and Patriarch of Alexandria, after his church's synodical decision to restore the order of deaconesses for their mission, published in my book *ΑΝΤΙΔΩΡΟΝ of Memory and Honour* (Thessaloniki: 8A CEMES Publications, 2019), 21–37.

with the editing of its proceedings.² I, therefore, feel compelled—not to say responsible—to attempt an Orthodox theological approach, especially after the courageous decision of the Patriarch of Alexandria Mgr. Theodoros II to revive the order of deaconesses in his church. Dedicating with gratitude this study to him, I will try to responsibly respond to the above delicate issues on the basis of both the latest decisions of the Holy and Great Council of the Orthodox Church, held in Crete in June 2016,³ and of the latest scientific results of contemporary Orthodox theology.

***

The Holy and Great Council in its mission document, "The Mission of the Orthodox Church in Today's World," declared that the hope of the church:

> Is experienced and foretasted by the Church, especially each time the Divine Eucharist is celebrated, bringing *together* (1 Cor 11:20) the *scattered children of God* (John 11:52) without regard to race, sex, age, social, or any other condition into a single body where there is neither Jew nor Greek, *there is neither slave nor free, there is neither male nor female* (Gal 3:28; cf. Col 3:11) (Preamble).

And in Section E on "The Attitude of the Church toward Discrimination," the Council stated that "The Orthodox Church . . . believes that God "has made from one blood every nation of men to dwell on all the face of the earth" (Acts 17:26) and that in Christ "there is neither Jew nor Greek, there is neither slave nor free, there is neither male nor female: for you are all one in Christ Jesus" (Gal 3:28)."

---

2. The above conference was organized by the Center for Ecumenical, Missiological, and Environmental Studies "Metropolitan Panteleimon Papageorgiou" (CEMES) and symbolically launched on July 22, 2014, the feast of St. Mary Magdalene, the "Equal to the Apostles" (or the "apostle to the apostles" by certain church fathers) in the liturgical tradition of the Orthodox Church.

3. All the documents/decisions of the Holy and Great Council of the Orthodox Church are displayed in various languages on the official website of the council, accessed June 24, 2022, http://www.holycouncil.org.

CHAPTER TWO

Of course, the issue of deaconesses (and indirectly the ordination of women) was not on the agenda of this vital pan-Orthodox council.[4] However, the issue of the revival of the order of deaconesses was high on the agenda of the Russian Orthodox Church's *Sobor* before the outbreak of the communist Bolshevik revolution and at the March 2014 *Synaxis* of the Primates of the Orthodox Church that decided this long-awaited council, Archbishop Chrysostomos of Cyprus had stated that we should ask ourselves the question of the status of women in the church and seriously study and proceed to the restoration of the order of deaconesses in the church, taking of course into account all aspects of the issue.

***

More than sixty-five years ago the late Evangelos Theodorou, a respected Orthodox scholar opened the discussion within Orthodox theological circles about the thorny issue of the ordination of women to the sacramental priesthood with his doctoral dissertation on deaconesses.[5] The semi-official position till now of the Orthodox Church on all the above issues, however, was expressed at an

---

4. Nevertheless, fifteen Orthodox missiologists in the preconciliar process made some recommendations to the synod in a document entitled "Some Comments by Orthodox Missiologists on 'The Mission of the Orthodox Church in Today's World.'" Point number 7 reads as follows: "In the chapter on human dignity no reference at all is made to women and their ministry, nor to the traditional and canonical institution of deaconesses. It will be a completely ineffective contemporary declaration on mission by the Orthodox Church, if it fails to reaffirm the dignity of women, given the Church's unique tradition of allowing their access even to the sacramental diaconal priesthood, in the still canonically valid institution of deaconesses. It is advisable, therefore, the sentence: 'The teaching of the Church is the source of all Christian striving to preserve the dignity and majesty of the human person' be followed by 'especially of women, so highly dignified in the patristic and liturgical tradition, that they were welcomed to the sacramental diaconal ministry as deaconesses, canonically testified and never annulled in times when a clear separation of duties and commissions of the different sexes permeated social reality throughout.' Accessed June 24, 2022, https://academia.edu/26833426 and eds. P. Vassiliadis, N. Dimitriadis, and D. Keramidas, *Theology at the Service of the Church, The CEMES Projects* [Thessaloniki: 30 CEMES, 2020], 15.

5. Evangelos D. Theodorou, Ἡ χειροτονία ἢ χειροθεσία τῶν διακονισσῶν [The "Ordination" or the "Laying-on of Hands" of Deaconesses] (Athens, 1954).

ad hoc inter-Orthodox Conference in 1988 on the Greek island of Rhodes. Convened on the initiative of the Ecumenical Patriarchate, this conference reached some preliminary conclusions,[6] including the following relevant points:

On the place of women, for the first time in official documents, an important self-critical assessment of the situation was made:

> While recognizing these facts, which witness to the promotion through the Church of the equality of honor between men and women, it is necessary to confess in honesty and with humility, that, owing to human weakness and sinfulness, the Christian communities have not always and in all places been able to suppress effectively ideas, manners and customs, historical developments and social conditions which have resulted in practical discrimination against women. Human sinfulness has thus led to practices which do not reflect the true nature of the Church in Jesus Christ (24).

Equally significant was the position taken regarding the order of deaconesses:

> The apostolic order of deaconesses should be revived. It was never altogether abandoned in the Orthodox Church though it has tended to fall into disuse. There is ample evidence, from apostolic times, from the patristic, canonical and liturgical tradition, well into the Byzantine period (and even in our own day) that this order was held in high honor (32).[7]

---

6. Gennadios Limouris, ed., *The Place of the Woman in the Orthodox Church and the Question of the Ordination of Women* (Katerini, 1992). The conclusions alone were also published in English as *Conclusions of the InterOrthodox Consultation on the Place of the Woman in the Orthodox Church and the Question of the Ordination of Women (Rhodes, Greece, October 30–November 7, 1988)* (Minneapolis: Light and Life, 1990), accessed June 24, 2022, https://orthodoxdeaconess.org/wp-content/uploads/2013/11/RhodesConsultation.pdf

7. With regard to the overall issue of the ordination of women, the Rhodes Consultation stated: "The impossibility of the ordination of women to the special priesthood as founded in the Tradition of the Church has been expressed in these ecclesiastically-rooted positions: (a) on the example of our Lord Jesus Christ, Who did not select any woman as one of His Apostles; (b) on the example of the Theotokos, who did not exercise the sacramental priestly function

Recently, reviews of the writings of His Eminence Metropolitan Kallistos (Ware) of Diokleia (the first modern Orthodox theologian to systematically formulate theological views on this issue);[8] the studies by Elisabeth Behr-Sigel[9] and Nikolaos Matsoukas (the Orthodox Dogmatic Theologian of the Aristotelian University of Thessaloniki),[10] as well as some recent doctoral dissertations[11] and postdoctoral monographs;[12] and especially the enormous developments in biblical, systematic, historical, patristic, and even socio-

---

in the Church, even though she was made worthy to become the Mother of the Incarnate Son and Word of God; (c) on the Apostolic Tradition, according to which the Apostles, following the example of the Lord, never ordained any women to this special priesthood in the Church; (d) on some Pauline teachings concerning the place of women in the Church, and (e) on the criterion of analogy, according to which, if the exercise of the sacramental priesthood by women were permitted, then it should have been exercised by the Theotokos" (14).

8. Metropolitan Kallistos first wrote on the subject in his article "Man, Woman, and Priesthood of Christ," in *Man, Woman, and Priesthood*, ed. Peter Moore (London: SPCK, 1978), 68–90, reprinted almost verbatim in the classic Orthodox theology collective work, Thomas Hopko, ed., *Women and the Priesthood* (Crestwood, NY: St. Vladimir's Seminary Press, 1983), 9–37. Nearly twenty years later (and ten years after the Rhodes conference) Metropolitan Kallistos, in the revised edition of *Women and the Priesthood* (Crestwood: SVS, 1999) and also in a booklet coedited with Elisabeth Behr-Sigel under the title *The Ordination of Women in the Orthodox Church* (Geneva, 2000), stated: "On the subject of women and the priesthood, *there exists as of yet no pan-Orthodox statement, possessing definitive ecumenical authority*," commenting on the Rhodes Consultation that "its conclusions do not possess a formal and final authority, binding upon the Orthodox Church as a whole; rather, they constitute a contribution to a continuing debate" (51).

9. See on her contribution Eleni Kasselouri-Hatzivassiliadi, "The personality of Elisabeth Behr-Sigel and the Order of Deaconesses," in *Deaconesses, Ordination of Women and Orthodox Theology*, eds. P. Vassiliadis, E. Amoiridou, and M. Goutzioudis (Thessaloniki: 12 CEMES, 2016), 349–55.

10. Ibid., Maria Hatziapostolou, "Deaconesses and Ordination of Women in the Theology of Nikos Matsoukas," 357–70.

11. Constantinos Yokarinis, Ἡ ἱερωσύνη τῶν γυναικῶν στό πλαίσιο τῆς Οἰκουμενικῆς Κίνησης [*The Priesthood of Women in the Framework of the Ecumenical Movement*], (Katerini, 1995). Maria Gwyn McDowell, *The Joy of Embodied Virtue: Toward the Ordination of Women to the Eastern Orthodox Priesthood*, PhD diss., Boston College, 2010.

12. Constantinos Yokarinis, Το έμφυλο ή άφυλο του σαρκωθέντος Χριστού [*The Genderness or Genderlessness of the Incarnate Christ*] (Athens, 2013).

logical studies, have all revealed the quite urgent need for better documentation of the official theological position of the Orthodox Church.

Several years ago, His Eminence Metropolitan John (Zizioulas) of Pergamon, representing the Ecumenical Patriarchate and addressing the Anglican Communion during its regular conference at Lambeth, noted that the solution to this thorny issue, which torments the Christian world and has divided vertically and horizontally the various Christian denominations, can be found neither by arguments from *sociology* nor exclusively by arguments from *tradition*. What the Christian community desperately needs is mainly *theological* arguments.

***

All these prompted the Center for Ecumenical, Missiological, and Environmental Studies (CEMES) to convene the aforementioned international conference, the main focus of which was the Orthodox theological approach to the revival of the traditional order of deaconesses. However, the conference also dealt with the thorny issue of the ordination of women, especially with the theological perspectives of the admission or not of women into the sacramental priesthood, reversing somewhat the wording of the patriarchal invitation to the conference in Rhodes late in the 1980s, with the emphasis shifting from "exclusion" to "admission."

This small but substantial change was prompted by the reflections of the international symposium, held one year earlier and based mainly on the thoughts and proposals of Evangelos Theodorou, to whom the conference was dedicated, who stated:

> In the debate on the general ordination of women, the Orthodox theology should not resort to inappropriate use of human, biological concepts about the alleged male or female sex of each of the persons of the Holy Trinity, thus destroying the apophatic and inaccessible-to-human-intellect character of the Trinitarian doctrine. Rather, ecclesiological criteria must be aimed at building the Church of Christ. We must also use Christological theology, which teaches about

a *Theanthropic* God and in God's salvific work, which incorporated and received the whole human nature, male and female. And so we must seek the division of responsibilities of the Church's ministers according to the variety of their charisms. This variety of charisms has particularly brought forward the ancient Church.[13]

Theodorou made another important observation, namely that the interpretation in our canonical sources that the deaconess was a symbol of the Holy Spirit, thus occupying a higher position than the presbyter, who were considered symbols of the apostles, should at least upgrade the status of women regarding the theological legitimacy of participation in the sacramental priesthood. None, of course, of the Orthodox theologians who have been involved or engaged in theological investigation of the matter (in addition to Theodorou, Metropolitan Kallistos of Diokleia, and Metropolitan Anthony (Bloom) of Sourozh of blessed memory) dispute, on the basis of "tradition" and the current canonical order of the Orthodox Church ("τό γε νυν έχον," as Theodorou brilliantly underlined), that women are excluded from the sacramental "hierourgic" priesthood but not from the "diaconal" one.

The argument, therefore, "from tradition" (a concept so important in the history of the Eastern Orthodox Church—for many unfortunately, even nowadays, over and above the teaching of Jesus Christ) continues to be, despite the warning by Metropolitan John of Pergamon mentioned above, a powerful and largely nonnegotiable criterion for reopening of the theological debate on the issue in many cases, even without the necessary distinction between the apostolic "Big T" Tradition and the various subsequent "little T" traditions.

But beyond this necessary distinction, which the Orthodox Church has officially adopted—namely the preeminence of the *apostolic* tradition and that the church is its authentic bearer and custodian—modern theological scholarship has advanced an equally

---

13. On many ecclesiastical websites and the CEMES YouTube channel, accessed June 24, 2022, https://www.youtube.com/watch?v=HWi84dPrR8w&t=234s.

important distinction: that of authentic but *latent* tradition, and that which was *historically* formed. A classic example of this is the institution of the order of deaconesses.

However, even if we adhere to this "historical" Orthodox tradition, how could we ignore the gradual degradation of women in the history of Western Christianity on three issues, the position of Mary Magdalene, St. Junia the Apostle, and the order of deaconesses, when the long tradition of the East took pride in these women and the institution? How can the most indisputable scientific evidence, the existence in the New Testament and the first Christian centuries of women bearing the solemn attribute "apostle" (e.g., Junia), be ignored by the Orthodox, especially in the list of the theological arguments on the issue of restoring the order of deaconesses, i.e., the admission of women into the sacramental "diaconal" priesthood—especially today, when it is indeed more urgently needed than ever, as the Rhodes Consultation has stated,[14] and the Ecumenical Patriarch has openly declared at an international meeting in Constantinople?[15]

Finally, it is worth mentioning what Patriarch Gregory of Antioch wrote in a speech on the myrrhbearers, as late as the sixth century AD. There he clearly connected women not only with the "ordination" but also with the "apostolic" office (Μαθέτω Πέτρος ὁ ἀρνησάμενός με, ὅτι δύναμαι καὶ γυναῖκας ἀποστόλους χειροτονεῖν, "Let

---

14. The reinstitution of the order "would represent a positive response to many of the needs and demands of the contemporary world. This would be all the more true if the diaconate in general (male as well as female) were restored in all places in its original, manifold services (*diakoniai*) with extension into the social sphere, in the spirit of the ancient tradition and in response to the increasing specific needs of our time," in Limouris, ed., *The Place of the Woman in the Orthodox Church*, 31ff.; also in Kyriaki Karidoyanes FitzGerald, *Women Deacons in the Orthodox Church: Called to Holiness and Ministry* (Brookline, MA: Holy Cross Orthodox Press, 1999), 160–67.

15. In his address to the Inter-Orthodox Conference for Women (Constantinople, May 12, 1997), His All-Holiness Ecumenical Patriarch Bartholomew said, "The order of ordained deaconesses is an undeniable part of tradition coming from the Early Church. Now, in many of our Churches, there is a growing desire to restore this order so that the spiritual needs of the People of God may be better served. There are already a number of women who appear to be called to this ministry."

Peter who has denied me learn that I am able to ordain also women as Apostles").[16] This textual evidence, an indirect reference to the *latent authentic tradition,* perhaps proves that evidence is not completely absent in Eastern Christian tradition for a different attitude regarding the liturgical status of women, at least different from the conventional one. Interestingly—even ironically—during the same period in the West another Gregory, the famous Pope Gregory the Great, had unconsciously been responsible for degrading the memory of St. Mary Magdalene from an outstanding female leader of the church to that of a repenting sinful woman.[17]

Notwithstanding what I very briefly mentioned so far, there are also difficulties and problems in the restoration of the order of the sacramental priesthood of deaconesses. Recently in the Orthodox diaspora, mainly among the converts from the extremely conservative Evangelical stream, the following argument is being developed: any rejuvenation of the order of deaconesses, although it is testified to in the ancient Eastern Orthodox tradition and despite its ecumenical, synodical, and canonical validity, is undesirable for the simple reason—the argument goes on—that it may also open wide a window for the adoption of the ordination of women. Such novel views, which develop around many issues imported into the Orthodox tradition, especially among conservative circles, justify the importance of a theological approach also to the general issue of women's ordination.[18]

And to return to the issue of deaconesses, such arguments—fortunately not officially formulated by the Orthodox Church—create a feeling of an unacceptable theological inconsistency, which will irreparably damage the reliability of Orthodox theology. How can

---

16. Gregory of Antioch, PG 88f.:1864b

17. More in my work, "Mary Magdalene: From a Prominent Apostle to a Symbol of Love and Sexuality," accessed June 24, 2022, http://www.academia.edu/2024999.

18. More in Valerie Karras, "Theological Presuppositions and Logical Fallacies in Much of the Contemporary Discussion of the Ordination of Women," in *Deaconesses, Ordination of Women and Orthodox Theology,* eds. P. Vassiliadis, E. Amoiridou, and M. Goutzioudis (Newcastle upon Tyne, UK: Cambridge Scholars Publishing, 2017), 93–103.

some theologians continue to rely basically on tradition for the general issue of the ordination of women and at the same time ignore or reject it in the case of the ordination of deaconesses?

With the exception of the recommendation that the then-anticipated pan-Orthodox council consider the restoration of the order of deaconesses,[19] the above CEMES conference in 2014 did not come to other conclusions, choosing to leave any final decision to the appropriate ecclesiastical authorities in the hope that they would also consider other relevant parameters. The majority of the speakers simply underlined the inconsistency in the current conventional Orthodox view. To this end, the following theological concerns were expressed in the final communique:

1. How important, for the Orthodox Church's theological arsenal, is the fact that the institution of deaconesses has a conciliar, ecumenical, and canonical foundation, which in fact has never been repealed by subsequent synodical decision?
2. Since deaconesses were installed into their ministry through ordination (*hierotonia*), which was the same as that for the major orders of the clergy, and not by simple laying on of hands (*hierothesia*), and their ordination had an absolute likeness in form and content with the ordinations of the major orders of the clergy, does not the reluctance by many Orthodox Churches to proceed to the rejuvenation of the order of deaconesses affect the witness of the Church today?
3. Can the clear assurance in the ancient prayers that Christ did not ban women *also* from having liturgical duties in the churches (see, "rejecting no woman . . . from serving in your holy houses" [ὁ μηδὲ γυναῖκας . . . λειτουργεῖν τοῖς ἁγίοις οἴκοις σου ἀποβαλλόμενος]) help the Orthodox Church to immediately proceed to the rejuvenation of the order of deaconesses?
4. Can the proposed distinction of the sacramental priesthood into "diaconal" and "hierourgic," i.e., a quantitative rather

---

19. See the "The Final Communique" in *Deaconesses, Ordination of Women and Orthodox Theology*, 497–502.

than qualitative distinction, help the Orthodox Church to restore her traditional ancient practice and ordain deaconesses?

5. How can the interpretation in the canonical sources that the deaconess, as a symbol of the Holy Spirit, held a higher position even than that of the presbyter, who was considered a symbol of the apostles, affect the possibility of upgrading the status of women in relation to the theological legitimacy of their participation in the diaconal sacramental priesthood?

6. Can Orthodox bishops at any time, without any relevant conciliar decision, ordain deaconesses and accept them into the major orders of the clergy?

7. If the Orthodox Church is characterized by its liturgical (and eucharistic) theology, how crucial is it today to revive the order of ordained deaconesses for their necessary missionary witness, particularly in the area of ministry?

8. If the human person is determined by their relationship with others, and if the Eucharistic community is for the Orthodox the primary framework for constructive and virtuous relationships, which are fully possible for both men and women, on what theological ground can one today exclude women from even the diaconal sacramental priesthood?

9. Does the presence of "demonic" elements (e.g., ideas about women being cursed for their culpability in the Fall and their eternal punishment in subjugation to the man, as well as about their impurity with their consequent marginalization in the Church's life of worship and administration, etc.) compromise the Church's witness to the world, additionally raising an enormous ethical problem?

10. Throughout Western Christian history, there has been a gradual, perhaps unconscious, degradation of women on three issues: the status and position of Mary Magdalene, of St. Junia, and of the institution of deaconesses. The long-standing tradition of the East, on the other hand, takes pride in these persons and institutions. How can this affect the position of the Orthodox Church?

11. How can the now-academically indisputable evidence in the New Testament and in the early Christian centuries of important women apostles (e.g., Junia) affect the Orthodox theological argument on the need for the rejuvenation of the order of deaconesses, and even on the discussion of women's ordination?
12. If great Orthodox theologians, such as St. Gregory the Theologian and St. John Chrysostom, speak about the priesthood with metaphors based not on male paternal models, but rather on examples of virtue for the community, and if both theses hierarchs use both masculine and feminine metaphors to describe the method and the ministry of the priesthood, what theological arguments can justify the exclusion today of women even from the diaconal priesthood?
13. Does Patriarch Gregory of Antioch's reference connecting women, until the sixth century, with the apostolic office and ordination ("Μαθέτω Πέτρος ὁ ἀρνησάμενός με, ὅτι δύναμαι καὶ γυναίκας ἀποστόλους χειροτονεῖν" PG 88, 1864b) not demonstrate that there is at least some evidence that the Church held a different attitude in the Eastern Christian tradition regarding the liturgical role of women?
14. Does the exclusive "male priesthood"—derived from the historically indisputable male form of the Incarnate God—constitute a binding element of divine grace? How strong is this theological argument, and how consistent is it to the dogma of Chalcedon?
15. Is the exclusion of women from the sacramental priesthood, especially from the "diaconal" one in the course of history, based on human law (*de jure humano*) or divine law (*de jure divino*)?
16. What impact can the close terminological connection that St. Basil the Great repeatedly makes in his anaphora between "diaconal" and "sacramental" have on the liturgical role of women?
17. On the thorny issue of the ordination of women, should the Orthodox Church and its theology use liturgical, canonical,

Trinitarian, Christological, ecclesiological, eschatological, or sociological criteria?
18. In selecting theological criteria, should priority be given—and if so, how much—to the long-standing "primary" *liturgical* tradition of the Church, over the various *doctrinal* expressions that were subsequently formulated?
19. Is it theologically legitimate to use human, biological concepts of gender and the supposedly masculine or feminine structures of each of the persons of the Holy Trinity?
20. How and to what extent does the basic Orthodox theological position that at the eschaton there will be no discrimination based on biological sex influence the debate about the liturgical and sacramental role of women?
21. Does the invocation of elements of ontological reduction and the division of the human being into two hierarchically superimposed sexes negate the doctrine of the Divine Incarnation and annul its objectives?
22. If, according to Orthodox Christian anthropology, the archetype of the human being is Christ, does the invocation then of the male sex of the Word of God provide theological, canonical, historical-critical, and liturgical grounds for the exclusion of women even from the diaconal sacramental priesthood?
23. If every human person is created unique, complete, and free, designed to achieve deification (theosis) through their virtuous life, how is it possible theologically to define the nature of the human being, or even the virtuous life, on the basis of gender? Does this not lead to a denial of the completeness of human nature at the crown of creation, as well as its call to the "likeness"?
24. Regarding the ministry of the priesthood, does not the selective use and transfer of practices based on gender—which theologically and anthropologically permit the impairment of the human person—substantially undermine rather

than encourage the achievement of the Orthodox ideal of theosis?[20]

***

A consideration, therefore, of these missiological, liturgical (i.e., eucharistic), anthropological, and ecological parameters, is what constitutes an "Orthodox theological approach" to this burning and divisive issue. More recently, Metropolitan Kallistos of Diokleia has clearly stated that "the focal point in the theological deliberations in the twenty-first century will be shifted from ecclesiology to anthropology. . . . The key question will not be only 'what is Church,' but also and more fundamentally 'what is the human being.'"[21] A prominent component of Christian anthropology is undoubtedly the overall *status of women,* especially their public role in the liturgical life. The same is true with another specific characteristic of contemporary Orthodox theology: the *ecological* one, the care of the environment, God's creation, on purely theological grounds. Ecumenical Patriarch Bartholomew, with his global ecological initiatives and his sensitivity for the environment, both at a liturgical level (establishment of the Feast of the protection of God's Creation on September 1) and at a scholarly and theological one (the series of the international ecological conferences), have rightly given him the nickname "the Green Patriarch." The consequences of *ecology*—as a projection of *anthropology*—for the status and role of women are not insignificant.

Except for extreme cases, Orthodox women are never entrusted with leading roles in the ritual, even though the early church—especially in the East— extensively made use of deaconesses. The gender ambivalence of ritual is revealed by the dichotomy between theology and practice. While the Orthodox liturgy includes female saint veneration and reputes the Theotokos as "more honorable than the Cherubim, and more glorious beyond compare than the Sera-

---

20. "The Final Communique" in *Deaconesses, Ordination of Women and Orthodox Theology,* 497–502.

21. Kallistos (Timothy) Ware, Η Ορθόδοξη θεολογία στον 21ο αιώνα [*Orthodox Theology in the Twenty-first Century*] (Athens, 2005), 25.

phim"—that is, above the world of the celestial beings—down on earth, women are excluded from joining the superior clergy, even to the rank of deaconesses.

At the bottom line, therefore, the issue at stake is not the ordination of women as such, in other words as a sociological issue and a demand of modernity, but the missiological, liturgical, anthropological, and ecological dimension of our understanding of the Christian priesthood.

***

(a) In a recent article I argue for the need to contextualize the eucharistic event so that the Orthodox Church can meaningfully witness to the gospel in our contemporary society.[22] The *missiological* consequences of eucharistic theology derive from a proper understanding of Christian worship, the basic characteristics of which are full of "prophetic" elements. The core of Jesus's teaching is based on the basic principles of the Old Testament, something that we Orthodox usually forget, using the First Testament only as an exclusive prefiguration of the Christ event. However, Jesus Christ himself had a different and more prophetic view (cf. e.g., his inaugural speech at the Nazareth synagogue, Luke 4:16ff.), and the early Christian community developed their liturgical, and especially their eucharistic, behavior in accordance with the idea of the covenant (or covenants), particularly through the obligation of the people to a *thanksgiving* worship to God and a commitment to one another in the memory of the liberating grace of God in Exodus.

While in the Old Testament the worship of God was primarily a *thanksgiving liturgy* for the liberation from the oppression of the Egyptians, at the same time it was also a constant reminder for a commitment to a moral and ethical life and an obligation for resistance against any oppression and exploitation of their fellow human beings. In this sense, the *worshiping* (and eucharistic, in the wider sense, thanksgiving) community was also a *witnessing* community.

---

22. "Eucharistic Theology Contextualized?" accessed June 24, 2022, https://www.academia.edu/32859534/.

The same is true with the Eucharist of the early Christians, which was incomprehensible without its social dimension.[23]

When, however, the social and political conditions in Israel began to change and a monarchical system was imposed upon God's people, there was also a tragic change in their concept of communion, and consequently in their liturgy. The latter lost its communal character and was gradually institutionalized. With the construction of the Temple of Solomon, the religious life of the community turned into a cult incumbent with the necessary professional priesthood and the necessary financial transactions. Jesus's action against the money changers is quite indicative of the new situation. His repeated appeal to "mercy/charity/*eleon*" instead of sacrifice is yet another reminder of the real purpose of the true worship.[24]

All these developments, as it is well known, resulted in the strong protest and reaction of the Old Testament prophets. Whereas previously the governing principle of the communal life was divine ownership of all the material wealth, according to the Psalmist's affirmation, "the Earth is the Lord's and everything in it" (24:1), now the focus shifted from the justice of God to the personal accumulation of wealth. Amos and Hosea in the Northern Kingdom before its dissolution in 722 BC, and Isaiah, Micah, Jeremiah, Habakkuk, and Ezekiel in Judea, began to speak of the main components of liturgy, i.e., law and justice, values that were lost because of the private ownership, which changed the traditional concept of society and their worship. For the prophets of the Old Testament the abolition of justice and cancellation rights of the poor above all meant rejection of God himself. Prophet Jeremiah insisted that knowing God was identical with being fair to the poor (22:16). Prophet Isaiah went even further in his criticism, on the issue of the greed and avarice, as manifested by the accumulation of land: "Woe to those who add

---

23. Cf. Acts 2:42ff., 1 Cor 11:1ff., Heb 13:10–16; Justin, 1 *Apology* 67; Irenaeus, Adver. Her. 18:1.

24. See more in W. Brueggemann, 8, *The Prophetic Imagination* (Philadelphia: Fortress Press, 1978). In 1 Kings 8, the conversation of Yahweh with Samuel is highly instructive underlining the implications of this radical change in the relationship between God and his people.

to their home and join the field with the field, so that now there is no other place for them to stay and the only country holding" (5:8). He did not hesitate to characterize the greedy landlords as "thieves" (1:23) and to characterize the confiscation of the land of indebted farmers as a grab at the expense of the poor.[25]

This highly social and prophetic dimension of an authentic Christian worship, clearly manifested in the teaching, life, and work of Jesus Christ, and of course in the early church's eucharistic gatherings, is the model of ethics that any consideration of the ordination of women should follow. As the official documents of the Holy and Great Council of the Orthodox Church underline,[26] the church does not exist for herself but for the world.

(b) In terms of extending the consideration of the ordination of women on the basis of a *liturgical* theology, of paramount importance is our understanding of the sacramental and/or sacrificial character of the Eucharist.

(i) The term *"μυστήριον"* (mystery), which in Latin was rendered *sacrament,* is a clearly religious *terminus technicus*, which is etymologically derived from the verb *"μύειν"* (meaning "to close the eyes and mouth"), and not from the verb *"μυεῖν"* (meaning "to dedicate").[27] In antiquity it is recorded (primarily in the plural) in rituals with secret teachings, both religious and political, and accompanied by a host of exotic activities and customs. These mysteries may have originated in the ritualistic activities of primitive peoples, but they took much of their shape from the Greek religious world (Dionysiac, Eleusinian, Orphic, etc., *mysteries*) and then combined creatively with

---

25. Isa 3:14–15. See the detailed analysis of the problem by Ulrich Duchrow and Franz Hinkelammert in their book *Property for People, Not for Profit: Alternatives to the Global Tyranny of Capital* (London: Bloomsbury Publishing, 2004), as well as their more recent one, *Transcending Greedy Money. Interreligious Solidarity for Just Relations, New Approaches to Religion and Power* (New York: Palgrave MacMillan), 2012.

26. The documents can be found on the council's official website, accessed June 24, 2022, https://www.holycouncil.org/home.

27. "They were called mysteries because they close their mouths and nothing is explained to anyone. And μύειν is the closing of the mouth" (*Scholia to Aristophanes*, 456).

various Eastern cults before assuming their final form during the Roman period. Because Christianity has spread during the height of the mystery cults, and because of some external resemblances with them, the history-of-religions school of thought formulated the theory of reciprocal dependence—and in particular the dependence of Christianity on the mystery cults. Today such a theory is less popular among historians as it was a few generations ago; after all, an "analogy" can hardly be identified with a "genealogy."

In biblical literature, as well as in the early post-biblical one, the term "mystery" was always connected with cultic ritual or with the liturgical expression of the people of God. In the Septuagint it appears for the first time in the Hellenistic literature (Tobit, Judith, Wisdom, Sirach, Daniel, Maccabees), where it is frequently used pejoratively to describe the ethnic mystery religions (cf. Wis 14:23: "secret mysteries . . . [connected with] child sacrifices"), or to imply idolatry.[28] In Daniel, the term "mystery" assumes, for the first time, a significant connotation, that of eschatology, with this meaning continuing to develop over time.[29]

The only use of the term in the Gospels occurs in the Synoptic tradition, in the famous interpretation of the parables: "the mystery [-ies] of the Kingdom of God [of heaven]" (Mark 4:11). Here, as well as in the *corpus paulinum*,[30] the term is connected with the *kerygma*, not with ritual (as in the various mystery cults), and it was very often used in connection with terms of *revelation*.[31] Generally, in the New Testament, *mystery* is never connected with secret teachings, nor do we encounter any admonitions against defiling the mystery, as is seen in the mystery cults.

There is ample evidence in the letters of the St. Paul that in certain circles of the early church the significance of the Lord's Supper,

---

28. G. Bornkamm, "μυστήριον, μυέω," in G. Kittel, et al, *Theological Dictionary of the New Testament*, vol. 4, (Grand Rapids, MI: Erdmans, 1977), 813.

29. Ibid., 814.

30. For more, cf. Walter Bauer, *A Greek-English Lexicon of the New Testament and Other Early Christian Literature*, revised and edited Frederick William Danker (Chicago, University of Chicago Press, 2000).

31. For more, cf. G. Bornkamm, "μυστήριον, μυέω," 821 ff.

and by extension the profound meaning of the Eucharist, was interpreted in light of the Hellenistic mystery cults' rituals, and thus the mystery was believed to transmit an irrevocable salvation. Paul attempts to correct this view on the basis of ecclesiological criteria through his teaching on spiritual gifts and the church as "the body of Christ."

According to the "sacramentalistic" view of the mystery cults, the person acquires, via the mysteries, a power of life that is never lost. In the mystery groups and the syncretistic environment of early Christianity, it was widely believed that the human beings were connected with the deity through the initiation; they could acquire eternal salvation only by participating in the deity's death and resurrection.[32] The Gnostics, being influenced by the mystery cults and adopting their sacramentalistic view, even performed baptism for the departed in an attempt to activate this indestructible power over death. St. Paul refuted this magical/sacramentalistic view of baptism in his Epistle to the Romans (6:3–11). It is of course true that he interprets baptism in theological terms as participation in Christ's death on the cross, but at the same time he insists that this must have consequences in the moral life of the faithful. For this reason, he exhorts the baptized to "walk in newness of life" (6:4) "so that (they) might no longer be enslaved to sin" (6:6).[33]

Ephesians 3:3–12 is characteristic of the Pauline (and the New Testament in general) understanding of μυστήριον. There Paul's mission to the Gentiles is clearly described as "the plan of the mystery hidden for ages in God who created all things through Jesus Christ; that through the Church the manifold wisdom of God might now be made known to the rulers and authorities in the heavenly places" (3:9–10). Mystery, therefore, is the *hidden plan of God for the salvation of the whole world*. The church, then, by extension, is consid-

---

32. Cf. S. Agouridis's commentary on 1 Cor 10 in *St. Paul's 1st Epistle to the Corinthians*, Hermeneia of the New Testament 7 (Thessaloniki, 1982), 161 ff. [in Greek], which he aptly titles: "The mysteries are not a guarantee for the future" and "Christianity is incompatible with idolatry."

33. E. Lohse, *Theology of the New Testament. An Epitome*, Greek translation (Athens, 1980), 155ff.

ered a "mystery" because in her the mystery of salvation is accomplished. And because the church is the collective manifestation of the Kingdom of God, the *Divine Eucharist* was also characterized as a "mystery," more precisely as the mystery par excellence. Until the fourth century AD, the term "mystery" and its derivatives were not connected in any way with that which later came to be called sacraments.[34]

Therefore, it is a myth that sacramentality in the conventional sense is the sine qua non characteristic, at least of the Orthodox Church.

(ii) As to the *sacrificial* (or not) character of the Eucharist, the prevailing liturgical language used in the Orthodox Church—e.g., Αγία τράπεζα (Holy Table), not altar; Ιερόν Βήμα (Holy Bema (tribunal), not sanctuary; *receiving communion*, not the sacraments; the eschatological perspective of the Eucharist, and not the Eucharist as an enactment of Christ's sacrifice on the cross—is quite revealing. Even from the time of the New Testament literature, several ideas worked simultaneously in the use of *priestly* and *sacrificial* vocabulary. People's obedience to the gospel, their deeds of charity toward each other, their prayer and thanksgiving, all were called "offerings" or "sacrifices," because in them honor was rendered to God in the freedom and power of the Holy Spirit; and their worship was called a "sacrifice of praise" (θυσία αἰνέσεως). And not only that: the people themselves as an eschatological community were considered a "living sacrifice," a "royal priesthood," a "temple holy to God" (1 Pet 2:4–10). Most importantly the church's ministers were not given priestly names: they rather bore secular designations, such as *presbyteros* (elder), *episkopos* (bishop), *diakonos* (deacon), or *proestos* (presider), all intended to underline their service to the community.[35]

---

34. Cf. G. Bornkamm, "μυστήριον, μυέω," 823 ff. More on the non-sacramental character of the so-called mysteries of our church in my article dedicated to my colleague, Fr. Paul Tarazi, entitled "Mysteriology: The Biblical Foundation of Sacramental Theology (Christian Mystery, Mystery Cults, and Contemporary Christian Witness)" in *Festschrift in Honor of Professor Paul Nadim Tarazi. vol. 2: Studies in the New Testament*, ed. B. Nassif (New York: 2015), 89–98.

35. David Power, *The Eucharistic Mystery: Revitalizing the Tradition* (New York: Herder & Herder, 1995), 115.

CHAPTER TWO

The most powerful argument some Catholics—and sometimes theologians from all the traditional churches, the Orthodox included—employ against the acceptance of women into the sacramental priesthood, is the cultural taboo of the uncleanness of women during childbearing, and the ensuing inability to perform *sacrifice*.[36]

Sacrifice from the anthropological perspective is an unnatural act that seeks to establish culture in the place of nature.[37] It is by its nature exclusive and conservative. Its function is to establish clear boundaries between the sacred and the profane, between those who are pure and those who are impure, between those who are in power and those who remain outside of it. The function of sacrifice is to support and preserve an alleged God-given social order. The problem is not simply that allowing women access to the upper class grants them also authority and power. Although this would be a reasonable interpretation of such an objective, it does not yet explain the strong resistance of the traditional churches to accept women in the ecclesiastical sacramental orders.

The overall evidence of the New Testament literature, as well as of early architecture and frescoes, especially in the catacombs, testify that *women did have leadership roles in Christian worship*. There is no doubt about this.[38] Women did occupy significant leadership roles

---

36. Sociologists and anthropologists argue that in all known cultures, the woman in her childbearing years was allowed to perform blood sacrifices, and that sacrifice is in fact a remedy for having been born of woman. And that only the bearing of male children establishes social genealogies, as opposed to merely natural ones, which also include bearing female children. One might think of the importance of apostolic succession for valid orders in this light. In the dialogue between Catholics and Anglican the question regularly raised to the Anglicans is how they accept at the same time sacrifice, and the ordination of women. It cannot be "sacrifice" in the way the Catholics (and one can mistakenly add the Orthodox) understand it. More in Nancy Jay, *Throughout Your Generations Forever: Sacrifice, Religion, and Paternity* (Chicago: University of Chicago Press, 1992).

37. More on this in Damien Casey, "The 'Fractio Panis' and the Eucharist as Eschatological Banquet," accessed June 24, 2022, https://womenpriests.org/?s=damien+casey (first appearance in the Macauley University Electronic Journal on August 18, 2002).

38. B. Witherington, *Women in the Ministry of Jesus* (Cambridge: Cambridge University Press, 1984); idem, *Women in the Earliest Churches* (Cambridge,

within the community, but only while Christianity remained primarily a religion of the private sphere.

However, the question should not be whether women *have been* or *can be* ordained. The question should rather be whether the one who presides—whatever their sex—acts not so much *in persona Christi* as *in persona ecclesiae*. Evidence of women presiding at the Eucharist does not necessarily translate into evidence that women were *priests*. Even more important is the question of whether their role is related to a certain non-sacrificial understanding of the Eucharist (as it is the case in the New Testament and the early church), and whether the ruling metaphors are eschatological.[39]

If the Eucharist was understood to be primarily a sacrifice, then there are all sorts of anthropological reasons why women would not preside over the Lord's Table. But the Eucharist originally was *not* understood as a sacrifice as such, but rather, as David Power put it, a "subversion of sacrifice";[40] or, as Robert Daly has convincingly argued, it is "an *incarnational spiritualization of sacrifice* that is operative in the New Testament and the early Church."[41]

(c) In the long history of the undivided church (the era of the ecumenical councils) the theological focus was on Christology, related of course to soteriology. In the twentieth century, as a result of

---

1988). Also, my paper "Η Πανορθόδοξη Σύνοδος και η παρακαταθήκη του Αποστόλου Παύλου για τον ρόλο των γυναικών" ["The Pan-Orthodox Council and St. Paul's Legacy on the Role of Women"], accessed June 24, 2022, https://www.academia.edu/26833053.

39. According to Damien Casey ("Fractio Panis"), there is a correlation between eschatological expectation of the outpouring of the Holy Spirit in the final days and women's prophetic leadership. In the ecclesial typology of the East, the bishop was said to be in the image of God the Father; the deacon, of Christ; the deaconess, of the Holy Spirit; and the priests, of the apostles. The priest, far from being *in persona Christi*, is only in the image of the apostles, holy men to be sure, but still only men, whereas the deaconess, as we stated above, are in the image of the Holy Spirit.

40. Power, *The Eucharistic Mystery*, 140ff.

41. Robert J. Daly, *The Origins of the Christian Doctrine of Sacrifice* (Philadelphia: Fortress Press, 1978), 138. Though, according to Casey "the question arises as to whether sacrifice can undergo an 'incarnational spiritualization' and still be sacrifice" ("Fractio Panis," n. 8).

the fragmentation of Christianity and the ensuing ineffectiveness of the Christian mission, the focus inevitably shifted to ecclesiology. The most urgent demands in today's witness to the gospel of Christ are undoubtedly of an *anthropological* character. However, in order to formulate an Orthodox anthropology, we need to go beyond the widely-accepted views in Christian literature. Metropolitan Kallistos argues that

> Many Fathers of the Church (Gregory the Theologian, Gregory of Nyssa, Isaac the Syrian, etc.) believe that "the divine image in the human being should be associated with the soul and not with the body, and even in the soul it is related to the power of self-knowledge and of speech." But there are others—who may be a minority but a significant minority—who adopt a more holistic approach, asserting that the divine image includes not only the soul but the whole being: body, soul, and spirit together. In this way they agree with the view expressed in the Fifth Ecumenical Council and the Christian Creed. St. Irenaeus of Lyons, e.g., writes: "The soul and the spirit can be part of, but not the entire, human being; a perfect human being is a clash and a union both of a soul, who has the spirit of the Father, and held in the image of God, a merciful flesh."[42] [Metropolitan Kallistos continues:] The reality of the (human) person is beyond and above whatever explanation we choose to give it. The inherent element of the person is the overcoming of him/herself, his/her ability to be always open, his/her ability to point always to the other. The human person, unlike the computer, is the

---

42. *Against Heresies* 5:6,1 (Ἡ δε ψυχή καί τό πνεῦμα μέρος τοῦ ἀνθρώπου δύναται εἶναι, ἄνθρωπος δε οὐδαμῶς· ὁ δε τέλειος ἄνθρωπος σύγκρασις καί ἕνωσίς ἐστι ψυχῆς τῆς ἐπιδεξαμένης τό πνεῦμα τοῦ Πατρός καί συγκραθείσης τῇ κατ' εἰκόνα Θεοῦ πεπλασμένῃ σαρκί). This same view is also to be found in the celebrated passage of Michael Choniatis, attributed wrongly to St Gregory Palamas, ". . . μή ἄν ψυχήν μόνην, μήτε σῶμα μόνον λέγεσθαι ἄνθρωπον, ἀλλά τό συναμφότερον, ὃν δή καί κατ' εἰκόνα πεποιηκέναι Θεός λέγεται" (Προσωποποιΐαι, PG 150, col. 1361C).

one that fires every new start. Being a human being means to be unpredictable, free, and creative.[43]

The very concept of human identity, as it is developed in recent years, is quite ambiguous. Previously, identity was considered as something "given." Now, after thorough scientific research—though these findings are being questioned by some—it is argued that identity is a "construction." That is why the secular scientific community discusses "shaping" the identity of a person or group in the sense of a "dynamic process" through which the individual (or the group) is constantly affected by the environment, thus developing a new ethos.

Modern and postmodern ethicists attempt in every way to impose an "inclusive ethos," while traditional societies, and especially religions, defend an "exclusive ethos." The former seek to integrate a group into its social context, which they often attempt to shape, while the latter seek the necessary distance with persistence in the traditional values. There are of course cases, even in the New Testament texts, where the ethos of all groups is mixed, so its "exclusive" side marks definite boundaries, outside of which everything is excluded as heretic, while its "inclusive" side expresses the manifold and constantly-developing community.[44]

Christian anthropology is related to human sexuality. On the secular side, a new ethos is being directly or indirectly affirmed:

> It is impossible to predict what will happen with sexual variations in the future, in two hundred or three hundred years. One thing should not be forgotten: men and women are involved in a web of centuries of cultural determinations that are almost impossible to analyze in their complexity. It is now impossible to talk about "woman" or "human"

---

43. From the first paragraph of Metropolitan Kallistos's ceremonial speech as an affiliated member of the Academy of Athens, "Ο άνθρωπος ως μυστήριον. Η έννοια του προσώπου στους Έλληνες Πατέρες" ["The Human Being as a Mystery. The Concept of the Person in the Greek Fathers"] (Academy of Athens Publications, 2006).

44. Eberhard Bons and Karin Finsterbusch, eds., *Konstruktionen individueller und kollektiver Identität* (Göttingen: Vandenhoeck & Ruprecht, 2016).

without being trapped in an ideological theater, where the multiplication of representations, reflections, recognitions, transformations, distortions, constant change of images, and fantasies cancels any appreciation in advance."[45]

Also, on the Christian side there is a similar concern. In a "Letter from Sheffield" (the city in which a World Council of Churches consultation was convened at the beginning of the Ecumenical Decade of Churches in Solidarity with Women), it was stated: "We welcome the recognition that human sexuality does not contradict the (Christian) spirituality, which is unified and relates to the body, the mind, and the spirit in their entirety. . . . Unfortunately, sexuality itself has been for centuries and continues to be problematic for Christians."[46]

In the Bible, of course, human beings are never defined by their nature, whether the physical self or the surrounding material world, but by their relationship with God and their fellow human beings. Therefore, salvation is not achieved through any denial of body, including sexuality, or through escape to a supposedly "spiritual" world. Their physical and spiritual functions are perceived as an inseparable unity, and both can either remove them from God or put them at his service, i.e., in communion with God. The human "flesh" does not lead to evil, nor is it extremely dangerous: it becomes so only when humans surrender the entire existence, not to God, who created them, but to it.

But also in Eastern Christian tradition, as John Meyendorff has long ago argued, human nature is not a static, closed, autonomous entity, but a dynamic reality. The human being is determined by its relationship with God.[47] The nature, therefore, of human beings did not lose its dynamism after the Fall, because by the grace of

---

45. Hélène Cixous and Catherine Clément, *La Jeune Née* (1975) [in French]; *The Newly Born Woman*, trans. Betsy Wing (Minneapolis: University of Minnesota Press, 1986).

46. Connie Parvey, ed., *The Community of Women and Men in the Church: The Sheffield Report* (Geneva: World Council of Churches, 1983), 83.

47. Meyendorff, *Byzantine Theology* (New York: Fordham University Press, 1974), 2.

God it can be transformed. Indeed, the role of God's grace is that it essentially provides them with their real and authentic nature.[48] Even more important and insightful, however, is Archbishop Lazar Puhalo's recent contribution, entitled *On the Neurobiology of Sin*.[49]

(d) In addition to the anthropological dimension in dealing with the role of women in church and society, an *ecological* approach can hardly be ignored. The male *and* (not "or") female interrelatedness is also mutually related to a Christian understanding of integral ecology.[50] There is an interesting concern in the Roman Catholic Church and its social doctrine[51] recognizing that an adequate theological anthropology is required for social/ecological justice. So far the Catholic Church (and I will add all the traditional ancient churches) shows an ambivalent admixture of natural law and patriarchal ideology. If man and woman complete each other in both church and society, why is patriarchal male headship still enshrined in the church hierarchy, given that man and woman are fully homogeneous in their "whole being"?[52]

Of course, this is something that has been consistently pursued by the secular ecofeminist movement and has long stemmed from a patriarchal ideology of male domination and female submission, which for many scholars was the consequence of the Augustinian doctrine of the original sin.[53] It is, however, also a Christian (and

---

48. Ibid.,143 and 138.

49. Lazar Puhalo, *On the Neurobiology of Sin* (Dewdney, Canada: Synaxis Press, 2011).

50. On integral ecology see my paper "The Witness of the Church in Today's World: Three Missiological Statements on Integral Ecology," accessed June 24, 2022, www.academia.edu/28268455.

51. Cf. *Compendium of the Social Doctrine of the Church*, accessed June 24, 2022, https://www.vatican.va/content/benedict-xvi/en/letters/2005/documents/hf_ben-xvi_let_20051119_rivera-carrera.html.

52. From a recent working draft—among so many others, encouraged by Pope Francis's willingness to promote gender equality in his church—by Luis T. Gutiérrez, "Gender Balance for Integral Humanism & Integral Ecology" (December 22, 2015).

53. Based mainly on Gen 3:16. See also my article "Ο ιερός Αυγουστίνος ως ερμηνευτής του Αποστόλου Παύλου και το πρόβλημα της ανθρώπινης σεξουαλικότητας" ["St. Augustine as Interpreter of St. Paul and the problem of Human

even ecclesiastical) anthropological concern. This is not about what women (or men) want. This is about discerning what Jesus Christ wants for the church in the twenty-first century, for the glory of God, for integral human development, for integral humanism, and for integral ecology in light of an adequate theological anthropology, based on the authentic, though latent, tradition of the church, and not just on the historically-established one.

As long as the patriarchal binary prevails, subjective human development remains defective, with pervasive repercussions in human relations as well as human-nature relations . . . there can be no fully integral ecology as long as humanity behaves as the dominant male and treats nature as a submissive female. There can be no lasting social justice, and there can be no lasting ecological justice, as long as human behavior is driven by the patriarchal mindset.[54]

The Old Testament exemplifies patriarchal bias in many ways, notably by the metaphor of woman coming *out of* man (Gen 1:22). It is inescapable, however, that this bias was corrected in the New Testament, notably by the Pauline explicit statement that "when the set time had fully come, God sent his Son, born *of* a woman" (Gal 4:4). God becoming incarnate "from a woman" is a reversal of woman "coming out of man." Not insignificantly, this seemingly innocuous clarification follows the summary of the cultural progression that is now attainable, but has yet to be fully attained, in human history: "There is neither Jew nor Gentile, neither slave nor free, nor is there male and female, for you are all one in Christ Jesus" (Gal 3:28).

What I have so far underlined is nothing more than a "contribution" to a theologically, historically, and scientifically permanent solution to a pending issue that hinders the authentic witness of the church in the twenty-first century. The age-old prejudices, pseudo-theological arguments, and cultural habits can no longer persuade a rapidly-changing society hungry and thirsty for the truth.

Sexuality"], posted with all publication details, accessed June 24, 2022, academia.edu/1992336/.

54. Luis T. Gutiérrez, "Gender Balance for Integral Humanism & Integral Ecology."

Chapter Three

FEMALE DEACONS IN THE BYZANTINE CHURCH[1]

Valerie A. Karras

Despite the energy devoted by American and Western European church historians and theologians to the question of the ordination of women in early Christianity[2] and in the (Western) medieval

---

1. This article is based in part on Valerie A. Karras, "The Liturgical Participation of Women in the Byzantine Church" (Ph.D. diss., The Catholic University of America, 2002), ch. 6, "Female Deacons in the Byzantine Church," and will be republished, in longer form, in the author's forthcoming book, tentatively titled *Women in the Byzantine Liturgy* (Oxford University Press, expected 2005). The author would like to express deep appreciation to her graduate assistants, Michael Farley, Brett Huebner, Julia Schneider, and Daniel Van Slyke, for their retrieval of books, proofreading, and so on, at various stages of this research; to her dissertation committee, George T. Dennis, S.J., Eustratios Papaioannou, and Dominic Serra, for their patience and suggestions; and to two anonymous reviewers for their extremely helpful comments. All errors are, of course, the author's. [*Editors' note:* Dr. Karras was unable to present at the January/February 2020 CEMES symposium; her seminal article, "Female Deacons in the Byzantine Church," in *Church History* 73:2 (June 2004): 272–316, is reprinted here with permission from her and Cambridge University Press.]

2. Relevant works include Ute E. Eisen, *Women Officeholders in Early Christianity: Epigraphical and Literary Studies*, trans. Linda M. Maloney (Collegeville, MN: Liturgical, 2000); Susanna Elm, "Vergini, vedove, diaconesse: alcuni osservazioni sullo sviluppo dei cosidetti 'ordini femminili' nel quarto secolo in oriente," *Codex Aquilarensis* 5 (1991): 77–90; Roger Gryson, T*he Ministry of Women in the Early Church*, trans. Jean Laporte and Mary Louise Hall (Collegeville: Liturgical, 1976); Giorgio Otranto, "Note sul sacerdozio femminile nell'antichita in margine a una testimonianza di Gelasio I," *Vetera Christianorum* 19 (1982): 341–60; Giorgio Otranto, *Italia meridionale e Puglia paleocristiane: Saggi storici* (Bari: Edipuglia, 1991); and Karen Jo Torjesen, *When Women*

Christian Church,³ these scholars have shown comparatively little interest toward the female diaconate in the Byzantine Church,⁴ even when comparative analysis could potentially help elucidate questions regarding the theology and practice of women's ordinations in the West.⁵ Most of the research on the female diaconate in the Byzantine Church has occurred in Mediterranean academic circles, usually within the field of Byzantine studies, or in the Eastern Orthodox theological community; sometimes the examination of the female diaconate in the Byzantine Church has been part of a broader examination of women's liturgical ministries.⁶

Were Priests: Women's Leadership in the Early Church and the Scandal of Their Subordination in the Rise of Christianity (San Francisco: Harper, 1993). As part of a broader examination of early church orders, see the discussion of deaconesses in J. G. Davies, "Deacons, Deaconesses, and the Minor Orders in the Patristic Period," *Journal of Ecclesiastical History* 14 (1963): 1–15. Early scholarship on the female diaconate, concentrating on the early church, includes Jan Chrysostom Pankowski, *De diaconissis* (Regensburg: George Joseph Manz, 1866); and A. Kalsbach, *Die altkirchliche Einrichtung der Diakonissen bis zu ihrem Erloschen* (Freiburg im Breisgau: Herder, 1926).

3. See, for example, Gary Macy, "The Ordination of Women in the Early Middle Ages," *Theological Studies* 61:3 (September 2000): 481–507; and J. Ysebaert, "The Deaconesses in the Western Church of Late Antiquity and their Origin," *Instrumenta Patristica* (Eulogia) 24 (1991): 421–36.

4. The "Byzantine Church" refers to the church of the East Roman (Byzantine) Empire, particularly the Church of Constantinople, in the period from 330 (the founding of Constantinople as the imperial capital of the Roman Empire) to 1453 (the fall of Constantinople to the Ottoman Turks).

5. For example, Macy draws on Eastern Church practice only in a footnote referencing the ordination of deaconesses in the early church, and does not discuss contemporaneous Byzantine practice at all, although it could help explain his observation that "some medievals, including bishops and popes, considered deaconesses and abbesses to be as ordained as any other cleric." Macy, "The Ordination of Women," 502 and 502, n. 93.

6. Works in whole or part on the Byzantine deaconess include Paul F. Bradshaw, *Ordination Rites of the Ancient Churches of East and West* (New York: Pueblo, 1990); Kyriaki Karidoyanes FitzGerald, *Women Deacons in the Orthodox Church: Called to Holiness and Ministry* (Brookline, MA: Holy Cross Orthodox Press, 1998); Aimé Georges Martimort, *Deaconesses: An Historical Study*, trans. K. D. Whitehead (San Francisco: Ignatius, 1986); Robert F. Taft, S.J., "Women at Church in Byzantium: Where, When—and Why?" *Dumbarton Oaks Papers* 52 (1998): 27–87; Evangelos Theodorou, " <χειροτονία> ἢ <χειροθεσία> τῶν διακονισσῶν," *Theologia* 25:3–4 and 26:1 (July–September and October–Decem-

CHAPTER THREE   41

The evidence for ordained female deacons in the early Christian period, at least in portions of the Eastern Church, is clear and unambiguous.[7] That deaconesses continued to exist from the early through the middle Byzantine period,[8] at least in Constantinople and Jerusalem, is also indisputable. (This is not to say that deaconesses were to be found throughout the Empire; there clearly were certain localities where deaconesses did not exist.[9])

---

ber 1954; January–March 1955): 430–601 and 56–76; and Cipriano Vagaggini, "L'ordinazione delle diaconesse nella tradizione greca e bizantina," *Orientalia Christiana Periodica* 40 (1974): 145–89.

7. Although it does not give ordination rites, the early-third-century *Didascalia Apostolorum*, extant in Syriac from a lost Greek original, parallels the ministry of female deacons to that of male deacons; A. Vööbus, *The Didascalia Apostolorum in Syriac*, Corpus Scriptorum Christianorum Orientalium, vols. 401 and 407, Syr. 175 and 179 (Louvain: Sécretariat du Corpus Scriptorum Christianorum Orientalium, 1979); Eng. trans. A. Vööbus, *The Didascalia Apostolorum in Syriac*, Corpus Scriptorum Christianorum Orientalium, vols. 402 and 408, Syr. 176 and 180 (Louvain: Sécretariat du Corpus Scriptorum Christianorum Orientalium, 1979). Book VIII, 3–5, 16–26, of the fourth-century Syriac *Apostolic Constitutions*, which is heavily dependent on the earlier *Didascalia*, gives the ordination rite for bishops, presbyters, deacons, deaconesses, subdeacons, and readers, and the consecration rite for confessors, virgins, widows, and exorcists. *Les Constitutions Apostoliques*, 3 vols., ed., trans., intro., critical text, notes Marcel Metzger, Sources Chrétiennes (hereafter SC), vols. 320, 329, and 336 (Paris: Éditions du Cerf, 1985–87); 3:138–48, 216–28; Eng. trans. "Apostolic Constitutions," in *Fathers of the Third and Fourth Centuries*, eds. Alexander Roberts and James Donaldson, Ante-Nicene Fathers, vol. 7, reprint ed. (Peabody, MA: Hendrickson, 1994), 481–83, 491–93. For a discussion of these and other early church documents relating to the female diaconate in the East, see Bradshaw, *Ordination Rites*, 83–92; Martimort, *Deaconesses*, 35–119.

8. The "early Byzantine period" denotes the fourth through sixth centuries. The turbulent seventh and eighth centuries, as the early part of the "middle Byzantine period," constitute a liminal phase marking the final transformation of society, state, and culture from late antiquity to what is characteristically considered "Byzantine." The "middle Byzantine period" thus extends from this transitional time through the ninth century (post-iconoclasm) to the fall of Constantinople to the Latins in 1204; the late period then dates from the Latin occupation until the Ottoman conquest in 1453.

9. See, for example, Martimort, *Deaconesses*, 132, regarding the area west of the Jordan in the early to mid-sixth century. Also, most scholars have assumed that ordained female deacons did not exist in Egypt, based on the scant literary evidence and on comments by Origen and Clement of Alexandria indicating a nonliturgical office; see Martimort, *Deaconesses*, 76–100; Otranto, "Note sul

While the literary record does not give a detailed and comprehensive picture of the female diaconate, especially with respect to liturgical activities, the order appears to have thrived in the early Byzantine period.[10] From the late fourth to the late seventh century, we have ample literary evidence of a female diaconate in the capital city, and archeological evidence of deaconesses in a number of other areas of the Empire, particularly Asia Minor.[11] During his tenure as archbishop of Constantinople, for instance, John Chrysostom counted as one of his closest friends and supporters the wealthy and influential deaconess Olympias.[12] Ecumenical councils set a minimum age

---

sacerdozio femminile," 343; Ysebaert, "*Deaconesses,*" 424. Ugo Zanetti, "Y eut-il des diaconesses en Égypte?" *Vetera Christianorum* 27 (1990): 369–73, shows through textual analysis that women deacons are specifically mentioned in the euchologion of the White Monastery in the tenth century, but nothing is known of their rank or functions, nor whether they were ordained.

10. There are numerous women titled "deacon" in late antique correspondence, saints' lives, and *apophthegmata* ("sayings" or short stories). For brief descriptions of some of these women, see Gillian Cloke, "*This Female Man of God": Women and Spiritual Power in the Patristic Age, AD 350–450* (London: Routledge, 1995), 208–09; Laura Swan, *The Forgotten Desert Mothers: Sayings, Lives, and Stories of Early Christian Women* (Mahwah, NJ: Paulist, 2001), 109–26.

11. While references to deaconesses (the Greek word is διάκονος with the feminine article, the significance of which will be discussed below) are scattered throughout the Greek-speaking Mediterranean, the most numerous epigraphic references to female deacons are Asia Minor inscriptions dating to the fourth through sixth centuries; see Eisen, *Women Officeholders,* 162–74.

12. Olympias had previously been a protégée of Gregory of Nazianzus as well. See Elizabeth A. Clark, *Jerome, Chrysostom, and Friends* (New York: Edwin Mellen, 1979), 107–57; Susanna Elm, *Virgins of God: The Making of Asceticism in Late Antiquity* (Oxford: Clarendon, 1994), 178–81. Elm (ibid., 174, 181–82) suggests that the ordained female diaconate developed, at least in part, as a method of simultaneously satisfying wealthy and powerful widows and controlling them as ordained clergy in a way that was not possible with the consecrated but nonordained order of widows. Her theory is plausible, in that the already existing office of deaconess—for which there is some evidence by the end of the first or early in the second century—came to be used as a method of rewarding and honoring (and simultaneously controlling) these wealthy, powerful, and influential aristocratic women. Certainly, early imperial legislation of the female diaconate shows its roots in the order of widows: Theodosius in June 390 promulgated a law requiring that deaconesses be widows of at least age sixty (the minimum age stipulated by the Apostle Paul for enrolled widows) and with children to whom they would leave most of their property. *Codex Theodosiani,*

for deaconesses,[13] and Justinianian legislation regarding clergy at the great imperial churches of Hagia Sophia and Blachernae in the mid-sixth century included female deacons, for whom he also promulgated strict laws enforcing chastity.[14] There was even a neighborhood of Constantinople, attested to from the eighth through at least the eleventh century, known as that "of the Deaconess"—presumably it was named after a deaconess of the seventh or eighth century, perhaps the sister of the seventh-century Patriarch Sergius.[15] The Barberini codex, containing a liturgical manual (*euchologion*) from the liminal period of the eighth century, provides an ordination rite for female deacons that is more analogous to that of male deacons than are the less-detailed, late antique Eastern Church orders of several

---

Lib. 16, t. 2, no. 27; in *Theodosiani Libri XVI*, eds. T. Mommsen and P. Meyer (Berlin: Weidmann, 1905), 843–44. See, too, Sozomen, *Historia ecclesiastica* 7, 16, 11, in Sozomenus, *Kirchengeschichte*, ed. Joseph Bidez with Gunther Christian Hansen. Griecheschen Christlichen Shriftsteller der Ersten Jahrhunderte, Neue Folge (Berlin: Academie, 1995), 4:324 (hereafter GCS).

13. For example, can. 15 of the Council of Chalcedon, held in 451, set the minimum age at forty, twenty years younger than the emperor Theodosius had required sixty years earlier; Ioannes Baptista Pitra, *Juris ecclesiastici Graecorum historia et monumenta iussu Pii ix. Pont. Max. Vol. 1: A primo ad VI saeculum* (Rome: S. Congregationis de Propagande Fide, 1864; reprint, Bardi Editore, 1963), 528; Carl J. Hefele, *Conciliengeschichte*, (Freiburg: Herder, 1875), 2:519. Can. 14 of the Council in Trullo (691–92) reiterated the same age requirement; Pitra, *Juris ecclesiastici Graecorum historia et monumenta iussu Pii ix. Pont. Max. Vol. 2: A VI ad IX saeculum* (Rome: S. Congregationis de Propagande Fide, 1868; reprint, Bardi Editore, 1963), 31–32. See Martimort, *Deaconesses*, 107–9. Imperial legislation also set minimum ages and otherwise regulated clergy, including deaconesses. In the sixth century, Justinian lowered Theodosius's minimum age for female deacons from sixty to forty (Nov. 123, chap. 13); this was reiterated in book 3, title 1, chap. 5 of the ninth-century *Basilics* (an abridged and somewhat updated version of the Justinianic legal corpus, compiled under the emperors Basil I and Leo VI). *Basilicorum libri LX. Series A*, 8 vols., eds. H.J. Scheltema and N. van der Wal (Groningen: Wolters, 1955–88).

14. See the discussion in Section IV, below, esp. nn. 109, 112, and 113.

15. The neighborhood was called "Τὰ τῆς Διακονίσσης." See R. Janin, *Constantinople byzantine: Développement urbain et répertoire topographique*, 2nd ed. (Paris: Institut Français d'Études Byzantines, 1964), 341.

centuries earlier; in fact, the ordination rite for female deacons in the Barberini codex is virtually identical to the male deacons' rite.[16]

The female diaconate continued to exist—at least within the capital city and in some women's monastic communities[17]—throughout the middle Byzantine period, with both liturgical and pastoral functions, although female deacons may not have continued to be ordained as late as the twelfth century, and their duties varied somewhat from those the order had in the early church.[18] Evidence of their continuing liturgical and pastoral roles is provided, respectively, by Constantine Porphyrogenitus's tenth-century manual of ceremonies, which refers to a special area for deaconesses in the Constantinopolitan cathedral of Hagia Sophia (the "Great Church"),[19] and by Anna Comnena's biographical panegyric to her father, the emperor

---

16. Barberini gr. 336 preserves the oldest extant Byzantine euchologion: *L'eucologio Barberini gr. 336 (Ff 1-263)*, eds. Stefano Parenti and Elena Velkovska, Bibliotheca "ephemerides Liturgicae" "subsidia," vol. 80 (Rome: C.L.V.–Edizioni Liturgiche, 1995). The ordination of the female deacon (secs. 163–34, in *Barberini*, 185–88) will be thoroughly examined in Section V, below.

17. According to Martimort, *Deaconesses*, 151–52, two manuscripts of liturgical service books (euchologia)—the Grottaferrata codex from the eleventh or twelfth century and the Cairo codex from the fourteenth century—specify that the deaconess, "according to the custom that prevails today, . . . must be a nun in habit, tonsured," thereby implying that the rubrics writer was aware that nonmonastic women had formerly been ordained as deaconesses, but this was no longer the practice. Martimort cites as his source A. Dimitrievskij, *Opisanie liturgitseskich rukopisej*, vol. 2, Εὐχολόγια (Kiev: Izd. Imperatorskago Universiteta Sv. Vladimira, 1901), 346, 996. Curiously, this instruction is missing from the ordination rite, taken from the Grottaferrata manuscript, which is reproduced in Jacobus Goar, ed., *Euchologion sive rituale Graecorum* (Graz: Akademische Druck-U. Verlagsanstalt, 1730; reprint 1960), 218–19. Goar's euchologion draws on a number of Greek manuscripts but relies principally on the Grottaferrata codex.

18. With respect to functions and duties, see the discussion in Section II, below, for instance, regarding the universality of infant baptism.

19. According to Constantine, *De ceremoniis* 44 (35), for the feast of the Annunciation, the emperor, after visiting the *skeuophylakion* (where relics and vessels were kept, and the Gifts prepared), "passes through the narthex of the gynaeceum where the deaconesses of the Great Church have their customary place." Constantine VII Porphyrogenitus, *Le livre des cérémonies*, ed. and trans. Albert Vogt (Paris: Société d'Édition "Les Belles Lettres," 1935), 171; Eng. trans. Taft, "Women at Church," 65.

Alexios I Comnenos, who ruled from 1081 to 1118: the princess mentions the emperor's concern to ensure that "the work of the deaconesses was carefully organized" in the church of St. Paul, attached to the large charitable complex Alexios had constructed in the capital city.[20] Two nearly contemporaneous canonists of the twelfth century, John Zonaras and Alexios Aristenos, in their commentaries on canon 15 of Chalcedon,[21] also discuss deaconesses as though still active. Their witness is confirmed, at least in the Great Church, at the turn of the thirteenth century by the eyewitness account of Anthony of Novgorod,[22] and a century later by an unpublished *entalma* (order) of Patriarch Athanasius I (1303–9) calling for the abolition of the "custom" of deaconesses.[23] The question of how long female deacons survived as an *ordained* order is murkier, however, and will be discussed in Section VI of this article; the extant evidence provides a *terminus ante quem* of the early twelfth century.[24]

I. The Ministry of Byzantine Deaconesses

The activities of Byzantine deaconesses varied over time. Anna Comnena's mention of deaconesses attached to the church serving her father's large philanthropic center implies that charitable and other pastoral activities remained an ongoing concern of at least some fe-

---

20. Anna Comnena, *Alexiad* 15, 7–8, in vol. 3 of Anna Comnena, *Alexiade (règne de l'empereur Alexis I Comnène, 1081–1118)*, trans. Bernard Leib (Paris: Les Belles Lettres, various), 217. These deaconesses may also have been the female chanters that Alexios ordered for the antiphonal chants in St. Paul's.

21. J.-P. Migne, ed., *Patrologiae cursus completus. Series Graeca* (hereafter PG) (Paris: Migne, 1857–66), 137:141–44. See the conclusion to this article for a discussion of their commentaries.

22. Anthony's description also confirms Constantine Porphyrogenitus's siting (n. 19, above) of a special location for deaconesses in Hagia Sophia. See nn. 49 and 50, below.

23. In codex Vat. gr. 2219, f. 132v–143r; see no. 1747, item 1, in V. Laurent, *Les regestes des actes du patriarcat de Constantinople, vol. I, Les actes des patriarches, fasc. IV, Les regestes de 1208 à 1309* (Paris: Institut Français d'Études Byzantines, 1971), 526: "Ils proscriront les monastères doubles et feront cesser la coutume des diaconesses." The author is grateful to an anonymous reviewer for citing this *entalma*.

24. See n. 53, below.

male deacons. However, the primary reason for ordination to the clergy is specific liturgical function, and that is the area for which we have the most information with respect to female deacons, especially in late antiquity. One of the most important sacramental duties of the deaconess in the early church in the East was conducting the physical anointing[25] and baptism of (nude) adult women, who were then "officially" baptized by the bishop's prayer over the just-baptized woman after she was either chastely robed or hidden from the male gaze.[26] This function of deaconesses was made obsolete by the increasing rarity of adult baptism from the end of the fourth century onward due to the combination of the dominance of Christianity as the state religion and the universal adoption of infant baptism.[27]

However, while the baptismal need for female deacons decreased as the church moved into the early Byzantine period, other liturgical and pastoral duties remained, particularly with respect to women who were housebound due to illness or childbirth. The early church's practice of sending a deaconess with the Eucharist to the homes of

---

25. For example, John Chrysostom, *Baptismal Instructions* 2, 24, describes this part of the rite as performed (for men) in Antioch in the late fourth century. Jean Chrysostome, *Huit catéchèses baptismales inédites,* intro., critical ed., trans., and notes Antoine Wenger, Sources Chrétiennes 50 (Paris: Éditions du Cerf, 1957), 147.

26. *Apostolic Constitutions, III,* 16, in Metzger, *Les Constitutions Apostoliques II,* 154–58; Francis X. Funk, *Didascalia et Constitutiones Apostolorum* (Paderbom: Schoningh, 1905), 201; cf. Vööbus, *Didascalia Apostolorum,* 53. The fifth-century *Testamentum Domini,* II, 8, prescribes a similar role for ordained widows and also instructs that women being baptized be shielded from the presbyter or bishop's view by a veil. I. Rahmani, ed., *Testamentum Domini Nostri Jesu Christi* (Mainz: Kirchheim, 1899; reprint, Hildesheim: George Olms, 1968), 128–31.

27. José Grosdidier de Matons, "La femme dans l'empire byzantin," in *Histoire mondiale de la femme,* ed. Pierre Grimal (Paris: Nouvelle Librairie de France, 1967), 40, connects the decline of deaconesses to this lessening need for them in adult baptisms.

The conversion to Christianity of foreign women still provided occasion for female deacons to assist in baptism, but, at least in rural Byzantine Palestine, that practice had fallen into disuse, although female deacons still existed in the Church of Jerusalem. See John Moschos, *Pratum spirituale,* chap. 3, in PG 87.3:2853–56.

housebound female parishioners,[28] although not specifically mentioned in texts dating from the middle Byzantine period, probably remained one of their functions well into this period. This is indicated by a letter of Patriarch Photios written between 877 and 886 to Leo, Bishop of Calabria, in southern Italy. Leo had consulted the Constantinopolitan patriarch about certain canonical matters; among them was a question about women who took Communion to Christians who had been imprisoned (perhaps held hostage?) by "Saracens," that is, Arabs. In his reply, Photios instructed Leo to choose noble women, either virgins or in chaste old age,[29] who were "worthy of being received into the diaconate and of being received into the rank of deacons."[30] Since Leo asked the question of Photios, evidently the order of female deacons was not known in his area of Calabria by this time, or at least so few deaconesses still existed that the Calabrian bishop was unfamiliar with the guidelines for and restrictions on candidates to the order.[31] Photios's response, on the other hand, indicates (1) that female deacons still existed (otherwise, his remarks about choosing women "worthy of being received into the diaconate" would make no sense), and (2) that he knew not only

---

28. For example, *Didascalia Apostolorum* 16: "For there are houses where you may not send deacons, on account of the pagans, but to which you may send deaconesses. And also because the service of a deaconess is required in many other domains." In Vööbus, *Didascalia Apostolorum*, 156.

29. Unlike the canons and civil legislation regulating female deacons, Photios does not specify virgins and widows, but perhaps that is implied by the phrase "σεμνῷ γήρατι."

30. Ep. 297, 4; in Photios, *Photii patriarchae Constantinopolitani epistulae et amphilochia*, eds. B. Laourdas and L. G. Westerink, vol. 3, *Bibliotheca Scriptorum Graecorum et Romanorum Teubneriana* (Leipzig: BSB B. G. Teubner, 1983), 166.

31. Calabria was part of Byzantine Italy and so generally had more in common with Constantinople than with Rome. In fact, there is evidence of women deacons in Byzantine Italy in the seventh and eighth centuries (see nn. 36, 42, and 47, below), though not in the ninth. It is unclear, moreover, if they still existed, whether they existed as their own order by this time in the Latin Church (that is, further north in Italy). Western deaconesses' ministry may have been connected to that of their husbands; they generally were the wives of deacons, and as such were also ordained and shared an active ministry with their husbands. See Gary Macy, "Ordination of Women," 493–94.

about the type of women who were ordained to the diaconate, but also that their ministry included taking the Eucharist to shut-ins.

In addition to the needs of laywomen (and imprisoned laymen), the seclusion of nuns precipitated special needs within the female monastic community. Thus, as noted above, deaconesses became particularly associated with female monasticism, from the fourth-century deaconess Lampadion[32] in charge of a choir of virgins in the monastic community founded by St. Macrina, who has been called the "Fourth Cappadocian,"[33] to St. Irene in the ninth century,[34] a

---

32. Gregory of Nyssa, *De vita Macrinae* 29, in *Grégoire de Nysse: Vie de Sainte Macrine*, intro., critical text, trans., notes Pierre Maraval, SC (Paris: Éditions du Cerf, 1971), 178:236; Eng. trans. Gregory of Nyssa, *The Life of Saint Macrina*, ed. and trans. Kevin Corrigan (Toronto: Peregrina, 1997), 45. Corrigan notes (68, n. 78) that the Greek term χορός may have either a general meaning (a group), or the specific meaning of a choir, as may be inferred from Hippolytus's *Apostolic Tradition*, 25, in Hippolytus, *On the Apostolic Tradition*, trans. John Behr (Crestwood, NY: St. Vladimir's Seminary Press, 2001), 134, or 26 in Hippolytus, *The Treatise on the Apostolic Tradition of St. Hippolytus of Rome, Bishop and Martyr*, 1968, trans. Gregory Dix, ed. Henry Chadwick, reprint with corrections from 2nd rev. ed. (London: Alban, 1991), vv. 18–32. See Johannes Quasten, *Music and Worship in Pagan and Christian Antiquity*, trans. Boniface Ramsey (Washington, D.C.: National Association of Pastoral Musicians, 1983), 78–81. Elm, *Virgins of God*, 177–78, n. 122, discussing the scholarly debate over the general or technical interpretation of the word in this context, observes that χορός is twice mentioned in the vita in a ceremonial sense, and cautiously raises Quasten's suggestion that it was in fact a musical chorus, while noting that Nyssa more commonly uses the word in its generic sense in the vita.

33. Jaroslav Pelikan, *Christianity and Classical Culture: The Metamorphosis of Natural Theology in the Christian Encounter with Hellenism* (New Haven, CT: Yale University Press, 1993), 89.

34. While the vita of St. Irene purports to tell the life of a ninth-century saint, the English translator of the vita finds the lack of chronological coherence so striking as not only to suggest that the text was composed in the tenth century (which the hagiographer readily admits), but also to call into question the very existence of the female saint. Jan O. Rosenqvist, *The Life of St Irene Abbess of Chrysobalanton* (Stockholm: Uppsala University, 1986), xxiii–xxix. While the latter conclusion is unwarranted given the Byzantine author's reference to the continuing veneration of Irene's tomb in his or her own day, Rosenqvist is no doubt correct in his theory that the description of Irene's life is a work of hagiographical fiction. However, that need not negate the value of the vita's description of Irene's ordination at the hands of the patriarch. It would have made little sense for the hagiographer to include a description of her diaconal ordination if the practice were completely unfamiliar to the average Byzantine layperson.

nun attached to the convent of Chrysobalanton in Constantinople who, according to her tenth-century hagiographer, was ordained as a deacon of the Great Church, that is, Hagia Sophia: "Without delay the patriarch rose from his throne at once and asked for a censer. Burning incense and praising God he initiated a hymn befitting the occasion. Then he first ordained Irene deaconess of the Great Church—for through the Spirit in him he knew her purity—and thereafter consecrated her with the seal of hegumenate."[35]

Three things are notable in the above account: (1) the (masculine) second-declension noun *diakonos* (διάκονος) was still being used, rather than the feminized *diakonissa* (διακόνισσα); (2) the word *cheirotonia* (χειροτονία) was used, a technical term for "ordination"; and (3) Irene was simultaneously consecrated as *hegoumene*, or abbess, of her monastery. The use of the title *diakonos* is significant since the alternative title, *diakonissa*, could also refer to the wife of a deacon.[36] Both the saint's personal background—Irene was a nun

---

Since ordination as a deacon was not a standard trope in middle Byzantine vitae of female saints, its inclusion in *The Life of St. Irene* points to either current or relatively recent actual practice and may be one of the few elements of the saint's life based in fact.

35. Rosenqvist, *Life of St Irene*, 26–29.

36. J. G. Davies, "Deacons, Deaconesses," 1, n. 1, states that the term διακόνισσα first appears in synodal literature in canon 19 of the Council of Nicaea, and the purely feminine term was sometimes used interchangeably with διάκονος (for example, in the fourth-century *Apostolic Constitutions* and in some of Justinian's sixth-century legislation). Archbishop Peter L'Huillier, *The Church of the Ancient Councils: The Disciplinary Work of the First Four Ecumenical Councils* (Crestwood: SVS, 1996), 244, observes that Justinian used the term διακόνισσα in legislation dealing with deaconesses alone; in legislation referring to both male and female deacons, however, he used the term διάκονος, with the adjective(s) for the appropriate sex. Nevertheless, διάκονος is the more common term used for a female deacon (leading to potential ambiguity with respect to the masculine plural form). Both canonical and civil legislation in late antiquity and the early Byzantine period more regularly use the term διάκονος for a woman deacon, as do the overwhelming majority of epigrams for women deacons compiled by Eisen, *Women Officeholders*, chap. 7. Surprisingly, the use of this term for female as well as male deacons has not been readily recognized by some scholars, leading to unfortunate "corrections." For example, Gustave Schlumberger, in his *Sigillographie de l'empire byzantin* (Paris: Société de l'Orient Latin, 1884; reprint, Turin: Bottega d'Erasmo, 1963), 232, incorrectly notes "sic" and

with no former husband—and the term *diakonos* make it patent that the patriarch was indeed ordaining Irene to a clerical order. Her ordained status is further reinforced both by the use of the term *cheirotonia* for "ordination" (the significance of which will be discussed in Section V) and by the patriarch's beginning the Divine Liturgy, the liturgical context for ordinations to major orders.[37]

As for the conjunction of the diaconate with Irene's consecration as abbess, this coincides with one of the two types of monastic women who typically were ordained to the diaconate in the early and middle Byzantine period:[38] (1) abbesses and nuns with liturgical functions, and (2) the wives of men who were being raised to the episcopacy.[39] By the fourth and fifth centuries, it was increasingly

---

emends to "Antonin" (that is, Antoninos, a male name) the feminine genitive name ντονίνης, which appears on the obverse of a seventh- or eighth-century seal from Byzantine Italy whose reverse shows the masculine/feminine genitive title διακόνου. In the CD-ROM *Prosopography of the Byzantine Empire I (641–867)*, ed. John Robert Martindale (London: King's College/Ashgate, 2001), Martindale does note that "it is possible that the feminine form 'Antonina' is correct and that the owner of the seal was a deaconess," yet the entry is listed as "Antoninos I," a male deacon, when in fact there is no legitimate reason to doubt that the owner of the seal was exactly what the seal indicates: a female deacon named Antonina.

37. The Greek phrase "τὸν θεὸν εὐλογήσας," which Rosenqvist translates merely as the bishop's "praising God," should be recognized as more likely referring to his beginning the divine liturgy: "Εὐλογημένη ἡ βασιλεία τοῦ Πατρός," that is, "Blessed is the kingdom of the Father," Goar, *Euchologion*, 52. (Alternatively, it could refer to the beginning blessing of several other services, "Εὐλογητὸς ὁ Θεὸς ἡμῶν," that is, "Blessed is our God.") The author thanks Eustratios Papaioannou for calling attention to this. Also, the order given, ordination first, followed by consecration as abbess, fits this interpretation since, although ordination to major orders occurred during the divine liturgy, ordination to lower orders, monastic tonsuring, and consecration to monastic offices were done outside of—hence, often after—the liturgy.

38. That the entalma of Patriarch Athanasius I, mentioned above (see n. 23), proscribed both double monasteries (that is, men's and women's joint communities) and deaconesses in the same item likely indicates that these deaconesses were nuns.

39. While most of the documentation for this latter category dates to the early and early-middle Byzantine periods, one possible late antique example of this second category is Theosebia, who may have been a deaconess, and who was either the wife or sister of Gregory of Nyssa, based on a condolence letter he received from Gregory of Nazianzus. See Elm, *Virgins of God*, 157–58, for

expected that men elevated as bishops would become celibate, even if married;[40] in the middle of the sixth century, the first civil legislation requiring this appeared, promulgated by Justinian in 531.[41] The first ecclesiastical legislation requiring bishops to separate from their wives was enacted over a century later. Canon 48 of the Council in Trullo, held in 691–92, calls for the wife of a bishop to take monastic vows after her husband's consecration as bishop and, if deemed worthy, to be ordained a deacon.[42] Perhaps the diaconate was expected since, as Cholij demonstrates with Theodore Balsamon[43] and others in the late middle Byzantine period, church officials believed "that the wife is, in some way, consecrated because of her union in marriage with her husband-priest."[44] By the middle Byzantine period, bishops typically took monastic vows, so the monastic tonsure combined with ordination to the female diaconate was as near as the wife of a bishop could get to her (former) husband's ecclesiastical

---

a discussion of the relative merits of the evidence; also, Michel Rene Barnes, "'The Burden of Marriage' and Other Notes on Gregory of Nyssa's *On Virginity*," *Studia Patristica*, v. 37, part II, eds. M. F. Wiles and E. J. Yarnold (Leuven: Peeters, 2001), 13, esp. n. 7.

40. C. Knetes, "Ordination and Matrimony in the Eastern Orthodox Church," *Journal of Theological Studies* 11 (1910): 481–90. Knetes attributes the development of the widespread expectation of episcopal celibacy to monastic influence.

41. *Code of Justinian* I, 3, 47 (48); in *Corpus iuris civilis* (hereafter CIC), 3 vols. (Berlin: Weidmann, 1954–59), vol. 2, *Codex Iustinianus*, ed. Paul Krueger, 34. Justinian's legislation on bishops and their wives and families is discussed in Knetes, "Ordination and Matrimony," 490–91. For more on the history of marriage within the ordained orders of clergy, see Roman Cholij, *Clerical Celibacy in East and West* (Leominster, U.K.: Fowler Wright Books, 1989).

42. Pitra, *Juris ecclesiastici*, 2:50. An example from eighth-century Byzantine Italy is recounted in Agnellus, *Liber pontificalis ecclesiae Ravennatis* 154, in *Le Liber pontificalis*, 3 vols., text, intro., and commentary L. Duchesne (Paris: E. Thorin; E. de Boccard, 1955–57), 1:483; cited in Martindale, *Prosopography*, "Euphemia 3" and "Sergios 54."

43. Balsamon, a canonist, was patriarch-in-exile of Antioch, residing in Constantinople in the late twelfth century.

44. Cholij, *Clerical Celibacy*, 28. This became the rationale for forbidding the widows of priests to remarry. Gary Macy's article, "Ordination of Women," esp. 490-94, demonstrates how a similar attitude was manifested differently in the medieval Latin Church, by ordaining or consecrating the spouses of clerics.

"rank."⁴⁵ There is no indication, however, that bishops' wives-cum-deaconesses were expected to have any particular liturgical or other ministry. Presumably they served the same functions as other deaconesses within a monastic setting.

These ministries of monastic female deacons were typically either liturgical or supervisory in nature. The simultaneous ordination and consecration of St. Irene of Chrysabalanton as both deacon and abbess reflects the continuation of a tradition evident from the early Byzantine period of combining these two offices; for example, Olympias and her successor, Elisanthia, were both abbess and deaconess.⁴⁶ This association of deaconess with abbess thus began by at least the late fourth century or early fifth century in the East, and occurred in the medieval period in the Latin as well as the Byzantine Church.⁴⁷

---

45. Cholij, *Clerical Celibacy*, 28–29, cites similar reasoning in a requirement of Pope Alexander III preserved in the *Decretals* of Gregory IX, which disallowed a married man from entering a monastery unless his wife also took monastic vows. Regarding the wife's assumption of a rank similar to her husband's, Macy, "Ordination of Women," 493–94, suggests that the wives of presbyters and deacons in the Western Church perhaps had "at times formed a liturgical team with their spouse." He notes that, "according to a Roman Ordinal from ca. 900, *presbyterae* and deaconesses received their commissioning at the same time and as part of the same ceremony as the priests and deacons who were their spouses. The prayers for the ordination of deaconesses in the several sacramentaries through the twelfth century are identical (apart from the use of the feminine form) to those used in the ordination of a deacon. Both deaconesses and presbyterae received special vestments as part of their ordination rites. These rites apparently did not distinguish between those deaconesses (or presbyterae) who had an active ministry and those who were merely the spouses of priests and deacons." A Latin rite of ordination for the female deacon is published in Cyrille Vogel and Reinhard Elze, *Le Pontifical Romano-Germanique du dixième siècle. Le Texte I. Studi e Testi* (Vatican City: Biblioteca Apostolica Vaticana, 1963), 226:54–59.

46. See Elm, *Virgins of God*, 180, who claims that "by the fifth century the *hegoumene*-deaconess nexus was common."

47. For example, Radegund of Poitiers; see Pauline Schmitt Pantel, ed., and Arthur Goldhammer, trans., "From Ancient Goddesses to Christian Saints," in *A History of Women in the West* (Cambridge, MA: The Belknap Press of Harvard University Press, 1992), 1:437–38; Macy, "Ordination of Women," 492–93. Another example, from mid-eighth century Byzantine Italy, is Euphrosyne, deaconess and abbess of the women's monastery of SS. Marcellinus and Petrus in

As for public liturgical functions, the one most commonly mentioned is that of chanting. The vita of St. Macrina shows that Lampadia was responsible for the women's choir, a liturgical duty, which would make ordination to the diaconate appropriate. By the late middle Byzantine period, the liturgical function of chanting appears to have become one of the ministries of female deacons not only in women's monasteries but also in the Great Church. Several *typika* (liturgical or monastic rules) and *euchologia* (liturgical manuals or service books) mention women's choirs, which chanted the first part of matins.[48] The eyewitness account of Anthony of Novgorod, during his visit to Constantinople in about the year 1200, confirms this as contemporary practice. His testimony is particularly compelling since, unlike the ritual manuals, which characteristically attempt to preserve a record of even outdated rites and practices, Anthony's primary concern was simply to describe his experience. He observed a group of women, whom he mistakenly called "myrrhbearers,"[49] par-

---

Naples; Bartolommeo Capasso, *Monumenta ad Neapolitani ducatus historiam pertinentia* (Naples: F. Giannini, 1881), 1:262–63; cited in Martindale, *Prosopography*, "Euphrosyne 5." The vita of Neilos of Rossano, chap. 79, provides a tenth-century example of an abbess-deacon in Byzantine Italy (Capua); Βίος καὶ πολιτεία τοῦ ὁσίου πατρὸς ἡμῶν Νείλου τοῦ Νέου, ed. G. Giovanelli (Grottaferrata: Badia di Grottaferrata, 1972), 118. My thanks to an anonymous reviewer for bringing the latter source to my attention.

48. Juan Mateos, *Le Typicon de la Grande Église. Ms. Sainte-Croix No 40, Xe siècle*, vols. 1–2, trans. Juan Mateos, *Orientalia Christiana Analecta*, vols. 165–66 (Rome: Pontificum Institutum Orientalium Studiorum, 1962–63), 1:4–5, 154, and 2:52 and 287; Miguel Arranz, "L'office de l'asmatikos hesperinos ('vêpres chantés') de l'ancien euchologe byzantin," *Orientalia Christiana Periodica* 44 (1978): 408.

49. The author is indebted to George Majeska, who noted that some Russian travelers to Constantinople, such as Anthony of Novgorod, mentioned "myrrhbearing women" who sang and who had a special place near the Great Church's "prothesis chapel," or *skeuophylakion*, which was located just outside the north door in the northeast bay, that is, the same place mentioned by Constantine Porphyrogenitus as the "deaconesses' narthex" (see n. 19). For this reason, despite Anthony's identification of these women as myrrhbearers, Majeska believes that the reference is to the deaconesses of the Great Church. He theorizes that the confusion of titles was due to the Russians' not having deaconesses; the title "myrrhbearer," however, was frequently used for women serving a wide variety of nonordained functions in the Russian Church. The Russian use of the term

ticipating in the matins service at Hagia Sophia. Matter-of-factly and in passing, Anthony revealed that these women chanted during the matins: "And not far from this prothesis the Myrrhbearers sing."[50] These "myrrhbearers" probably were deaconesses since he located them in exactly the same spot as Constantine Porphyrogenitus had located the deaconesses more than two hundred years earlier.[51] These women, also called *askētriai* (so named after their communal ascetic lifestyle), in addition to Balsamon's description of their maintaining order in the women's aisle, sang during matins and for funerals, for which they also sometimes served as mourners.[52] It is likely that these are the women to whom Balsamon dismissively referred when he commented: "[t]oday deaconesses are no longer ordained although certain members of ascetical religious communities are erroneously styled deaconesses."[53]

In addition to the Great Church, this liturgical ministry of chanting was mirrored in other important churches, if not by deaconesses, then by monastic women following the same liturgical pattern. For example, a twelfth-century satirical account of a pilgrimage to Thessaloniki for the feast of its patron, St. Demetrios, describes

---

"myrrhbearer" should not, however, be confused with the consecrated or ordained order of myrrhbearers in the Church of Jerusalem, which participated with the rest of the clergy in the Paschal services at the Church of the Holy Sepulchre. See nn. 57 and 59, below.

50. A.III.8; in *Kniga Palomnika: Skazanie mest svjatykh vo Tsaregrade Antonija Arkhiepiskopa Novgorodskago v 1200 godu*, ed. Kh. M. Loparev, Pravoslavnij Palestinskij Sbornik (St. Petersburg: Izd. Imp. Pravoslavnago palestinskago ob va, 1899), 51:2–9; trans. Taft, "Women at Church," 67. Taft identifies the prothesis with the cylindrical *skeuophylakion* of the Great Church, just outside the walls of the church on the northeast side.

51. See above, n. 19; Taft, "Women at Church," 65–70.

52. R. Janin, *Les églises et les monastères,* La géographie ecclésiastique de l'Empire byzantin (Paris: Institut Français d'Études Byzantines, 1975), 3:549–50; Gilbert Dagron, *Constantinople imaginaire: Études sur le recueil des Patria*, Bibliothèque Byzantine Études (Paris: Presses Universitaires de France, 1984), 8:252, n. 177. Earlier, until at least the ninth century, ordained female deacons were distinct from the *askētriai* (ἀσκήτριαι); see the citation from the *Basilics* in n. 115, below. Perhaps some of the σκήτριαι were deaconesses.

53. Theodore Balsamon, *Scholia in Concilium Chalcedonense*, in PG 137:41; Eng. trans. Martimort, *Deaconesses*, 171.

the liturgical participation of nuns during the basilica's festal service as follows: "Then from those who had specially practiced the rituals of the festival—what a congregation they had there—there was heard a most divine psalmody, most gracefully varied in its rhythm, order, and artistic alternations. For it was not only men who were singing; *the holy nuns in the left wing of the church, divided into two antiphonal choirs*, also offered up the Holy of Holies to the martyr."[54]

Commenting on this description, Sharon Gerstel notes that the wing where the nuns were located "must refer to the widened eastern end of the north aisle adjacent to the sanctuary."[55] In other words, the nuns in St. Demetrios in Thessaloniki were stationed in the area corresponding to the *gynaeceum* (women's aisle) of the deaconesses in Hagia Sophia; moreover, like the deaconesses, they chanted from there during services.

It appears, then, that certain leadership positions within the monastery—at a minimum, those of abbess and of director of the liturgical choir—were associated with the female diaconate, recognition of the supervisory or liturgical functions of these women. In addition, at least some deaconesses—and, later, nuns who served as their successors—attached to urban foundations served the broader community liturgically by chanting during the services in the great cathedrals.

Other specific activities of deaconesses during worship, whether in monasteries or in cathedrals and parish churches, are for the most part unknown, with one exception. A liturgical manual from the Church of Jerusalem[56] dating to the tenth century includes in its

---

54. R. Romano, ed., *Timarione: Testa critico, introduzione, traduzione, commentario e lessico* (Naples, 1974), 59. Eng. trans. *Timarion*, trans. B. Baldwin (Detroit: Wayne State University Press, 1984), 48–49; quoted in Gerstel, "Painted Sources," 92–93 (emphasis in Gerstel).

55. Gerstel, "Painted Sources," 93, n. 18.

56. The Church of Jerusalem, although a patriarchate in its own right and politically subject to Arab Muslim rule from the seventh century, nevertheless maintained spiritual ties to the Byzantine Church and continued to be a Greek Byzantine Church. Because of pilgrimage traffic, the rites and calendar of the Church of Jerusalem, particularly in the early Byzantine period, were extensive and elaborate, and "exerted a strong liturgical influence on the other churches of

paschal rubrics two orders of ordained or consecrated women: female deacons and *myrophoroi* (myrrhbearers).[57] According to the rubrics, near the end of the paschal matins there was a procession to the solea,[58] which included two of various orders of clergy: deacons, subdeacons, myrophoroi, and deaconesses. While the myrophoroi followed the deacons, holding *triskelia* (three-legged reading stands), the deaconesses carried two *manoualia* (single candleholders) with lit candles.[59]

In general, however, female deacons did not have the public processional and other liturgical functions of male deacons. For example, the ordination rite, to be discussed in Section V below, does not provide for the deaconess to read petitions and explicitly prohibits her from distributing Communion during the Divine Liturgy, both of which were typical functions of the male deacon. Therefore, although they were ordained at the altar and received Communion

---

the East." Hans-Joachim Schulz, *The Byzantine Liturgy: Symbolic Structure and Faith Expression,* trans. Matthew J. O'Connell, intro. Robert Taft (New York: Pueblo, 1980), 139. The hymnographic tradition of the monastery of St. Sabas in Palestine during the middle Byzantine period was equally influential on the Byzantine Church.

57. The *typikon* (liturgical rule or manual) describing these rites, "Τυπικὸν τῆς ἐν Ἱεροσολύμοις Ἐκκλησίας," is reproduced in A. Papadopoulos-Kerameus, Ἀνάλεκτα ἱεροσολυμιτικῆς σταχυολογίας, vol. 2 (St. Petersburg: V. Kirvaoum, 1894); see especially 179–99. The manuscript dates to 1122, but in the prologue (iii) Papadopoulos-Kerameus argues that it is a copy of an earlier work from the late ninth or early tenth century, based on a prayer commemorating Patriarch Nicholas, whose patriarchate lasted from 932 to 947 (the two Latin patriarchs named Nicholas reigned several decades after the written date of the manuscript, so the commemoration cannot refer to either of them). The typikon in general provides the texts and rubrics (some of which may have been added in the twelfth century) for the liturgical services of the Church of Jerusalem. A summary of the material on the *myrophoroi* contained in the Jerusalem typikon can be found in Gabriel Bertoniere, *The Historical Development of the Easter Vigil and Related Services in the Greek Church*, Orientalia Christiana Analecta (Rome: Pontifical Institutum Studiorum Orientalium, 1972), 193:50, n. 108. For a fuller discussion, see Karras, "Liturgical Participation," 153–62.

58. The solea is the part of the nave, often set off from the rest of the nave, directly in front of (that is, to the west of) the altar area. By the tenth to twelfth century, this is typically where one would find the chanter's stand and the bishop's throne.

59. Papadopoulos-Kerameus, Ἀνάλεκτα, 199.

there, there was no need for them to remain in the altar throughout the service; in fact, it would not have been practicable—or even possible—for all the large number of clergy attached to the Constantinopolitan cathedral to remain in the sanctuary throughout the liturgy.[60]

Rather, according to several accounts from the middle Byzantine period, the deaconesses of the Great Church of Hagia Sophia participated in the liturgy not from within the sanctuary, but from an area just outside the sanctuary on the north aisle.[61] This location, adjacent to the northern women's aisle (*gynaeceum*[62]) on the ground floor, indicates that their duties included general oversight or management of the gynaeceum, just as the *Apostolic Constitutions* prescribed for deaconesses in the early church.[63] In fact, in the late middle Byzantine period, at a time when female deacons had presumably devolved to a nonordained monastic order, Balsamon summed up their duties in just this way in a letter to Patriarch Mark III of Alexandria: "they ecclesiastically manage the gynaeceum."[64]

By this time, that is, the end of the twelfth century, while deaconesses remained in the same location as earlier, they were no longer ordained and so would no longer have entered the sanctuary

---

60. See n. 96, below.

61. See n. 19, above; also, Taft, "Women at Church," 65–70.

62. In the Great Church, as in all the large churches in the East, women and men were segregated for cultural and moral reasons; in most churches, women occupied the north side and men the south side (churches were always oriented to the east). See Sharon E. J. Gerstel, "Painted Sources for Female Piety in Medieval Byzantium," *Dumbarton Oaks Papers* 52 (1998): 91–92. Taft, "Women at Church," 57, even notes a funeral rubric in an eleventh-century codex that calls for the body of the deceased to be placed on the right (south) side of the church if male, on the left (north) side if female. However, most of the textual evidence for Hagia Sophia indicates that women occupied both the north and south aisles, with men in the central portion of the nave. See Taft, "Women at Church," 34–39; and T. F. Mathews, *The Early Churches of Constantinople: Architecture and Liturgy* (University Park: University of Pennsylvania Press, 1971), 130–33.

63. *Apostolic Constitutions* II, 57, 10, in SC, 320:314.

64. "τὴν γυναικωνῖτιν ἐκκλησιαστικῶς διορθούμεναι" (my translation). Theodore Balsamon, *Responsa ad interrogationes Marci 35*, in PG 138:988. Cf. Martimort, *Deaconesses*, 172.

to receive the Eucharist. This is probably the foundation for Balsamon's assertion, in his response to Mark of Alexandria, that deaconesses did not participate (or receive Communion) at the altar[65] and that in general they were simply part of the congregation.[66] Balsamon's description of the liturgical functions of Byzantine deaconesses is overly narrow, though, since he omits mention of their role as chanters, as witnessed by Anthony of Novgorod.

In fact, the location of the deaconesses, adjacent to the sanctuary, was not the most practical place for women whose only duty was to keep order in the women's section of the church. On the other hand, it would have served as an indication of their clerical status. More importantly, in terms of liturgical function, it was a practical location from which to sing (directly opposite to the male readers and chanters) and also from which to approach the altar in order to receive the Eucharist with the other clergy, as the ordination rite prescribed.[67] This special liturgical space for the deaconesses, then, both remained as an institutional memory of an earlier time when female deacons were ordained and received the Eucharist as clergy, and provided an appropriate location from which to chant for women who continued to be known as deaconesses even when the title had become a monastic honorific rather than an indication of a substantively clerical office.

Given both the number and variety of primary sources attesting to the female diaconate, there is general agreement as to both the existence of deaconesses in the Byzantine Church and the nature of their various liturgical and pastoral functions. However, there has been considerable disagreement and even controversy, in academic as well as ecclesiastical circles, over such questions as (1) whether the female deacon was considered part of the clergy; (2) if so, whether the deaconess was included among the "major orders" of clergy; and

---

65. "παρὰ δὲ τῇ ἁγιωτάτῃ Ἐκκλησίᾳ τοῦ θρόνου τῶν Κωνσταντινουπολιτῶν διακόνισσαι προχειρίζονται, μίαν μὲν μετουσίαν μὴ ἔχουσαι ἐν τῷ βήματι"; Balsamon, *Responsa* 35, in PG 138:988.

66. "ἐκκλησιάζουσαι δὲ τὰ πολλά"; ibid.

67. See Section V, below.

(3) what light the ordination rite of the female deacon might shed on the previous two questions. It is to these issues that we now turn.

II. The Female Deacon As Clergy

The clerical status of the female deacon in the Byzantine Church is clear for the early period. Even a canon from the Council of Nicaea (the first ecumenical council), held in 325, stating that certain deaconesses were not ordained, interpreted in its context implies the clerical, ordained status of female deacons in the catholic Church. This canon 19 regulated the manner in which Paulianist clergy were to be received into the catholic Church, requiring rebaptism and reordination, and administering the latter only for those who are found worthy.[68] Deaconesses were specifically banned from ordination because, the canon states, "since they have received no laying on of hands [*cheirothesian tina*], [they] are thus therefore to be counted among the laity."[69]

The pertinent question here is *which* deaconesses "have received no laying on of hands"? Aimé Georges Martimort, rather than considering the question of which deaconesses are the subject of the final sentence of the canon,[70] focuses instead on a phrase from the previous sentence, which calls for the same form to be observed for deaconesses and all other clergy. Then, rather than applying this clause to the rebaptism and potential reordination of Paulianist clergy, which has just been discussed, he instead interprets it as indication that the manner of ordination in the catholic and Paulianist Churches was the same for deaconesses and other clergy, thus reading the canon to

---

68. Pitra, *Juris ecclesiastici*, 2:435; Carl J. Hefele, *Conciliengeschichte* (Freiburg: Herder, 1873), 1:427.

69. Ibid.; Eng. trans. Martimort, *Deaconesses*, 102.

70. By contrast, Jerome Cotsonis, "A Contribution to the Interpretation of the 10th Canon of the First Ecumenical Council," *Revue des études byzantines* (*Mélanges Raymond Janin*) 19 (1961): 190, immediately observes that one of the important questions in this canon is "whether the word refers to the deaconesses of the Paulianists only or to those of the Church too." Unfortunately, Martimort nowhere refers to or cites in his discussion the Cotsonis article, although it was published two decades before Martimort's work. See also Theodorou, "<Χειροτονία> ἤ <Χειροθεσία>," 27–32.

mean that *neither* the Paulianists nor the catholic Church ordained women as deacons: "No more than before, however, did they receive any laying on of hands or become a part of the κλῆρος [clergy]."⁷¹ However, the fact that deaconesses were singled out for special mention precisely *because* they had not been ordained makes it clear that there was a difference in practice here between the two churches; that is, either the Paulianists or the catholic Church considered deaconesses a nonclerical order and hence did not confer ordination on them. If both churches had viewed them as nonclergy, there would have been no reason to mention them at all.⁷²

Furthermore, if it were the catholic Church that did not ordain deaconesses or consider them to be clergy, there would have been no reason to mention them since the required reordination for Paulianist clergy would have been impossible in the case of the deaconess; everyone would already know that they had lay status.⁷³ The

---

71. Martimort, *Deaconesses*, 103. Kalsbach, *Altkirchliche Einrichtung*, 46–49, and Gryson, *Ministry of Women*, 48–49, reason similarly. See Cipriano Vagaggini, "L'ordinazione," 155–56.

72. Cotsonis, "Contribution," 190, observes that an assumption that deaconesses in general were not ordained "makes the rest of the text of the canon contradictory to itself. For at the beginning of the same sentence it appears that the canon regards deaconesses as members of the clergy while later it would seem prepared to consider them as being classed merely among the laity." Similarly, Vagaggini, "L'ordinazione," 155–60, notes the illogical contortions to which other, earlier scholars have gone in order to interpret this canon in a way that excludes deaconesses from the clergy, including theorizing different types of deaconesses.

73. This is the problem with the interpretation of the canon suggested by L'Huillier, *Church of the Ancient Councils*, 82–83. L'Huillier argues that, since there is no extant ordination rite for female deacons before the *Apostolic Constitutions* (citing the lack of one in the *Apostolic Tradition*), it was probably the Paulianists who had ordained female deacons as opposed to the catholic Church. He furthermore suggests that, "if this phrase concerns deaconesses in general, maybe the fathers of Nicaea wanted to remind people that this type of ministry did not have a priestly character properly speaking," 83. However, the *Apostolic Tradition* is the only extant document containing ordination rites earlier than the *Apostolic Constitutions*; the absence of an ordination rite for deaconesses in this one work does not exclude the possibility of the ordination of deaconesses in other geographic areas, particularly the East. Indeed, it is unlikely that the *Apostolic Constitutions* would include an ordination rite for female deacons only a couple of decades—at most—after the Council of Nicaea in 325 if canon 19

logical inference, then, is that the canon excluded Paulianist deaconesses from the reordination possible for other orders because, since they were not ordained in the Paulianist Church, they were considered laypersons, not ordained clergy, even in the heretical church. In other words, the purpose of this canon, as with many of those dealing with the Montanist Church in North Africa, was to try as much as possible to integrate heretical clergy into the catholic clergy so that they could remain with their communities; in the case of deaconesses, however, whereas it was possible for them to continue their ministry, it was impossible to consider their ministry to be a clerical one, as in the catholic Church, since the Paulianist deaconesses were not ordained clergy.

Jerome Cotsonis provides a particularly attractive solution along these lines by proposing that the text of the canon was corrupted early in its manuscript history. He suggests replacing *tina* [feminine accusative singular of the indefinite article] in the final sentence with *tines* [feminine nominative plural], so that the final sentence would read, "since *some of these women* have received no laying on of hands [*cheirothesian tines*], [they] are thus therefore to be counted among the laity."[74] Thus, it is apparent that, already by the time of the First Ecumenical Council, female deacons were ordained members of the clergy, thus necessitating the special provision in canon 19 for women called "deaconesses" in the Paulianist Church who, however, were not ordained. The clerical status of deaconesses is even clearer in canon 15 of the Council of Chalcedon, in the middle of the fifth century, which clearly assumed female deacons were ordained clergy who exercised a ministry.[75]

---

were truly meant to be interpreted as a reminder of a long-standing blanket exclusion of ordained women deacons. (As with Martimort, L'Huillier appears unaware of the Cotsonis article.)

74. Cotsonis, "Contribution," 197. His solution is more plausible than the attempt of Gelasius, in his *Church History*, and two ancient Latin translators to solve the problem by changing the first reference from "deaconesses" to "deacons." See the discussion in L'Huillier, *Church of the Ancient Councils*, 82 and 99, nn. 392 and 393.

75. "Διάκονον μὴ χειροτονεῖσθαι γυναῖκα πρὸ ἐτῶν τεσσαράκοντα καὶ ταύτην μετὰ ἀκριβοῦς δοκιμασίας." See n. 13, above. In this regard, L'Huillier, *Church*

III. The Female Diaconate As a "Major Order"

That the deaconess was included not just among the clergy, but also specifically among the major orders of clergy, is even more indisputable as one moves further into the Byzantine period. First it is necessary to review the distinction between the two general levels of ordained orders.[76] All ordained orders had liturgical and/or sacramental functions more or less unique to each. Nevertheless, there were differences in ordination rite and in liturgical function that allow several orders to be grouped together. In the case of the distinction between "major" and "minor" orders, to use more modern terminology, the differences appear to be ones of degree or centrality of function, especially liturgical or sacramental function.[77] For instance, in the Byzantine Church,[78] only bishops, presbyters, and deacons could read the petitions of the liturgy.[79] Those three orders

---

of the Ancient Councils, 245, argues that "the text of canon 15 of Chalcedon leaves no doubt about the sacramental nature of the feminine diaconate. . . . It is, therefore, clear that at least at this period in the East, we are not dealing with an inferior order."

76. The distinctions which are clear by the end of the middle Byzantine period are incipient but not so clear in the late antique period. In a response to Martimort, written as an appendix to the English translation of his book, Gryson, *Ministry of Women*, 117–18, notes that distinctions between levels of clergy are evident in such early texts as the *Apostolic Constitutions*, but faults Martimort (*Deaconesses*, 75) for failing to consider the differences on their own terms, instead anachronistically applying modern views of ordination and of levels of clergy to the early period: "I believe that 'the concepts of our modern theology' have nothing to do with determining how the *Apostolic Constitutions* regarded the ordination of deaconesses. One cannot say that because our theology is reluctant to accept this ordination as sacramental, the same as that of the male deacons, the *Apostolic Constitutions* could not consider it such." It is possible, however, to recognize differences in clerical levels based on contemporaneous evidence, not on anachronistic applications of modern theology and practice.

77. See, for example, Frank Hawkins, "Orders and Ordination in the New Testament," in *The Study of Liturgy*, eds. Cheslyn Jones, Geoffrey Wainwright, and Edward Yarnold (New York: Oxford University Press, 1978), 301–20.

78. While this discussion concerns the historical Byzantine Church, the distinctions drawn in this and the following paragraph apply to the modern Eastern Orthodox Church as well.

79. See, for example, the Divine Liturgy of St. John Chrysostom in Goar, *Euchologion*, 47–69.

also received the Eucharist at the altar and could distribute it to others, while those in minor orders received Communion with the laity and could not commune others. These differences in liturgical function were reflected in the various rites of ordination.[80]

Moreover, beyond the distinction between major and minor orders, a further distinction must be drawn within the major orders between the diaconate, on the one hand, and the presbytery and episcopacy, on the other hand. Of course, each order had its own character and uniqueness. However, there was a liturgical and sacramental connection between bishop and presbyter that excluded the deacon already evident in the early church.[81] So, for example, while the deacon could give a blessing in a nonliturgical context, he did not do so during the liturgy, where only the presbyter or bishop could formally bless.[82] Also, although deacons read the petitions at liturgical services, they did not read the liturgical prayers (including the consecration prayer during the liturgy), which were for presbyter or bishop only; nor could deacons baptize.[83] At times, the diaconate seemed to straddle not only the division between major and minor orders, but even the distinction between clergy and laity. For instance, the rites of the Byzantine Church provided a distinct funeral

---

80. Goar, *Euchologion*, 65–67; the text of the liturgy assumes that both a presbyter and a deacon are serving. Functions of lower orders may be assumed by higher orders, but not vice versa. Thus, the deacon's role (petitions, and so on) would be assumed by a presbyter or bishop serving alone; by contrast, a deacon could not baptize or celebrate the Eucharist. The specific characteristics of the ordination rites are discussed in Section IV, below.

81. Hawkins, "Orders and Ordination," 304.

82. This was typically seen in those few instances where the bishop or presbyter turned to the faithful (the celebrant typically stood at the altar facing east in the same manner as the laity), perhaps made a gesture of blessing (the rubrics are not always specific), and said to the congregation, "Peace be with you" (Εἰρήνη πᾶσι). According to the *Apostolic Constitutions*, VIII, 3, 28, in SC 336:230, blessing was reserved to bishops and presbyters; neither the male nor the female deacon was to bless congregants.

83. *Apostolic Constitutions*, III, 11, in SC 329:146; deacons were permitted only to assist bishops and presbyters. The Latin Church by the medieval period allowed deacons to baptize, but this expansion of the diaconal role never occurred in the East.

service for presbyters and, by extension, bishops;[84] deacons, by contrast, were buried according to the rubrics for the laity.

These limitations on the deacon's liturgical role were manifestations of a fundamental liturgical difference between the diaconate and the other two major orders: the deacon could not act as celebrant of any of the sacraments.[85] After all, in its origin, the diaconate's primary ministry—as the name suggests—was meant to be pastoral.[86] By contrast, both presbyter and bishop exercised primary sacramental and liturgical functions, although the distinction between the two orders was unclear (and perhaps nonexistent) in the New Testament church.[87] Gradually, the presbyters clearly came to be under the authority of the bishop[88] and to celebrate the sacraments in the stead of the bishop, who alone retained the sacramental authority to ordain.[89] Thus, it was not coincidental that the presbyter acquired the name "priest" (*hiereus*) and that one of the alternatives to the standard term for "bishop" (*episkopos*) became "archpriest" (*archiereus*).

Where, then, did the Byzantine deaconess fit in this distinction between major and minor orders? The organization of ordination rites in the Byzantine euchologia is informative. Most are

---

84. Goar, *Euchologion*, 451–65.

85. This may be seen in the numerous sacraments and other services in the Goar euchologion. Unlike the Latin Church, the Byzantine Church did not allow a deacon to serve as a witness to matrimony. This was because, as an Orthodox sacramental theology of marriage developed, the cleric marrying the couple was, as with the other sacraments, viewed as the celebrant (note the structure of the wedding— "crowning"—service, in ibid., 314–25). By contrast, the Latin Church continued the late antique philosophy embedded in civil law that viewed marriage essentially as an oath or contract; thus, the celebrants were the couple itself, with the cleric acting primarily as witness.

86. *Diakonos* (διάκονος) means "servant"; Acts 6:1–6. For a somewhat controversial revisionist interpretation of the meaning of the term, see John N. Collins, *Diakonia: Reinterpreting the Ancient Sources* (New York: Oxford University Press, 1990).

87. Hawkins, "Orders and Ordination," 293–97.

88. This had occurred for at least some of the churches of Asia Minor by the end of the first century, to judge by the letters of Ignatius of Antioch.

89. *Apostolic Constitutions*, III, 11, in SC 329:146.

organized in descending order,[90] that is, from presbyter to deacon and deaconess, then to the lower orders of subdeacon, chanter, and reader. Others reverse the order; thus, Goar's euchologion, relying principally on the eleventh-century Grottaferrata euchologion from Constantinople, organizes the ordination rites in ascending order, from reader and chanter, to deputy and candle-bearer, to subdeacon, and then within "major orders" from deacon to deaconess to various ecclesiastical officials (such as archdeacon), to presbyter and finally bishop.[91] What is striking is that, even when the rites are organized in ascending order, the ordination of the female deacon is always placed directly after that of the male deacon. This consistent placement manifestly demonstrates that male and female deacons were considered to be of essentially the same rank or order.[92]

Moreover, the mid-sixth-century legislation of Justinian provides perhaps the most incontrovertible evidence, outside of the rubrics of the ordination rite itself, that the female deacon in the Byzantine Church not only was regarded as a member of the clergy, but was also ranked with the major orders of clergy.[93] In his Novel 3, the emperor included female deacons among the clergy whose numbers he regulated for the Great Church of Hagia Sophia,[94] in the prologue listing male and female deacons together,[95] and later specifying one hundred male and forty female deacons for Hagia Sophia.[96]

---

90. For example, the ordination rites in the eighth-century Barberini euchologion, contained in secs. 159–66, follow this descending order; *Barberini*, 178–90.

91. Goar, *Euchologion*, 194–261.

92. Martimort, *Deaconesses*, 151, notes that, in all but one manuscript from the Byzantine period (Sinai gr. 956), this is the case. He draws no conclusions from this, however.

93. Martimort, *Deaconesses*, 109–12, discusses Justinian's novellae, but in this context completely sidesteps the question of whether the female diaconate was considered a major order.

94. CIC, vol. 3, *Novellae*, eds. Rudolf Schoell and Guilelmus Kroll (Berlin: Weidmann, 1959), 18.

95. "πόσους δὲ διακόνους, ἄρρενάς τε καὶ θηλείας"; CIC 3:19.

96. Nov. 3, 1, in CIC 3:21. Since the novel limits presbyters to 60, male deacons to 100, female deacons to 40, subdeacons to 90, readers to 110, and chant-

66   CHAPTER THREE

Of course, the term "clergy" included both major and minor orders; thus, Novel 3 regulated subdeacons, readers, and chanters as well as presbyters and deacons (doorkeepers are listed after the total of clergy). However, it is clear, for two reasons, that Justinian ranked the female deacon among the major orders of clergy. First, he consistently listed the female deacon together with the male deacon when discussing clergy in general, normally using the first-declension *diakonos* with the feminine article, although occasionally the feminized noun *diakonissa* was used (sometimes within the same piece of legislation).[97]

Secondly, in Novel 6, the emperor set forth the rules regarding the ordination[98] of higher clergy, limiting the novel to bishops, presbyters, and deacons, both male and female. In fact, the novel is entitled, "Regarding how it is necessary for bishops and presbyters and male and female deacons to be ordained."[99] That Justinian—and, thus, presumably the Byzantine Church as a whole[100]—considered deaconesses to be part of the higher clergy is further underscored by his prefatory remarks in this novel about the *hierosynē*, or "priesthood" in its broad sense.[101] Considering that the novel was limited to the episcopacy, presbyterate, and diaconate, this indicates Justinian's *hierosynē* to be analogous to what today is termed "major orders."

However, it appears from other legislation that, although deaconesses were obviously considered part of the clergy, and the higher clergy at that, Justinian and others were not entirely comfortable with the idea. The cultural notions that female nature was morally

---

ers to 25, it is clear that female deacons are included among the "most reverend clergy" totaling 425 persons. This novel was reiterated in the *Basilics* III, 2, 1.

97. For example, Nov. 6, 6, in CIC 3:43–45.

98. The Greek word consistently used is χειροτονία, not χειροθεσία; the potential significance of these two terms will be discussed in Section IV, below; see especially n. 124.

99. CIC 3:35.

100. There is no indication that Justinian or any other emperor attempted to impose drastic liturgical change on the church through legislation; therefore, the logical assumption is that his categorization of the female diaconate reflects the theology of orders of the Byzantine Church generally.

101. CIC 3 :35–36.

"weaker,"[102] and that male headship—especially in church affairs—needed to be exercised over women who were either lustful or susceptible to seduction,[103] no doubt influenced Justinian as well as the church as a whole. That women were ordained to major orders likely multiplied the trepidation hierarchs and emperors felt in this regard.

Such cultural biases account for the double standards adhered to for male and female deacons. The requirements for entry to the female diaconate were far more restrictive than for the male diaconate, even in late antiquity, and the penalties for misconduct by female deacons were far more severe than for their male counterparts. As with the other clergy in major orders, female deacons could not marry after their ordination (by contrast, members of all minor orders except subdeacons were permitted to marry).[104] Unlike the male clergy, however, married women could not become deaconesses unless they were separated from their husbands (as with the wives of bishops). As mentioned earlier, deaconesses—just as en-

---

102. For more on late-antique and Byzantine notions of the inherent weakness of women, see, for example, part 2, chap. 1, "Incapacités ou exclusions?" in Joëlle Beaucamp, *Le statut de la femme à Byzance (4e–7e siècle)*, vol. 2, *Les pratiques sociales*, Trauvaux et mémoires, Monograph 6 (Paris: De Boccard, 1992), 273–93; and Hélène Saradi Mendelovici, "L' 'infirmitas sexus' présumée de la moniale Byzantine: doctrine ascetique et pratique juridique," in *Les femmes et le monachisme byzantin*, ed. Jacques Perreault (Athens: Canadian Archeological Institute, 1991), 87–97. Gillian Clark, *Women in Late Antiquity: Pagan and Christian Lifestyles* (Oxford: Clarendon, 1993), 56–62, discusses for late antiquity in general the ambivalence toward the notion of female weakness expressed in law and practice.

103. This philosophy was rooted biblically in 1 Tim 2:11–12, where women are forbidden to teach because Eve was deceived (hence, she "taught" Adam badly). See, for example, John Chrysostom, *On the Priesthood*, 3, 2, in PG 48:633.

104. Can. 15 of Chalcedon; in Pitra, *Juris ecclesiastici*, 1:528. Justinian's Nov. 6, 6, in CIC 3:43–44. See Joëlle Beaucamp, *Le statut de la femme à Byzance* (4e–7e siècle), vol. 1, *Le droit impérial*. Travaux et mémoires, Monograph 5 (Paris: De Boccard, 1990), 183; Gryson, *Ministry of Women*, 109–10. For a more general discussion of the restriction on higher clergy's marrying after ordination, see Patrick Demetrios Viscuso, "A Byzantine Theology of Marriage: The 'Syntagma kata stoicheion' of Matthew Blastares" (Ph.D. diss., The Catholic University of America, 1989), 90–92.

rolled widows—originally had to be at least sixty years old;[105] later the age was lowered first to fifty[106] and then to forty.[107]

Judging from the age and marital restrictions, it would appear that the purpose of these restrictions was to ensure that female deacons were as chaste and sexually nonthreatening—perhaps even asexual—as possible.[108] This would also explain why the punishment for sexual misconduct was far harsher for deaconesses than for the

---

105. See n.12, above. Theodosius specifically refers to the Apostle Paul's minimum for Widows. Gryson, *Ministry of Women*, 70, notes that the fifth-century Byzantine historian Sozomen, in his *Ecclesiastical History,* 7, 16, 8–11 (Sozomen, GCS, 4:323–24), credits a scandal in the capital with provoking Theodosius to set such a high minimum age. The connection is unclear since, according to Sozomen, the incident involved not a deaconess but an upper-class woman who accused a male deacon of sexual misconduct in connection with a penance prescribed to her by a priest, who was defrocked. See Gryson, *Ministry of Women*, 148, n. 246; Beaucamp, *Le statut de la femme*, 2:355.

106. Nov. 6, 6, in CIC 3:43.

107. However, there were exceptions, such as Olympias, the close friend of St. John Chrysostom, who was widowed quite young and was ordained a deaconess at the age of twenty-nine or thirty, at about the same time that Theodosius enacted the law setting the minimum age at sixty. Clark, *Jerome, Chrysostom,* 112; Elm, *Virgins of God,* 179. Another exception was Irene of Chrysobalanton, who was probably in her early to mid-twenties at the time of her ordination. Rosenqvist, *The Life of St Irene*, 28–29, n. 8.

108. It would be anachronistic, particularly for the Constantinopolitan Church, to read into these age restrictions the issue of ritual impurity associated with menstruation. Except for a longstanding, highly restrictive tradition in Alexandria and a caution in the fifth-century *Testamentum Domini*, of Syrian provenance, against ordained widows approaching the altar during their menses, there is no indication of liturgical restrictions on menstruants in the Byzantine Church prior to the ninth century. To the contrary, church orders from the early Byzantine period in the area of Antioch denounced the imposition of Levitical notions of impurity, explicitly including menstruation. See Section V, below. For more on this subject, see Joan Branham, "Bloody Women and Bloody Spaces: Menses and the Eucharist in Late Antiquity and the Early Middle Ages," *Harvard Divinity Bulletin* 30:4 (spring 2002): 15–22; Shaye J. D. Cohen, "Menstruants and the Sacred in Judaism and Christianity," in *Women's History and Ancient History*, ed. Sarah B. Pomeroy (Chapel Hill: The University of North Carolina Press, 1991), 273–99; G. L. C. Frank, "Menstruation and Motherhood: Christian Attitudes in Late Antiquity," *Studia Historiae Ecclesiasticae* 19:2 (1993): 185–208; Karras, "The Liturgical Participation of Women," chap. 3, "The Ritual Impurity of Women: Blood and Birth," 88–135; and Patrick Viscuso, "Menstruation: A Problem in Late Byzantine Canon Law," *Études*

male clergy, exemplified most starkly by a provision in Justinian's Novel 6, promulgated in 535, which prescribed the death penalty for any deaconess who broke her vow of celibacy by marrying or engaging in fornication.[109] Such a penalty was far harsher than for laywomen guilty of fornication;[110] it was also far harsher than for fornicating subdeacons, deacons, and priests, who were simply reduced to lay status.[111] Justinian asserted that the deaconess's crime was similar to that of unchaste vestal virgins in pagan times and thus deserved the same capital punishment.[112] Later emperors lessened the severity of punishment, but even confiscation of property was more severe than the penalty for males committing the same crime.[113] In practice, however, misbehaving deaconesses may have been treated more similarly to male clergy than the imperial legislation would suggest; Joëlle Beaucamp observes that the punishment usually found in the hagiographic literature for sexually misbehaving deaconesses and nuns is defrocking or expulsion from the monastery, respectively.[114] Eleven years after Novel 6, Justinian himself, through Novel 123, reduced the penalties in cases where sexual impropriety was unclear. Nevertheless, while the penalties in such cases were similar to those

---

byzantines 4 (1999). Note that Cohen and Frank treat only the late antique period.

109. "αὑταί τε ἔνοχοι γενήσονται θανάτου." Nov. 6, 6, in CIC 3:44–45. See Beaucamp, *Le statut de la femme*, 1:183.

110. Ibid.

111. Nov. 6, 5, in CIC 3:42–43; see also Nov. 22, 42, in CIC 3:176.

112. CIC 3:45. By contrast, canon 44 of Basil prescribes seven years' excommunication for a deaconess guilty of fornication with a pagan; Pitra, *Juris ecclesiastici*, 1:593. See Beaucamp, *Le statut de la femme*, 2:354; Martimort, *Deaconesses*, 105.

113. Cf. Novel 123, chaps. 14, 29, and 30, in CIC 3:605, 616. Confiscation of the property of a wayward deaconess was retained in the *Basilics* III, 1, 46. For any man who raped a deaconess, nun, or other consecrated woman, the penalty was confiscation of the rapist's property; Nov. 123, chap. 43; *Basilics* IV, 1, 15.

114. Beaucamp, *Le statut de la femme*, 2:340. Beaucamp, ibid., 276, n. 34, also cites Sozomen (*Ecclesiastical History* IV, 24, 16, in GCS, 4:181), who mentions a deaconess named Nektaria, who was excommunicated for violating her "contracts" (συνθῆκαι) and "vows" (ὅρκοι).

for adultery for laywomen, they were still more severe than for male clerics guilty of the same misconduct.[115]

Thus, female deacons in the Byzantine Church were restricted in a number of ways in which male deacons were not, apparently because of their incongruous position as women clergy. At the same time, however, it appears that the severity with which deaconesses were regulated was itself a further indication of their rank as members of the higher clergy. Ultimately, however, while the legislative and other material above points clearly to their status as members of major orders, the most telling evidence comes from the ordination rite itself.

IV. The Ordination of the Byzantine Deaconess

While the categorization of ordained orders into "major" and "minor" is anachronistic, distinguishing ranks of clergy by differences in the rite of ordination as well as by liturgical function is not a novel concept. Hence, the crucible for the controversy over the status of the female diaconate in the early and Byzantine Church has been the rite of ordination. As early as the fourth-century *Apostolic Constitutions*,[116] there are clear differences between the ordinations of presbyter and deacon, on the one hand, and those of subdeacon and

---

115. The penalties under Novel 123 were similar to those that soon after would be instituted for adultery (that is, imprisonment in a monastery and loss of property). But Beaucamp notes that this novel (chaps. 14 and 29), as with Novel 6, again is more lenient with male clerics (priests, deacons, and subdeacons), requiring only their defrocking and turning over their property to the diocese that they served. In other words, male clerics retained their personal freedom, including their freedom to marry. Beaucamp, *Le statut de la femme*, 2:184; see also 210. L'Huillier, *The Church of the Ancient Councils*, 247, similarly comments on the severity of canonical punishment in canon 15 of Chalcedon for deaconesses who marry (defrocking and excommunication) vis-à-vis their male counterparts (defrocking only), but he theorizes unconvincingly that its rationale lies in the maturity expected of the deaconess because of her greater age.

The symbolic status of deaconesses and other consecrated women with respect to the honor of the church, "as the bride of Christ," can also be discerned in the harsh penalty (cutting off the nose) prescribed in the ninth-century *Basilics* for those who behaved lewdly toward these women. *Basilics* LX, 37, 76.

116. VIII, 16–21, in SC 336:216–22.

reader, on the other hand.¹¹⁷ The ordination rites in the document are brief, omitting most rubrics and not even describing when the ordination is to be performed (that is, its larger liturgical context).

Nevertheless, there are discernible differences for different levels of clergy. The rubrics for the ordination of presbyter and deacon call for the candidate to be ordained "in the presence of" those of their own order and above.¹¹⁸ For example, the deacon is to be ordained by the bishop's laying hands on him "in the presence of the whole presbytery, and of the deacons."¹¹⁹ By contrast, the rites for subdeacon and reader call for the bishop simply to lay hands upon the candidate.¹²⁰ Although there are no rubrics describing where these ordinations take place, the phrase "in the presence of" the other higher clergy implies that the ordinations of presbyter, deacon, and deaconess probably were performed in the altar area, where the other clergy would have been present at the *synthronon*.¹²¹ In the case of the

---

117. The liminal position of the deaconess has engendered vociferous disagreement over her status. Bradshaw, *Ordination Rites*, 84, declines to participate in the debate between Gryson and Martimort over whether the deaconess in the *Apostolic Constitutions* was sacramentally ordained, arguing that such a debate "may not only be anachronistic but also over simplistic: the categorization of the liturgical ministries of the early Church cannot be reduced to a simple division between clergy and laity."

118. Martimort, *Deaconesses*, 69, notes this distinction, but fails to comment on it with respect to the ordination of the deaconess, whereas Gryson, Ministry of Women, 115–20, finds it suggestive of the higher clerical status of the deaconess. Bradshaw, *Ordination Rites*, 85, notes the similarities between the *Apostolic Constitutions* and the later Byzantine rite both in the analogous general structure and in the minor differences between the ordination rites of deacon and deaconess.

119. *Apostolic Constitutions*, VIII, 17, in SC 336:218; Eng. trans. "Apostolic Constitutions," in *Fathers of the Third and Fourth Centuries*, eds. Alexander Roberts and James Donaldson, *Ante-Nicene Fathers* (hereafter ANF), vol. 7, reprint ed. (Peabody, MA: Hendrickson, 1994), 492.

120. VIII, 20–21, in SC 336:220–22.

121. The *synthronon* was a type of mini-amphitheater, that is, a series of raised levels in a semicircular shape, lining the sanctuary apse in early Christian churches in the East. This architectural feature may still be seen in certain ancient churches, such as Hagia Eirene in Constantinople (Istanbul). See Thomas F. Mathews, *The Early Churches of Constantinople: Architecture and Liturgy* (University Park: University of Pennsylvania Press, 1971), 143–52.

deaconess, the *Apostolic Constitutions* calls for the bishop to "lay thy hands upon in the presence of the presbytery, and of the deacons and deaconesses."[122] Thus, even the meager information gleaned from the *Apostolic Constitutions*' ordination rite for the deaconess suggests that the deaconess was placed among the major orders.[123]

By the middle Byzantine period, the distinction is clearer between major and minor orders, in part through increasing, though not yet complete, consistency in the use of the ordination terms *cheirotonia* and *cheirothesia*.[124] In his seminal work on the distinctions between these two types of ordination, Greek theologian and church historian Panayiotes Trembelas notes that the cheirothesia rite—for ordination to lower orders—is characterized principally by (1) its physical location outside the *bema* (altar area); and (2) its temporal location outside of the divine liturgy.[125] By contrast, the

---

122. VIII, 19, in SC 336:220; Eng. trans. ANF 7:492.

123. Bradshaw, *Ordination Rites*, observes that "the word 'ordination' [*cheirotonia*] does not appear at the beginning of the instruction concerning deaconesses" and suggests that "this omission may be intended to indicate a subtle distinction in status." However, he does not respond to Gryson, *Ministry of Women*, 118, who, upon examination of the critical apparatus, concluded "that the formulas in question *peri de cheirotonias presbyterōn* and others were wrongly inserted by Funk in the current text, and that in fact, these titles had been introduced later on into part of the manuscript tradition." See Francis X. Funk, *Didascalia et Constitutiones Apostolorum* (Paderborn: Schöningh, 1905). Marcel Metzger's more recent critical edition, in SC 336, reproduces the same titles. The apparatus shows that the wording in these section titles is variable in the manuscript traditions, so Gryson may be correct; Funk and Metzger's editorial choices could have been predicated on the assumption that women were not truly ordained.

124. For a thorough discussion of the history of the use of these two terms and of their significance in terms of the distinction in ordination rites, see Panagiotis Trembelas, "Τάξεις χειροθεσιῶν καὶ χειροτονιῶν," *Theologia* 19:2–3; 20:1 (1941–48; 1949); Cyrille Vogel, "Chirotonie et chirothésie: Importance et relativité du geste de l'imposition des mains dans la collation des ordres," *Irénikon* 45 (1972): 7–21, 207–38; and Vagaggini, "L'ordinazione," 179–80, esp. n. 2. Vogel, 10, observes that the distinction in meaning between these two heretofore interchangeable terms begins in the eighth century and even then only in some juridical and didactic works. L'Huillier, *Church of the Ancient Councils*, 243, agrees with Vogel regarding the instability of the two terms prior to the Second Ecumenical Council of Nicaea (787).

125. Trembelas, "Τάξεις," 452.

cheirotonia type of ordination—that is, for major orders—occurs at the bema and in the course of the Divine Liturgy;[126] in addition, there is an allusion to the candidate's election to the clerical order. The terms were still in flux in the middle Byzantine period—for example, "cheirotonia" was used in the euchologia for the subdeacon's ordination, although it followed the cheirothesia format[127]—but the distinction Trembelas draws on the basis of physical and liturgical location is clear and consistent. Bishops, presbyters, and deacons were ordained at the altar in the course of the liturgy; subdeacons, readers, and so on, were not.

It is easier to distinguish among the orders for the middle Byzantine period than for the early church or early Byzantine period based on these ritual characteristics because the rubrics for the various ordinations are much fuller and more specific in the Byzantine euchologia than in the earlier *Apostolic Constitutions*. Two important euchologia from the middle Byzantine period that preserve the ordination rite of the female deacon together with other major and minor orders are the eighth-century Barberini codex 336128 from a Greek-speaking region of Italy and an eleventh-century codex from Constantinople, Grottaferrata G.b.l., the primary manuscript source for the massive euchologion collection published by Goar in the seventeenth century.[129] The rites and prayers for the ordination of the deaconess in the two manuscripts are identical. Given

---

126. Trembelas, "Τάξεις," 456; Taft, "Women at Church," 63–64.

127. *Barberini*, 188; Goar, *Euchologion*, 203.

128. The ordination rite for the deaconess is found in secs. 163–64, in *Barberini*, 185–88.

129. This manuscript is also known as the Bessarion codex; the ordination of the deaconess appears in Goar, *Euchologion*, 218–22. The ordination rites are preserved in a third principal euchologion, Paris BN Coislin 213, written in 1027, but it is very similar to the Grottaferrata manuscript; Bradshaw, *Ordination Rites*, 7. There is also a tenth-century manuscript from the library of the monastery of St. Katherine, known as Sinai 956, and several late Byzantine manuscripts. For a discussion of these, see Miguel Arranz, "Les sacrements de l'ancien euchologe constantinopolitain (1)," *Orientalia Christiana Periodica* 48 (1982): 284–335, and Martimort, *Deaconesses*, 150, regarding the placement of the ordination rite. Theodorou, "<Χειροτονία> ἢ <Χειροθεσία>," 576–88, analyzes the texts specifically with reference to the ordination rite for the deaconess.

their geographic and chronological separation, this indicates that in the Byzantine period the ordination rite for the female diaconate was widespread and standardized, thereby suggesting that so was the order itself.[130]

As for the content of the ordination rite for the female deacon, the most outstanding feature is that, far more explicitly than in the *Apostolic Constitutions*, its structure is analogous to the ordination of the male deacon; in fact, while the prayers are distinct for the two ordinations, the wording of the rubrics is virtually identical,[131] a point underscored in Goar by a separate, short set of rubrics that instructed that "One must perform [the ordination rite] for the deaconess as for male deacons, except for a few things."[132]

According to the Barberini and Grottaferrata euchologia, the deaconess was ordained during the Eucharist, at exactly the same point in the liturgy as for the male deacon—that is, immediately following the end of the *anaphora* section, after the royal doors are reopened.[133] As with the male deacon, she was brought to the arch-

---

130. Caution should be exercised due to the archaizing tendency of the Byzantines; thus, the tendency to preserve texts intact may simply mean that the female diaconate was indeed widespread in the early Byzantine period but may not necessarily indicate that this was still the case at the time the *euchologia* were written. For instance, regarding Constantine Porphyrogenitus's *De administrando imperio*, sister volume to his *De ceremoniis*, Alexander Kazhdan notes in Alexander P. Kazhdan et al., eds., *The Oxford Dictionary of Byzantium* (New York: Oxford University Press, 1991), 1:593, that "one must distinguish between the date of compilation . . . and the date of texts included." Nevertheless, on the basis of the vita of St. Irene Chrysobalanton, as well as the fragmentary but presumably reliable sigillographic and diplomatic evidence from Byzantine Italy (see nn. 36, 42, and 47, above), we know that at least through the eighth century in southern Italy and the ninth or tenth century in Constantinople and Jerusalem, some women were still being ordained as deacons.

131. Taft, "Women at Church," 63, asserts that "the detailed rubrics . . . show an almost exact parallelism between the rite for instituting deacons and deaconesses."

132. Goar, *Euchologion*, 219. A canonist of the fourteenth century, Matthew Blastares, *Collectio alphabetica*, letter Γ, chap. 11, quotes this text almost verbatim; in PG 144:1176.

133. Bar. 163.2, in *Barberini*, 185; Goar, *Euchologion*, 218. The *anaphora* is the central portion of the Divine Liturgy, culminating in the consecration of the bread and wine.

bishop[134] (an indication that the ordination occurred at the altar, where he would be at that point in the liturgy[135]). She bent her head as the archbishop placed his hand on it; then, making a cross three times (presumably, over her head), the archbishop read the following prayer:

> Holy and almighty God, who through the birth of your only-begotten Son and our God from the Virgin according to the flesh sanctified the female, and not to men alone but also to women bestowed grace and the advent of your Holy Spirit; now, Lord, look upon this your servant and call her to the work of your diaconate, and send down upon her the abundant gift of your Holy Spirit; keep her in orthodox faith, in blameless conduct, always fulfilling her ministry according to your pleasure; because to you is due all glory and honor . . .[136]

There followed a litany, with the sixth petition specifically on behalf of the "now appointed deaconess, and her salvation. That our loving God will bestow on her a spotless and irreproachable diaconate, [let us pray] to the Lord."[137] With the archbishop again

---

134. The Barberini codex consistently uses the word "archbishop" (ρχιεπίσκοπος), while the Grottaferrata manuscript used by Goar primarily uses "archbishop," but occasionally "bishop." The use of the word "archbishop" probably indicates the euchologion's original provenance of Constantinople.

135. Literally, she is "offered" (προσφέρεται), or perhaps "offers herself"; Bar. 163.2, in *Barberini*, 185; *Euchologion*, 218. Martimort, *Deaconesses*, 172, quotes Balsamon, *Responsa* 35, in PG 138:988, as asserting, in answer to a question posed him by Patriarch Mark III of Alexandria, that "formerly [πάλαι] there were sometimes recognized orders [τάγματα] of deaconesses, and they too had their place in the sanctuary [βαθμὸν ἐν τῷ βήματι]." Remarkably, Martimort states that Theodore is wrong because "at no time did deaconesses in the Byzantine rite ever have access to the sanctuary," despite his earlier admission (152) that, "even if the place of ordination was not always specified, . . . that place was evidently the sanctuary, because the doors remained open and the candidate had to advance toward the bishop; nowhere is it specified that the bishop had to leave the altar."

136. Bar. 163.3, in *Barberini*, 185–86; Goar, *Euchologion*, 218; Eng. trans. Bradshaw, *Ordination Rites*, 138.

137. Bar. 164.6, in *Barberini*, 186; Goar, *Euchologion*, 218; Eng. trans. Bradshaw, *Ordination Rites*, 138.

placing his hand on the head of the woman he was ordaining, he followed the litany with a second consecration prayer:

> Lord, Lord, who do not reject women offering themselves and wishing to minister in your holy houses in accordance with what is fitting, but receive them in an order of ministers; bestow the grace of your Holy Spirit also on this your servant who wishes to offer herself to you, and fill her with the grace of the diaconate, as you gave the grace of your diaconate to Phoebe whom you called to the work of ministry. Grant to her, O God, to persevere blamelessly in your holy temples, to cultivate appropriate conduct, and especially moderation, and make your servant perfect, that standing at the judgment seat of your Christ she may receive the worthy reward of her good conduct. By the mercy and love for humanity of your only-begotten Son ...[138]

After the "amen," the archbishop then vested the ordinand with the diaconal *orarion* (a long stole symbolic of the diaconal office), placing it around her neck, under her *maphorion*, and bringing the two ends of the stole around to the front.[139] Finally, the newly ordained female deacon received Communion at the hand of the archbishop, who then gave her the chalice, which she received and placed back on the altar.[140] In addition, at the end of the ordination rite for the male deacon (that is, immediately before the ordination rite for the deaconess), there is a postscript in both the Barberini and Grottaferrata codices noting that this is the ritual for ordaining a deacon or deaconess during the normal divine liturgy,[141] but that

---

138. Bar. 164.10, in *Barberini*, 187–88; Goar, *Euchologion*, 218; Eng. trans. Bradshaw, *Ordination Rites*, 138.

139. Bar. 164.11, in *Barberini*, 188; Goar, *Euchologion*, 218–19. The *maphorion* was a loose garment covering the head and shoulders worn by respectable Byzantine women. Byzantine icons usually show the Virgin Mary and female saints so attired (certain ascetic saints, such as Mary of Egypt, being obvious exceptions).

140. Bar. 164.13, in *Barberini*, 188; Goar, *Euchologion*, 219.

141. Literally, "when there is a *proskomide* service," that is, a service of preparation of the bread and wine for consecration during the Eucharist. Bar. 162.14, in *Barberini*, 184; Goar, *Euchologion*, 211.

the ordination may also be done during a presanctified liturgy, the only difference being that the placement of the ordination during the service is slightly different because there is no anaphora in a presanctified liturgy.[142]

The similarities between the texts for the ordination of deacon and deaconess are striking. The prayers are different[143] but contain the same basic elements, including an *epiclesis* (invocation of the Holy Spirit) and a reference to God's calling them to this office. The litany is identical, with the obvious exception of the use of the feminine form when referring to the ordinand in the sixth petition. In terms of rubrics, there are only a few differences: (1) the deaconess bowed her head instead of kneeling; (2) she was not vested with a liturgical tunic,[144] and the way in which she was vested with the orarion was different from the male deacon; (3) the deaconess was not given a kiss by the archbishop; (4) she was not given a *ripidion* (liturgical fan) to carry in procession or with which to fan the Holy Gifts; and (5) when the archbishop gave the deaconess the chalice after she had received Communion, she placed it back on the altar rather than taking it out of the sanctuary in order to distribute Communion to the laity.

As noted earlier, modern scholars have been far from unanimous in their analysis of this ordination rite, variously weighing the significance of the differences between the male and female deacons' ordinations. Some scholars find the similarities strong enough to assert that the female diaconate in the Byzantine Church constituted a major order.[145] Others have focused on the differences noted above

---

142. Bar. 162.15, in *Barberini*, 185; Goar, *Euchologion*, 211.

143. The differences in the two sets of prayers are discussed below.

144. The text for the ordination of the male deacon says that the bishop "ἐπαίρεται τὸ φελώνιν" ("lifts up and sets on [the deacon] the *phelonin*"); Bar. 162.11, in *Barberini*, 184. This garment is apparently what would become known as the *stikharion*, and should not be confused with the *phelonion*, or chasuble, worn by presbyters.

145. Among the first who argued for its placement among the major orders was Theodorou, "<Χειροτονία> ἢ <Χειροθεσία>," 576–601. FitzGerald, *Women Deacons*, 78–110, while presenting the opposing view of John Karmiris, relies heavily on Theodorou's conclusions, and agrees with him. See also Vagaggini,

and claim that it definitely was not,¹⁴⁶ while a few express ambivalence or simply avoid dealing with the issue, considering the female diaconate so unique and anomalous in the history and theology of clerical orders that they cannot place it definitively within either the major or minor category.¹⁴⁷

It is worth examining the differences that do occur between the rites for male and female deacons to ascertain if they are significant in terms of a theology of orders, or if they are relatively minor and may be accounted for by other reasons. The most significant difference is in the consecration prayers;¹⁴⁸ in fact, unlike the rest of the rite, there is almost no textual correspondence between the prayers for male and female deacons. Martimort argues that the difference in content between the two sets of prayers is substantial and indicates a considerable difference in function,¹⁴⁹ but his arguments are strained and unconvincing. For instance, he claims that the prayers for the male deacon refer specifically to his being a deacon by using the word "deacon" (*diakonos*), for example "the work of the deacon" (*to tou diakonou ergon*), but that, in the prayers for the female deacon, "reference was made only to διακονία, which was a very general and very imprecise term, translated as readily by 'service' as by 'diaconate.'"¹⁵⁰

"L'ordinazione," 177–85, and Taft, "Women at Church," 63–64, who supports this position since he clearly understands the ordination to be a "cheirotonia rite."

146. Opponents of the view that women deacons in the Byzantine Church were members of major orders include Vlassios Pheidas, "The Question of the Priesthood of Women," in *The Place of the Woman in the Orthodox Church and the Question of the Ordination of Women*, ed. Gennadios Limouris (Katerini, Greece: Tertios, 1992), 186–89, and Martimort, *Deaconesses*, 156.

147. Bradshaw, *Ordination Rites*, 88–89, may fall into this category since he makes no comment on the level of the order and, regarding the earlier *Apostolic Constitutions*, expresses his disquiet with anachronistic and oversimplistic categorizations of historical clerical orders (see n. 117, above). Nevertheless, in his review of the ordination rites of various orders, he treats the deaconess immediately after the deacon and before what he titles "minor orders"; Bradshaw, *Ordination Rites*, 83–103.

148. FitzGerald, *Women Deacons*, 82–101, offers a combination of theological with pastoral reflection on the two consecration prayers.

149. Martimort, *Deaconesses*, 155–56.

150. Ibid., 156.

It is true that *diakonia* and *diakonos* have both generic and technical meanings. In this case, however, it strains common sense and violates the liturgical context of the prayers to understand the word diakonia as generic rather than technical when the prayers are for someone being ordained a diakonos. Certainly, Bradshaw feels that the term refers specifically to the diaconate in these prayers; hence, his translation of the key passages in the two consecration prayers: "the work of your diaconate" and "the grace of the diaconate."[151]

On the other hand, Martimort discounts two very important similarities in the consecration prayers. One is the epiclesis, which in the case of the female ordination rite, according to Martimort, indicated "that deaconesses were entering upon a state of life aimed at perfection,"[152] as opposed to their receiving a specific grace conferred at ordination. His attempt to relativize its importance in the deaconess's ordination by reference to an epiclesis for minor orders in the *Apostolic Constitutions* is undercut, however, by his own admission that, "in the Byzantine rite, the Holy Spirit is invoked upon neither lectors nor subdeacons."[153] The second similarity is God's call to the ordinand, which Martimort implies was given to Phoebe but not to the candidate since the deaconess's willingness and desire is explicitly mentioned in her second prayer;[154] however, Martimort neglects to mention that the first prayer specifically asks God to "call her to the work of your diaconate," followed by the epiclesis, "and send down upon her the abundant gift of your Holy Spirit."[155]

However, perhaps the most astounding example of Martimort's bias is his attempt to impose a difference where one does not exist, namely, at the beginning of the rite, where in the case of both male and female deacon, the rubrics state that the bishop intoned a prayer

---

151. Bradshaw, *Ordination Rites*, 138.
152. Martimort, *Deaconesses*, 155.
153. Ibid.
154. Ibid.
155. Bar. 163.3, in *Barberini*, 186; Goar, *Euchologion*, 218. Eng. trans. Bradshaw, *Ordination Rites*, 138.

beginning *"Hē theia charis"* ("The divine grace").[156] For neither sex is the full text of the prayer given in the euchologia,[157] but it is common to the ordination rite for all three major orders in the middle Byzantine period.[158] Martimort, however, seizes upon the opportunity presented by the omission of the full text of the prayer to extrapolate from a sixteenth-century euchologion that uses, for the consecration of abbots and stewards, a prayer beginning the same way but with different content since those are consecrations as opposed to ordinations. He justifies by tautological reasoning this backward projection from what is clearly not an ordination: "Surely this text could not have been the same one as was used at other ordinations, where the supposition always existed that the candidate already possessed the preceding degree of ministry."[159] However, it is unreasonable to infer a different prayer for the female deacon's ordination, particularly since the full text of the prayer is not given. That the euchologia cite only the incipit clearly indicates that it was the same prayer for both male and female deacon, as well as for presbyter and bishop.[160]

While there is no theologically significant difference in the ordination prayers, Martimort is correct, however, in noting that there are differences in the liturgical functions of male and female deacons in the Byzantine Church. Not all differences in the rubrics, however, may be ascribed to differences in liturgical function, much less to differences in the level of ordination implied. For instance,

---

156. Bar. 161.3 for the deacon, 163.2 for the deaconess, in *Barberini*, 181 and 185; Goar, *Euchologion*, 211 and 218. FitzGerald, *Women Deacons*, 80–82, gives the full text of the prayer from other sources and comments upon its significance.

157. In fact, Martimort, *Deaconesses*, 153, notes that no existing manuscript contains the complete text.

158. See, for example, Goar, *Euchologion*, 242 and 244, for the presbyter and bishop, respectively.

159. Martimort, *Deaconesses*, 153.

160. In fact, L'Huillier, 244, argues the opposite from Martimort based on this very prayer. He notes that, although the ordination status of the deaconess in the early church may be ambiguous, the Byzantine female deacon clearly "acquired all the characteristics of accession to higher orders, as professor E. Theodorou has noted, since the formula 'the grace divine' is used." Taft, "Women at Church," 64, also finds the prayer incipit significant; see n. 126, above.

with respect to the first and third differences noted above, Bradshaw has suggested that both the female ordinand's kneeling before the bishop and her receiving a kiss from him may have been considered inappropriate actions within Byzantine society; even a late Byzantine canonist, Matthew Blastares, saw nothing substantive in the female deacon's failure to kneel, instead assigning the rubrical difference to the deaconess's "weakness."[161] As has already been made evident in other areas of deaconesses' historical liturgical participation, such as baptism and receiving the Eucharist at home, propriety has played an important role both in excluding women and including them in various ways. Thus, while it is conceivable that the rubrics for the deaconess to remain standing reflect her lack of public ministry at the altar, it more likely is simply a matter of propriety or "chivalry." In any case, Martimort's invocation of the symbolism of pseudo-Dionysius in stressing the importance of the act of kneeling appears misplaced.

Nevertheless, the remaining three differences are indeed connected to liturgical function. The female deacon in the Byzantine Church did not perform the public liturgical functions of the male deacon in the Divine Liturgy; thus, she was not given a ripidion in order to fan the Holy Gifts.[162] Similarly, while the female deacon delivered the Eucharist to housebound women, she did not distribute it during the Divine Liturgy; therefore, when the bishop gave her the chalice after administering Communion to her, she simply returned it to the altar.[163]

---

161. Bradshaw, *Ordination Rites*, 88. Similar concerns are apparent in the requirement that even the female deacon wear the *maphorion*, which was considered proper women's attire among the Byzantines and which reflected the Apostle Paul's injunction in 1 Cor 11 that women prophesy with their heads covered. As for Matthew Blastares's allusion to the deaconess's "weakness," this may refer either to generic "feminine weakness" (see n. 102, above) or to the more advanced age of female deacons relative to male deacons at the time of ordination; Blastares, *Collectio alphabetica*, letter Γ, chap. 11, in PG 144:1176.

162. Cf. Bar. 161.11 and 164.11, in *Barberini*, 184 and 188; Goar, *Euchologion*, 209 and 218–19; cf. Martimort, *Deaconesses*, 156.

163. Cf. Bar. 161.13 and 164.13, in *Barberini*, 184 and 188; Goar, *Euchologion*, 209 and 219; see Martimort, *Deaconesses*, 154. Since there was no liturgical reason for the bishop to give the chalice to the deaconess, FitzGerald, *Women*

The final difference—that the female deacon does not wear a liturgical tunic and that she is vested with the orarion[164] in a different manner from the male deacon—similarly reflects a difference in liturgical function, but does not indicate a difference in the clerical orders' respective rank.[165] As mentioned in the previous paragraph, the female deacon did not perform the public liturgical functions of the male deacon; these included reading petitions as well as participating in liturgical processions and distributing the Eucharist during the Divine Liturgy. Therefore, as with presbyters or male deacons who were not among the clerical celebrants for a particular liturgy,[166] she wore no liturgical tunic; in the case of the deaconess, there was no need to vest her with the tunic at all since her duties would never require her to wear it.

As for the orarion, the deaconess essentially wore it in the same manner as the subdeacon (that is, with both ends brought to the front), while the male deacon's stole hung from one shoulder or, for an archdeacon, circled diagonally around the body from one shoulder, with the two ends crossing and hanging down, front and back, from the shoulder. This difference, too, had a functional basis,

---

Deacons, 102, cites a Swedish scholar named Brodd who suggests that it may have been a relic of an earlier practice of deaconesses distributing the Eucharist at the liturgy. However, there is no contemporaneous evidence to support this hypothesis. It seems likelier that it was simply a desire to parallel the male and female deacons' ordination rites as closely as possible to each other, limiting differences to those necessitated either by propriety or by differing liturgical functions.

164. For a fuller discussion of the orarion, see S. Salaville and G. Nowack, *Le rôle du diacre dans la liturgie orientale: Étude d'histoire et de liturgie*, Archives de l'orient chrétien, vol. 3 (Paris; Athens: Institut Français d'Études Byzantines, 1962); and especially G. A. Soteriou, "Τὸ ὀράριον τοῦ διακόνου ἐν τῇ Ἀνατολικῇ Ἐκκλησίᾳ," Ἐπετηρὶς Θεολογικῆς Σχολῆς τοῦ ἐν Ἀθήνῃσι Πανεπιστημίου, 1:3 (1926): 405–90.

165. Martimort, *Deaconesses*, 154, suggests this by commenting on the extension of the orarion to the subdeacon, in contravention of canon 22 of the fourth-century council of Laodicea.

166. A presbyter not serving at the liturgy, or one officiating at a noneucharistic service such as those from the liturgy of the hours, would not be fully vested, but would wear only the *epitrachelion*, which was the particular stole symbolizing his priesthood.

since the male deacon held up the front half of his orarion while reciting petitions;[167] the deaconess would not be reading petitions. Conversely, the male deacon did not always wear his stole over one shoulder. During the Lord's Prayer he rewrapped it around himself so that he then was vested with it in the same manner as the subdeacon and deaconess.[168]

Again, the reason for changing the manner in which the male deacon wore the orarion was liturgical function. While neither middle Byzantine liturgical commentaries nor the rubrics of the euchologia of that period make any mention of this, frescoes mimicking liturgical acts, such as the Communion of the Apostles, show that typically the hands were covered when handling liturgical vessels (see the figure on the left in Figure 1). Neither deacon nor deaconess wore the large, cape-like *phelonion*, which the presbyter used to cover his hands; rather, they would have used the two ends of the orarion for that purpose.[169] Thus, male and female deacons in fact *were* vested identically with the orarion at the time of Communion in order to hold the chalice during reception of the Eucharist.

It deserves mention in this context that, in contrast to the extensive literary evidence of the female diaconate in the Byzantine Church, there is a complete lack of visual evidence. No vested deaconess saints appear in Byzantine-era frescoes, although their male counterparts, such as Stephen and Laurence, are typically

---

167. Balsamon, in PG 137:1369; in Soteriou, "Τὸ ὀράριον," 457.

168. Peter D. Day, *The Liturgical Dictionary of Eastern Christianity* (Collegeville, MN: Liturgical [A Michael Glazier Book], 1993), 213.

169. See Soteriou, "Τὸ ὀράριον," 433. In addition to the occasional evidence provided by such illuminated manuscripts as the tenth-century Athens gr. 211, fol. 110v, and the fourteenth-century Brit. Mus. Add. 39627, fol. 202r, numerous frescos from the eleventh to fourteenth centuries of the Communion of the Apostles depict apostles approaching the chalice with their hands veiled, including St. Sophia in Ochrid (eleventh century); and monastic churches in Studenica (thirteenth and fourteenth centuries), and Gračanica and Čučer (fourteenth century). Photos of many of these frescoes (including Figure 1 below) appear in Richard Hamann-Mac Lean and Horst Hallensleben, *Die Monumentalmalerei in Serbien und Makedonien vom 11 bis zum frühen 14 Jahrhundert*, Osteuropastudien der Hochschulen des Landes Hessen, Reihe 2, Band 3 (Giessen: W. Schmitz, 1963).

shown vested. For example, the north (funerary) chapel of a monastic church in Cappadocia known as Ayvali Kilise preserves a rare tenth-century fresco of St. Olympias, friend and patron of St. John Chrysostom.[170] The fresco is rather badly deteriorated; nevertheless, it appears that she is dressed identically to the other holy women, not vested as a deaconess.

It is difficult to form any conclusions from her secular attire, however. On the one hand, certainly she would have been known to be a deaconess since that information was contained in the *menaion* and *synaxarion*[171] accounts of her life (she must have been familiar to the monks for them to have commemorated her on the wall of the church, although she might have been included because a relative of the founder or other monk shared the same name). On the other hand, the fresco is dated to sometime between 913 and 920,[172] by which time the lack of provincial evidence shows the female diaconate in the Byzantine Church to be in decline, at least outside of Constantinople and Jerusalem, and possibly Byzantine Italy. It is quite likely that monks in tenth-century Cappadocia, in central Asia Minor, would never actually have seen an ordained deaconess. Therefore, the iconographer (who may even have been a member of the community, although the quality of the work is far from primitive[173]) would not have known how to depict one.

In addition, the rite of ordination examined above shows that the female deacon did not wear a liturgical tunic. It also indicates that the bishop placed the orarion under the maphorion that covered the deaconess's head and shoulders, making the orarion rather difficult to see in an icon, particularly given the pattern of fabric folds common in Byzantine iconography. Therefore, the lack of

---

170. Nicole Thierry and Michel Thierry, "Ayvali Kilise ou Pigeonnier de Gülli Dere: Église inédite de Cappadoce," *Cahiers archéologiques* 15 (1965): 126–27.

171. The *menaion* (from the Greek word for "month"—there were twelve *menaia*) contained the special hymns and readings, including short vitae of the relevant saints, associated with the calendar feasts. The synaxarion provided only the saints' lives, but at greater length.

172. Thierry and Thierry, "Ayvali Kilise," 101.

173. Thierry and Thierry, "Ayvali Kilise," 99.

visual evidence of vested deaconesses, particularly since relatively little pre-iconoclastic religious art remains extant, is probably not significant.

Perhaps the most striking aspect of the ordination rite for the female deacon, and the one that most obviously demonstrates that the female diaconate was considered a major order, is that the deaconess received the Eucharist at the altar with the rest of the higher clergy.[174] Although the euchologia do not give the order of reception of Communion in the rubrics for the normal celebration of the Divine Liturgy,[175] the order followed at ordination would have been followed more generally. It is possible, of course, that female deacons, not having the liturgical altar duties of their male counterparts, remained outside the altar area and communed with the laity and noncelebrating clergy. On the other hand, it seems incongruous to postulate that the female deacon in the Byzantine Church was vested with the orarion and received Communion at the altar at her ordination, but then functioned liturgically completely as a layperson thereafter. Rather, it is reasonable to assume that female deacons—at least those "on duty" for a particular liturgy—were vested with the orarion and thus received Communion at the altar as the last of the major orders of clergy to do so. At some later point, when deaconesses were no longer ordained, they would have remained outside the altar and received Communion with the rest of the laity.

V. The Disappearance of the Female Diaconate

The question of how long the female diaconate did survive as an ordained order is difficult to answer. Since euchologia often retained archaic and obsolete practices, the mere appearance of an ordination rite for female deacons, as discussed previously, does not necessarily

---

174. This differs from the *Apostolic Constitutions*, VIII, 13, 14, in SC 336:208–10, whose rubrics place the deaconess at the head of the ordained and consecrated women who receive the Eucharist, after all the ordained and consecrated men, including lower orders and monks. This may simply reflect the segregation of the sexes, however, since all the ordained and consecrated men are listed first (in descending order), followed by the ordained and consecrated women, then by the children and the rest of the laity.

175. As mentioned earlier, the rubrics assume only a presbyter and deacon.

confirm the existence of ordained female deacons at the time the liturgical manual was written. On the other hand, the euchologia *did* change over time,[176] so defunct rituals that new manuscripts continued to include were probably not so far removed from the time of the manuscript's creation as to be beyond some oral tradition or collective memory, particularly when that ritual was as unique as the ordination, at the altar, of a female deacon.

Moreover, the fact that one of the liturgical functions of Byzantine deaconesses in the late middle period was chanting indicates the likelihood of their ordained status continuing well into that period, since chanting duties were normally performed by ordained clergy, particularly in the large cathedrals. Male chanters were ordained to the minor order of reader; the only order of female chanters (apart from nuns) for which we have information are in fact deaconesses. Of course, the documentary evidence demonstrates that Byzantine deaconesses continued liturgical chanting—for a time, at least—even after they ceased to be ordained, but Patriarch Athanasius's entalma in the early fourteenth century demonstrates the suspicion and discomfort with which the church viewed an order that was no longer actually an ordained order. In all probability, the Constantinopolitan patriarch's proscription against the "custom" of deaconesses evidences the final loss of any widespread institutional memory of the *ordained* order of female deacons.[177]

---

176. Martimort, *Deaconesses*, 173, provides two examples of euchologia from the late and post-Byzantine period that do not contain the ordination rite for female deacons, observing that "not all of the copyists, of course, were slaves to routine to the same degree." The Goar *euchologion* includes variations in ordination and other rites based on several manuscripts. Moreover, there are some striking differences between the eighth-century Barberini 336 codex and the tenth-century Grottaferrata manuscript, for example, in the service of the forty-day blessing after the birth of a child. See nn. 188 and 189, below.

177. Further evidence of the loss of institutional memory of ordained deaconesses may be the lack of any mention of them in Symeon of Thessaloniki's *De sacris ordinationibus*, in PG 155:361–470; deacons are treated in cols. 361–84, along (in part) with other major orders. Symeon was born in Constantinople in the latter half of the fourteenth century and became archbishop of Thessaloniki, the second most important city in the Byzantine Empire, in the early fifteenth century. His massive works describe in detail the liturgical practices of Thessa-

Thus, female deacons in the Byzantine Church appear to have reached their zenith in the early Byzantine period, where there is a plethora of archaeological, canonical, legislative, liturgical, and hagiographic evidence not only for Constantinople but for Asia Minor as well. By contrast, in the middle Byzantine period, particularly following iconoclasm, the evidence becomes increasingly scanty and simultaneously more ambiguous. Especially outside the capital city of Constantinople and holy city of Jerusalem, there is almost no indication of a female diaconate beyond a seal and a few passing references emanating from Byzantine Italy in the liminal seventh and eighth centuries. Did the social, political, and military upheavals of the iconoclastic period have a negative effect on the female diaconate? There is no specific evidence to support such a hypothesis, but the apparent decline of the order at this time, especially in the provinces, probably is not sheer coincidence. Female monasticism, like its male counterpart, played an important role in the resistance to imperial iconoclastic policy;[178] the female diaconate, by this time largely tied to female monasticism, may have suffered as a consequence. Moreover, the active female diaconate may have been just another of the many practices and institutions of late antiquity and the early Byzantine period that fell into oblivion during this critical period as provincial cities contracted and refashioned themselves and their civic and religious way of life.[179] However, given the continuation of male clerical orders virtually unchanged, the discontinuities of the iconoclastic period probably did not in themselves play a major role in the decline of the female diaconate.

---

loniki in his time, yet in this treatise on clerical ordinations he never mentions female deacons. See Martimort, *Deaconesses*, 174.

178. For example, popular tradition held that the first iconophile martyr was a nun. For women's roles during iconoclasm, consult Alice-Mary Talbot, ed., *Byzantine Defenders of Images: Eight Saints' Lives in Translation* (Washington, DC: Dumbarton Oaks, 1998).

179. See, for example, Cyril Mango, *Byzantium: The Empire of New Rome* (London: Weidenfeld and Nicolson, 1980), esp. 60–87. The Eastern provinces in particular were seriously affected by, first, Arab incursions beginning in the seventh century and, later, repeated Turkish onslaughts, particularly in Asia Minor, from the eleventh century on.

By at least the ninth or tenth century, it appears that only nuns were ordained as female deacons. While the evidence for female diaconal ordination itself is less conclusive for the ninth through early twelfth centuries than for earlier eras, there is enough to hypothesize that the female diaconate probably continued to exist as an ordained order in Constantinople and Jerusalem for most if not all of this period. Judging by John Zonaras's implication that the ordained order still existed in his time (early to mid-twelfth century),[180] it may be further hypothesized that the ordination of female deacons in the Byzantine Church ceased at about this time since, according to Theodore Balsamon's statement in the late twelfth century, "[t]oday deaconesses are no longer ordained although certain members of ascetical religious communities are erroneously styled deaconesses."[181] At the same time, Balsamon noted that the (no longer ordained) order continued to exist as a special group of nuns, and Anthony of Novgorod described them as participating in the chanting of the matins service.

No one knows exactly when or why the female diaconate disappeared from the life of the Byzantine Church in the late middle Byzantine period since there are no extant sources calling for its abolition (with the exception of Patriarch Athanasius's *entalma*, which however was promulgated after the order ceased to be an ordained one). Most scholars have chosen not to hypothesize on it, although a few theories have been advanced.[182] In the absence of any documen-

---

180. Martimort, *Deaconesses*, 171, n. 36, remarks that both John Zonaras and Alexius Aristhenes (mid-twelfth century) "commented on this canon as if it were still in force," yet discounts the value of these witnesses since, he claims, "that was the typical proceeding of that age." Nevertheless, the fact that Balsamon, near the end of the same century, did not attempt to pretend that an extinct order still existed seems to challenge Martimort's denial. Zonaras and Aristhenes are probably as reliable about the practice of their day as are Balsamon and, later, Blastares, for theirs. It is also possible that female deacons were no longer being ordained by the mid–twelfth century, but that Zonaras and Aristhenes knew of women who had been ordained slightly earlier.

181. See n. 53.

182. For example, Martimort, *Deaconesses*, 171–74, recounts the evidence from Balsamon of the disappearance of the female diaconate but suggests no rationale for it. By contrast, FitzGerald, *Women Deacons*, 134–48, suggests several

tary evidence pointing to other causes, the most likely answer—both for the decline beginning in the iconoclastic period and the eventual vanishing of the ordained order in the twelfth century—is the introduction into the Byzantine Church beginning in the late seventh century of severe liturgical restrictions on menstruating women.

The extant evidence for the early church shows a dichotomy between Alexandria and Antioch in attitudes toward menstruation and other bodily functions associated by Levitical law with ritual impurity.[183] The restrictions on menstruants that surfaced first within Christianity in the canonical letters of Dionysius of Alexandria[184] in the mid-third century became canon law for the Byzantine Church

---

possible reasons, but most do not answer the question of why the female diaconate declined in the Byzantine Church at the end of the middle Byzantine period. For example, changing liturgical practices (including the universality of infant baptism) and reactions to gnosticism might have been relevant in late antiquity and the early Byzantine period, but not in the twelfth century; conversely, the effect of the Church's captivity under Islam might have influenced provincial practices, but would not have been a factor in Constantinople as it was not conquered by the Ottoman Turks until at least three centuries after the disappearance of the deaconess. The presumed negative influence of Islam on women's liturgical orders is also contraindicated by Jerusalem's retention of the female diaconate as well as its unique office of *myrophoroi*. As for the prohibitions of various Western Church councils, those were no more likely to be followed by the Byzantine Church than were Western prohibitions against married clergy. FitzGerald (143–45) does raise the issue of menstruation in the context of the writings of Theodore Balsamon and Matthew Blastares, but draws no specific conclusions; "women's sexuality" is simply one possibility among several.

183. See n. 108, above. It should be noted, however, that even in Syria, where women per se were not excluded from the altar, they were at times restricted from both it and the Eucharist when menstruous. See Branham, "Bloody Women and Bloody Spaces," 20. Branham's thesis is that restrictions against menstruous women in Jewish temple worship and Christian eucharistic worship in late antiquity and the early medieval period were based on the notion of eliminating competing bloods, menstrual and sacred (that is, the Eucharist). Her thesis might provide at least a partial explanation for the ease with which canonists such as Balsamon and Blastares rationalized away for ejaculant men the Levitical notions of ritual impurity that they so eagerly applied to menstruating and postpartum women. See Patrick Viscuso, "Purity and Sexual Defilement in Late Byzantine Theology," *Orientalia Christiana Periodica* 57 (1991): 400–02.

184. Can. 2, in PG 10:1281A; Pitra, *Juris ecclesiastici,* 1:544; G. A. Rhalles and M. Potles, Σύνταγμα τῶν θείων καὶ ἱερῶν κανόνων (Athens: G. Chartophylax, 1854), 4:7–9, including the commentaries of Zonaras and Balsamon. See

in 692 through the Council in Trullo,[185] which adopted wholesale the canonical writings of a dozen bishops, including Dionysius and his later successor, Timothy, who similarly restricted menstruous women from receiving the Eucharist or even entering the church.[186]

It probably took some time for the private canons given ecumenical authority by the Council in Trullo to gain such widespread acceptance as to alter liturgical practice and be taken for granted by the twelfth and fourteenth-century canonists Theodore Balsamon and Matthew Blastares, respectively.[187] It is in this same period—between the eighth and eleventh centuries—that fragmentary evidence indicates the rise of ritual impurity notions associated with childbirth,

---

Branham, "Bloody Women and Bloody Spaces," 19–20; Cohen, "Menstruants and the Sacred," 288–89; Frank, "Menstruation and Motherhood," 198–201.

185. Can. 2, in Pitra, *Juris ecclesiastici*, 2:21–23.

186. Pitra, *Juris ecclesiastici*, 1:631. This is Question 7 in a series of eighteen questions and answers, referred to as "the 18 canons of Timothy" or the "Canonical Replies." Frank, "Menstruation and Motherhood," 200, notes that, in Question 6 (requiring a woman to defer baptism until after her menstrual cycle) as well as in Question 7, Timothy adds that the menstruant should wait "until she has been purified of it" (ὡς οὗ καθαρισθῇ—but note that Taft, "Women at Church," 75, reads ἕως ἂν καθαρισθῇ, although this does not substantively change the meaning of the text). Taft wonders whether "there was a specific Christian ritual of purification for women, or only that there was a period of time that had to elapse in order to effect purification?" Since the church would not have required the sacrifice of pigeons as prescribed in the Levitical law, it is not unreasonable to assume that the purification was a bath of some sort, similar to that which the fifth-century *Testamentum Domini* (I, 42) required of widows following their menstrual period before they returned to the altar. I. Rahmani, *Testamentum Domini*, 100; Eng. trans. Grant S. Sperry-White, "Daily Prayer in Its Ascetic Context in the Syriac and Ethiopic *Testamentum Domini*" (Ph.D. diss., University of Notre Dame, 1993), 59. However, this does not mean that such bathing was a church ritual. The term could just as easily refer either to some homespun ritual or even to a woman's visiting the public baths at the end of her menstrual cycle, in which case καθαρισθῇ might more accurately be translated simply as "made clean" than "purified," which has ritual connotations. Regarding this provision in the *Testamentum Domini*, also see Taft, "Women at Church," 75.

187. See Branham, "Bloody Women and Bloody Spaces," 20–21. Moreover, given Balsamon's complaint, in PG 138:465C, that women often ignored the full proscription by participating in the liturgy from the narthex, one wonders just how widespread—or at least heartfelt—the acceptance of restrictions on menstruants was even in the twelfth century. See Taft, "Women at Church," 50.

the other "women-and-blood" nexus. The eighth-century Barberini codex gives only a single prayer for a newborn child's presentation at church forty days after birth, with no rubrics attached and no mention of the mother.[188] By contrast, in the eleventh-century Grottaferrata manuscript, there is a full forty-day rite commemorating not only the entrance of the child into the church but also the mother's return to it; the service is named for the mother[189] and includes two prayers for her as well as two prayers for the child. In addition to this liturgical evidence, there is the startling canonical opinion of the early-ninth century Constantinopolitan Patriarch Nikephoros, who advised that an infant who received emergency baptism before the forty-day rite could not be cared for, or even approached, by its mother until the mother had been "purified."[190]

Thus, by the eleventh century, if not earlier, the Byzantine Church had developed a theology of women's ritual impurity associated with menstruation and childbirth, and even expressed this liturgically through the expansion of the forty-day blessing service previously offered exclusively for the newborn child. So, it is not surprising that Balsamon erroneously argued, against the evidence to the contrary (of which he was aware), that women deacons in earlier times could not have attended at the altar because "the impurity of their menstrual periods dictated their separation from the divine and holy sanctuary,"[191] his assumption of unchanging ecclesiastical tradition leading him to extrapolate anachronistically back to earlier

---

188. Bar. 336, 113, in *Barberini*, 97. See Miguel Arranz, "Les sacrements de l'ancien Euchologe constantinopolitain (3)," *Orientalia Christiana Periodica* 49 (1983): 292–93.

189. "Εὐχαὶ εἰς γυναίκα λεχώ, μετὰ μ' ἡμέρας." Goar, *Euchologion*, 267–71.

190. Pitra, *Juris ecclesiastici*, 2:335. José Grosdidier de Matons, "La femme dans l'empire byzantin," in *Histoire mondiale de la femme*, ed. Pierre Grimal (Paris: Nouvelle librairie de France, 1967), 36, appears to be aware of this canon of Nikephoros when he comments on the differing effects of the mother's ritual uncleanness on the newborn, depending on the infant's baptismal status. This would explain why infants normally were not baptized before forty days.

191. Theodore Balsamon, *Responsa* 35, in PG 138:988; Eng. trans. Martimort, *Deaconesses*, 172.

church history the theology and practice of the late-twelfth-century Byzantine Church.

However, the fourteenth-century Byzantine canonist Matthew Blastares did not go so far as to argue that women had never been permitted per se into the altar area. Indeed, Blastares was obviously familiar with much of the late antique and early-to-middle Byzantine literature regarding the female diaconate, including the ordination rite.[192] The canonist even stated that some people believed that female deacons "were permitted to approach the altar [θυσιαστήριον] and to share a role with male deacons pretty much on an equal basis with them."[193] While admitting that little was now known of the ministry of women deacons, Blastares nevertheless found the latter proposition improbable, arguing that women could not have served liturgically at the altar since they were not permitted to teach publicly; rather, they were appointed as deacons in order to assist at baptism. As for women at the altar, Blastares observed that women in earlier times had been permitted to approach the altar, giving as an example Gorgonia, the sister of Gregory of Nazianzus.[194] Therefore, Matthew Blastares stands out as the rare Byzantine who not only acknowledged that ordained female deacons had at one time existed but who, at least through the opinion of "others," recognized that they may have disappeared because of a change in the church's theology and practice: "Later, however, the Fathers forbade them to approach the altar and carry out any service [πηρεσίας] there because of their menstrual periods."[195]

VI. Conclusion

As for the modern scholarly debate over whether the female deacon was considered "ordained" and whether that ordination was considered a major order, the naysayers predicate their opposition on

---

192. Blastares, *Collectio alphabetica*, letter Γ, chap. 11, in PG 144:1176, summarizes the ordination rite as it appears in the *Barberini* and *Grottaferrata* euchologia.
193. Ibid., col. 1173; Eng. trans. Martimort, *Deaconesses*, 173.
194. Ibid.
195. Ibid.; Eng. trans. Martimort, *Deaconesses*, 173.

CHAPTER THREE 93

two erroneous postulates. The first is the unsubstantiated presupposition—in truth, a tautological argument—that women were always excluded from major orders in the history of the church, and that to admit that they had been ordained to one major order then would open the door for their admission to the other two.[196] The second is the assumption that, if the female diaconate was not identical to the male diaconate in liturgical function, then it was not a true diaconal office.[197]

However, both presuppositions fail on their merits. With respect to the first one, in reality all three major orders are distinct and unique, but the diaconate is particularly distinct vis-à-vis both the presbytery and the episcopacy. As noted earlier in this article, even male deacons were not permitted to celebrate any of the sacraments, including baptism. Their liturgical function was to assist the presbyter or bishop, and the deacon was even buried as a layperson, there being no special funeral rite for him as there was for presbyters and bishops.[198] That women were ordained to the diaconate in the Byzantine Church does not thereby lead to the conclusion that they could (at least in theory) also have been ordained to the presbytery and episcopacy. There is no evidence to support such a conclusion, and modern concerns about whether or not women should be ordained to these orders should not influence current scholarly interpretations of the historical record.[199]

As for the second presupposition, limiting the choices for understanding the female diaconate in the Byzantine Church to "equal to the male diaconate" or "not a true diaconate" creates a false and

---

196. For example, Pheidas, "The Question of the Priesthood of Women," 181–89.

197. This second argument, below the surface, appears to be based on the first one; that is, it has more to do with modern ecclesiastical debates over the role of women in the church than with a dispassionate scholarly view of the historical record. See Martimort, *Deaconesses*, 148–56, 243–50.

198. See n. 84, above.

199. L'Huillier, *Church of the Ancient Councils*, 316, n. 392, echoes this sentiment.

overly simplistic dichotomy.[200] The female diaconate obviously was not the exact equivalent to the male diaconate since the deaconess did not serve the public liturgical role that the male deacon did—she neither chanted the diaconal petitions, nor processed at the Great Entrance (an assumption based on her not receiving the ripidion during her ordination), nor distributed the Eucharist to the laity during the liturgy. This should not be surprising given the Byzantines' ideology of the private role of women versus the public role of men.[201] This same distinction was clear in the respective functions of male and female deacons in the early church. In other words, the female deacon's liturgical ministry mirrored the public/private space segregation of roles and functions endemic in both late antique and Byzantine cultures.

However, although the female diaconate in the Byzantine Church was not simply the mirror image of the male diaconate, it was considered equivalent to the male diaconate in terms of clerical ranking. Certainly, that is how the Byzantines treated it, as evidenced from the sixth through the twelfth centuries in imperial legislation, church orders, ordination rites, and even the order in which the ordination rites were organized in euchologia. The ordination rite itself, including vesting with the diaconal orarion and reception of Communion at the altar with the deacons, presbyters, and bishop, further underscores the Byzantines' assumption that the deaconess was part of the higher clergy of the church. It was related to the male diaconate in a manner analogous, perhaps, to the relationship between the orders of the episcopacy and the presbytery.[202] Just as

---

200. L'Huillier, *Church of the Ancient Councils*, 245, raises a similar caution in his discussion of the significance of canon 15 of Chalcedon with respect to the status of the female diaconate.

201. Ideology and actual practice often differed, of course. See Judith Herrin, "In Search of Byzantine Women: Three Avenues of Approach," 167–89, in *Images of Women in Antiquity*, eds. Averil Cameron and Amélie Kuhrt (Detroit: Wayne State University Press, 1983; rev. ed. 1993), esp. 168–70; Alice-Mary Talbot, "Women," 117–43, in *The Byzantines*, ed. Guglielmo Cavallo, trans. Thomas Dunlap, Teresa Lavender Fagan, and Charles Lambert (Chicago: University of Chicago Press, 1997), esp. 129–40.

202. See n. 81.

the bishop's role more actively involved him in the larger church than did the presbyter's, so the male deacon's role more actively involved him, particularly liturgically, in the larger parish community than did the deaconess's. Thus, the Byzantine female diaconate was a liminal and unique clerical office that operated as a distinct order, at the diaconal level, focused on pastoral and liturgical ministry to women and recognized as a major clerical order in both the civil and ecclesiastical literature of the Byzantine period.

Figure 1. Fresco of the Communion of the Apostles, Hagia Sophia, Ochrid, 1037–56. Courtesy of Wilhelm Schmutz Verlag.

Chapter Four

ORTHODOX RESPONSES TO THE POSSIBILITY OF A REJUVENATED FEMALE DIACONATE: THE UNITED STATES CONTEXT

Teva Regule

The female diaconate is a part of Orthodox history. For more than one thousand years, the Orthodox Church ordained women to serve as deaconesses. As the Orthodox theologian and author of *Women Deacons in the Orthodox Church* Kyriaki Karidoyanes FitzGerald writes,

> According to Byzantine liturgical texts, the ordination of the woman deacon occurred as any other ordination to major orders. It took place during the celebration of the Eucharist and at the same point in the service that the male deacon was ordained.
>
> She was ordained at the altar by the bishop, and later in the service, received Holy Communion at the altar with the other clergy.
>
> Depending upon the need, location, and situation in history, the deaconess ministered primarily to the women in the community in much the same way that the male deacon ministered to men. . . .
>
> [The order] was gradually deemphasized sometime after the twelfth century. It should be noted, however, that there

does not exist any canon or church regulation that opposes or suppresses the order. . .[1]

For more than one hundred years, various voices within the church have been calling for the restoration of the female diaconate. This is not a new issue within the life of the church, and yet the church has not moved significantly to revive this ministry. The possibility of doing so is received variously by the faithful. For some, the idea of rejuvenating the female diaconate is met with enthusiasm, for others, caution, and for still others, disdain. However, it is fair to say that many faithful Orthodox Christians are only obliquely aware that this ministry even existed within the church. They have yet to form an opinion on the issue.

This paper will explore some of the positive and less-positive responses to the possibility of rejuvenating the female diaconate in the American context. I will begin by reviewing the recent history of calls for a revival of this ministry and their reception, address objections that still exist to doing so, and note the general difference in the reception of this possibility from the reaction of some via social media compared to in-person presentations.

First Suggestions

To my knowledge, the first official mention of the need for a reinstitution of the female diaconate in the North American context was proclaimed in 1953 by Archbishop Michael of what was then the Greek Orthodox Archdiocese of North and South America. In a letter to the members of his diocese he suggested that in order to meet the ministerial needs of the faithful, [the Synod] was considering reviving this ministry:

---

1. Kyriaki Karidoyanes FitzGerald, "Orthodox Women and Pastoral Praxis: Observations and Concerns for the Church in America," in *Orthodox Perspectives on Pastoral Praxis* (Brookline, MA: Holy Cross Orthodox Press, 1988). Dr. FitzGerald references the work of Evangelos Theodorou, "The 'Ordination' or 'Appointment' of Deaconesses (in Greek) as well as the *Didascalia Apostolorum* (Syriac Version) 4.3.12 and 4.3.13, ed. and trans. Richard Connolly (Oxford: Clarendon Press, 1929), 146, 148.

There is so much to be done in each community that the endeavors of these priests alone do not suffice. For should the priest wish to know, as he must, his spiritual children by name, their problems, and their spiritual and moral needs, this would certainly be beyond his physical and spiritual resources. . . .

These tremendous needs of our Greek Orthodox Church in America have urged us to make a fervent appeal such as this to our daughters-in-Christ. . . .

With the future welfare of our Church and membership at heart, we are considering the establishment in this country of an order of deaconess.[2]

In the 1960s, his successor, Archbishop Iakovos, expressed the same desire in two keynote addresses to the Clergy-Laity Congress of the Greek Orthodox Archdiocese.[3] Although nothing came of these aspirations, the seed of the possible renewal of this office was planted.

Initial Reception

Momentum for the possible revival of the female diaconate gained strength in the years immediately following the 1988 Rhodes Consultation. For those who may be unaware, this conference was called by the Ecumenical Patriarch (Demetrios I) as part of the preconciliar work of what was to have been the "Great and Holy Council of the Orthodox Church" at the time. It was attended by approximately seventy people and included official church delegates (including many bishops and priests) and expert advisors from the Eastern Orthodox Churches from all over the world (with the exception of the Patriarchates of Antioch and Jerusalem). It was originally organized

---

2. Quoted in Kyriaki Karidoyanes FitzGerald, *Women Deacons in the Orthodox Church: Called to Holiness and Ministry* (Brookline: Holy Cross Orthodox Press, 1998), 154–55.

3. Archbishop Iakovos (Koukouzis), *Visions and Expectations for a Living Church: Addresses to Clergy Laity Congresses, 1960–1966*, ed. Demetrios J. Constantelos (Brookline MA: Holy Cross Orthodox Press, 1998), 20–21 in St. Catherine's Vision, "A Call for the Rejuvenation of the Ministry of the Ordained Deaconess" (2014), 5.

in response to the challenge posed to the Orthodox Churches by ecumenical partners who had begun ordaining women to ministry and strove to articulate an Orthodox answer to this question. While the consultation was not in favor of ordaining women to the presbyterate (or episcopacy), it did state that the "order of deaconesses should be revived."[4] The consultation concluded that there was ample evidence for this ministry from apostolic times well into the Byzantine period, that the deaconess was ordained (*cheriotonia*) to higher orders, and that such a revival would "represent a positive response to the many needs and demands of the contemporary world."[5] The consultation at Rhodes was a pivotal event. It marked the first international consensus among Orthodox thinkers and leaders on the revival of the female diaconate in the modern period.

In the ten to fifteen years after Rhodes, books were written about the order,[6] conferences convened[7] to explore the ministry, and subsequent calls for its revival were made.[8] Anecdotal evidence suggests that the reception among the laity was positive. In 1990,

---

4. "Conclusions of the Consultation," in *The Place of the Woman in the Orthodox Church and the Question of the Ordination of Women*, ed. Gennadios Limouris (Katerini: "Tertios" Publications, 1990), 31. Henceforth, "Conclusions."

5. Ibid., 31.

6. For example, Ellen Gvosdev, *The Female Diaconate: An Historical Perspective* (Minneapolis, MN: Light and Life, 1991) and Kyriaki Karidoyanes FitzGerald, *Women Deacons in the Orthodox Church*.

7. For example, in 2000, the *St. Nina Quarterly* sponsored a large conference entitled "Gifts of the Spirit" in Dedham, Massachusetts, at which a revival of this ministry was discussed. Likewise, a similar discussion was held in 2004 at a conference cosponsored by the Antiochian Village Heritage and Learning Center and the Women's Orthodox Ministries and Education Network, "Women: Where are you in the Life of the Church?" These conferences were in addition to the international conferences for Orthodox women that confirmed a need for a renewal of this order (e.g., Crete, 1990, Damascus, 1996, Istanbul, 1997).

8. For example, the Orthodox Christian Laity (OCL) called for the restoration of the deaconess as part of its *Project for Spiritual Renewal*, accessed January 30, 2020, https://ocl.org/oclpublications/proiect-for-orthodox-renewal/. For a more complete listing of calls for the rejuvenation of the female diaconate in the modern era, see *Deaconesses, The Ordination of Women and Orthodox Theology*, eds. Petros Vassiliadis, Niki Papageorgiou, and Eleni Kasselouri-Hatzivassiliadi (England: Cambridge Scholars Publishing, 2017), 274–76. Henceforth, *Deaconesses, The Ordination of Women and Orthodox Theology*.

Ellen Gvosdev (a matushka in the Orthodox Church in America) conducted a small survey among the laity to qualify this reception.[9] Among her respondents were men and women of various ages and ethnic backgrounds as well as both cradle Orthodox and those who joined the faith later in life. Notably, they all saw the need for a revival of the female diaconate, especially for pastoral care and spiritual guidance of the faithful. Unfortunately, the reaction of the clergy and hierarchy was less positive. No bishop answered the survey and those with whom she spoke did not see a need for this ministry. Other clerical opinions "ranged from clear disdain for the mention of women's ministry to those who used jurisdictional disarray in America as a reason for not being able to do anything concrete about it."[10] In 2004, Demetra Jaquet conducted a similar study as part of her doctoral work. The results, included in her Doctor of Ministry thesis, showed that more than seventy-five percent of respondents answered positively to the statement, "I think the re-institution of the order of deaconess would benefit the Church."[11] Despite the laity being positively inclined to support such a move by the church, no steps were taken and momentum for the revival of the ministry stalled.

Recent Reception

The possibility of the revival of the female diaconate began to attract interest again in the lead-up to the Great and Holy Council that was eventually held in Crete in 2016. In November 2014, St. Catherine's Vision, an international, pan-Orthodox Christian fellowship of women theologians and other lay servant-leaders, published a "Call for the Rejuvenation of the Ministry of the Ordained

---

9. See Ellen Gvosdev, *The Female Diaconate: An Historical Perspective* (Minneapolis: Light and Life), 40–44 for a description of the survey and a summary of the results. Henceforth, Gvosdev, *The Female Diaconate*.

10. Gvosdev, *The Female Diaconate*, 44.

11. Demetra Velisarios Jaquet, "Attending the Flame of Feminine Holiness: Women in Christ in Community," [Unpublished DMin thesis] (Antiochian House of Studies/Pittsburgh Theological Seminary, 2004).

Deaconess."[12] It was addressed to His All-Holiness Ecumenical Patriarch Bartholomew and the Secretariat of the Great and Holy Council. Building upon the consensus of the Rhodes Consultation, the twenty-page proposal summarized the history of the order, confirmed that the deaconess was actually ordained to higher orders (e.g., *cheriotonia*) by highlighting various aspects of the Byzantine ordination rite, emphasized a need for such a ministry, and outlined the possible duties of a future female deacon. The document also pointed to the need to revive the entire diaconate in the life of the church. Lastly, it outlined the parameters of a pilot program to begin the process. The document was disseminated widely and provoked an immediate negative reaction among some, notably Fr. Chad Hatfield (President of St. Vladimir's Orthodox Seminary) and Fr. Lawrence Farley (a priest in the OCA and frequent blogger on social media), both converts to the Orthodox Church from the Anglican tradition. Farley questioned[13] the biblical foundation of the female diaconate, challenged her ordination as a deacon based on slight differences in the rite between the male and female deacon (e.g., standing vs. kneeling at one point), critiqued the proposal for deviating from canonical proscriptions of the office (e.g., age and marital status, although the parameters for the pilot program did not mention these explicitly), and posited that the call was proposing a "new order" of ministry rather than a rejuvenation of an old one. He also questioned the need for an "ordained" office. Finally, he suggested that ordination of women to the diaconate would (automatically) lead to women being ordained to the presbyterate and episcopacy and charged that this was really the hidden "feminist" agenda of those advocating for the renewal of the female diaconate.

---

12. "Call for the Rejuvenation of the Ministry of the Ordained Deaconess," accessed January 30, 2020, http://saintcatherinesvision.org/assets/files/December%20SCV%20Call.pdf.

13. Chad Hatfield interviews Lawrence Farley, "Deaconess" (podcast), December 3, 2014, accessed January 30, 2020, https://www.ancientfaith.com/podcasts/svsvoices/deaconesses and Lawrence Farley, "A Second Look at the Rejuvenation of the Deaconess," December 4, 2014, accessed January 30, 2020, http://myocn.net/second-look-rejuvenation-ministry-ordained-deaconess. Henceforth, Lawrence Farley, podcast and blog post (2014).

In her presentation to the participants of the last conference sponsored by the Center for Ecumenical, Missiological, and Environmental Studies (CEMES) on this issue, "Deaconess, Ordination of Women and Orthodox theology" (2015), Valerie Karras critiqued some of Farley's arguments,[14] emphasizing that women fully ranked as deacons and not some lesser office. She explained more fully the parameters of the office and warned against conflating the orders of the diaconate and presbyterate. Ironically, Karras affirmed Farley's "enculturated understanding of how holy orders should be organized and function."[15] However, whereas Farley claimed that the female diaconate is no longer needed since the segregation of the sexes that gave rise to the order no longer exists in the modern world, Karras argued for the opposite conclusion. She suggested that a more appropriate question for the debate should be,

> Given that, even in a patriarchal, segregated society [Byzantium] where women had no public roles, the church fully ordained women to the diaconate with a ministry that paralleled the public/private segregation of the sexes that existed in other areas of life, why is the church today *not* ordaining women to the diaconate . . . [with] the same diaconal ministries and functions, reflective of the integration of women and men in today's society[?]"[16]

I also presented at that same conference.[17] In order to respond to the proposition put forth by Farley and others that an ordained ministry for women was not necessary, I addressed the meaning of ordination to help us understand more fully what an ordination confers versus a similarly functional lay ministry. To summarize, I empha-

---

14. Valerie Karras, "Theological Presuppositions and Logical Fallacies in much of the Contemporary Discussion on the Ordination of Women" in *Deaconesses, The Ordination of Women and Orthodox Theology*, 85–97. Henceforth, Karras, "Theological Presuppositions."

15. Karras, "Theological Presuppositions," 93.

16. Karras, "Theological Presuppositions," 94.

17. See Teva Regule, "Rejuvenating the Diaconate: Building up the Body of Christ" in *Deaconesses, The Ordination of Women and Orthodox Theology*, 263–73.

sized that it is a setting apart of someone for ministry that establishes a new relationship with the community; it confers a reciprocity between the church and the ordained, giving the ordained not only the support and authority *of* the church, but also the responsibility *to* the church; and that it connects the faithful to the sacramental life of the church. I also emphasized the need for this ministry, citing overburdened parish priests and neglected pastoral needs of the faithful. Lastly, I outlined some ways that a fully-functioning diaconate (both male and female), a ministry of service that has historically focused particularly on pastoral care, philanthropy, Word, and liturgy, could benefit the church.

To recapitulate: First, it could strengthen the pastoral care of the faithful and enhance this care through the sacramental life of the church (e.g., bringing communion to the sick and infirm). In addition, a fully functioning diaconate could help to provide much needed spiritual direction to the faithful. Furthermore, a female deacon, in particular, could serve as an intercessor between the clergy and laity (especially women) to, among other things, guard against abuse or false charges of the same.

Second, a rejuvenated diaconate could help to recapture the philanthropic dimension of liturgy by connecting good works with liturgical celebration.

Third, it could help to uplift the Word of God. The church could benefit greatly from those who study scripture more particularly and use their education to help to edify the lives of those in the liturgical assembly.

Finally, a renewed diaconate would help to connect the pastoral, social, and liturgical dimensions of the diaconate more fully. Quoting Fr. John Chryssavgis, I reminded the conference participants that "the decision as to whether or not women deacons perform [public] liturgical functions arguably remains the exclusive prerogative of bishops in synod, in order that the catholic mind of the church may gradually mature in and collectively seal this critical aspect of the female diaconate."[18] I have continued to emphasize these points at various conference and parish presentations with stories of my own ministerial experience over these past five years with a positive result.[19] It is these more positive aspects that have helped to move people's hearts and minds on the issue.

Recent Reception Continued

In February 2016, Patriarch Theodoros of Alexandria took steps to revive the female diaconate, consecrating five women as "deaconesses" to help meet the ministerial needs of his diocese.[20] In some quarters of the United States, this announcement was met with support and hope. In other quarters, it was met with confusion. And in still other quarters, it was met with vocal opposition. As an example of the former, in October 2017 a group of renowned Orthodox liturgists (i.e., seminary and theological school professors) from the United States and Greece expressed their support for the Patriarchate of Alexandria to "restore in a timely fashion the order of deaconess within the borders of the Patriarchate."[21] They emphasized that the reinstitution of the female diaconate does "not constitute an innovation . . . but the revitalization of a once functioning, vibrant, and effectual ministry."[22] They also clarified that the "restoration of the female diaconate is such that neither doctrinal issues nor author-

---

18. John Chryssavgis, *Remembering and Reclaiming Diakonia: The Diaconate Yesterday and Today* (Brookline: Holy Cross, 2009), 19.

19. For example, I have spoken at a number of conferences sponsored by the St. Phoebe Center for the Deaconess (e.g., New York City, 2014, and Chicago, 2018) and the International Orthodox Theological Association (Iasi, Romania, 2019) as well as local parish talks in Rhode Island and Massachusetts.

20. "Patriarch Theodoros of Alexandria performs first consecration of deaconesses," accessed January 30, 2020, https://orthodoxdeaconess.org/contemporary-orthodox-deaconesses/patriarch-theodoros-of-alexandria-performs-first-consecration-of-deaconesses/.

21. "Documentation: Orthodox Liturgists Support Ordination of Women Deacons," accessed January 30, 2020, https://www.praytellblog.com/index.php/2017/10/25/documentation-orthodox-liturgists-support-ordination-of-women-deacons/. Henceforth, "Orthodox Liturgists Support Ordination of Women Deacons."

22. "Orthodox Liturgists Support Ordination of Women Deacons."

itative precedents are at stake."[23] They concluded by applauding the Patriarchate of Alexandria for "giving flesh to an idea that has been discussed and studied by pastors and theologians for decades."[24]

The backlash against the move by the Patriarchate of Alexandria and the support from the liturgists came in the form of a public letter and petition drive entitled "A Public Statement on Orthodox Deaconesses by Concerned Clergy and Laity."[25] This initiative was driven mostly, but not exclusively, by converts to the faith, many of whom had left their former ecclesial tradition because of, among other reasons, the ordination of women. As stated, the purpose of the letter was to (1) question what was accomplished in the Congo, (2) "clarify" the historical record on the place of the deaconesses in the Orthodox tradition, and (3) point out "serious doctrinal" issues raised by the appointment of deaconesses. (Tellingly, the tone of the response was set by the foreword to the letter and suggested that those in favor of the reinstitution of the female diaconate were "poorly informed and politically driven."[26])

The drafters of the document questioned whether a true ordination (to the diaconate) took place, ironically, referring to some of the major features of the Byzantine ordination rite that Farley had previously discounted in his initial reaction to the proposed ordination of deaconesses.[27] Here they have a point, as the *consecration* of the deaconesses in Africa did not follow the Byzantine ordination rite of the female deacon and was more akin to ordination to the subdiaconate. However, it could be argued that the drafters of this statement did not understand that this was part of *a process* of reinstituting the female diaconate as was implied in the liturgists' statement.

---

23. Ibid.
24. Ibid.
25. "A Public Statement on Orthodox Deaconesses by Concerned Clergy and Laity," accessed January 30, 2020, https://www.aoiusa.ore/a-public-statement-on-orthodox-deaconesses-by-concerned-clergy-and-laity-2/. Henceforth: "A Public Statement on Orthodox Deaconesses by Concerned Clergy and Laity."
26. Johannes Jacobse, Preface, "A Public Statement on Orthodox Deaconesses by Concerned Clergy and Laity."
27. Farley, podcast and blog post (2014).

In trying to "clarify" the historical record, the drafters relied heavily on the work of Aimé Georges Martimort, a Roman Catholic theologian, emphasizing, among other things, that the presence of deaconesses was never ubiquitous and therefore not universally accepted. The text also noted that a number of local Western councils prohibited their appointment (e.g., Orange in 441, Orléans in 533). However, it failed to mention that the Orthodox Church does not regard these local Western councils as authoritative.

The drafters also made the claim that there are "serious doctrinal issues" raised by the appointment of deaconesses. In particular, the document posited that a parallel diaconate for women blurs the distinction between male and female and "upends the natural and economic order of male and female to raise women over men in the hierarchy of the Church."[28] This point has no basis in the history of the order and the theological anthropology of the patristic tradition. Furthermore, as the board of the St. Phoebe Center for the Deaconess has written, "while all ordained orders bear the authority of the Church by their very nature, the work of the diaconate is service, and its characterization as one wherein one group exercises authority over another misconstrues and subverts this truth."[29]

Embedded in the text is the fear that this move will be the beginning of the "slippery slope" toward the ordination of women to all ranks of clergy. The document reads, "Neither can we accept [the liturgists'] assurances that deaconesses today will not lead to priestesses tomorrow, knowing where similar incremental innovations have led in heterodox communions."[30] While this may be a popular concern, it does not take into consideration the long history of the female diaconate within the Orthodox Church (with no history of ordaining women to the presbyterate) nor the differences in the theological

---

28. "A Public Statement on Orthodox Deaconesses by Concerned Clergy and Laity."

29. St. Phoebe Center for the Deaconess Board, "Towards a Reasoned and Respectful Conversation about Deaconesses," accessed January 30, 2020, https://orthodoxdeaconess.org/wp-content/uploads/2018/09/Towards-9-11.pdf.

30. "A Public Statement on Orthodox Deaconesses by Concerned Clergy and Laity."

understanding of orders or ecclesial polity within other Christian communities outside of the Orthodox Church. Furthermore, the claim in the document that those who advocate for the revival of the female diaconate "covet the rank, honor, and authority of the clergy"[31] reveals, perhaps, a greater motivation or fear of those opposed to such a move.

Advocacy for the revival of the female diaconate continues in the church today. So what are we to make of all of this? Positively, the debate has raised the awareness of the need for a fully functioning diaconate in the church. For some this includes only men, but others are open to the possibility of women in this ministry as well. More people are understanding and advocating for a diaconate that is not just a stepping-stone toward the presbyterate nor just a liturgical functionary, but a ministry of service that is grounded in the way that the church meets the world.[32]

Less positively, this debate exposes the lack of education regarding the historical deaconess and understanding of it and how ministries can develop to meet the needs of the faithful. This is especially the case regarding the possible public, liturgical role of a future female deacon. The main fear of those opposed to the reestablishment of the female diaconate is that this will lead to women exercising the ministry in this fashion as well as women entering the presbyterate and episcopacy and a subsequent unraveling of the tradition at large. While one can be sympathetic to this concern, it conflates our understanding of the orders of "priesthood"—deacon, presbyter, and bishop—and, ironically, reveals that many of those opposed to the female diaconate see no theological reason why women could not be ordained to higher office if admitting them to the diaconate would automatically do so. But, most importantly, I think it reveals a lack of confidence in the mind of the church.

---

31. "A Public Statement on Orthodox Deaconesses by Concerned Clergy and Laity."

32. Lawrence Farley, "Do We Really Need Deacons?" accessed January 30, 2020, https://www.oca.org/reflections/fr.-lawrence-farley/do-we-really-need-deacons.

Most of the loud voices in opposition to the ordination of women to the diaconate raise their concerns in online forums and social media. But, what about the "person in the pew?"—those faithful members of the church who are just trying to work out their salvation within the community? From the numerous conferences and parish talks that I (and others) have given, I have found a refreshing openness to the possibility of rejuvenating this ministry. When people are presented with the history of the order, are able to discuss their concerns, and, most importantly, realize the potential benefits to the church and the world, they are open to it. I close with a quote from an observer who attended a recent symposium on the female diaconate sponsored by the Archons of the Ecumenical Patriarchate (Philadelphia region) last spring,

> As the day proceeded, the talks gave a holistic view of the diaconate, what it has been, what it has deteriorated into, and what a wholehearted and unstinting revitalization of the order could create for the church. We were presented with a vision of a church whose members are cared for pastorally, energetically, joyfully, thoughtfully, and wisely in a way that few of us can ever have experienced but would love to see. The evolution of reactions was striking. By the end of the day, the audience had shifted from lukewarm to positively radiant with enthusiasm. . . . It was inspiring to see so many people who love their church energized by this new and exciting way of serving it, our communities, and the world.[33]

I pray that one day it will be so.

---

33. Patricia Bouteneff, "Letter from Philadephia," *The Wheel* online, April 6, 2019, accessed January 30, 2020, https://www.wheeljournal.com/blog/2019/4/6/patricia-bouteneff-letter-from-philadelphia.

II

Scriptural Perspectives

Chapter Five

CHRISTIAN WOMEN AT THE ALTAR TABLE:
ANCIENT PRECEDENT FOR THE REINSTITUTION OF THE ORDER OF DEACONESSES

Ally Kateusz

Extremely important for the reinstitution of the order of deaconesses is the evidence of ancient Christian art that demonstrates women taking a far greater role in ministries and the liturgy than previously thought. Yes, Christian women were present at church altars, and the altars had crosses on them.

Why is art so important? Paul Bradshaw, University of Notre Dame Professor of Liturgy, points out that virtually no liturgical manuscripts have survived from the first seven centuries.[1] Given this long gap in the written record, these artifacts provide precious *windows* through which we can see the early Christian liturgy as it was once performed. Three artifacts (fig. 1) are to my knowledge the three oldest to portray people at the altar table of a real church. Two, an ivory reliquary box and a huge sarcophagus front, are both usually dated around the year 430, and they are the two oldest. An ivory pyx is the third oldest, dated to the 500s, yet it is the oldest to portray only one sex at the altar table.

---

1. Paul Bradshaw, *The Search for the Origins of Christian Worship: Sources and Methods for the Study of Early Liturgy* (Oxford: Oxford University Press, 2002), 3.

Figure 1. The three ancient artifacts: reliquary box, sarcophagus, and pyx.

The ivory pyx is thought to have been carved in the eastern Mediterranean, probably Palestine (fig. 2). After that, its provenance is uncertain until it appeared at an auction in Paris in 1906.[2] Here we see a tripod table with a gospel book on it, a big lamp above, a procession of women, and a cross on the back (detail).

This altar area is usually identified as that of the Anastasis Church, partly because the round shape of the pyx evokes the Anastasis rotunda, but also because other artifacts similarly represent the Anastasis shrine that was over the cave of the Holy Sepulchre inside the rotunda.[3] For example, both the ivory pyx and a pewter ampoule made a century later in Jerusalem, and today in

---

2. [alc] Emile Molinier, ed., *Catalogue des Objets d'Art et de Haute Curiosite de l'Antiquite du Moyen-Age et de la Renaissance: Collection de M. D. Schevitch* (Paris: Galerie Georges Petit, April 46, 1906), 16–18, 120–21.

3. Archer St. Clair, "The Visit to the Tomb: Narrative and Liturgy on Three Early Christian Pyxides," Gesta 18, no. 1 (1979): 127–35, esp. 129–31, figs. 7 and 8; for more on the altar, see Weitzmann, Age of Spirituality, 581; and A. Goldschmidt, "Mittelstücke fünfteiliger Elfenbeintafeln des VI.–VII. *Jahrhunderts,*" *Jahrbuch für Kunstwissenschaft* (1923): 30–33, esp. 32–33.

the Monza Cathedral Museum, depict spiral columns holding up a three-sided canopy (fig.3).⁴

Figure 2 and detail. Ivory pyx depicting a procession of women to a tripod altar table with Gospel and cross. Anastasis in Jerusalem, 500s. Metropolitan Museum of Art, New York. CC0.

Figure 3. Two women at Anastasis shrine with spiral columns and half hexagon canopy. Ampoule from Palestine, ca. 600s. Monza Cathedral Treasury Museum. Garrucci, *Storia,* pl. 6:434.5.

---

4. Andre Grabar, *Les ampoules de Terre Sainte (Monza-Bobbio)* (Paris: C. Klincksieck, 1958), 20–23, 34–36, 39–40; see esp. plate 9, but also plates 11 and 14. For image, see Raffaele Garrucci, *Storia della arte cristiana nei primi otto secoli della chiesa,* 5 vols. (Prato: Gaetano Guasti, 1872–1881), pl. 6:434.5.

Both also depict two women carrying censers. The ampoule portrays them as the two Marys approaching the shrine over the Holy Sepulchre with an angel opposite, as if about to tell the women that the Lord had risen. The pyx by contrast portrays two women with censers approaching the altar itself.[5]

Around the back of the pyx, the sculptor carved three more women in a procession to the altar, each with her arms raised. Russian Orthodox art historian Alexei Lidov says the arms-raised pose "is interpreted in monographic studies as a liturgical one."[6] During this era the clergy wore everyday clothes, which only over time became clerical fashion. Yet hanging from each woman's waist is a narrow strip of doubled cloth. According to Lidov this cloth, sometimes fringed, sometimes with delicate stripes at the end, later was called a "maniple" in the West, but in the East the *enchirion* (literally "handy")—a white handkerchief hanging at the girdle of an archpriest, he says, and later called *epigonation*."[7] Due to its various names over time in both East and West, I call it simply the eucharistic cloth. Church officiants used it only during the performance of the Eucharist, for example to wipe excess wine from the rim of the chalice.

The rise of priestly insignia is seen in two wall mosaics that flank the altar in the Holy of Holies of the Basilica of San Vitale in Ravenna. Dated around the year 550, these mosaics are usually identified as a liturgical procession in the famous Hagia Sophia basilica in Constantinople, because on the left they portray Emperor Justinian holding the paten for the bread, and on the right, Empress Theodora holding the chalice for the wine (figs. 4 and 5).[8]

---

5. St. Clair, "Visit to the Tomb," 130.

6. Alexei Lidov, "The Priesthood of the Virgin Mary as an Image-Paradigm of Christian Visual Culture," *IKON* 10 (2017): 9–26, 10.

7. A. Lidov, "Priesthood of the Virgin Mary," 20.

8. Otto G. von Simson, *Sacred Fortress: Byzantine Art and Statecraft in Ravenna* (Princeton, NJ: Princeton University Press, 1987), 27–39, pl. 2, 4, 18. For the images here, see Josef Wilpert, *Die romischen Mosaiken und Malereien der kirchlichen Bauten vom IV. bis XIII. Jahrhundert* (Freiburg: Herder, 1976), pl.109, 110.

Figure 4. Justinian holds the golden paten. Mosaics in the altar apse, Basilica of San Vitale, Ravenna. Source: Wilpert, *Romischen Mosaiken*, pl. 109.

Figure 5. Theodora holds the golden chalice. Source: Wilpert, *Romischen Mosaiken*, pl. 110.

The mosaic that portrays Justinian also portrays Bishop Maximianus, his name over his head, wearing the episcopal pallium—a long white band with a cross on it, worn only during the Eucharist. The decade around 550 is the very first time we see the episcopal pallium on a man in art. On the right are two more clergy, a man carrying a large book and a man carrying a censer. This is the first time that we see a Christian man carrying a liturgical censer in church art.

The opposite mosaic portrays Theodora lifting the chalice and standing between two eunuchs on the left and seven women on the right. Two of the women wear the fringed white cloth hanging from their girdles, as seen on the ivory pyx. A third appears to hold it folded, much as Pope Clement holds it folded in an eleventh-century wall painting in old St. Clement Basilica in Rome, where he also wears an episcopal pallium while he performs the mass in front of an altar table laden with a chalice and paten (fig. 6).⁹

Figure 6. Pope Clement holds the cloth as he officiates the Eucharist at the altar. Basilica San Clemente, Rome, ca. 1000. Source: Wilpert, *Romischen Mosaiken*, pl. 240.

Alexei Lidov contradicts anyone who might argue that the cloth in this mosaic must mean something different just because it is seen with a woman. He says, "Let me remind those who are convinced of the lay provenance of the handkerchief that Theodora with her

---

9. A. Lidov, "Priesthood of the Virgin Mary," 17, fig. 19. For image, see Wilpert, *Romischen Mosaiken*, pl. 240.

retinue, as well as Justinian, are presented in San Vitale in a liturgical procession in the sanctuary, both holding liturgical vessels."[10]

Returning to the pyx, the technical name for the beautiful columned structure over its altar is a *ciborium*, sometimes called a "balduchin." Today the vast majority of ciboria over altars are square, and a review of the photos and diagrams in Jelena Bogdanovic's 2017 book, *The Framing of Sacred Space*, demonstrates that in antiquity, the same was true—almost all ciboria over altars were square.[11]

An example of a square ciborium is seen on one of the two oldest artifacts to depict people at the altar of a real church, in this case the second Hagia Sophia in Constantinople that replaced the first basilica of 415 that burned in 542, after which Justinian built the huge Hagia Sophia, which still stands today.

This sarcophagus front was discovered in 1988 in Istanbul in an underground tomb structure (fig. 7).

Figure 7. Sarcophagus with liturgical scene inside the second Hagia Sophia. Constantinople, ca. 430s. Photo courtesy of the author.

---

10. A. Lidov, "Priesthood of the Virgin Mary," 17–23, esp. 17, fig. 18.

11. Jelena Bogdanovic, *The Framing of Sacred Space: The Canopy and the Byzantine Church* (New York: Oxford University Press, 2017).

Johannes Deckers and Ümit Serdaroglu published the find, and noted that the column capitals on this carving were the same as the column capitals of the second Hagia Sophia. Based on where it was found, the style of the man's bulb clasp, and the early Christian cross, they dated the carving very tightly around the year 430.[12] They described a ciborium with columns framing the table, an early Christian cross set upon it, and curtains pulled back.[13] An arms-raised man and woman flank the table, with the man on the left and the woman on the right, the same gendered placement seen a century later in the mosaics depicting the liturgy in Justinian's Hagia Sophia. A boy is beside the woman, much as two eunuchs were beside Theodora, but otherwise the arms-raised man and woman have almost symmetrical poses, down to the pointing of their feet.

Remarkably, the dating around the year 430 corresponds to a conflict that took place in the second Hagia Sophia, a conflict between the imperial princess, Pulcheria, who was regent for her younger brother, and the new Patriarch, Nestorius. According to the *Letter of Cosmas*, Pulcheria was accustomed to being with her younger brother in the Holy of Holies during the Eucharist. Nestorius opposed Pulcheria's custom, and on Easter Sunday in 428, he stopped her at the door of the Holy of Holies.[14] Three years later, the Council of Ephesus deposed Nestorius and exiled him. We may assume that afterward, Pulcheria resumed her custom.

---

12. Johannes G. Deckers and Ümit Serdaroglu, "Das Hypogäum beim Silivri-Kapi in Istanbul," *Jahrbuch für Antike und Christentum* 36 (1993): 140–63, esp. 160–63.

13. Deckers, "Hypogäum beim Silivri-Kapi," 147–48.

14. *Letter to Cosmas 6*, trans. Frangois Nau in *Histoire de Nestorius d'après la lettre à Cosme et l'Hymne de Sliba de Mansourya sur les docteurs grecs, Patrologia Orientalis 13* (Paris: Firmin-Didot, 1916), 275–86, esp. 279.

Returning to the square ciborium, Figure 8 provides a three-dimensional drawing of one.[15] As we can see, the artist's perspective means that the two closest, or front, columns appear widest, and that the two back columns appear more distant and thus, closer together. This would have represented a typical ciborium, although most did not have spiral columns.

Figure 8. A square ciborium.

As we can see, however, the ciborium on the ivory pyx does not appear to be square, but more like a slightly rounded trapezoid, a half hexagon. The placement of its columns appear opposite to what is seen on a square ciborium. The back columns are wider, set against what seems to be the wall of the Shrine of the Holy Sepul-

---

15. The drawing of a square ciborium in an apse, copyright author, is a composite of drawings of a square ciborium, ostensibly representing the ciborium in Old Saint Peter's basilica, in Jocelyn Toynbee and John Ward Perkins, *The Shrine of St. Peter and the Vatican Excavations* (New York: Pantheon, 1957), 202, fig. 20, and in the Vatican excavators' report, Bruno M. Apollonj Ghetti, Antonio Ferrua, Enrico Josi, and Engelbert Kirschbaum, *Esplorazioni sotto la confessione di San Pietro in Vaticano, eseguite negli anni 1940–1949*, 2 vols. (Vatican City: Citta del Vaticano, 1951) vol. 1, fig. 121, and Ghetti, *Esplorazioni*, vol. 1, plate H; also see Kirschbaum, *Tombs*, fig. 10, pl. 29.

chre, while its two front columns frame the altar table. The unusual half-hexagon shape of this ciborium, along with its spiral columns, is important because we see a similar half-hexagon ciborium with spiral columns on the ivory reliquary box that depicts the altar area of Old St. Peter's Basilica (fig. 9).

Figure 9. Liturgical scene inside Old St. Peter's Basilica, Rome. Ivory reliquary box, ca. 400s. Museo Archeologico, Venice. Source: Scala/Art Resource.

This ivory box is the second of the two oldest artifacts to depict people at the altar of a real church. It was discovered in 1906 beneath a Roman-era church near the city of Pola in what is now Croatia. It is often dated around the year 430 because Galla Placidia is thought to be portrayed on one of its sides.[16] Here again we see a half-hexagon ciborium supported by spiral columns, plus a large hanging lamp above an altar table and cur-

---

16. Davide Longhi, *La capsella eburnea di Samagher: Iconografia e committenza* (Ravenna: Girasole, 2006), 112; and Margherita Guarducci, *La capsella eburnea di Samagher: Un cimelio di arte paleocristiana nella storia del tardo impero* (Trieste: Società Istriana di Archeologia e Storia Patria, 1978), 123.

tains pulled back. In Old St. Peter's, the second-century shrine of St. Peter was on the ciborium's back face. Just as the two front columns of the Anastasis ciborium framed its altar table, so also the two front columns in Old St. Peter's framed a second-century stone table that was embedded in the shrine. Figure 10 shows the half-hexagon ciborium, plus the beams that continued over to two more columns set against the walls of the apse.[17] It was set on the chord of the apse, where it was beautifully proportionate.

Figure 10. A half-hexagon ciborium. Columns from the Pola ivory. Old St. Peter's Basilica, Rome, ca. 400s. Source: Scala/Art Resource, New York, author.

As on the ivory pyx, the ivory reliquary box (fig. 9) portrays women in the liturgy, but in this case a gender parallel liturgy, such as seen in Constantinople. In 1908, Anton Gnirs, the first to publish the box, said that this scene had extraordinary value for understanding the early Christian liturgy. He identified two men and two women with their arms raised flanking the ciborium, and, be-

---

17. The drawing of the half hexagon ciborium, copyright author, is taken from the ciborium sculpted on the Pola ivory, with the columns from a photograph of the ivory applied to the drawing of the apse. See also n. 15 here.

neath the ciborium, a man and a woman on either side of the *mensa dell'altare*, as he called it, the altar table.[18] Virtually all subsequent art historians have agreed three men are on the left and three women on the right.[19]

Gnirs himself did not recognize the six famous spiral columns sculpted on the ivory, but other scholars soon suggested that they were the very same six spiral columns today in the galleries of the modern St. Peter's.[20] That they were the same was confirmed in 1941, when the Vatican excavated beneath the modern basilica's high altar. At the bottom of a stack of medieval altars, Vatican excavators discovered the second-century shrine, which they believed was the shrine dedicated to Peter near the site of his martyrdom in Rome.[21] Fourth-century architects had built Old St.

---

18. Anton Gnirs, "La basilica ed il reliquiario d'avorio di Samagher presso Pola," in *Atti e memorie della Societá Istriana di Archeologia e Storia Patria* 24 (1908): 5–48, esp. 32–33.

19. Pietro Toesca, *Storia dell'arte italiana*, vol. 1 (Turin: Unione, 1927), 322; Pericle Ducati, *L'arte in Roma dalle origini al sec. VIII* (Bologna: Cappelli, 1938), 380; Alexander Coburn Soper, "The Italo-Gallic School of Early Christian Art," *The Art Bulletin* 20, no. 2 (June 1938): 145–92, esp. 157; Henri Leclercq, "Pola" in *Dictionnaire d'archéologie chrétienne et de liturgie*, vol. 14 part 1, eds. Fernand Cabrol and Henri Leclercq (Paris: Letouzey et Ane. 1939), cols. 1342–46, esp. 1345; Giuseppe Wilpert, "Le due piu antiche rappresentazioni della Adoratio Crucis," *Atti della Pontificia Accademia romana di archeologia*, series 3, Memorie 2 (1928): 135–55, esp. 148, where he describes husband and wife at the altar adoring the cross, although he prefers to imagine they were the two apostles on the lid; and Carlo Cecchelli, *Le arti minori e il costume*, vol. 1 of *La vita di Roma nel Medioevo* (Rome: Palandi, 1951–52), 208, published in 1951 but likely sent to publication before the Vatican excavation report because he still saw a married couple at an altar. Guarducci, *Capsella eburnea*, 126–27 (Constantine and Helena); Longhi, *Capsella eburnea*, 109–12 (Galla Placidia and Valentinian II); Ally Kateusz, "'She sacrificed herself as the priest': Early Christian Female and Male Co-Priests," *Journal of Feminist Studies in Religion* 33, no. 1 (Spring 2017), 45–67, esp. 63 (Galla Placidia and Valentinian II); and Fabrizio Bisconti, "La Capsella di Samagher: Il quadro delle interpretazioni," *Il cristianesimo in Istria fra tarda antichità e alto Medioevo* (2009): 217–31, esp. 230–31.

20. Alice Baird, "La Colonna Santa," *The Burlington Magazine* 24 (1913–14): 128–31; and Leclercq, "Pola," cols. 1342–1346, esp. 1345, fig. 10429.

21. Engelbert Kirschbaum, *The Tombs of St. Peter and St. Paul*, trans. John Murray (New York: St. Martin's, 1959), 53–57, fig. 7 for the stack of altars, and see figs. 12, 13, and 35 for cross-section diagrams of the shrine and its travertine

CHAPTER FIVE

Peter's around this shrine, which was the focal point of the whole basilica.[22] Both Jerome in the late 300s and Gregory of Tours in the late 500s had reported that Peter's tomb was beneath the altar in Old St. Peter's Basilica[23]—and the excavators discovered a stone tomb below.[24]

The shape and size of the second-century shrine matched what was carved on the ivory, down to the arched niche seen behind its stone table (fig. 10).[25] Englebert Kirschbaum, one of the Vatican excavators, later wrote that the scene on the ivory was "so striking even in its details as to confirm conclusively its interpretation as the Constantinian apse in Saint Peter's."[26] Gnirs had speculated: *Could the man and woman at the altar table be participating in a ceremony of the sacrament of matrimony?*[27]

---

mensa, plus fig. 35 for a reconstruction of the shrine in context with the apse of Old Saint Peter's.

22. Jocelyn Toynbee and John Ward Perkins, *The Shrine of St. Peter and the Vatican Excavation*, 201.

23. Jerome, *Contra Vigilantium* 1.8; Gregory of Tours, *Liber in gloria martyrum*, 27.

24. E. Kirschbaum, *Tombs*, 81–94, 113–19.

25. For a reconstruction of the shrine illustrating the niche over the *mensa*, see Toynbee, *Shrine,* fig. 17; for a diagram, see Kirschbaum, *Tombs*, figs. 13 and 37.

26. E. Kirschbaum, *Tombs*, 60.

27. Gnirs, "Basilica," 37.

Figure 11. (detail of Figure 9). Man and woman at the second-century shrine's table.

In the next decades other art historians followed his suggestion.[28] Others have since proposed that they could be mother and son.[29] Some people have suggested that they might be venerating the cross in the niche behind the altar table, but in 1928 the famous Vatican specialist Joseph Wilpert entirely rejected that suggestion,

---

28. Pietro Toesca, *Storia dell'arte italiana*, vol. 1 (Turin: Unione, 1927), 322; Pericle Ducati, *L'arte in Roma dalle origini al sec. VIII* (Bologna: Cappelli, 1938), 380; Alexander Coburn Soper, "The Italo-Gallic School of Early Christian Art," *The Art Bulletin* 20, no. 2 (June 1938): 145–92, esp. 157; Leclercq, "Pola," col. 1345; Giuseppe Wilpert, "Le due più antiche rappresentazioni della Adoratio Crucis," *Atti della Pontificia Accademia romana di archeologia*, series 3, Memorie 2 (1928): 135–55, esp. 148, where he describes husband and wife at the altar adoring the cross, although he prefers to imagine they were the two apostles on the lid; and Carlo Cecchelli, *La vita di Roma nel Medioevo, volume 1: Le arti minori e il costume* (Rome: Palandi, 1951–52), 208, published in 1951 but likely sent to publication before the Vatican excavation report because he still identified a married couple at an altar.

29. Guarducci, *Capsella eburnea*, 126–27 (Constantine and Helena); Longhi, *Capsella eburnea*, 109–12 (Galla Placidia and Valentinian II); Kateusz, "'She sacrificed herself as the priest'," 63 (Galla Placidia and Valentinian II); and Bisconti, "Capsella di Samagher," 230–31.

saying, "In Saint Peter's Basilica the cross was not venerated in such a pronounced fashion as depicted in this scene."[30] The reason is that Old St. Peter's Basilica did not have a relic of the True Cross and thus such veneration did not occur there.[31] Other art historians have pointed out that the woman was sculpted raising some kind of container, perhaps a pyx or a bowl.[32] If she had been a man, from the beginning she almost certainly would have been identified as a priest raising the chalice.

The Vatican excavators took almost ten years to write their final report, yet never mentioned in it that earlier scholars had identified a woman at this altar.[33] Instead, they tried to move the altar away from the woman. For four decades virtually every scholar had identified the table as the basilica's altar.[34] The Vatican authors, however, proposed that the shrine's table was not the altar and argued that instead the basilica had a portable altar table. They proposed the ciborium must have been a 20-by-20-foot square, which they illustrated as seen in Figure 8. Vatican excavator Englebert Kirschbaum later explained why a square ciborium was so important to them. A square ciborium's overhead ribs would cross in the middle of the square, he said, and the lamp would hang from that midpoint—over empty floor, ten feet in front of the second-century shrine and its stone table. The altar would have sat under the lamp's light, he said, and concluded: "We have to suppose a *portable* altar table."[35]

---

30. Wilpert, "Due più antiche rappresentazioni," 149.

31. Leclercq, "Pola," col. 1345.

32. Longhi, *Capsella*, 100; Angiolini, *Capsella*, 29; Buddensieg, "Coffret en ivoire de Pola," 163; Robin Jensen, "Saints' Relics and the Consecration of Church Buildings in Rome" in *Studia Patristica, ol. LXXI – Including papers presented at the Conferences on "Early Roman Liturgy to 600" (November 14, 2009 and February 27, 2010) at Blackfriars Hall, Oxford, UK*, eds. Juliette Day and Markus Vinzent (Leuven: Peeters, 2014), 153–69, esp. 162–63; and Bogdanović, *Framing of Sacred Space*, 185.

33. Gnirs, "Basilica," 37.

34. Gnirs, "Basilica," 34, 36–37, fig. 28; Toesca, *Storia dell'arte italiana*, 322; Ducati, *Arte in Roma*, 380; Soper, "Italo-Gallic School of Early Christian Art," 157; Leclercq, "Pola," col. 1345; Wilpert, "Due piu antiche rappresentazioni," 148; and Cecchelli, *Vita di Roma*, 208.

35. Kirschbaum, *Tombs*, 61, italics added.

I discuss this fabrication in my new book, *Mary and Early Christian Women: Hidden Leadership*; but, in short, the ciborium was not square.[36] There was no portable altar. The lamp hung above the second-century shrine and its stone table—the focal point of the entire basilica.

The half-hexagon ciborium over Peter's tomb, with the shrine at the back and the half dome above, reflected the image of the half-hexagon ciborium at the Holy Sepulchre, with the dome of the rotunda above. The architects of Old St. Peter's reproduced the architecture of the famous Anastasis shrine, thereby visually invoking the sacral power of Jerusalem in Rome and symbolically linking Peter's tomb to Christ's.

Worthy of consideration is the possibility that the gender-parallel liturgy seen in Old St. Peter's Basilica suggests not only that the architecture of Jerusalem was sacred in Rome, but also that Jewish ritual tradition was. Philo of Alexandria described the first-century gender-parallel ritual of Jews whom he called Therapeutae. He said some were near Alexandria as well as in other areas. He detailed their all-night ritual with two leaders, a man who represented Moses and a woman who represented Miriam.[37] Their ritual invoked the Jerusalem Temple, with altar table, bread, libation, and priests.[38] Joan E. Taylor in her study on the Therapeutae says, "Both men and women saw themselves not only as attendants or suppliants but as priests in this Temple."[39] Philo also said their ritual had two choirs, one male and one female, which sang all night and lifted their arms when the sun rose.[40] On the ivory, the men and women appear to be singing with open mouths,

---

36. Kateusz, *Mary*, 167–72; see also Ally Kateusz, "'She sacrificed herself as the priest': Early Christian Female and Male Co-Priests," *Journal of Feminist Studies in Religion* 33, no. 1 (Spring 2017): 45–67, esp. 56–64.

37. Philo of Alexandria, *On the Contemplative Life*, 1–90, esp. 68–69; and *On Agriculture* 80–81.

38. Philo of Alexandria, *On the Contemplative Life*, 83–89.

39. Joan E. Taylor, *Jewish Women Philosophers of First-Century Alexandria: Philo's "Therapeutae" Reconsidered* (New York: Oxford University Press, 2003), 343.

40. Philo of Alexandria, *On the Contemplative Life*, 83–89.

CHAPTER FIVE 129

as if a male choir and a female choir. Remarkably, the mass for which Old St. Peter's was most famous was the annual all-night mass commemorating Peter. The ivory sculptor, thus, could have captured the men and women singing and raising their arms during the very moment that the sun rose.

Affirming that the liturgy we see here in Old St. Peter's Basilica indeed could have had its roots in the Jewish traditions of the Therapeutae, Eusebius of Caesarea wrote that the Therapeutae's meetings, not only their rituals, but also their separate places for women and men, were still popular in the churches of his time.[41] We have no cause to doubt Eusebius.

Archeology further supports his claim. For example, the Megiddo church in Palestine is the very oldest church ruins known in Israel, dated between the years 230 and 305. Megiddo is fifteen miles from Caesaria, where Eusebius was bishop. Only the pillar of its stone table has survived, but it is flanked by floor mosaics, with women's names on one side and men's on the other.[42] This church was next to a bakery, which suggests that bread could have been shared at this stone table. The gendered mosaics flanking the table suggest these Jesus followers may have had a gender-parallel ritual for breaking the bread.

Frescoes in the Christian catacombs of Rome suggest the same tradition of male and female leaders at the offering table. For example, a fresco in the Cubiculum of the Sacraments in the Catacomb of Callistus portrays a man and an arms-raised woman flanking a tripod table laden with a plate and bread (fig. 12).[43] The man is on the left and the woman on the right, the same as seen two centuries later in the liturgy above ground in Old St. Peter's Basilica.

---

41. Eusebius of Caesarea, *Ecclesiastical History* 2 17.21–23
42. Joan E. Taylor, "Christian Archaeology in Palestine: The Roman and Byzantine Periods," in *Oxford Handbook of Early Christian Archaeology*, eds. David K. Pettegrew and William Caraher (Oxford University Press, 2019) 36989, esp. 371–72.
43. Joseph Wilpert, *Die Malereien der Katakomben Roms*, 2 vols. (Freiburg im Breisgau: Herdersche, 1903), pl. 41.1.

Figure 12. Man and woman at a tripod mensa, Callistus Catacomb, Rome. Source: Wilpert, *Malereien,* pl. 41.1.

Janet Tulloch analyzed other Christian catacomb frescoes that portray male and female pairs with both holding cups, with the woman raising hers as the leader.[44] Tulloch says in Christian frescoes, "Female figures dominate the cup action."[45] She says that this *greatly* contrasts with *pagan* funerary art in Rome, where virtually always the *man* is seen raising the cup. For example, as seen in Figure 13, a woman on the right raises the cup above the tripod table, while on the far left, a seated man also holds a cup on the table.[46] This pair, both with cups, resonates with the bishop Irenaeus of Lyons's report around the year 170 that in one community of Jesus followers, both a man and a woman consecrated the wine. Notably, when Irenaeus described the actions of the woman as she consecrated the cup of

---

44. Janet H. Tulloch, "Women Leaders in Family Funerary Banquets," in *A Woman's Place: House Churches in Earliest Christianity*, eds. Carolyn Osiek, Margaret Y. MacDonald (Fortress, 2006), 164–93.

45. Tulloch, "Women Leaders," 182.

46. See Tulloch, "Women Leaders," 178, 184–85, figs. 8.3 and 8.3 detail. Image from Wilpert, *Malereien*, pl. 157.2.

wine, he used the verb *eucharistein*.[47] Further suggesting that these catacomb frescoes represent eucharistic ritual, the *Latin Didascalia apostolorum* instructed that the Eucharist be performed in cemeteries, and indeed these catacombs were cemeteries.[48]

Figure 13. Seated man holds cup (left) and standing woman raises cup (right). Marcellino and Pietro catacomb. Late third to early fourth century. Source: Wilpert, *Malereien*, pl. 157.2.

A tradition of women raising the eucharistic cup thus is continually witnessed, from Irenaeus of Lyon's report around 170—to the Christian catacomb frescoes in Rome that portray women raising the cup above the table, to the woman seen raising the cup above the altar table in Old St. Peter's Basilica, to Theodora seen lifting the golden chalice in the Hagia Sophia in Constantinople around the year 550 (fig. 14).

---

47. This ritual was not innovative, but archaic, per Cecile and Alexandre Faivre, La place des femmes dans le rituel eucharistique des marcosiens: déviance ou archaïsme?," *RevScRel* 71 (1997): 310–28.

48. Latin *Didascalia apostolorum* 26; *Didascalia Apostolorum: The Syriac Version Translated and Accompanied by the Verona Latin Fragments*, trans. R. Hugh Connolly (Clarendon, 1929), 253.

Figure 14. Christian women raise the cup. From Rome to Constantinople, late third to mid-sixth centuries. Detail of figures 13, 11, and 5.

These ancient artifacts, the three very oldest to depict people at the altar in real churches, are *windows* that show us early Christian women at the altar table and performing liturgical functions. Through these windows we also see that Christians treasured their roots in Israel—not only the architecture of Jerusalem, not only Jewish scripture, but also, it seems, Jewish ritual traditions. The parting of the ways, between Christian and Jew, was long.

Galatians 3:28, a baptismal formula itself, preserved by a Jewish teacher named Paul, may have been based on a Jewish model. In any case, the earliest Jesus followers appear to have observed it in their assemblies. Both Jew and Greek were leaders in their assemblies. Both slave and free were leaders in the assemblies. So also, both male and female were leaders in their assemblies—for, *they said*, we are all one in Christ Jesus.

***

CHAPTER FIVE

If any conclusion regarding the urgent need for the reinstitution of the ancient priestly and liturgical order of deaconesses can be drawn from the above analysis of the historical and archeological evidence of a leading liturgical role of women in early Christianity from its very beginning down to the sixth century CE, it would be the uncontested evidence of women's presence around the altar of real churches. Although this was attested in all three major centers of early Christianity (Jerusalem, Rome, Constantinople), i.e., both in the East and in the West, the majority of the artifacts, as we have shown, appear to have been mainly originated or modeled after Eastern (Christian or Jewish) ritual and architectural traditions. Therefore, it may not be a coincidence that a female diaconal presence in the Christian East lasted much longer than in the West. And although the liturgical priestly order of deaconesses in the second millennium has fallen into disuse, it has never been canonically or theologically annulled, with appearances continuing well into the twentieth century.

Chapter Six

A SOCIOLOGICAL APPROACH TO THE INVISIBILITY OF DEACONESSES

Niki Papageorgiou

The recommendation to reinstitute the order of deaconesses (including their liturgical role) is most certainly the result of scholarly research affirming the institutional role of women deacons in the Orthodox and other churches in the historical field through the evidence of biblical and apocryphal sources, liturgical texts, early, proto-Byzantine and mid-Byzantine liturgical practices of the church, as well as the early Christian art. But most importantly, the reinstitution of the order of deaconesses is not foreign to Orthodox Church history, but in accordance with its authentic, though latent, tradition.

The role of research proves to be of paramount importance here. Painstaking theological, canonical, historical, philological, and in particular archaeological research, functions as a kind of archeology of knowledge: the research "digs" under the "embankments," i.e., the social additions that cover women's faces, hide their activities, silence their role and make them invisible. The role of the research is to "dig" in order to reveal the active and dynamic presence of women and to give shape and form to their activities, almost forgotten under the weight of the historical conditions that unfairly reduced their importance. Under the burden of historically unjust and demeaning conditions, women are often treated as quasi-absent, silent, and invisible. Of course, they are present, but society's gaze and hearing are not focused on them; no one sees them, and no one hears them. Research can give voice to women and make them visible, present, and influential again in the process of the church community.

This is what Ally Kateusz's research did in two of her last studies on the subject. The first in this volume, and the second in her recent Open Public Lecture, dedicated to "The Unity of the One Church of Christ."[1] With Kateusz's contribution, the testimony of art strengthen the results of the biblical and historical research in recent years, reminding us of the forgotten institutional and liturgical role of women, when the church functioned as a body of Christ around the altar and not as a hierarchical and patriarchal institution as it had evolved under the influence of the social and cultural environment of late antiquity. The depictions of women around the holy altar, according to Kateusz's analysis, testify to the fact that women had a leading liturgical role in the Christian communities during the first centuries. It is even remarkable that the women are not simply present, together with men, around the altar; they are also presented in a symmetrical way, demonstrating the equally participatory and eucharistic character of the primary community, compared to the later hierarchical and patriarchal one.

Art illuminates in its own revelatory way the unseen aspects of a forgotten, but clearly existing tradition, concerning the role of women in the early church. The deaconesses actively participated in the process of the church's operation, i.e., in its liturgical, pastoral, and social work. However, over the centuries their participation faded away and fell into oblivion. Societies had to change, the debate on the role of women had to be reopened, and the perspective of research renewed to ascertain and recognize the "invisible" figures of women hidden and invisible under the weight of social conditions. The interesting thing is that the more the subject is researched, the more we discover examples of women ministers who are there

---

1. "Images in Art of Women Deacons in East and West," in *For the Unity of the One Church of Christ*, eds. Archbishop Lazar Puhalo, P. Vassiliadis, N. Dimitriadis, and K. Drosia, (Ottawa: Synaxis Press, 2022), ch. 22.

waiting silently and invisibly for the help of research in order for women to gain a voice and a face, appreciation, and recognition.

The invisibility of women, closely related to non- or under-recognition, is emerging as a focal point in social science research. It derives from an idea of American sociologist Robert Merton that certain psychosocial processes affect the allocation of rewards to scientists for their contributions that in turn affect the flow of ideas and finding through the communication networks of science.[2] The American feminist Matilda Gage, "replying" to Merton, promoted the idea that women scientists are under-recognized in some scientific fields having been ignored, denied credit, or otherwise dropped from sight.[3] Since then, the issue of the invisibility and under-recognition of women has become an analytical tool for the study of the position of women in the academic field,[4] as well as in the sociopolitical and labor field.[5]

Invisibility is considered a form of abuse of their identity and underestimation of their value to the detriment, of course, not only of the women themselves, but also of the healthy functioning of the community and society in general. Behind the invisibility of women, the patriarchal and male-dominated structures of traditional societies are hidden, which are supported by the dominant members of the group (men) who developed this construct.[6] Practices used in order for one group of individuals to dominate others

---

2. See Robert K. Merton, "The Matthew Effect in Science. The reward and communication systems of science are considered," *Science* 159 (3810), 1968: 56–63.

3. See Margaret W. Rossiter, "The Matthew Matilda Effect in Science," *Social Studies of Science*, 23 (2), 1993: 325–41.

4. See indicatively, Ann Oakley, "The Invisible Woman: Sexism in Sociology," in Ann Oakley, *The Sociology of Housework* (reissue), 1st ed, (Bristol University Press, 2018), 1–26, accessed July 24, 2022 https://www.jstor.org/stable/j.ctv75d8k9; Chara Karagiannopoulou, "Visibility and Invisibility of Gender in International Relations," in *A Century of International Relations,* eds. A. Gofas, G. Evagelopoulos, M. Koppa (Athens: Pedio, 2020), 364–74 [in Greek].

5. See Caroline Criado Pérez, *Invisible Women: Data Bias in a World Designed for Men* (New York: Abrams Press, 2019).

6. See Margaret W. Rossiter, "The Matthew Matilda Effect in Science," *Social Studies of Science*, 23 (2), 1993: 325–41.

are obscurity, ridicule, withholding information, inducing feelings of shame and guilt, as well as devaluing them.[7] In this context, the impression is created that those who belong to the dominant social group speak more, so their contribution and value is recognized.[8] On the contrary, the social contribution of women, as in general of individuals or groups coming from non-dominant social categories, is underestimated. The dominant group usually sets the rules and norms, with the result that marginalized group members are put at a disadvantage: once they become invisible, they are deprived of recognition, appreciation, power, and voice.[9]

On the contrary, women's visibility allows recognition,[10] authenticity, self-determination.[11] Visibility implies that a person is accepted for their skills and abilities, rather than being categorized by others in a stereotypical way.[12] Both visibility and invisibility are embedded in power relations because those in power also have the ability to make others visible or invisible. These two situations reflect social hierarchies and social boundaries and are then used to reinforce these arbitrary boundaries, ensuring the maintenance of social hierarchy between groups.[13] Because they are socially constructed,

---

7. See B. Kanjara, Professional Options, Equalities and the "equalizing" Potential of the School, 2007, accessed July 24, 2022, http://www.isotitaepeaek.gr/iliko_sxetikes_ereunes/ekpedeusi/SEP_School%20possibilities.pdf.

8. P. Lewis and R. Simpson, *Revealing and Concealing Gender: Issues of Visibility in Organizations* (New York: Palgrave Macmillan, 2010); R. Simpson and P. Lewis, "An Investigation of Silence and a Scrutiny of Transparency: Re-examining Gender in Organization Literature through the Concepts of Voice and Visibility," *Human Relations*, 58 (10), 2005: 1253–75.

9. A. Brighenti, "Visibility: A Category for Social Science," *Current Sociology* 55 (3) (2007), 323–42; R. Simpson and P. Lewis, "An Investigation of Silence and a Scrutiny of Transparency," 1253–75.

10. L. M. Roberts, "Changing Faces: Professional Image Construction in Diverse Organizational Settings," *The Academy of Management Review*, 30 (4), 2005: 685–711.

11. N. T. Buchanan, I. H. Settles, *Managing (In)visibility and Hypervisibility in the Workplace, Journal of Vocational Behavior*, 113 (August 2019): 1–5, accessed July 24, 2022 https://doi.org/10.1016/j.jvb.2018.11.001.

12. Ibid.

13. A. Smedley and B. D. Smedley, "Race as Biology is Fiction, Racism as a Social Problem is Real," *American Psychologist*, 60, 2005: 16–26.

when social conditions change, so does the nature and function of conditions of visibility.

Let us hope that this continuous and persistent revelation of the institutional role of women in the church in the first centuries, will also reveal the dynamic presence of modern women in the church and open ways for the institutional recognition they earn and deserve that suits them. To this end, testimonies, such as the artifacts brought to the surface by early Christian and early Byzantine archeologists, are of enormous importance.

[Editors' note: Niki Papageorgiou, an editor of this volume, did not present at the 2020 conference, but has added this commentary on the previous chapter by Ally Kateusz.]

Chapter Seven

THE GOSPEL REFERENCES TO WOMEN: A SOCIOLOGICAL REMINDER

Dimitrios Passakos

Introduction: Women in Jewish Society

From which part of the man should I take the woman out? the Almighty wondered. From the head? She will become very imaginative. From the eye? She will become very strange. From the ear? She will eavesdrop on the doors. From the mouth? She will talk. From the hand? She will be wasted. He finally got a very dark part, a very occult part of the body, hoping to make her modest.[1]

The above rabbinical aphorism is a small occasion to think about the current perceptions of woman in the time of Christ and to be able to more safely evaluate the corresponding image presented by the Gospel narratives.

In a theocratic society such as the Jewish world of Christ, which based its very existence on the Law, it was inevitable that the requirements of the Law would determine not only the relationship of the Jew with Yahweh and his fellow man, but also project a specific structure of society, which in turn found its legitimacy in the Bible. The choice of specific interpretations of critical passages in the

---

1. Cf. Bereishit Rabbah 18.2 in a rough and concise translation, accessed on August 21, 2020, https://www.sefaria.org/Bereishit_Rabbah.18.2?lang=bi.

scriptures is not surprising, since this approach was the safest way to "sanctify" established notions and practices in the Jewish society of the day.

One can cite as an example the famous passage about the creation of man. The narrative is delivered, as is well known, in two variants: A Priestly and a Yahwist.[2] The first (Gen 1:26–28):

> Then God said, "Let us make humankind in our image, according to our likeness; and let them have dominion over the fish of the sea, and over the birds of the air, and over the cattle, and over all the wild animals of the earth, and over every creeping thing that creeps upon the earth. So God created humankind in his image, in the image of God he created them; male and female he created them. God blessed them, and God said to them, "Be fruitful and multiply, and fill the earth and subdue it; and have dominion over the fish of the sea and over the birds of the air and over every living thing that moves upon the earth."

This passage exudes an atmosphere of equality and complementarity between man and woman: both constitute the original human being, created in the image and likeness of God. The second (Gen 2:21–23):

> So, the Lord God caused a deep sleep to fall upon the man, and he slept; then he took one of his ribs and closed up its place with flesh. And the rib that the Lord God had taken from the man he made into a woman and brought her to the man. Then the man said, "This at last is bone of my bones and flesh of my flesh; this one shall be called Woman, for out of Man this one was taken.

This passage conveys exactly the same truths, except that in rabbinic interpretation the text has now succumbed to the dominant social conception of the position of women in Jewish society: she is

---

2. See M. Konstantinou, *Του συνιέναι τας Γραφάς: 13 + 1 steps of introduction to the Old Testament* (Thessaloniki: Barbounakis, 2014), 135–165. Cf. E. X. Adamtziloglou, Ἦσαν δε εκεί γυναίκες πολλαί [*There were many women there*] (Thessaloniki: Simbo, 1997), 43–80.

"extracted from" the man (the "very dark" and "occult" part of the body referenced above). Therefore, one is tempted to conclude that she is created not in the image and likeness of God, like Adam, but in the image and likeness of Adam, with all that this may mean at the level of salvation. The most interesting aspect of this interpretation lies in the fact that Genesis first mentions the word "man" at 2:23 after the famous incision in the original man, Adam, which effortlessly leads to the conclusion that man and woman begin to exist as distinct beings—after the intersection in Adam or, to put it differently, they are both created at the same time and no one precedes the other, as the first narrative of creation suggests. Needless to say, the clandestine act of Adam's identification with the man sanctifies a particular view of the position of women in Jewish society, which has proved so resilient that it dominates through Christian patriarchal interpretation to this day.

A second example of the militarization of the interpretation of the text in the legitimation of the specific social institution is observed in the command of the Decalogue in Deut 5:21 (cf. Exod 20:17): "Neither shall you covet your neighbor's wife. Neither shall you desire your neighbor's house, or field, or male or female slave, or ox, or donkey, or anything that belongs to your neighbor." The report of the forbidden desires (the house, the field, the slave, the ox, the donkey, the living and everything else that belongs to the neighbor) includes his wife. The layout of the mandate leaves the window open to a sexist interpretation: the woman "belongs" to the man, like any of his other assets. Such an approach is also confirmed by Exod 21:2–3: "When you buy a male Hebrew slave, he shall serve six years, but in the seventh he shall go out a free person, without debt. If he comes in single, he shall go out single; if he comes in married, then his wife shall go out with him," where it seems that the release of a Jewish slave also implies the release of his wife.

In such a strictly patriarchal environment, the Jewish woman is under the jurisdiction of either her father or her husband.[3] The wife

---

3. In what follows about the position of women in the Jewish society of the time of Christ, much is due to the classic work of Daniel Ropes, *Everyday life in*

owed absolute obedience and loyalty to her husband, but she could not demand fidelity from her husband either. Her social position was inferior, since her contact with the public space was made only through her husband, she always stood aside on the street and it was indecent for someone to talk to her; she did not eat with men, her position and the "kingdom" was her home and many times the windows of the house facing the street were latticed so that she could not be seen outside.[4] The housework was in her absolute responsibility, especially the care to knead bread, to provide with her pitcher water for the needs of the house and to make sure that there was always pure oil available for the Saturday lamp.

Legally, the woman was treated as a minor, and her testimony was not valid in court. Her husband could easily divorce her ("because he found a fault in her") by simply giving her the divorce document (αποστάσιον). If, unfortunately, her second husband divorced her, then she was now considered unclean. She could not inherit from either her father or her husband, as the deceased's assets were usually returned to his closest relative. But it was not forbidden for a worthy woman to have personal gains, which she could manage.[5]

In the religious space, women were not obliged to attend the reading of the Torah, to live in tents during the Feast of Tabernacles, or to hang amulets and fringes on their mantles. They were also exempted from the obligations of the Law that were formulated with the "debts" and from those that had to be done in a certain time. This does not mean, however, that they were not subject to the orders of the Law. In fact, many rabbis urged women to know the Law well, to teach it to their children, and to push their husbands to faithfully apply its provisions. The access of the women to the Temple was limited to the special outer courtyard for them. In the synagogues they sat in a special space separated by a lattice so that they were not with the men, and of course they were not allowed to

---

Palestine in the time of Jesus (translated into Greek from French by Elli Angelou) (Athens: Papadimas, 1990), 151–64.
    4. Song 2:9. Judg 5:28, and Deut 24:1–4. Cf. Matt 5:31.
    5. Prov 31:16.

speak, as some rabbis said, "A woman's singing voice is considered nakedness."[6]

The situation became even more difficult for the Jewish woman in matters of sexuality and honor. It was necessary to confirm her purity on the first night of the wedding. If she could not have children, she was socially stigmatized; and in matters of honor, the Law was relentless with her. If a woman was suspected of adultery, she had to go through the humiliating process of swallowing bitter water, which is described in the book of Numbers (5:11–31). But if she was arrested on the spot, she was sentenced to death by stoning in front of the crowd. In rabbinic thought, women were a not insignificant source of danger because their sexual attraction to men could lead to social disintegration.

The above image of the position of women in the time of Christ was the rule, which of course had its exceptions (the heroine Deborah, the mother of the Maccabees, Ruth, Judith, Esther, and others). But the rule was so deeply rooted in Jewish society and culture that the rabbis' prayer "Thank you, my God, for not making me a pagan, a slave, or a woman" did not seem absurd. The occult secretariat often reached extreme formulations. Note this excerpt from the Testament of the XII Patriarchs (Testament of Reuben 5:1–5):

> For evil are women, my children; and since they have no power or strength over man, they use wiles by outward attractions, that they may draw him to themselves. And whom they cannot bewitch by outward attractions, him they overcome by craft. For moreover, concerning them, the angel of the Lord told me, and taught me, that women are overcome by the spirit of fornication more than men, and in their heart they plot against men; and by means of their adornment they deceive first their minds, and by the glance of the eye instill the poison, and then through the accomplished act they take them captive. For a woman cannot force a man openly, but by a harlot's bearing she beguiles him. Flee, therefore, for-

---

6. See accessed August 21, 2020, https://www.sefaria.org/Berakhot.24a?lang-bi.

nication, my children, and command your wives and your daughters, that they adorn not their heads and faces to deceive the mind: because every woman . . ."[7]

Women in the Time of Christ

It is true that the story of Jesus was written by men, but it is not just for men. Although the Jewish society of the first century AD is deeply patriarchal, Jesus's attitude toward women is in stark contrast to the culture of the time. By his teachings and miracles, he shows that he refuses to consider them inferior to men, but treats them with respect, acknowledging their particularities, their talents, and their desires, often in a way that is in direct opposition to cultural and religious assumptions and norms of Jewish society. All four evangelists, each depending on the purpose of writing his gospel, provide valuable information, sometimes indirectly and modestly, like Mark and Matthew, sometimes almost declaratively, like John and especially Luke, with his "social" gospel.

Some typical cases:

- Jesus talks to the women in a public place (with the widow of Nain,[8] the concubine,[9] the bleeding one[10]) when he heals or teaches.[11]
- He denies the usefulness of the laws of purity of Leviticus, rewarding the bleeding woman, addressing her as his daugh-

---

7. Accessed July 12, 2022, https://www.sefaria.org/The_Testaments_of_the_Twelve_Patriarchs%2C_The_Testament_of_Reuben_the_First_born_Son_of_Jacob_and_Leah.

8. Luke 7:11–17.

9. Luke 13:10–17.

10. Matt 9:20–22, Mark 5:25–34, Luke 8:43–48.

11. See S. Agouridis, *The Apocrypha of the Old Testament*, vol. 1, (Athens, 1974), 185–86 (in our free translation, "My children, women are wicked, because having no power or authority over man (sic.). They think wickedly because of their shape, how to distract him from them. And the one who cannot be paid by force is defeated by fraud. Because the angel of God told me about them and taught me that women defeat man (sic.). With the passion of prostitution, and they plot against men (sic.). And with their ornaments they first deceive the mind and with their eyes they spread the virus and then with their actions they capture them."

ter, even though she, by touching him, has made him ritually infected.[12]
- He refers to a woman with the phrase "daughter of Abraham" (Luke 13:16), which in the context clearly has the meaning of title and refers to the salvation of women on an equal footing with men.
- He recognizes the dignity of sinful women and shows them compassion where the Law requires judgment and condemnation. The two cases are typical, of the sinful woman who anoints Jesus's feet with myrrh and wipes them with her hair[13] and of the woman caught in adultery, which leads to stoning.[14] In the first, the host Simon the Pharisee inwardly disputes that Jesus is a prophet, since he does not discern that the one leaning on him is a sinful woman. Jesus not only forgives her many sins because of her great gratitude, but sets her as a model for Simon to teach. In the second, Jesus aborts the stoning of the adulteress (which, remarkably, is imposed by the Law) and not only avoids the trap set by the scribes and Pharisees, but also without acknowledging her sin, he refuses to condemn her as well, calling her to a new life.
- He reveals deep truths to the Samaritan woman,[15] seeing her thirst for truth; and so he transcends national, religious, moral, and social taboos so blatantly that his disciples wonder when they see it, but without externalizing their questions. This case is unique, because Jesus is revealed as the Messiah to a woman, a woman of dubious morality and even a Samaritan woman, who then ends up becoming a preacher to her fellow villagers. To Martha, Lazarus's sister, who knows that only Jesus can do something for her brother, he is revealed as the resurrection and life.[16]

In the Pharisees' attempt to tempt him about the possibility of divorce given by the Law (why did they want to tease him especially with the Law? Maybe because they saw his positive attitude toward

---

12. See footnote 9.
13. Luke 7:36–50, Matt 26:6–13, cf. John 12:3–8.
14. John 8:3–11.
15. John 4:1–42.
16. John 11:25.

women?), Jesus completely relativizes the Law, limiting its power only in the case of prostitution and to the Pharisees' statement that this Law was given by Moses. Jesus notes that he allowed them to divorce their wives because they were hard-hearted and that this was not the original order of things.

In the history and teaching of Jesus, especially as narrated by the Evangelist Luke,[17] female figures and images from the life and representations of women are used: Mary and Elizabeth (Luke 1), the prophetess Anna (2:36–38), the widow of Zarephath (4:25–26), the mother-in-law of Simon (4:38–39), the women in the service of Jesus (8:1–3), Martha and Mary (10:38–42), the parable of the leaven (13:20–21), the parable of the lost coin (15:8–10), the parable of the unjust judge and the widow (18:1–8), the question of the Sadducees about the resurrection (20:27–40), the widow's two small coins (21:1–4), the women mourning his condemnation (23:26–31), and the women watching his crucifixion, who prepare perfumes and myrrh and become witnesses of his resurrection (23:55 ff).

Finally, in all the Gospels, women are the first witnesses of the resurrection of Jesus. This is especially important in light of the fact that the woman's testimony was not valid before the court and is made even more important by the information that the male disciples of Jesus are unable to believe in the fact of the resurrection and the testimony of the women.[18]

The subversive image presented above of Jesus's attitude toward women seems to fade with the election of the twelve apostles. But is that the whole reality? Let's look at the female disciples of Jesus.

In the oldest gospel of the canon, Mark, there is seldom any mention of women and even of women disciples of Jesus, until the reader reaches the end of the text, almost at the death of Jesus. There (Mark 15:40–41) the reader is suddenly informed, "There were also women looking on from a distance; among them were Mary Magdalene, and Mary the mother of James the younger and of Joses,

---

17. See R. McLaughlin, *Confronting Christianity: 12 Hard Questions for the World's Largest Religion* (Illinois: Crossway, 2019), esp. ch. 8, 131–52.
18. Mark 16; Matt 28; Luke 24; John 20.

and Salome. These used to follow him and provided for him when he was in Galilee; and there were many other women who had come up with him to Jerusalem." Where did so many women come from? Joan Taylor, a professor of Christianity and Judaism at the Second Temple at King's College London, was right in pointing out very recently that one should reread Mark's Gospel from the beginning and imagine literally every scene with the presence of women inside it.[19] After all, Mark indirectly invites us to do this, when he notes that these women "when he was in Galilee followed him [i.e., Jesus] and served him."

Luke—again—who, as has been previously noted, has a special sensitivity to illuminate the role of women in the story of Jesus, quotes a piece of information (8:1–3) that comes to supplement and expand that of Mark: "Mary, called Magdalene, from whom seven demons had gone out, and Joanna, the wife of Herod's steward Chuza, and Susanna, and many others, who provided for them out of their resources." Luke also notes with absolute naturalness that in the sermon on the kingdom of God that Jesus preached from city to city, he was accompanied not only by the twelve, but also by some "women who had been healed of evil spirits and infirmities." These women are obviously not mentioned as part of the throng that probably followed Jesus, but as a group of Jesus's disciples next to the twelve. Three named female disciples seem to have a distinct position in this group. Let's look at each one separately:

Mary Magdalene: A Jewish woman was commonly known as her father's daughter or her husband's wife. Here one finds a woman known by a nickname, Magdalene. It has been speculated that the nickname refers to Magdala, on the west shore of Lake Tiberias, its place of origin. Taylor claims that the Aramaic root of her nickname refers to the word "tower," so one has Peter ("rock") in the twelve

---

19. Cf., Michael Collett "The story of Jesus has been told by men for men–but it's not just about men," Australian Broadcasting Corporation (ABC News), September 9, 2019, accessed January 28, 2020, https://www.abc.net.au/news/2019-09-10/the-story-of-jesus-isnt-just-about-men/11481632.

and Magdalene ("tower") in the female disciples.[20] Magdalene, like the other two, seems to be an independent woman who followed Jesus as a disciple and supported his work with her belongings. She is present at the crucifixion with Jesus's mother and other women (see Mark's text above), and she sees where Jesus's corpse is placed and then joins the group of women who go to anoint his body with perfume and myrrh.[21] This process was performed by the close relatives of the deceased, which shows that Magdalene had a special connection with Jesus. According to the Gospel of John, she is the first witness of the resurrection of Jesus (20:1–18) and the one who undertakes the task of becoming a preacher of the resurrection—that is, an apostle—to the twelve. This dynamic presence of Magdalene seems to create a problem, which is vaguely erased in the texts of the New Testament: While for John this is the only first witness of the resurrection who sees and converses with the risen Christ, in Matthew he is with another Mary, while in Luke the disciples are the first to see the risen Christ. In contrast to the apocryphal literature,[22] which reserves for Magdalene a prominent place in early Christianity in the fourth and fifth centuries, Magdalene will be reduced into a repentant prostitute.

b. Joanna, the wife of Chouza (an official of Herod's household): She participates, according to Luke 24:1, together with Magdalene, in the group of myrrhbearing women. The most interesting thing here is that she is a female disciple of Jesus who has apparently abandoned the high life offered to her by her husband's place near Herod, follows Jesus on his tours, and supports his work with her own financial means: a completely subversive image of a woman in first-century Jewish society.

---

20. See Anna Cox, dir., *Jesus' Female Disciples: The New Evidence* (2018), Web-Based Streaming, accessed January 28, 2020, https://topdocumentaryfilms.com/jesus-female-disciples-new-evidence.

21. Matt 28:1–8; Mark 16:1–8; Luke 24:1–12.

22. See "Dialogue of the Savior, Wisdom of Jesus Christ, Gospel of Philip, Faith Wisdom, Gospel of Mary," in J. M. Robinson, *The Nag Hammadi Library*, 3rd rev. ed. (San Francisco: Harper & Row, 1988); and in Greek, S. Agouridis, ed., *Christian Gnosticism. The Coptic texts of Nag Hammadi in Egypt* (Athens: Artos Zoes), 2004.

CHAPTER SEVEN

c. Susanna: Everything known about her comes from Luke's reference. She was apparently a female disciple of Jesus with possessions, which she had to provide for the needs of preaching.

The scene evidently presented is that, next to the circle of the twelve, there is a group of female disciples of Jesus. Some of them have their belongings to financially support the work of their teacher. Joan Taylor even makes a remark: In the pericope of the mission of the disciples by Jesus to preach (Mark 6:7), "He called the twelve and began to send them out two by two, and gave them authority over the unclean spirit," there is a reference to a mission of the disciples in pairs (two by two), a reference reminiscent of the story of Noah:

> I will establish my covenant with you; and you shall come into the ark, you, your sons, your wife, and your sons' wives with you. And of every living thing, of all flesh, you shall bring two of every kind into the ark, to keep them alive with you; they shall be male and female. Of the birds according to their kinds, and of the animals according to their kinds, of every creeping thing of the ground according to its kind, two of every kind shall come into you, to keep them alive. (Gen 6:18–20)

In Genesis 7:2–16 the animals enter the ark in pairs, that is, one male and one female. One could, Taylor wonders, assume that something similar is implied in Jesus's disciples' mission: in pairs, that is, a male and a female apostle?

Luke has preserved another text that speaks, albeit indirectly, of Jesus's disciples. It is the well-known story of Martha and Mary (10:38–42):

> Now as they went on their way, he entered a certain village, where a woman named Martha welcomed him into her home. She had a sister named Mary, who sat at the Lord's feet and listened to what he was saying. But Martha was distracted by her many tasks; so she came to him and asked, "Lord, do you not care that my sister has left me to do all the work by myself? Tell her then to help me." But the

Lord answered her, "Martha, Martha, you are worried and distracted by many things; there is need of only one thing. Mary has chosen the better part, which will not be taken away from her."

The passage shows Martha adopting the role of hostess, accepted by the Jewish society of the time, who takes care of the diakonia of the guests of the house, and Maria fulfilling a "male" role, that of the disciple sitting next to the teacher's feet and listens to his teaching. In Martha's complaint to Jesus that her sister left her alone in the duties of a woman, Jesus praises this choice of Mary to take on the role of a disciple, a choice that no one is going to take away from her.

Conclusion

A consensus has now been reached among scholars of the social history of Christianity that it has emerged in history as a sectarian movement.[23] Werner Stark studied the causes of sectarianism, the role of the sect leader, the sect's relationship with the state, the nature, the diversity and the disintegration of the sects.[24] The findings from this work of the professor of sociology at Fordham University were utilized by Robin Scroggs, then New Testament professor at Chicago Theological Seminary, to show that the movement created by Jesus met all the requirements and had all the hallmarks of a religious sect:[25] It starts as a protest, rejects the established view of reality, a spirit of equality prevails among its members, offers love and acceptance within it, relies on a voluntary basis, demands absolute commitment from its members and is sometimes apoca-

---

23. The terms "sect," "sectarian," etc., are used here in the established sociological meaning.

24. See Werner Stark, *The Sociology of Religion: A Study of Christendom*, in three volumes: *Established Religion* (New York: Fordham University Press, 1967); *Sectarian Religion* (New York: Fordham University Press, 1967); *The Universal Church* (UK: Routledge and Kegan Paul, 1967).

25. See "The Earliest Christian Communities as Sectarian Movement," in J. Neusner, ed., *Christianity, Judaism and Other Greco-Roman Cults, Part 2: Early Christianity* (Oregon: Wipf and Stock Publishers, 2004), 2–23.

lyptic, in the sense that it looks forward to the final establishment of the kingdom of God.[26]

It is important that Scroggs's conclusions refer to the original rural, Palestinian form of Christian communities and not to the later communities created in the urban environment of the Greco-Roman cities. That is, they are based primarily on data from the gospels. It is also crucial to note that the term "sect" should not be treated, as sociologists often do, in opposition to the institutionally-organized church, but to its wider social environment.

Indeed, the image of a religious group, where a spirit of equality prevails among its members and offers love and acceptance within it, is the image given in the gospels about the movement of Jesus. That is, whatever the differences of its members for the outside world, economic, class, origin, age, and sex, they are transcended within the sect, where the farmer is equal to the landowner, the slave to the master, the man to the woman, the young to the old. In such a spirit of equality, it would not be possible to distinguish between male and female discipleship. The image of an equal participation of disciples around Jesus is the image that fits into an apocalyptic Jewish sect, such as Palestinian Christianity.

This image seems to have begun to fade from the fourth century onward. Of course, the discussion about this development is outside the scope of my specialty. I suspect, however, that the "necessary" compromises made by the church when she decided to join the Byzantine Commonwealth and become one of its two pillars gradually led to the secularization of the original apocalyptic sect[27] and the inevitable adoption of the empire's authoritarian model to the detriment of the spirit of equality that prevailed before. Thus, the more the church promotes her institutional manifestation, the more she will conform to the world and reproduce its authoritarian-patriarchal model. However, whenever she realizes her eschatological-communal identity, she will be manifested as

---

26. Ibid., 3–7.
27. See the excellent study of A.N. Papathanasiou, *Η Εκκλησία γίνεται όταν ανοίγεται. Η ιεραποστολή ως ελπίδα και ως εφιάλτης* [*The Church Becomes When It Opens Up. Mission as Hope and as Nightmare*] (Athens: En plo, 2008), 126–54.

a transformed world of equality and justice, not only among her members, women and men, but also as an enviable alternative to the "outside" world.

Chapter Eight

THE NEW THEORIES ABOUT MARY MAGDALENE

Aikaterini Drosia

Introduction

The figure of Mary Magdalene constitutes an important symbol of the importance of the female presence within the first Christian community. Based on the data not only from the New Testament, but also from the apocryphal texts that have been preserved, Mary Magdalene constitutes a typical example of female ministry.

Although the references to her name are rare, the importance of her presence and her contribution to the history of Christianity, mainly as an evangelist of the resurrection message, make her extremely important. Inside a traditionally androcentric community, Mary Magdalene is displayed as a role model of female presence. Her biblical image is summarized from a formerly demonized person to a loyal disciple of Jesus. According to other sources, she has been characterized as a sinner, a prostitute, and Jesus's partner. The minimum amount of historical documents about the "Magdalene in history" and the fragmentary information that ancient Christian texts provides us, were the occasion for her name to be connected with a series of fictional accounts, which as a result led to the truth about her historical face to remain a riddle until today.

The historical face of Mary Magdalene gathered the timeless interest of studies, mainly because of the incorrect characterization of her as a sinner, prostitute, and Jesus's partner. The identification of

Mary Magdalene with two different women, Mary from Bethany who was Lazarus's sister, and the sinful woman who anointed Jesus at Simon's house, contributed to this fact. Moreover, in the context of literature and myth she prevailed as a feminist symbol; and books, articles, and movies were inspired by her, mostly from her misunderstood relationship with Jesus.

In the last few years, new data has come to the light about the position of women in the church with the revelation of sources that belong to early Christianity. It is worth mentioning the recent publication of Ally Kateusz's book *Mary and Early Christian Women*,[1] which provides important evidence from early Christianity that Mary Magdalene assumes a model of female leadership and was honored as an apostle. Early Christian art shows Mary and other women as deacons, or even church leaders. Kateusz's research is important because it brings to light arguments against the position that prevailed for centuries, i.e., that only men were apostles and church leaders. Her analysis of illustrations that came to the light in the twentieth century is also important. These clues make the woman's presence clear in the early church's traditions.

The revival in interest, especially about Mary Magdalene—either as an effort for the reconstruction of her profile, of which little is known, or as a recognition of her great offering to Christianity—led to Dan Brown's novel and resulting movie *The Da Vinci Code*, as well as to the discovery of the Gospel of Judas.

Subsequently, two examples that took place during the last decade will be presented. The first one is about a papyrus fragment discovery known as "The Gospel of Jesus's Wife" and the second one is about the attitude of the Roman Catholic Church about the position of women within the church and Mary Magdalene's role.

---

1. Ally Kateusz, *Mary and Early Christian Women. Hidden Leadership* (Switzerland: Palgrave Macmillan, 2019). See also her contribution in this volume.

CHAPTER EIGHT

The Papyrus: "The Gospel of Jesus's Wife"

Recently, the name of Mary Magdalene returned to the forefront, this time through a little papyrus fragment that was announced at the Tenth International Coptic Congress in Rome as a falsely entitled part of "The Gospel of Jesus's Wife."[2] This specific fragment in Shaheen Coptic writing of unknown origin comes to be added to previous discoveries that confirm the leadership role of women.[3]

This discovery was presented by Karen King, a Harvard University professor of church history. The authenticity (or not) of the fragment provoked a storm of reactions, but from the first moment the researcher argued that nothing changes the data about the Jesus of history. The interdisciplinary conclusion of three scientific institutes proves its authenticity, but it is dated between the fourth and eighth centuries AD. The interest in the fragment is the word "TAZIME" (woman). In Greek translation, it means "my mother gave me life" (line 1). "Students told Jesus" (line 2). "Mary [probably Magdalene] worth's that" (line 3). "Jesus told them: my wife. . ." (line 4). "She might be my disciple" (line 5). This new discovery, according to Karen King herself, doesn't change the historical documents about Jesus's family situation and the wording "my wife" probably has metaphorical meaning. Although it is added to the already existing discoveries of apocryphal texts about the leadership role of women and the relationship between Mary Magdalene and Jesus, nowhere does it exist as a historical sign that she was Jesus's partner.[4]

So the conflict about what the position of women was in Jesus's time comes back again.[5]

---

2. More in Karen King, "Jesus said to them, 'My wife . . .'": A New Coptic Papyrus Fragment" in *Harvard Theological Review*, vol. 107, no. 2 (April 2014): 131–59.

3. Petros Vassiliadis, "Mary Magdalene and the Papyrus with Magdalene," in his Ρινίσματα Καθημερινότητας: *Theological and Social* (E-Book 3) (Thessaloniki, 2019).

4. Petros Vassiliadis, "Mary Magdalene and the Papyrus with Magdalene," 59–60.

5. The content of the fragment after its presentation at the International Conference of Coptic Studies in Rome was of particular concern to the Roman Catholic Church; but despite calls for change, the Vatican reiterated its position

This controversial "Gospel of Jesus's Wife," alongside the other gospels that have come to the light, includes deviations from the officially recognized gospels, as for example the Gospel of Judas and the Gospel of Mary, and was the reason for a new circle of theological and scientific conversations to begin about Christ's human nature.[6]

The Example of the Roman Catholic Church and the Model of Mary Magdalene at the Preaching of the Previous Popes

The twenty-first century, with its main characteristic of volatile evolution in every sector, brought many changes concerning women too, which had begun during the last century. The changes in both their mentality and their way of living couldn't leave unaffected religion and theology in general. Specifically, the contribution of the Second Vatican Council was very positive for the change of how women were projected in the church. In addition, through texts, speeches, and letters from previous popes of the Roman Catholic Church, the evolution of their attitude about the ordination of women, their rights, and their general position within the church is obvious.

Pope Paul VI, having in mind the problems that the generation of the 1960s brought with it, in his "Apostolic Letter on the Occasion of the Eightieth Anniversary of the Encyclical Rerum Novarum," Paragraph 13 (May 14, 1971), he distinguishes positive and negative elements in the issue of women's liberation, stressing that the positives must be reinforced, and the negatives must be prevented.[7] The commission that he recommended on May 3, 1973, about the study of the position of women in the church and the

---

that the priesthood could not be open to women or married men, but one must follow the model Jesus himself pointed out. Laurie Goodstein, "A Faded Piece of Papyrus Refers to Jesus's Wife" in *New York Times*, A1, September 19, 2012.

6. Aikaterina Drosia, "Mary Magdalene in the Biblical and Later Christian Tradition: History-Theology-Legend," (Doctoral dissertation), 21 (Thessaloniki: CEMES publications, 2018).

7. Pope Paul VI, "Octogesima Adveniens: Apostolic Letter of Pope Paul VI" May 14, 1971, accessed August 3, 2022, https://www.vatican.va/content/paul-

community was also important.[8] He awarded the title "Church's Teacher" to St. Theresa of the Infant Jesus and to St. Catherine of Siena, and he additionally set up in 1971 a special committee for the study of contemporary issues related to "effective promotion of the dignity and responsibility of women." In addition, in one of his speeches he pointed out that "the female enjoys special dignity in Christianity more than in any other religion, which is confirmed in many places by the New Testament and is called to constitute the active and living force of Christianity."[9]

Pope John Paul II is the first pope of the Catholic Church who dedicated an entire pontifical text to the position of woman. It is the Apostolic Letter of August 15, 1988, "The Dignity and Vocation of Women."[10] The text refers to the relationship between man and woman, a relationship that reflects the communion of love between the persons of the Holy Trinity. It also refers to the uncertainty of gender relations. In addition, it positively interprets the third chapter of the book of Genesis, setting aside the issue of woman's relationship with original sin. The woman for man according to God's original plan is at the center of salvation mystery.[11]

However, the important role of women after Jesus's death seems to be weakening in Pope John Paul II's encyclicals, as he appears to have forgotten the important role that women played during the earthly action of Jesus, which was equal to that of male disciples. The reaction that erupted in ecclesiastical circles in both the United States and Great Britain after the ordination in America of

---

vi/en/apost_letters/documents/hf_p-vi_apl_19710514_octogesima-adveniens.html.

8. Eleni Pavlidou, "The Treatment of Women in the Catholic Church, from the Second Vatican Council until Today," in AAS (*Acta Apostolicae Sedis. Commentarium officiale Città del Vaticano*, 1909) 65 (1973): 125, 284.

9. Pope Paul VI, "To the members of the National Plenary Session of the Centro Italiano Femminile (6 Dec 1976)" in *Insegnamenti* XIV (1976).

10. Pope John Paul II, "The Dignity and Vocation of Women," accessed October 10, 2021, https://www.vatican.va/content/john-paul-ii/en/apost_letters/1988/documents/hf_jp-ii_apl_19880815_mulieris-dignitatem.html

11. Eleni Pavlidou, "The Treatment of Women in the Catholic Church," 126–27.

the first female bishop, Barbara Harris, in the Episcopal Church in the United States has its roots in male-dominated society. An interesting letter in *The Times of London* compares Mary Magdalene to Barbara Harris and seeks to present the inappropriateness of their positions. It states: "The election of Barbara Harris in the diocese is extremely shocking, as is the action of Mary Magdalene in the close circle of disciples."[12]

On the contrary, nowadays one encounters more open reactions to the issue of women diaconal services. Specifically, in the person of Pope Francis, as a head of the Roman Catholic Church, there exists a clear attitude of recognition of the female sex and her capacity to serve and not an effort to silence and conceal.

Extremely important for the recognition of the title of "apostle" by the Roman Catholic Church for Magdalene was the decree (*decreto*)[13] issued by the Congregation for Divine Worship and the Discipline of the Sacraments on June 3, 2016. As per the will of Pope Francis, the day of remembrance of Magdalene was exalted. Pope Francis continued to honor this commemoration, in the context of the jubilee of compassion, to praise the value of this woman who gave great devotion to Jesus and who was also greatly honored by him, after giving her the honor of being the witness of his resurrection. It is worth noting that the publication of another article, in the title of which Magdalene is mentioned as an apostle, clearly states that Jesus himself gave that title to her.[14]

Pope Francis, in his speech to his people at St. Peter's Basilica on May 10, 2017, on the subject of the power of Christian hope, focuses on the presence of Magdalene at the tomb of Jesus. He pres-

---

12. Ibid., 397. More about the latest developments in the Catholic Church can be found in Dimitrios Keramidas, "The Problem of the Catholic Church on Deaconesses and the Ordination of Women," in *Deaconess, Ordination of Women and Orthodox Theology* eds. P. Vassiliadis, E. Amoiridou, M. Goutzioudis (Thessaloniki: CEMES Publications 12, 2016), 397–416.

13. Accessed July 12, 2022, https://www.catholicnewsagency.com/news/34020/mary-magdalene---apostle-to-the-apostles---gets-upgraded-feast-day

14. Alexander Fischer, "Was Bedeutet: Maria Magdalena ist 'Apostolin der Apostel'?," Katholische Nachrichten, July 22, 2016, accessed July 12, 2022, http://www.kath.net/news/56067 [in German].

ents Mary Magdalene as an apostle of hope. He uses her example to show how personal the relationship between Jesus and humanity is. He presents the fact of the first appearance of the resurrected Jesus as wonderful, after taking place on a personal level. Jesus appears to a person he already knew, calling her by her name. Magdalene's reaction, when she realizes who is talking to her, is to want to touch Jesus; but he doesn't allow her, and the scene of the famous "do not touch me" follows. But she herself is sent by Jesus to announce the news of the resurrection to the other disciples. In this way, Pope Francis emphasizes, Magdalene is proclaimed as "the apostle of the new great hope."[15]

Jesus, as Pope Francis mentions in his speech, surprises Magdalene in the most unexpected way when she believes that his body was stolen. He repeatedly emphasizes Jesus's personal interest in humankind, which is captured in many parts of the gospel. By the fact that Jesus personally addresses Magdalene and calls her by her name, the pope wants to point out that Jesus knows each of us personally, forgives us, waits for us, and has patience with us. Mary Magdalene, as an example of hope and her experience, highlights the change from tears to joy and the announcement that she saw the resurrected Jesus.[16]

This is not the first time that Pope Francis has used the example of Mary Magdalene for the edification of his people, thus highlighting the emphasis and value he gives to a woman's testimony, which he uses to support and strengthen the Christian faith. Mary Magdalene, taking into account the data we have about her from the New Testament and apocryphal texts that have been preserved for us, can be a typical example of female ministry.

---

15. Elise Harris, "Pope Points to Mary Magdalene as an Apostle of Hope," Catholic News Agency, May 17, 2017, accessed July 12, 2022, https://www.catholicnewsagency.com/news/36050/pope-points-to-mary-magdalene-as-an-apostle-of-hope.

16. Ibid.

III

HISTORICAL PERSPECTIVES

Chapter Nine

THE PERSON OF DEACONESS PHOEBE IN THE WORK OF CHURCH FATHERS AND ECCLESIASTICAL WRITERS IN EARLY CHRISTIANITY

Eirini Artemi

Phoebe As One of Paul's Coworkers Mentioned in the Epistle to the Romans

The sixteenth chapter of Paul's Epistle to the Romans contains a reference to Phoebe, the deaconess in the church at Cenchreae, the port of Corinth.[1] She was probably Paul's assistant who carried the apostle's letter from Corinth to Rome. This particular woman was a prototype of a deaconess: "I commend to you our sister Phoebe, a deaconess of the church at Cenchreae, that you may receive her in the Lord as befits the saints . . . for she has been a helper of many and of myself as well."[2] She is the only deaconess we know by name in the first century AD, and the only woman then who is identified as a "deacon" (διάκονος).

---

1. In Acts 18:18, Paul visited and preached the gospel at Cenchreae, the port of Corinth, on his second missionary journey. M. Mowczko, "What did Phoebe's position and ministry as διάκονος of the church at Cenchrea involve?" in *Deacons and Diakonia in Early Christianity: The First Two Centuries*, eds. Bart J. Koet, Edwina Murphy, and Esko Ryokas (Tuebingen: Mohr Siebeck, 2018), 91–102.

2. Rom 16:1–2 RSV.

Phoebe's name is mentioned only once in the entire New Testament. Nothing is known about her family. It is assumed, however, that she was unmarried or a widow, because her name includes no mention of a husband, which functioned as a surname does today. D. Kyrtatas believes that Phoebe's name indicates that she was a free slave,[3] but I do not concur. What is sure is that, based on the meaning of her name,[4] one can assume that she was a pagan before she became Christian. Moreover, it is believed that she and Tabitha were the first women—or at least among the first women—to preach the gospel.[5] Indeed, Paul refers to her as: 1) co-worker, 2) sister, 3) patron, and 4) deacon. Paul, the Apostle to the Gentiles, seems to have insisted upon the following criteria contained in 1 Timothy 3:8–11 to call someone a deaconess: 1) the woman must be modest, 2) must not be hypocritical or insincere, 3) must not be a drunkard, 4) must not be greedy for financial gain, 5) must be above reproach such that no one could accuse her of anything unethical, 6) must not be a gossip, 7) must have self-restraint, and 8) must be faithful in all areas of life, such as religion, family, society, and more generally the nation as a whole.

With regard to the characterization of Phoebe as a "coworker," it must be noted that she had all the qualities of the Apostle Paul's male coworkers. Specifically, she would have been tested in various hardships, and she would have the will to endure any trial for faith in Christ.[6] She had to behave like a good soldier of Christ, which

---

3. D. Kyrtatas, "Evidence for the Christianization of Pontos," 45–69, esp. 58, ref. 18, accessed January 5, 2020, https://ejournals.epublishing.ekt.gr/index.php/deltiokms/article/viewFile/2587/2352.pdf. J. Danielou and H.I. Marrou, *The Christian Centuries: A New History of the Catholic Church*, vol. 1: *The First Six Hundred Years* (New York: McGraw Hill, 1964), 50–55.

4. Hesiod, *Theogony*, 132–36: "But later she slept with Ouranos and bore Ocean with its deep currents, And also: Coios, Crios, Hyperion, Iapetos, Theia, Rheia, Themis, Mnemosyne, Gold-crowned Phoibe, and lovely Tethys," 406–10: "And Phoibe came to Coios, and in the sensual embrace Of the god she loved, the goddess became pregnant And bore Leto, robed in midnight blue, gentle always, Mild to mortal men and to immortal gods."

5. B. Witherington III, *Women in the Earliest Churches* (Cambridge University Press, 1989), 150–51.

6. 2 Cor 8:16–24.

meant to have faith and trust in Jesus Christ and his church and to have a good conscience.[7] In addition, she should be a good soldier, "that inspired by them you may wage the good warfare, holding faith and a good conscience. By rejecting conscience, certain persons have made shipwreck of their faith."[8] At the same time, she was to be a good student, i.e., to pay attention and to be perfect in the eyes of God. She must also work for her continuous improvement, so that she might not be ashamed of any omission in the completion of her work, nor any oversight, great or small. Finally, as a good disciple, she must follow the teachings of the gospel without adopting any heretical teachings.[9] Additionally, she would have had the role of teacher, one who teaches others what she learned and heard about Christ from the Apostle Paul and the other apostles.[10] Of course, she had to teach Christ's words without fear of any difficulties, threats, or persecutions.

In addition to all the aforementioned characteristics that the Apostle Paul believed any of his coworkers should have, he also calls Phoebe "sister," "patron," and "deacon." The apostles frequently used the terms "brother" and "sister" to refer to members of Christ's church, demonstrating thus their unity. So also here the term "sister" denotes the spiritual relationship between Paul and Phoebe, since they are both Christians and both have been reborn from a common "womb," meaning the incarnation of the Lord and the common cup of the Holy Eucharist. After all, according to Christian teaching, all human beings are considered brothers and sisters, with all equal before their common father, God. All the more so for Christians who are members of the body of Christ. As Lynn Cohick observes: "Phoebe, as a sister in the house of God the Father, used her property and personal time to improve the lives of the other brothers and sisters, men or women of this particular Cenchrean community."[11]

---

7. 2 Tim 2: 1–13.
8. 1 Tim 1:18–19.
9. 2 Tim 2:15–23.
10. 2 Tim 2:1–13.
11. L. H. Cohick, *Women in the World of the Earliest Christians: Illuminating Ancient Ways of Life* (Grand Rapids, MI: Baker Academic, 2009), 304. Cp.

As for the term "patron," it is widely assumed that Phoebe was a wealthy woman who offered food at the common meals—the so-called *agape* meals—of the Christians in Cenchreae, after the Holy Eucharist. It is the only time the word "patron" is used in the whole New Testament. It is not considered a religious term, but rather in Roman society referred to someone with legal authority to defend the rights of foreigners living in the empire or of destitute Roman citizens.[12]

There is no indication that this word functioned as a title for someone with a prominent role in the church. But outside the church, this term unequivocally described a person of influence who could intervene effectively on behalf of people in difficult circumstances.[13] It seems that Phoebe had the opportunity to use her position to protect or help several Christians who were in such circumstances, including Paul himself. As a result, she was worthy of the care of the Christians in Rome.[14]

Finally, Phoebe was called a "deacon." She was the first woman to be referred to as a deaconess in the New Testament, and this ministry was entrusted to her by Paul. Based on the way the apostle praised her, it seems that she carried out her duties quite successfully. One cannot, as demonstrated by the texts of the fathers, define in detail the term "deacon"—a term that is found without the femi-

---

Gregory Palamas, *Homily 1– One Peace with One Another*, PG 151, 9: "We are all brethren in that we have one Creator and Lord, who is Father to us all. That brotherhood we share with animals and inanimate nature. We are also brethren one to another as descendants of one earthly father, Adam, and the only creatures made in God's images. But even this is common to all nations. More especially, however, we are brethren in that we are of the same race and live in the same place; and above and else, share one mother, the Holy Church and true piety, the author and finisher of which is Christ, the rightful Son of God. Not only is He our God, but He was well-pleased to be our Brother, our Father and our Head, bringing us all together into one body and making us members of one another and of Himself." J. C. Campbell, *Phoebe: Patron and Emissary* (Collegeville, MN: Liturgical Press: 2009), 25.

12. G. Bilezikian, *Beyond Sex Roles What the Bible Says about a Woman's Place in Church and Family* (Grand Rapids, MI: Baker Academic, 2006), 157.

13. Ibid.

14. Ibid.

nine ending in this substantive adjective—but it seems that it was a ministry with a broad scope of activities.[15] Of course, it should be noted that the use of the term "deacon" in the Apostle Paul's letters had the meaning of minister, servant, and helper.[16] A deacon was one whose responsibilities lay between prophecy and teaching, according to Romans 12:7, and who had many responsibilities for the benefit of either the church of Christ or the local churches. The verb διακονώ is used with the same meaning in the Gospel of John.[17] Additionally, it must be emphasized that the verb διακονώ—and not the noun διάκονος—was used for the seven men who were chosen to serve the church.[18] Generally speaking, according to Mary Evans, the New Testament nowhere refers to a woman as either an επίσκοπος (bishop/overseer) or as a πρεσβυτέρα (elder) connected with the Divine Liturgy.[19] Grenz agrees with Evans, noting that the New Testament may not describe women's ministry in terms of ordained deaconesses with liturgical duties, but neither does the New Testament exclude it. Consequently, one cannot reject either the role of assistant or the role of ordained deaconess.[20]

For his part, Paul seems to have great admiration for Phoebe, since he asked the Christians in Rome to welcome her " that you may receive her in the Lord as befits the saints, and help her in whatever she may require from you."[21] At this point, it must be stressed that it is unknown whether Phoebe traveled to preach the word of God as an apostle commissioned by the church at Corinth or at Cenchreae, or whether she traveled because she had to carry out

---

15. 1 Cor 3:5, 6; Eph 3:7, 6:21; Col 1:7, 23, 25, 4:7; Rom 15:8, 16:1, 13:4; Phil 1:1; 2 Cor 3:6, 6:4, 11:5, 15, 23; Gal 2:17.

16. C. Keener, "Women in Ministry: The Egalitarian View," in *Two Views on Women in Ministry*, eds. J. Beck and C. Blomberg (Grand Rapids, MI: Zondervan, 2001), 39.

17. John 12:26.

18. Acts 6:1–6.

19. M. J. Evans, *Woman in the Bible* (Downers Grove, IL: InterVarsity Press, 1983), 124.

20. S. Grenz and D. M. Kjesbo, *Women in the Church* (Downers Grove, IL: Intervarsity Press, 1995), 90.

21. Rom 16:2.

some of her own business. The apostle treated her equally with his male deacons and disciples, since he used the same language to entreat the Christians in Corinth to receive Timothy[22] and with the Philippians to receive Epaphroditus.[23]

Generally, Paul's attitude to Phoebe demonstrates in practice that for Christ and consequently for his apostles and for all members of his body—laity and clergy—there is only the application of the Lord's teaching: "There is neither Jew nor Greek, there is neither slave nor free, there is neither male nor female; for you are all one in Christ Jesus."[24]

Phoebe Through the Texts of the Church Fathers and Ecclesiastical Writers of the First Centuries of Christianity

Many church fathers and ecclesiastical writers mention Phoebe, not as the subject of individual inquiry but rather within the context of their commentaries on the New Testament and particularly their commentaries on Paul's Epistle to the Romans.

Moving chronologically, we begin with the indefatigable theologian Origen (185–253), who lived in a milieu in which deaconesses played an active role in the church and Christian communities. After his father's martyrdom in 202, he was taken under the protection of a wealthy Christian woman, thereby experiencing firsthand women's contributions.[25] Based on Origen's commentary on Romans, Marg Mowczko,[26] like Joan Cecelia Campbell,[27] has suggested that Phoebe may have been formally ordained as a deacon and had an institu-

---

22. 1 Cor 16:10–11.
23. Phil 2:29.
24. Gal 3:28.
25. Eusebius of Caesarea, *Church History*, 6.2.12–15.
26. M. Mowczko, "Women Church Leaders in the New Testament," July 28, 2010, accessed January 5, 2020, https://margmowczko.com/new-testament-women-church-leaders/. Idem, "Phoebe: Deacon of the Church in Cenchrea," November 13, 2014, accessed January 5, 2020, https://margmowczko.com/new-testament-women-church-leaders/.
27. J. C. Campbell, *Phoebe: Patron and Emissary*, 61.

tional role as a deaconess in the church at Cenchreae.[28] Of course, Mowczko does not seem to fully embrace this position, highlighting some doubts later in her work, since she admits Origen may have been anachronistically projecting Phoebe as an ordained deaconess. Nevertheless, there were ordained deaconesses in the following centuries. Elsewhere, however, Mowczko took an ambiguous view, arguing that this might not apply to Origen's commentary on Romans in particular.[29] Generally, in most of her work, Mowczko tends to accept that Origen considered Phoebe an ordained deacon.[30]

Aime Georges Martimort and Roger Gryson, on the other hand, do not believe that Phoebe was ever ordained. They maintain that Origen never mentions Phoebe being ordained as a deaconess, but rather speaks of her active participation in the charity work of the local church at Cenchreae. This role of women—who serve the church and perform charity—was a very honored one, which was

---

28. Origen of Alexandria, *Commentaries on the Epistle to the Romans*, 10.17, PG 14, 1278B: "Ita et haec religiosa Phoebe dum astat omnibus et omnibus obsequitur, assitere et obsequi etiam Apostolo meruit. Et ideo locus hic duo pariter docet, et haberi, ut diximus, feminas ministras in Ecclesia, et tales debere assumi in ministerium, quae adstiterint multis, et per bona officia usque ad apostolicam laudem meruerint pervenire. Hortatur etiam illud, ut qui bonis operibus in Ecclesiis dant operam, vicem recipiant a ftatibus et honorem, ut in quibuscumque neccesarium fuerit sive carnalibus officiis, honorifice habeantur."

29. M. Mowczko, "Phoebe: Deacon of the Church in Cenchrea," accessed January 5, 2020, https://margmowczko.com/was-phoebe-a-deacon-of-the-church-at-cenchrea-part-2, November 13, 2014, "While several Post-Nicene Christian writers unequivocally regarded Phoebe as an ordained deaconess, they seem to have been projecting customs of a later female diaconate back onto the New Testament church. Care must be taken not to make a similar mistake by projecting modern customs and roles of deacons onto the first-century church. On the other hand, one must also not make the mistake of thinking that *diakonos* simply means 'servant' in Romans 16:1, which is how the translators of the KJV, NKJV, NASB, ESV, HCSB, CEB, etc., have rendered the word here. Phoebe simply cannot have been both 'a servant,' in the usual sense of the word, as well as being 'a patroness (*prostatis*) of many,' as patronesses were wealthy and influential women in Greco-Roman society, and would have had servants of their own, rather than being servants themselves. Newer editions of the NIV, NLT, and NRSV translate *diakonos* as 'deacon' in Romans 16:1, which reflects a growing consensus among scholars that Phoebe was a deacon."

30. Ibid.

why Paul makes special mention of her.³¹ On this point, Origen is not clear whether he is referring to ordained female deaconesses or not. To make things more opaque, Origen also considered the wives of male deacons to be deacons, and apparently honorarily addressed them as such.³²

In their work *Ordained Women in the Early Church: A Documentary History*, Kevin Madigan and Carolyn Osiek agree that, in his commentary on Romans, Origen viewed Phoebe as a deaconess in the general sense of the term.³³ The general meaning of the term "deacon" can also be ascertained from the words of Paul himself in Colossians 1:25, "I was born a deacon." Unfortunately, it is difficult to understand what Origen understood about Phoebe's designation as a "deacon," since his commentary was preserved in Latin. In Latin, for example, the term "ministra" can be translated as "one in service" or "deaconess."

In his texts, Tertullian reveals that widows who served as deacons in the local church and the wives of priests had the privilege to sit with the priests in formal gatherings and to be considered as members of the clergy, even though they were not ordained. In his work *Testamentum Domini*, when he refers to deaconesses who were ordained, he does not indicate that they had any liturgical role at the holy altar.³⁴ On this point, Madigan and Osiek counter that just because these ordained deaconesses were not associated with the holy altar does not necessarily mean that they had no other role in the Divine Liturgy. These authors thus make a distinction between a priestly-sacramental role and a liturgical one.³⁵

---

31. A. G. Martimort, *Deaconesses: An historical study*, trans. K. D. Whitehead (San Francisco: Ignatius Press, 1986), 83. R. Gryson, *Ministère des femmes dans l'Eglise ancienne* (Gembloux: Duculot, 1972), 60–64.

32. Martimort, *Deaconesses*, 83.

33. M. Madigan and C. Osiek, *Ordained Women in the Early Church: A Documentary History* (Baltimore: Johns Hopkins University Press, 2005), 14.

34. Ibid. 5.

35. Ibid. 5.

CHAPTER NINE

In Homily XXX in his *Commentary on the Epistle to the Romans,*[36] and more specifically on 16:1–2, John Chrysostom considers Phoebe as belonging officially to the rank of ordained deaconesses, similar to Olympias, his faithful deaconess at the time. This perspective was, of course, anachronistic, since the position of a female deacon in the first century was quite different than that at the end of the third and beginning of the fourth centuries.[37]

Later, another ecclesiastical writer, Theodoret of Cyrus, in his *Commentary on Romans,* mentions much more about both the church at Cenchreae and Phoebe. The information he relays about Cenchreae may be derived from his own personal knowledge at the time he lived. He assumes the church at Cenchreae was large because they had a female deacon.[38] Theodoret also supplies another bit of information about Phoebe that cannot be found anywhere else. He believed that Phoebe was known not only to the Greeks but also to the so-called "Barbarians," which probably refers to the

---

36. John Chrysostom, *Commentary on Epistle to the Romans,* 30, PG 60, 663C–664A: «Συνίστημι δὲ ὑμῖν Φοίβην τὴν ἀδελφήν, διάκονον οὖσαν τῆς Ἐκκλησίας τῆς ἐν Κεγχρεαῖς. Ὅρα διὰ πόσων αὐτὴν σεμνύνει· καὶ γὰρ πρὸ τῶν ἄλλων αὐτῆς ἐμνήσθη πάντων, καὶ ἀδελφὴν ἐκάλεσεν· οὐ μικρὸν δὲ Παύλου κληθῆναι ἀδελφήν. Καὶ τὸ ἀξίωμα προσέθηκε, διάκονον εἰπών· Ἵνα αὐτὴν προσδέξησθε ἐν Κυρίῳ ἀξίως τῶν ἁγίων. Τουτέστι, διὰ τὸν Κύριον, ἵνα τιμῆς ἀπολαύσῃ παρ' ὑμῖν. Ὁ γὰρ διὰ τὸν Κύριον δεχόμενος, κἂν μὴ μέγαν τινὰ δέξηται, μετὰ σπουδῆς δέχεται· ὅταν δὲ καὶ ἁγία ᾖ, ἐννόησον ἡλίκης αὐτὴν ἀπολαῦσαι δίκαιον θεραπείας. Διὰ τοῦτο προσέθηκε, Ἀξίως τῶν ἁγίων, ὡς δεῖ τοὺς τοιούτους ὑποδέχεσθαι. Διπλῆν γὰρ ἔχει ἀφορμὴν τοῦ θεραπευθῆναι παρ' ὑμῶν, καὶ τὸ διὰ τὸν Κύριον δεχθῆναι, καὶ τὸ αὐτὴν ἁγίαν εἶναι. Καὶ παραστῆτε αὐτῇ ἐν ᾧ ἂν ὑμῶν πράγματι χρῄζῃ. Εἶδες τὸ ἀνεπαχθές; Οὐδὲ γὰρ εἶπεν, Ἵνα ἀπαλλάξητε, ἀλλ', Ἵνα τὰ παρ' ὑμῶν εἰσενέγκητε, καὶ χεῖρα ὀρέξητε, καὶ ἐν ᾧ ἂν ὑμῶν χρῄζῃ· οὐκ ἐν οἷς ἂν ᾖ πάντως, ἀλλ' ἐν οἷς ἂν ὑμῶν δέηται· δεήσεται δὲ ἐν ἐκείνοις, ἐν οἷς ἂν ὑμεῖς ἦτε κύριοι. Εἶτα πάλιν ὁ ἔπαινος ἄφατος· Καὶ γὰρ αὐτὴ προστάτις πολλῶν ἐγενήθη, καὶ αὐτοῦ ἐμοῦ. Εἶδες τὴν σύνεσιν; Πρῶτον μὲν τὰ ἐγκώμια, εἶτα μέσην τὴν παράκλησιν, εἶτα πάλιν τὰ ἐγκώμια τέθεικεν, ἑκατέρωθεν περιστέλλων τὴν χρείαν τοῖς ἐπαίνοις τῆς γυναικὸς τῆς μακαρίας ἐκείνης. Πῶς γὰρ οὐ μακαρία ἡ τοσαύτης ἀπολαύσασα παρὰ Παύλου μαρτυρίας, ἡ καὶ αὐτῷ βοηθῆσαι δυνηθεῖσα τῷ τὴν οἰκουμένην διορθώσαντι; Τοῦτο γὰρ ὁ κολοφὼν αὐτῆς τῶν ἀγαθῶν· διὸ καὶ ὕστερον αὐτὸ τέθεικε λέγων, Καὶ αὐτοῦ ἐμοῦ. Τί δέ ἐστι, Καὶ αὐτοῦ ἐμοῦ; Τοῦ κήρυκος τῆς οἰκουμένης, τοῦ τοσαῦτα παθόντος, τοῦ μυρίοις ἀρκοῦντος».

37. S. Grenz and D.M. Kjesbo, *Women in the Church,* 88.

38. Theodoret of Cyrus, *Commentary on Romans* 16, PG 83, 220A.

inhabitants of Spain, who spoke neither Greek nor Latin: "[Paul] has opened the whole world to her, and in every land and sea is that woman become celebrated, so that not the Romans only and the Greeks have known her, but even every barbarian nation."[39] There, Paul intended to preach the word of God[40] and probably did preach it,[41] with Theodoret implying that Paul had Phoebe with him as an assistant,[42] since he says "he has opened the whole world to her."[43] Based on this passage of Theodoret, Jewett argues that Phoebe may have been the organizer of the entire mission and preaching of the Apostle Paul in Spain.[44] He considered, therefore, that Phoebe had the following responsibilities for the preparation of the mission to the Iberian Peninsula: "a. to present the letter to the various local churches in Rome and to discuss its contents regarding the mission to Spain and the expected developments from this project that will

---

39. Ibid. English translation from "The Christian Remembrancer, or, The churchman's biblical, ecclesiastical & literary miscellany," 22 (1840) 30ff, accessed on September 1, 2021, https://www.tertullian.org/fathers/theodoret_commentary_on_romans_02.htm

40. Rom 15:23–29.

41. While it is not clear whether Paul preached in Spain after his release, there is some evidence that indicates the Apostle to the Gentiles spread the gospel in Spain: Romans 1 was written in 57 AD. In Romans 15:23 and 15:28, Paul expresses his desire to teach the gospel in the West, and particularly Spain, since the gospel was already being spread in the East. In 2 Timothy, which would have been written between 62–64 AD, he notes that he completed all his plans for the evangelization of the Gentiles (2 Tim 4:17); and since he accomplished his work, he would wait to be rewarded with the crown of glory and justice by the righteous Judge (2 Tim 4: 8). The first letter of Clement of Rome 5: 5–7 was a testimony that Paul preached at the end of the West, which meant Spain at that time. John Chrysostom also mentioned Paul's preaching in Spain in his commentary on the Second Epistle to Timothy, Sermon 10.

42. Theodoret of Cyrus, *Commentary on Romans* 16, PG 83, 220A.

43. Ibid.

44. R. Jewett, "Paul, Phoebe, and Spanish Mission," in *The Social World of Formative Christianity and Judaism: Essays in Tribute to Howard Clark Kee*, eds. J. Neusner, et al. (Philadelphia: Fortress, 1988), 144–64; R. Jewett, *Romans* (Minneapolis: Fortress, 2007), 89–91, 941–48. S. Mathew, "Women in the Greetings of Rom 16:1–16: A Study of Mutuality and Women's Ministry in the Letter to the Romans," Doctoral thesis (Durham University, 2010), 21. Available at Durham e-Theses, http://etheses.dur.ac.uk/369/.

arise with the "heads" (people who were in charge) of these churches, b. to convince the Christians of Rome that Paul was the most reliable man to carry out the Spanish Mission, and c. to seek the advice of the churches of Rome on finding financial resources for the realization of this mission."[45]

In the Ambrosian collection of Pseudo-Ambrose, it was noted that Phoebe was not an ordained deaconess and even excluded the possibility of a special order of ordained deaconesses not only in Paul's time, but also later.[46]

In his own commentary on the Epistle to the Romans, Pelagius notes that he is unaware of the existence of ordained deaconesses at least in the West, but cannot speak for the East. Nevertheless, he believes these deaconesses—and, therefore, specifically Phoebe—were dedicated to preaching the word of God in private settings, without a particularly large audience.[47]

Generally, most church fathers avoided analyzing and interpreting this passage in the Epistle to the Romans concerning Phoebe and the term "deacon." For example, Cyril of Alexandria carefully avoided commenting on the Phoebe passage in his commentary on Romans. Cyril's only recorded reference to Phoebe was in his work *Against Julian,* where he speaks about the Phoebe of Greek mythology.[48]

In conclusion, it is characteristic that the majority of church fathers made no reference to the passage in question characterizing Phoebe as a deaconess. Obviously, they knew that they could not give a complete answer as to whether the word "deacon" indicated an institutional role or not, so they preferred to pass it over in silence.

---

45. R. Jewett, "Paul, Phoebe, and Spanish Mission," 144–64; R. Jewett, *Romans,* 89–91, 941–48.

46. Ambrosiaster, *Commentarius in epistulas Paulinas (ad Romanos),* ed. H. J. Vogels, 1966, CSEL 81/1 (CSEL: Critical Editions of the Works of the Latin Church Fathers) 1966, 476–77.

47. Pseudo-Jerome, *Operum Mantissa,* PL 30, 714: "sicut etiam nunc in Orientalibus diaconissae in suo sexu ministrae videntur in baptismo, sive in ministerio verbi, quia privatim docuisse feminas invenimus, sicut Priscillam."

48. Cyril of Alexandria, *Against Julian,* 2, 25, SC 222, 256.

CHAPTER NINE

Conclusions

The word "deacon" was not often mentioned by many church fathers. It was used synonymously with "servant." The fact that the word "deacon" appeared only in the masculine led to the assumption that it was a special category of people who served the church, without implying ordination. Of course, there is the view that Phoebe was ordained, without necessarily meaning that she served at the holy altar but rather participated in some other parts of the Divine Liturgy.

Some of the fathers, such as John Chrysostom, explained Romans 16:1–2 based on their own era. In this way, Phoebe was anachronistically accepted as an ordained deaconess like Olympias.

Based on the above, one assumes that Phoebe was one of the Apostle Paul's coworkers and that she was involved in ministry, offering whatever services she could to the members of the community, just as did many men and widows.

Chapter Ten

ST. NINO AND ORDINATION OF WOMEN DEACONS IN GEORGIAN TRADITION

Leonide B. Ebralidze

The most ancient versions of the Life of St. Nino (†338/340) are preserved in the composite historical work Conversion of Kartli (formerly Iberia). In different manuscripts of Conversion of Kartli there are three complementary versions of the vita of Nino: Sinai (tenth-century manuscript), Shatberdi (tenth-century manuscript), and Chelishi (fourteenth-century manuscript).[1]

The text of the vita is clearly problematic: specifically, the story is alternated with the narrations of the different authors, as well as Nino herself, and of other personages. The textual analysis shows that the earliest versions originate from the same proto-version, which can "go back to written material at least as early as the seventh century, to judge by the occasionally very archaic verbal

---

1. The paper mainly follows the Sinai version of the vita, from the edited collection of all existing redactions: *Vita*, ed. D.M. Glonti, წმიდა ნინო ემბაზი ქართლისა [*St. Nino, Baptismal font of Kartli*] (Mtskheta: 2015). The available English translation of the vita is carried out from the late redaction, further elaborated in the eleventh century by Georgian historian Leonti Mroveli; therefore it is a little different from the ancient redactions. See M. Wardrop, ed., "Life of St. Nino" in *Studia Biblica: Essays in Biblical Archaeology and Criticism*, vol. 5 (Oxford: 1885). On the ancient redactions of the vita, see S. Rapp and P. Crego, *The Conversion of K'art'li:* The Shatberdi Variant (Kek. Inst. S–1141), in *Le Muséon* 119 (2006): 187–88. For the brief discussion of non-Georgian historical sources, see J.M. Sauget, "Nino," in *Bibliotheca Sanctorum*, vol. 9 (Rome 1967), 1018–21. For the brief popular version of the vita, see D.M. Lang, *Lives and Legends of the Georgian Saints* (London: 1956), 13–39.

forms which [the compiler] employs."² Another opinion expressed by scholars is that in the fifth century the primitive version of the vita was written, amplified in the seventh, and finally redacted in the ninth century.³

This paper will not discuss textual particularities of the vita. Rather, it will review one significant passage that contains important information about the imposition of the laying on of hands on women in the early church.⁴

As the hagiographical text recounts, St. Nino grew up in the court of her uncle, the Patriarch of Jerusalem, who anachronistically is named as Juvenal of Jerusalem (†458). It is noted by scholars that the presence of Patriarch Juvenal in the text is caused by pro-Chalcedonian intentions of its compiler. On this issue M. Van Esbroeck writes, "Certainly, the introduction of Juvenal in the story of St. Nino is intended to correct an earlier redaction where his familiarity with Rhipsimé and Gaiané was likely to lead to a justification of anti-Chalcedonism."⁵

---

2. D. Rayfield, *The Literature of Georgia: A History* (Oxford: 1994), 49.

3. Cf. G. Shurgaia, "La vita della Kartli nel contesto storico-politico caucasico," in *Al crocevia delle civiltà. Ricerche su Caucaso e Asia Centrale*, eds. A. Ferrari and D. Guizzo (Venice: 2014), 89–91.

4. After the presentation of the present paper at the international symposium "Deaconesses: Past, Present, and Future" held in Thessaloniki January 31–February 2, 2020, and organized by CEMES and the International Hellenic University, it turned out that a similar paper titled "The 'Ordination' of St. Nino, with Reference to the Prayers for Women Deacons in the Archieratikon of Manuscript A–86" had been presented by Paul Crego at the First International Symposium: Georgian Manuscripts in Tbilisi in 2009. Unfortunately, this paper is not available as it probably has not been published yet. As evidenced by the abstract, Crego, having recognized a possible ordination in the gesture of the Patriarch of Jerusalem, compares the hagiographic content with the pre-Byzantine euchological one, which, according to him, "includes language much stronger than Byzantine Greek prayers." For the abstract of Crego's paper, see *First International Symposium: Georgian Manuscripts, Abstracts of Papers*, ed. B. Kudava (Tbilisi: 2009), 39–40.

5. M. Van Esbroeck, "La place de Jerusalem dans la 'Conversion de la Georgie,'" in *Ancient Christianity in the Caucasus*, ed. T. Mgaloblishvili (Richmond: 1998), 63–64. The same opinion is expressed by Shurgaia: "It is true that the kinship relationship—albeit anachronistic—with the Patriarch Juvenal (422–458) betrays a precise political intent to make the illuminator of Georgia descend

To understand this passage it must be remembered that Rhipsimé and Gaiané were martyred and venerated in the Armenian Church, which chose anti-Chalcedonian positions, whereas the Georgian Church from the end of the sixth century definitely adheres to the Chalcedonian confession.[6] It seems that in the contest of the Georgian–Armenian church conflict, the compiler of the vita tries to distance himself from the Armenian Church by introducing in the story the Chalcedonian father, Juvenal of Jerusalem.

Besides the confessional problems, the author of the hagiographical text also had to resolve some of the sociocultural challenges in the face of a male-dominated society.

It was well demonstrated by M. Tarchnišvili that in the early Middle Ages, the role and legal status of women in Georgian society was minimal, and for Georgians it was difficult to accept a woman as an apostle and illuminator.[7] Moreover, in correlated Georgian,

---

from the most conspicuous representative of the Byzantine Chalcedonians; but it is also significant that the well-known representative of the Chalcedonian doctrine is sought in the very context of Jerusalem and not elsewhere," G. Shurgaia, "Mcxeta, la capitale rifondata," in *Santa Nino e la Georgia, Storia e spiritualità Cristiana nel Paese del Vello d'oro, Atti del I convegno Internazionale di Studi georgiani, Roma 30 gennaio 1999,* ed. G. Surgaia (Rome: 2000), 84.

6. On the issue of Georgian–Armenian Church conflict, briefly see T. Grdzelidze, "Georgia, Patriarchal Orthodox Church," in *The Encyclopedia of Eastern Orthodox Christianity,* ed. J.A. McGuckin (Oxford: 2011), 267–68.

7. Cf. M. Tarchnišvili, "Die Legende der heiligen Nino und die Geschichte des georgischen Nationalbewusstseins," in *Byzantinische Zeitschrift,* 40 (1940), 48–75.

Greek, and Armenian sources,[8] Nino is mentioned as a slave or captive woman: *mulier quaedam captiva*.[9]

Consequently, in hagiographical texts, during the different moments of her life, Nino received some kind of legitimization, such as the letter from Empress Elena, who called her "Queen and Equal to the Apostles": "ნეტარსა ნინოს ელენე სურვილით უწოდა დედოფლად და თვსსა სწორად და სწორად წმიდათა მოციქულთა" (Elena warmly addresses Nino as "equal to herself and equal to the apostles").[10] Mention of such a letter should be understood as a "political legitimization" for Nino's mission: even though she was a captive woman, she was elevated by the hagiographer to the rank of queen.

Elsewhere, in another passage at the time when she was entering in the Georgian era, she had a divine vision: a sealed book was given to her with ten sayings. The words reported missionary commandments from the Bible, including four words particularly concerning women:

---

8. Some scholars speculate that the ancient brief version of the vita was known by Latin and Greek writers through contacts with Georgians in the holy land: "At the cusp of the fourth and fifth centuries there existed a version of the Life of St. Nino which was known in Palestine. This version is reflected in the church history of Rufinus. . . . Rufinus had lived for twenty-four years both in Egypt and Jerusalem, where he may well have come in contact with Iberians. Rufinus's version of the Conversion of Kartli was later copied by the Greek historians Socrates, Sozomen, and Theodoret. Recent scholarship has also traced links between Rufinus's Greek version and Gelasius of Caesarea," T. Grdzelidze, *Georgia, Patriarchal Orthodox Church*, 266.

9. Rufinus of Aquileia, *Historia Ecclesiastica* 1,10, PL 21:480B. For the allegorical interpretation of Nino's captivity, see L. Pataridze, "La schiavitù di Santa Nino," in *Santa Nino e la Georgia*, ed. G. Shurgaia, 61–68.

10. *Vita* 122 (preserved in Chelishi version). See also *Life of St. Nino*, trans. Margery Wardrop (Gorgias Press, 2006), 64.

CHAPTER TEN

მაშინ განვსნა წიგნი იგი და მომცა მე კითხვად. დაწერილი იყო ჰრომაელებრ და დაბეჭდული იყო იესუსი.

დაწერილნი იყ[ვ]ნეს ათნი სიტყუანი, ვითარცა-იგი პირველ ფიც[არ]თა ქვის[ა]- თა.

პირველი სიტყუაჲ: სადაცა იქადაგოს სახარებაჲ ესე, მუნცა ითქუმოდის დედა- კაცი ესე.

ბ. „არცა მამაკაცებაჲ, არცა დედა- კაცებაჲ, არამედ თქუენ ყოველნი ერთ ხართ".

ზ. ფრიად უყ[უა]რდა მარიამ უფალსა, რამეთუ მარადის ისმენდა მისსა სიბრძნესა ჭეშმარიტსა.

თ. ჰრქუა მარიამ მაგდალენელსა იესუ: „წარვედ, დედაკაცო, და ახარე ძმ[ა]თა ჩემთა".

Then the man undid and gave me the book, on which was the seal of Jesus, and in it were written, in the Roman tongue, ten sayings, as on the first tables of stone [delivered to Moses]:

1. Wherever they preach this gospel, there shall they speak of this woman (Matt 26:13);

2. Neither male nor female, but you are all one (Gal 3:28); [...]

7. Now Mary was greatly beloved of the Lord, so that He always hearkened to her truth and wisdom; [...]

9. Jesus said to Mary Magdalene: "Go, O woman, and tell the good news to My brethren" (John 20:17).[11]

This passage can be understood as a "divine legitimization": Jesus paid attention not only to man, but also to woman; and Nino, as male apostles, was called to announce his word.

Prior to this adventure and "divine legitimization," in the very beginning of her missionary trip, Nino as a woman received an "ecclesiastical legitimization" of her mission by the patriarch of Jerusalem. The text reports:

---

11. *Vita* [Chelishi], 70–71. *Life of St. Nino*, trans. M. Wardrop, 17–18.

[ნიამფორმა] აუწყა პატრიაქსა. ხოლო მე მიწოდა წმიდამან მამამან ჩემმან პატრიაქმან, ძმამან დედისა ჩემისამან, და დამადგინა აღსავალსა საკურთხევლისასა და დამასხნა წმიდანი ჴელნი მისნი მჴართა ჩემთა ზედა, და სულითითქუნა ცად მიმართ და თქუა:
„უფალო, ღმერთო ჩემო, ღმერთო მამათაო და საუკუნეთაო, ჴელთა შენთა შევჰვედრებ ობოლსა ამას შვილსა დისა ჩემისასა და წარვავლინებ ქადაგებად შენისა ღმრთეებისა და რაგთა ახაროს აღგომაჲ შენი, სადაცა შენ სათნო-იყო სრბად მისი; ექმენ, ქრისტე, ამას გზა-მოგზაურ, მოძღუარ, ენა-მეცნიერ, ვითარცა-იგი წინათა მათ მოშიშთა სახელისა შენისათა".
და მიჯმნა დედისაგან ჩემისა და მომცა ჯუარი და კურთხევაჲ.

The Niamphori [Nino's nurse] told the patriarch what I desired and intended, and the patriarch, my uncle, called me, and placed me on the steps of the holy altar. He laid his holy hands upon my shoulders, sighed towards heaven from the depths of his heart, and said:

"O Everlasting Lord, God, I entreat Thine aid for my sister's orphan child, and I send her to preach Thy divinity. May she spread the good tidings of Thy Resurrection; wherever it pleases Thee may her course be; may this wanderer become, O Christ God, a haven of rest, a leader, wise in speech, since she goes forth in Thy name."

And my mother gave me a farewell kiss, and [the Patriarch] gave me the sign of the cross and blessing.[12]

In most instances, few pay attention to this small prayer, pronounced by the patriarch of Jerusalem, which usually is perceived as a small simple good wish. But it should not be forgotten that often hagiographers are inspired by liturgical texts,[13] and frequently hagiographic texts are hiding liturgical texts in themselves, even though in a particular way. As A. Kazdan pointed out: "If the *euchologia* describes the ideal system, the 'theory' of liturgy, hagiographers shed

---

12. *Vita* [Chelishi], 66–67. See also *Life of St. Nino*, trans. M. Wardrop, 12.
13. Hagiographers' inspiration from the liturgical texts was not an unusual method of composing. One of the most famous examples of the euchological text hidden in the hagiographical or historical one is founded in neighboring Armenia: one of the oldest fragments of the Anaphora of Basil is preserved in the *Epic Histories (Buzandran Patmut'iwnk')*, attributed to Pʻawstos Buzand, a fifth-century Armenian historian. Cf. G. Winkler, "Armenia's Liturgy at the Crossroads of Neighboring Traditions," in OCP 74 (2008): 372–78.

light on individual, 'patchy' phenomena as they saw them in real life, in everyday practice."[14]

Of course, there is no explicit euchological text in the vita of St. Nino, and it should be remembered that it is an *euchologia hagiographica*. Indeed, there are some layers, which reveal the liturgical structure of this passage:

1. Placing of Nino on the steps of the holy altar;
2. Laying of the hands upon her;
3. The prayer which invokes upon her the name of God and the grace of preaching and witnessing the resurrection.
4. Kiss and sign of the holy cross.

The above listed four elements can elsewhere be found in the ordination rites of different traditions. For example, the placing of the candidate in front of the altar is provided by an earlier Byzantine source, the famous Barberini euchologion.[15] The laying on of hands upon the candidate is provided in an earlier fourth-century source, the *Constitutiones Apostolorum*, where the bishop is required by Apostle Bartholomew: ἐπιθήσεις αὐτῇ τὰς χεῖρας ("you shall lay hands on her").[16] The prayer over the candidate is provided by all existent traditions of the ordination of deaconesses in Byzantine, Georgian, Armenian, and East Syrian rites.[17] Even though there is no explicit mention of the kiss in known ordination rites for women deacons, the kiss of newly-ordained ministers is one of the ancient elements of the ordination rites, which should not be confused with the kiss of peace.[18] Likewise, concerning the sign of the cross, there

---

14. A. Kazdan, "A Strange Liturgical Habit in a Strange Hagiographical Work," in *Eulogēma: Studies in Honor of Robert Taft, S.J.*, eds. E. Carr, S. Parenti, A.A. Thiermeyer, E. Velkovska, and R. Taft (Roma: Centro Studi S. Anselmo, 1993), 245.

15. Cf. S. Parenti and E. Velkovska, eds., *L'eucologio Barberini gr. 336* (Roma: 2000), 172–74.

16. Cf. F.X. Funk, *Didascalia et Constitutiones Apostolorum,* vol. 1 (Paderbornae, Germany: 1906), 524.

17. Cf. P.F. Bradshaw, *Ordination Rites of the Ancient Churches of East and West* (New York: Pueblo Publishing Co., 1990), 88–92.

18. Cf. Ibid, 34–36.

are no direct witnesses to the issue of female deacon ordination. However, generally it is one of the signs of ordination, as noted by P. Bradshaw: "The earliest allusion to use of the sign of the cross in ordination is found in the *Canons of Hippolytus*. . . . Its existence at Antioch is confirmed by John Chrysostom. . . . The 'cruciform seal' immediately after the initial imposition of the hand is mentioned by Pseudo-Dionysius."[19]

In this way, in the *Life of St. Nino* there is found a clear structure for ordination, even if in the text itself it does not mention explicitly ordination or deaconesses.

Notwithstanding, another more important detail is given in vita, immediately after the narration of the *laying of hands*, when she comes back to the house of Niamphori:

| ოდეს მივიწიენით სახლად დედაკაცისა მის, მუნ ვპოვეთ დედაკაცი ვინმე, მეფეთა ევადავი, სახელით რიფსიმე, რომელი იერუსალიმით ნათლისღებასა, ქრისტესა აღსარებისათვს ჰსურდა. [...] და მივეც მას ნათელი ჴელითა მღდელისაითა ჴელსა ქუეშე ჩემსა და ორმეოცდაათისა სულსა მის თანა სახლისა მისისაითა. | When we arrived in the house of that woman [Niamphori] I saw a woman courtesan of kings by name Riphsimé, longing to confess Christ, and waiting for baptism in Jerusalem [...] and I gave to her baptism with the hands of the priest and under my hands, and with her, others of her household, to the number of fifty souls.[20] |

Comparing this passage with the data of the *Life of St. Irene*,[21] A. Kateusz hypothesizes that the phrase "with the hand of the priest" must be a later interpolation.[22] Indeed, the Shatberdi version of vita omits mention of the priest: "მივეც მას ნათელი ჴელსა ქუეშე ჩემსა"

---

19. Ibid., 32.
20. *Vita* [Sinai], 36. See also *Life of St. Nino*, trans. M. Wardrop, 13.
21. For the discussion of the hagiographical sources, see R. Janin, "Irene," in *Bibliotheca Sanctorum,* vol. VII (Rome: 1966), 888–89.
22. Cf. A. Kateusz, *Mary and Early Christian Women: Hidden Leadership* (Cham, Switzerland: Palgrave MacMillian, 2019), 56–57.

("and I gave to her baptism under my hands").²³ Moreover in all the three oldest versions of the vita (Sinai, Shatberdi, and Chelishi), the Jewish priest Abiathar is mentioned as the one who "ნათელ-იღო ველსა შინა ნინოსსა" ("is baptized in the hands of Nino").²⁴ This, therefore, poses the question how one can interpret *the giving of baptism under the hands of Nino* unless in the context of the diaconal ministry of women?²⁵

While the authentic source of this hagiographical passage is unknown, there can be found some similarities with one of the three ancient Georgian prayers of ordination of "დედათ-დიაკონისა" ("woman deacon") in the pre-Byzantine Georgian rite.²⁶ These prayers are preserved in the tenth-century manuscript (A86 of Georgian National Center of Manuscripts) and have no antecedents in other traditions:

---

23. *Vita*, 67. The same absence of the priest in this passage is witnessed also in the later composition of her life, by Leonti Mroveli. See *Vita*, 151.

24. *Vita*, 51 (Sinai Version); Vita, 100 (Shatberdi and Chelishi versions).

25. Nowadays, Susan, mother of Nino, who devoted herself to the service of poor people (Cf. *Vita*, 34) is often interpreted as a deaconess, especially in the Russian sources., see, for example, V. Markovin, "Святая равноапостольная Нина и крещение Грузии" (Saint Nino equal to the Apostles and baptism of Georgia), in *Страницы: богословие, культура, образование* (Pages: theology, culture, education), 4/3 (1999), 415. This interpretation is likely to be true, but there is no further information to confirm such a conviction. Probably, M. Arranz was inspired by Russian literature when he wrote that the mother of Nino was a deaconess, but more interesting is his intuition to interpret the statute of *servant* of Nino, as her *diakonia*. Cf. M. Arranz, "Tre liturgisti georgiani della prima metà del XX secolo," in *Santa Nino e la Georgia*, ed. G. Shurgaia, 151.

26. It is well known that the Georgian Church adhered to the liturgical tradition of Jerusalem from the beginning of the fifth-century, via monastic foundations in the holy land. From the tenth to the eleventh centuries the process called *Byzantinization* took effect, which means replacing the Hagiopolitan Rite with the Constantinopolitan Rite. While the majority of Greek texts of the Hagiopolitan Rite disappeared, the Georgian-written source assumes an essential importance for studying the liturgy of Jerusalem in the first millennium. See S.R. Frøyshov, "The Georgian Witness to the Jerusalem Liturgy: New Sources and Studies," in *Inquiries into Eastern Christian Worship: Selected Papers of the Second International Congress of the Society of Oriental Liturgy* (Rome, September 17-21, 2008), eds. B. Groen, S. Hawkes-Teeples, and S. Alexopoulos (Leuven, 2012), 227-67.

უფალო, ღმერთო ძალთაო [...] შენ თავადმან განაწესე მჲევალიცა ესე შენი ცხებად ზეთისა მოსრულთა ამათ წმიდასა მას ნათლის-ღებასა და მოყვანებად იჳინი წმიდასა შენსა ემბაზსა [...] მოეც ამასცა განკრძალვით მხილებად და განსწავლად ახალ-ჰასაკთა, შრომაჲ საქმეთა შენთაჲ, მოჰმადლე ამას ყოველივე თქუმაჲ ყოფად სახელითა შენითა.	O Lord, God of Hosts [...] do thou thyself promote this thy handmaid to the grade, to the end that she may anoint with oil them that come to thy holy baptism and bring them to thy holy font [...] give also to her with vigilance to convince and instruct the young folk; in the performing thy duties; give grace unto her to utter all things in thy name.[27]

It is to be noted that in this prayer is not an explicit invocation of the Holy Spirit as in the hagiographical text. Moreover, enumerated are some of the duties of deaconesses, such as the participation in the administration of the holy baptism, *instructing the people, and announcing all things in the Lord's name*[28] It is easy to observe the similarities of these duties and those in the hagiographical text.

Another important link between these two texts is the liturgical tradition of Jerusalem. First of all, according to the vita, Nino received laying on of hands in Jerusalem, and there she gave baptism to Riphsimé and her household. On the other hand, the tenth-century manuscript A86, which contains the above-mentioned prayer of the ordination of women deacons, also contains the Liturgy of St. James and different rites of ordination, some of them deriving from the liturgical tradition of Jerusalem.[29] Because of a lack of sufficient available data, it is impossible to demonstrate that this concrete

---

27. On the base of the current A86 manuscript of the Georgian National Centre of Manuscripts, the text was edited by K. Kekelidze, Древнегрузинский архиератикон [*Old Georgian Archieratikon*] (Tbilisi: 1912), 96–97. The English translation is available in F.C. Conybeare and O. Wardrop, "The Georgian version of the Liturgy of St. James," in *Revue de l'Orient Chrétien* 19 (1914): 165.

28. Cf. P.F. Bradshaw, *Ordination Rites of the Ancient Churches,* 89–90.

29. Cf. H. Brakmann, "Die altkirchlichen Ordinationsgebete Jerusalems: Mit liturgiegeschichtlichen Beobachtungen zur christlichen Euchologie in Palaestina, Syria, Iberia und im Sasanidenreich," in *Jahrbuch für Antike und Christentum* 47 (2004): 110–11, 118–27.

prayer was used in Jerusalem;[30] but it is probable, if the Georgian liturgy was drawn from Jerusalem and the manuscript A86 contains a large number of the hagiopolitan prayers.

It could be put forward that the compiler of the vita was inspired by this ordination prayer. One thing is certain: in the sixth to seventh centuries when the text of the vita was compiled, the hagiographer had a clear model of the ordination of women and their liturgical function, certainly as it relates to the administration of baptism and their catechetical function "to instruct the young folk" or "spread the good tidings of the resurrection." Additionally, the tenth-century manuscript contains the pre-Byzantine rites of the diaconal ordination of women, and in Georgia at least six manuscript writings can be found from the fifteenth to seventeenth centuries containing those rites.[31] These liturgical dates are still in need of a detailed comparative study.

Thus, in the Georgian tradition there is historical evidence on women deacons from the sixth to seventeenth centuries, but current witness to diaconal ordination of women in the Georgian context dates as recently as 2015. As reported by the *Journal of Alaverdi Diocese* of the Georgian Orthodox Church on November 10, 2015, Metropolitan David Makharadze of Alaverdi had performed the laying on of hands of two deaconesses, Hegumenia Joanna and Nun Thecla, during the Divine Liturgy at the New Shuamta Monastery. The reported news tries to justify such an act: "In the female monastery there is a particular need for the ministry of deaconesses, for 'instructing in godliness, so that it might be an example of all that is pleasing.' Besides serving the priest during the worship, they are required to teach young people with awe. The prayer of ordination of deaconess reports 'You gave the grace of your Holy Spirit not only

---

30. Ibid., Brakmann also notes some similarities of the above-mentioned prayer with the prayer of *Constitutiones Apostolorum*, 119.

31. Cf. E. Gabidzashvili, ძველი ქართული მწერლობის ნათარგმნი ძეგლები, ტ. 5, ლიტურგია, ჰიმნოგრაფია, [*Translated Works of Ancient Georgian Literature*, vol. 5, *Liturgy, Hymnography*] (Tbilisi: 2011), 101.

to men but to women.'"³² It is important to note the quotations from the prayers, which reveal that the ancient, pre-Byzantine rite of ordination, discussed above,³³ were used.

As evidenced from the reported news, there is no perception of equality between the ordination of male deacons and female deacons. Further, it is to be argued that there is a lack of recognition of the sacramental nature of such an ordination. Notwithstanding, the significance of finding deaconesses in such a stern religious society as the Georgian one should not be underappreciated. In this way, the tradition that began with St. Nino continues.

---

32. "დიაკონისებად კურთხევა" ("The blessing of deaconesses"), in ალავერდი - ალავერდის ეპარქიის სეზონური გამოცემა *(Alaverdi – the Seasonal Edition of Alaverdi Diocese)*, 3/11 (2015), 14.

33. The first quotation is reported from the first (above-mentioned) prayer from the *A86* manuscript, while the second one is quoted from the second prayer of ordination of women deacons. Cf. F.C. Conybeare and O. Wardrop, "The Georgian version of the Liturgy of St. James," 165.

Chapter Eleven

FEMALE DIACONIA IN THE CONTEXT OF ECCLESIOLOGY

Zoya Dashevskaya

The question of women's ministry is, in the current day and age, well discussed in the academic literature. From the perspective of early Christian, patristic, liturgical, and canonical sources, the question has been well researched and examined; from a historical standpoint, the issue from each of these perspectives is fairly well delineated. In the Russian language, thanks to the works of Elena Belyakova and her colleagues,[1] Fr. Andrey Posternak[2] and many others, a significant amount of material has been gathered on the ministry of women during the time of the Russian Empire in the nineteenth and twentieth centuries—and of even more value are the materials from the Soviet period, given the broad context of church/state relations, data on canonical rights, the sociological perspective, etc. Attempts have been made to gather information on the service of women during difficult periods of persecution against the church, insofar as these materials are mainly disparate and available only as part of the oral history.

---

1. E. V. Belyakova, N. A. Belyakova, and E. B. Emchenko, *Zhenshchina v pravoslavii: tserkovnoje parvo i rossijskaja praktika* [*Woman in Orthodoxy: Canon Law and Russian Experience*] (Moscow: Kuchkovo pole, 2011).

2. *Sluzhenije zhenshchin v tserkvi: Issledovanija* [*The Ministry of Women in the Church: Research*], compiled by A. Posternak, S. N. Bakonin, A. V. Belousov (Moscow: Tikhon's Orthodox Humanitarian University Press, 2011).

In modern theological reflections from the twentieth and twenty-first centuries, women's ministry is considered not from a sociological point of view, for the most part, but rather from the perspective of an embodiment of the gifts of the Holy Spirit; see, for instance, Fr. Nicholas Afanasiev, Metropolitan Kallistos (Ware), Fr. Thomas Hopko, Elisabeth Behr-Sigel, Olivier Clément, Kyriaki Karidoyanes FitzGerald, Despina Prassas, and Metropolitan Anthony (Bloom). During the second half of the twentieth century, in various ecumenical circles, the question of ordaining women deaconesses (via sacramental ordination or the laying on of hands) was discussed with Orthodox participation; and scholars have examples of use of the rite for ordaining deaconesses not only in the nineteenth-century Russian church, but also in the twentieth century during the period of persecution. But it seems as if consideration of the questions of the status of women in the church and appropriate women's ministries are really only stepping-stones toward the consideration of much deeper aspects of a fundamental issue. As Professor Petros Vassiliadis notes, today, as ever, the contemporary situation absolutely requires "a constant search for theological, historical, and academically respectable answers to an open issue which is inhibiting the church's witness in the twenty-first century. Centuries-old prejudices, pseudo-theological arguments, and cultural habits are no longer sufficiently convincing for our fast-changing world, which hungers and thirsts for truth."[3] According to Elena Belyakova, "today Western-European experience of women's ministry remains key for the Orthodox tradition, while Orthodox women's experience of tenacity, persistence, and remaining firm in their faith is of particular significance for the European Christian world."[4] In my opinion, today's church is being called to answer a more general question that forms the broader context for this paper's question

---

3. Petros Vassiliadis, "Rolj zhenshchin v tserkvi, zhenskoje rukopolzhenije i chin diakoniss: pravoslavnyij bogoslovskij podkhod" ["The Role of Women in the Church, Women's Ordination, and the Order of Deaconesses: An Orthodox Theological Approach"], *The Quarterly Journal of St. Philaret's Institute*, no. 26 (Spring 2018): 83 [in Russian].

4. Belyakova, et al, *Women in Orthodoxy*, 532.

about women's ministries. The question that is vital to answer is this: Does current church practice and order really enable the action of the Spirit of God and promote the flourishing of the fullness of spiritual gifts within the contemporary church? For as the Holy Martyr St. Irenaeus of Lyon has said, "For where the Church is, there is the Spirit of God; and where the Spirit of God is, there is the Church, and every kind of grace" (*Adv. Haereses* III, 24), which implies the gifts of the Spirit, and church ministries.

Ecclesiological Context and the Question of Women's Ministries: What Do Women's Ministries Look Like in Different Manifestations of Church?

The following short summary in no way aspires to be a qualified and detailed analysis of all aspects of the question of women's ministries within the church; it's more a stepping-stone to setting the theological stage for considering all aspects of the question. It is by no means a coincidence that the question of women's diakonia is at present being considered primarily as a question of ordination, i.e., of the fixed, institutionalized position of a minister of the church, and also the degree to which women can participate in the celebration of the Holy Mysteries. It is probably for this reason that the question of women priests has been practically shunted entirely outside the framework of current discussion, insofar as the question of noninstitutional eldership is difficult even to speak about or describe within the framework of the discourse about canons.

The experience of the Old Believers in Russia, as well as that of the new martyrs and confessors of the Russian Church during the period of persecution, paves the way for broadening the theological context of the issue. It would seem that it is ecclesiological context, i.e., assumptions about the form that church can take that dictates one's approach to considering women's service in the church and its possible parameters, insofar as this offering of service—as with any ministry—exists only within the church. It logically follows that the contents of this ministry and its place in the church are determined by one's views and personal experiences related to church and the fullness of the ministries therein.

At the present time, from the perspective of contemporary Orthodox theology and church practice, it is possible to identify various, differing ecclesiological models that are coexisting—though not always in perfect peace—and one does sometimes witness "arguing." In this case, support is drawn from recent developments that represent private theological opinion and do not pretend to be some sort of ultimate knowledge regarding the question at hand. One authority on ecclesiology in modern Russia is Fr. Georgy Kochetkov, a scholar who is known to many because of his work in developing an integral and consistent system of introducing the foundations of the Christian faith, prayer, and life (i.e., catechesis) to adults in the modern world. Thanks to this system, thousands (even tens of thousands) of people in Russia have come into the church and become "practicing Christians" over the last forty-five years. The final stage of catechesis—a traditional introduction to the mysteries of the church (mystagogy), the central theme of which is "ecclesiology"—forms the foundation of personal faith and the church's faith in the New Testament church. Within the framework of this stage of catechesis, Fr. Georgy teaches that there are various "types" of Orthodox ecclesiology, drawing attention to the following: clerical-hierarchical, localized-parish (diocesan), localized-eucharistic, and community-brotherhood, suggesting that there are theological foundations and basic traits by which each of the types can be characterized. Various other theologians have also separately considered various ecclesiological "types," including Fr. John Behr,[5] Fr. John Erikson,[6] and Fr.

---

5. Types of Ecclesiology as a Reflection of the Experience of Church Life: David Gzgzian's interview with Fr. John Behr // "Evkharisticheskaya ekklesiologia segodnja: vosprijatije, voploshchenije, razvitije" ["The Eucharistic Ecclesiology Today and Its Perception, Development and Evolution"]: Materials from an international theological research conference (Moscow–Moscow Region, May 10–12, 2017) (Moscow: St. Philaret's Institute (SFI), 2018), 149–59. For information on St. Philaret's Institute see, accessed July 26, 2022, https://sfi.ru/en.

6. Fr. John Erikson, "Toward a Baptismal Ecclesiology: Faith Content and Ecclesial Context" [*The Quarterly Journal of St. Philaret's Institute*], no. 34 (Spring 2020): 19–45.

Valentin Asmus.[7] Insofar as Fr. Georgy's proposed approach to typological classification is more highly differentiated and developed, it will be used as a reference point in this paper. Fr. Georgy believes that one characteristic of our era—as of every other era of the church's existence in history—is that "in real life there has never been, is not, and never can be only one ecclesiological model."[8] It follows that in every era there exists a complex combination, intersection, and mixture of different ecclesiological models, and it is important to note, therefore, all the complexity and variation in the ecclesiological context under which the question is posed in the continuing endeavor to consider women's ministry at the level of the church in general.

Thus, let us look at the opportunities for making the women's diakonia a reality within the framework of different ecclesiological models.

It is completely clear that within the framework of a clerical-hierarchical understanding of church order that women's ministry doesn't find a place in the church in any form, whether institutional or outside the framework of one or another ordained position. Within this type of church structure, a woman is an unpaid employee for your lampstand and no more, i.e., she can work as a cleaner in the church (though not in the altar!), sell candles, and collect prayer lists to pass on to the priests. She can also sing in the choir; and in post-Soviet Russia this was, perhaps, the only place in which she could really serve God, and even this was only because of the fact that in the immediate aftermath of the 1000th anniversary of the Baptism of Rus, many churches were suddenly opened, and

---

7. "Contemporary Orthodox Ecclesiology: The Nature of the Church and Its Boundaries Interview with Metropolitan Kallistos (Ware), Fr. Georgy Kochetkov, Archpriest Valentin Asmus, A. G. Dunayev, A. V. Shishkov," *The Quarterly Journal of St. Philaret's Institute*, no. 26 (Spring 2018): 9–37, 26.

8. Georgy Kochetkov, *Tajny i tainstva cheloveka i Tservkvi: Opyt sovremennoj mistagogii pervoj stupeni: Posobije dlja mistagogov* [*The Mysteries and the Sacraments of the Person and of the Church: An Essay of the Modern Mystagogy of the 1st Stage: The Manual for the Mystagogues*] (Moscow: SFI, 2019), 310–11.

there were hardly any men in the Russian church. Within the framework of this ecclesiological model, woman is assigned a subordinate role and the only field in which she can manifest herself with appropriate dignity is as a mother and wife within the family—in giving birth to children, raising them, and in caring for her husband.[9]

Within the context of a localized-parish (diocesan) ecclesial order, Fr. Georgy believes that "life on all levels within the church—whether parish, diocesan, or localized/autonomous—is directly tied to the administrative-housekeeping, social-political (state governmental or national) borders."[10] Moreover, he stresses, local division into dioceses is expressed through the inviolable "one city, one bishop rule and the localized parish order through the parish, for which a localized territorial community is understood as the primary cellular building block of the entire church organism or the entire church organization."[11] As such, within the framework of localized-parish ecclesiology, a woman can realize her ministry to God only in rigid, institutional forms, and this takes the particular form of monasticism and no more. All other forms of women's ministry are rejected as being suspicious in some way or another, insofar as they are not recognized by either church or state.

Thus the well-known nineteenth-century church luminary Metropolitan Philaret (Drozdov) initially reacted very carefully to the

---

9. As such, Fr. Andrey Tkachyov, who is now popular in fundamentalist circles in the Russian Orthodox Church (ROC), says directly in his sermons, which are published via the Elitsy Orthodox website, accessed July 26, 2022, https://www.elitsy.ru, that "there were no women among the apostles, and no female people are ever called to be apostles. There are deep, Divine foundations for this, and it is also true that priesthood is not given to women." However, he notes that "women are not barred from spreading the Gospel," accessed July 26, 2022, https://www.youtube.com/watch?v=Y-geUDeVpDQ. And deceased Fr. Dimitry Smirnov, former head of the Patriarchal Commission for Family Issues and the Defense of Motherhood and Childhood, is one more name from the same camp. He, a well-known critic of birth control, declared on public radio that "women are 'weaker of mind' than men," making an exception only for Marie Curie, accessed July 26, 2022, https://www.ntv.ru/novosti/2211424/. We note, however, that Smirnov's statement earned a publicly announced negative reaction from official ROC representatives.

10. Georgy Kochetkov, *The Mysteries and the Sacraments*, 313.

11. Ibid.

idea of restoring the women's deaconesses when it seemed necessary for building a mission in the Altai and other activities explained by Archimandrite Macharij (Glukharev). The metropolitan did not forbid women from acting as missionaries under Archimandrite Machary; nevertheless, at a later date, he himself came to the point of taking decisive action in 1840 when he consecrated the head of the Spaso-Borodinskij Monastery, Mother Maria (Margarita Mikhailovna Tuchkova), as abbess using the rite for the ordination of a deaconess making use of the words "poveli" and povelite" (various imperative forms of the very "lead/shepherd") and pronouncing her *"axia"* three times after which she was adorned with the orarion of a deacon. Her memoirs of that occasion have been preserved. It is also important to mention the proposals of Archimandrite Makary that were partially put into practice: It was common for women to prepare other women for baptism, and those who performed this ministry (e.g., Sofia de Balmon) were not given any institutional office, but as a result became members of monastic communities (although originally Archimandrite Makary had envisaged the creation of communities for deaconesses). And it is no coincidence that another remarkable priest, Fr. Aleksandr Vasilievich Gumilevsky from the Church of the Birth of Christ on the Sands in St. Petersburg was having similar thoughts. Fr. Aleksandr put a great deal of effort into transforming the charitable sisterhood of the Elevation of the Holy Cross into a "community of Orthodox deaconesses."[12] Deeply convinced of the traditional nature of the institution of deaconess within the Orthodox Church, he tried to bring it back to life, though he was unsuccessful in doing so. He laid out a plan for the constitution of the Elevation of the Holy Cross Community of Orthodox Deaconesses[13] and tried hard to get it approved in the upper echelons of the church, knowing that there are devoted and self-sacrificial women ready to follow that path. Fr. Aleksandr thought that a restoration of the office of deaconess would be sup-

---

12. *Sluzhenije zhenshchin v tserkvi: Issledovanija*, [*The Ministry of Women in the Church: Research*], 317–18.
13. Ibid., 318–20.

ported by the Orthodox Church "because the unified voice of all the universal church councils supports the institution."[14] He was certain that women's monasticism did not solve the problem of women's ministry in general, and therefore strove to create a community of parish deaconesses; but with this attempt he was also unsuccessful. Fr. Aleksandr died in 1869 without having received permission to create a community of deaconesses.

The examples described above bear witness to the fact that within the context of a localized-parish ecclesiology, the idea of the restoration of the institution of women's ministry may gather some private support, though, particularly under conditions in which the church is dependent upon the state, these private initiatives are unlikely to be embodied or find any sort of longevity. To all such initiatives arising within Russia during the nineteenth and twentieth centuries and before the coup of 1917 the synod reacted with one question: Why create the institute of the diaconate for women when the Orthodox Church already has women's monasteries on the one hand and charitable sisterhoods on the other? So it seems there is no room for any institution of women's *church* ministry other than that which implies the taking of monastic vows within the framework of a localized-parish ecclesiology; this statement holds true even at the parish level because the parish is not self-sufficient and independent enough to make decisions in matters regarding such questions. Insofar as any ministry under this type of ecclesial model presupposes attachment to institutional forms, and these same forms 'lost' women's ministry over the course of history, they can no longer 'perceive' women's ministry when it is needful (the ministry of a deaconess rather than a monastic or a sister of charity). Drawing some preliminary conclusions, it can be said that the order of deaconesses during Russia's synodal period had no prospects of being restored on the level of the church as a whole, and the collection of unsuccessful attempts at its restoration during the nineteenth and early twentieth centuries bear witness to this fact.

---

14. Ibid., 322.

One finds a contrasting perspective during the post-Constantinian period, and it is no accident that the integral concept of *eucharistic* ecclesiology poses the question of women's ministry anew, and not only from the institutional standpoint.

As Fr. Georgy Kochetkov understands it, "*localized-Eucharistic* ecclesiology . . . is based upon the central significance of the unified mystery of the Eucharist (which . . . is understood as the Mystery of Mysteries) and the corresponding united Eucharistic assembly of the church, as well as on the practice of territoriality ('one city, one bishop, one Eucharist, one Eucharistic assembly'), although eucharistic locality is more linked to local common mutual spiritual life (sobornost),"[15] and the church community itself is more "the church in all its fullness, that it is some part of some universal whole,"[16] in line with the ancient Christian principle, "where the Eucharist is, there also is the Church."[17]

Eucharistic ecclesiology as an integral and well-developed theological concept arises from the work of Fr. Sergei Bulgakov and Fr. Nikolaj Afanasiev, i.e., out of the Russian emigration in Paris. Fr. John Behr believes that the appearance of eucharistic ecclesiology out of the Paris theological academic was, to a great degree, tied to the fate of the emigration itself and, as a result, the gathering of all the strengths of the church around the Eucharist;[18] it was the Eucharist in particular that became the means of uniting Russian people who had lost their fatherland and habitual world order, having found themselves in a foreign land. At that moment, for representatives of the Russian church in emigration, the Eucharist concentrated within itself the embodiment of the sobornal principles of church life, and logically, therefore, Fr. Sergei Bulgakov called the conference of the youth movement in Psherov, "Pentecost."

It is within the context of a eucharistic ecclesiology that the future new martyr Mother Maria (Skobtsova) sets up her work: her

---

15. Georgy Kochetkov, *The Mysteries and the Sacraments*, 318.
16. Ibid.
17. Ibid.
18. "Eucharistic Ecclesiology Today" conference materials, Moscow-Moscow Region, May 10–12, 2017 (Moscow: SFI, 2018), 151–52.

diaconia—located at a house at Rue Lourmel in Paris and the organization that she founded "Pravoslavnoye Delo"—was inspired by the idea of "liturgy outside of church." She herself described the work using liturgical language, stating that "on the level known to the public 'Pravoslavnoye Delo' can only be a 'Common Affair,' a sort of liturgy projected from the church into the world"[19] and that "We love one another, and confess unity of thought. Loving one another means not only unity in thought, but unity in action—it means a common life."[20] Moreover, in describing the fairly difficult work of going to market in the predawn darkness and coming back toting a heavy sack of inexpensive food on her back for those in her shelter, when something begins to leak out of the bag, she describes it using the word "liturgy." She will take anyone at all into her shelter, thereby expanding the mystical boundaries of the church; for the diaconia conceived of by her as a sort of all-expansive "new motherhood," there are no canonical, juridical, or faith-confessional divisions and borders. Mother Maria was also verbally talented. Thus, Metropolitan Evlogij (Georgievsky) blessed her to preach at the end of the liturgy.

Fr. Georgy Kochetkov believes that "it is this type of ecclesiology in particular which best of all perceives and brings into relief the mystical-dogmatic borders of the church,"[21] though it seems that in her ministry Mother Maria even surpasses these—to which her martyr's death bears eloquent witness. It is therefore natural that Mother Maria spoke of "evangelical" ecclesiology, which in essence surpasses a eucharistic ecclesiology that has its limitations.

This type of ecclesiological model is well documented in church history: women deaconesses can concelebrate in the Eucharist, take Holy Communion to those who are ill, perform chrismation of women in completing the mystery of baptism, and pass on catechetical teaching. The church's history contains many examples of such

---

19. Mother Maria (Skobtsova), *Memoires. Articles. Sketches*, vol. 1 (Paris: YMCA-Press, 1992), 222.
20. Ibid., 151.
21. Georgy Kochetkov, *The Mysteries and the Sacraments*, 320.

ministry, and they appear in liturgical-canonical records. It is within a eucharistic understanding of church sobornost and the fullness of church life in particular that women during the Soviet period were entrusted with the Holy Gifts and passed them to those in prison.[22]

On the whole, women's ministry within the context of this type of ecclesiology opens the door for Christian sisters to act *within* the sacramental boundaries of the church, and the central place in this type of ministry and its theological understanding is occupied by the Eucharist itself. Here, of course, a woman's sex is a particular limitation for her, though the character of women's diaconia are known to contemporary Orthodox thought specifically in the context of eucharistic ecclesiology. As one endeavors to understand the boundaries of women's ministry and simultaneously facilitate the manifestation of women's ministries to the fullest extent possible, the theological question more often than not presupposes the context of the mysteries of the church, which means one naturally runs into the issue of how to theologically reconcile hierarchical and non-hierarchical understandings of ministry.

Evangelical (Mother Maria, N.A. Berdyaev), or trinitarian (Fr. Dimitru Staniloae), or community-brotherhood ecclesiology (Holy Martyr Anatoly Zurakovsky, Fr. Vitaly Borovoj, and Fr. Georgy Kochetkov) was unveiled somewhat earlier than eucharistic ecclesiology according to Fr. Georgy Kochetkov.[23] Within the framework of this ecclesiological model, each is called to serve according to the gifts they have been given (1 Pt 4:10), independent of sex. One might characterize this ecclesiological model as theocentric and simultaneously trinitarian. Ecclesiology "addressed to the Father, Son, and Holy Spirit is also addressed to the human Person born again in the Holy Trinity, insofar as we believe in one indivisible God expressed in three non-intermingled hypostases and in Mankind in Christ."[24] This ecclesiological model is simultaneously Christocen-

---

22. A. Ya. Vasilevskaya, Katakomby XX veka [Catacombs of the 20th century]. *Memoires* (Moscow, 2001), 209–306.
23. Georgy Kochetkov, *The Mysteries and the Sacraments*, 321.
24. Ibid., 323.

tric and Pneumatocentric, having simultaneous communal and personal traits, and the church and its borders, on this understanding, are determined primarily in existential categories: "where Love and Freedom, Truth and Life are, there, too, is the Church."[25] Within the framework of this ecclesiological model, the ministry of each is called out in accordance with their spiritual gifts, insofar as these spiritual gifts are undertaken "in Christ" (Gal 3:28); and only in serving God and the church is the unsolvable opposition of "male" and "female" solved. Here is an example from the twentieth century: Maria Nikolayevna Umanets became the Guardian of the Elevation of the Holy Cross Brotherhood of Labour, founded by her brother, church luminary Nikolay Nepluyev. Being an aristocrat and the brotherhood's guardian member as per internal status, he invited graduates of agricultural schools (which he had founded) to join the brotherhood, and later passed all his wealth and property to the brothers. At the 1917–1918 Local Church Council of the Russian Orthodox Church, future new martyr and member of the governing body of the brotherhood, Fr. Aleksandr Sekundov (who had been chosen by his diocese to attend the council) greeted the council in the name of the Guardian of the Elevation of the Holy Cross Brotherhood, Maria Umanets. She was the leader of their governing body and the elder within the brotherhood right up until the time of the repression that made her execution of the office impossible. The text of the greeting is published in a series of documents from the Volume V of the Moscow Council of 1917–18 at 57–58.

On January 9, 1918, Patriarch Tikhon appealed to Orthodox Christians to form spiritual unions and brotherhoods; his call was heard by clerics and lay people, and received an energetic response. In the communities and brotherhoods founded by Bishop-catechist Makarij (Opotsky) and which lived under his unquestionable spiritual leadership, elderhood was often born by sisters, despite the fact that these brotherhoods also had male members. It is known that Bishop Makarij ordained one such woman as a deaconess. Unfortunately, the exact date of her consecration and the rite used are

---

25. Ibid., 325.

impossible to recover, though it was likely before 1941. In one of the prayers written in this brotherhood by a sister and addressed to the Mother of God, she requests "the gift of the apostles, having received strength from above . . . to go and proclaim the Gospel of the Kingdom of God."[26] There are also other testimonies to the consecration of deaconesses during the period of persecution.[27]

Under conditions of persecution, it was women, in particular, who became the guardians of not only the church's practice, but of the faith, of prayers and the Christian life in general, i.e., of the church's Holy Tradition. In the work of Elena Belyakova, as well as in memoires and testimonies published over the course of the last twenty years in Russia, one finds many examples *of spiritual mentoring* being exercised by women— more often than not by those who had chosen a monastic path, to remain unmarried, or even the path of the holy fool. These women gathered believers around themselves, e.g., the Krasheninnikov sisters, who voluntarily chose a life of celibacy and directly served the assembly of the church.

As such, in allowing the exercise of the feminine diaconia, the community and brotherhood ecclesiological model does not undermine hierarchical eldership. The female diaconia is exercised not within the framework of the parish, but in communities and brotherhoods, i.e., it assumes particular quality traits, obligations, and demands. The church ministry of women corresponds to the realities of church life and to the existing local and hierarchical church structure, but has freedom of expression, insofar as it simply presupposes a correspondence between hierarchical and spiritual eldership.

Within the framework of the community and brotherhood ecclesiological model, women can carry the apostles' ministry of preaching and spreading the good news of the gospel about Christ, which differs from mentoring others to live a pious and virtuous life according to the commandments. Women who are accordingly spiritually gifted may serve the community of the faithful; teach the

---

26. *Selected prayers: From the inheritance of Bishop Makary Opotsky's Brotherhood* (Moscow: KPF Preobrazhenije, 2015), 5.
27. Belyakova, et al, *Woman in Orthodoxy*, 461–63.

foundations of the faith, prayer, and life; bear the burden of spiritual eldership within the church (i.e., be the guardian of the gathering of the faithful); and "washing the feet" of their neighbors. Detecting and identifying the fullness of the sisters' spiritual gifts and the question of their consecration—which may not be liturgical as in some cases a simple blessing may suffice—as well as the reception of each specific ministry are matters that remain outside the scope of this paper as they require a more detailed analysis.

Diversity of Ministries in the Context of the Community-Brotherhood Ecclesiological Model: What Does This Look Like in Practice?

In this section, I will try to share some practical observations and firsthand experience. These are my own observations and experience over twenty-five years of participation in brotherhood life. In the Transfiguration Brotherhood, which will celebrate its thirtieth birthday in 2020, there is a great diversity of ministries exercised by Christian women.[28] Among them, not one of these women has been ordained or consecrated to their ministry. Some of us are married, and some have consciously chosen not to marry. As of today, we can give testimony responsibly before God to the good fruits that these women have brought and continue to bring on their path of service as members of living church communities and brotherhoods. Here is a list some of the more significant examples.

All the faithful are called to witness Christ to unbelievers, the unbaptized, and those of other faiths, as is read out—as a consecration to ministry—within the liturgical portion of the rite of baptism itself. Our sisters have the experience of personal witness to unbelieving family members, loved ones, and coworkers; we would note that witness within the family is one of the most complicated forms of witness in modern Russia, but practice shows that often children come to the faith first, and are followed by their parents.

---

28. For information on the Transfiguration Brotherhood, see, accessed July 26, 2022, https://psmb.ru/en.

CHAPTER ELEVEN

The experience of running a full course of catechesis for adults—both men and women—can also be called a ministry in its own right, to which we might add the instruction of children, teenagers, and people with various developmental particularities or difficult psychiatric diagnoses. I stress that I am speaking about bringing these people fully into the church so that they become real members of a church fellowship. A full catechetical cycle takes up to a year and a half, although in cases where the catechumen has special needs, the length of the course is shorter. After members come into the church, the catechist is responsible for continuing to oversee the group for an additional year, until members find their own footing on their path within the church.

Christian women who have not only a secular but also a spiritual education are catechists. Their groups generally have between fifteen and twenty-five people in them. The first part of the program for "listeners" incorporates weekly meetings, questions and answers on scripture, teaching people to pray individually and with the church, and helping them to change their lives to come into accordance with the standards of God's law and gospel ethics, i.e., helping people begin to live the scripture and the gospel. As part of the second stage, catechists relate and explain salvation history. In the third and final stage (*mystagogia*), they teach Orthodox dogmatics and introduce people to the Holy Mysteries.

Sisters of the Transfiguration Brotherhood may also bear the ministry of church eldership, under conditions where the elder member of the small Christian group (generally formed of those who went through the lengthy period of catechesis together) is chosen to serve for a period of one year, either by unanimous or simple majority vote. The group's decision must meet various criteria relating to their life in the church, responsibility, ability to care for all, not only for "one's own," but also for the community in a broader context (the brotherhood, the local church). The elder must also have the blessing of the spiritual leader of the Transfiguration Brotherhood. All of this relates to eldership in small fellowship groups (up to twenty or twenty-five people, including people of different ages) as well as to the eldership of brotherhoods (up to 100 people). The question of elder selection must not be understood as a question of pure "democracy," insofar as the church criteria in this selection are extremely important. Sisters who are small group leaders or the chairpeople of brotherhoods, together with their brothers, may lead at worship services of lay people in their communities and brotherhoods; read the scripture at fellowship meetings and preach; and gather to discuss questions of practical and church order relating to their communities and brotherhoods, i.e., bear the *ministry of council*. Naturally, this ministry presupposes care for the young and the elderly, helping to prepare children and youth to enter the church, concern for the church life of elderly brothers and sisters, as well as the care of more serious church affairs outside the boundaries of their local fellowship.

It is worth noting that from the perspective of today's practice of the division of gender roles within society, this state of affairs aligns with the contemporary societal role of women in the Russian Federation, although experience shows that in post-Soviet Russia women are often stricter leaders than men. Sometimes these qualities also manifest in church life; and, in such cases, sisters turn out to be "the scourge of God." Unfortunately, at times there are more sisters than brothers, and the catholic balance is somewhat compromised. I can attest to the fact that in the Transfiguration Brotherhood there are small groups made up of only sisters, though we don't yet have a single group made up only of brothers. (In total, there are about 130 small communities and groups, and sisters are elders in seventy-six of these cases.) Unfortunately, all of this is the result of the Communist genocide of the male population, and in particular of the Russian population during the years of repression, collectivization, forced hunger, mass deportation, and war. I want to hope that this is only temporary, only because the force of inertia is often greater in our brothers than in our sisters in the context of our modern Russian discourse.

During *church worship services* sisters may not only sing and read the Holy Scripture; the primary concern of sisters who are choir leaders and members is to help people pray, i.e., fully enter into the church's tradition of communing with God and of communal prayer for which purpose they must themselves know and understand this tradition; sing in their native language; pay attention to how accessible the worship texts are to the worshippers, including the use of quality modern translations; and in cases of necessity, translate these independently. In the context of home and community prayers in which collected church prayers are used and in cases where no clergy or brothers are present, sisters may lead prayers, read Holy Scripture, and preach. There are also cases in which sisters have been robed in a *stikharion* for the reading of scripture or for preaching during church worship when the assembly was headed by a priest of the ROC.

Also of note is the service of spiritual teaching and the education of lay people in forms recognized by the state government: sisters who are members of the brotherhood not only receive a spiritual education in their own right, but also organize the educational process (which in light of the current Russian law is something of a spiritual achievement (*podvig*) at the level of primary, secondary, and higher spiritual educations, teaching various disciplines including holy scripture, liturgics, church history, and other subjects. We also have sisters who are research scholars.

And sisters have in recent times acquired a very particular role in service in dialogue between church and society: this involves putting forward various initiatives that have a Christian basis and the expression of a well-thought-through Christian position in non-church (and sometimes anti-church) circles, both in arenas in the church and in society at large. This, for instance, takes the form of promoting various specific church initiatives on the level of the cities where they live. Among such initiatives, we note our Prayer for Remembrance initiative, which the Transfiguration Brotherhood organizes annually on the thirtieth of October, the day when victims of the Soviet repression are remembered on the streets and squares of cities across Russia and abroad.[29] Within the context of this initiative, during which litanies are served all day for the innocent victims, incorporating the reading of lists of thousands of those who were executed, many sisters are responsible for organizing the entire

---

29. See, accessed July 26, 2022, https://molitvapamyaty.ru [in Russian].

event. This includes contacting municipal authorities, receiving the blessing of local bishops, interaction with the priests of local parishes, speaking with those who live in nearby buildings, and actual participation in the all-day event. These events attract public attention to the question of how Russia remembers its own history, given that after a century of persecution and effort to create a new 'Soviet' man both the physical and the spiritual memory of our generations has been practically destroyed.

Here you have an incomplete list of ministries that have their root in Christ and their action in the Holy Spirit, which many Christian women, members of the Transfiguration Brotherhood, assume and carry in an effective and inspired fashion. It goes without saying that the execution of these ministries is not always sweetness and light, and does not always go perfectly. But it is a labor of joy, as the remarkable church confessor of the 1960s and 70s, Fr. Vsevolod Shpiller said, just as is the cross of our Lord and Savior.[30]

Conclusion

A short review of ecclesiological types of church order bears witness to the fact that in practice, the restoration of the fullness of women's ministry cannot happen simply, definitively, and/or uniformly in all instances and churches. However, there are spiritually sensitive examples from past years (for instance the initiatives to ordain deaconesses in the Alexandrian church) that show us that institutional ordination is possible when there is a pre-existing church ministry already attested to within a specific church assembly. A number of questions remain, i.e., the form of Christian women's participation in church administration and their church representation within

---

30. Archpriest Vsevolod Shpiller. Sermon on the day of the Exaltation of the Cross of the Lord September 27, 1980: ["You and I completely forget that always, as soon as we raise the cross, as soon as we stand next to Simon the Cyrene, in order to carry this cross together with Christ, it fills us with joy! Meanwhile, only where the cross of the Lord is, where is sacrificial love, only there is heavenly light, heavenly sweetness. Only the path of cross love leads to this heavenly sweetness, bliss both there and here on earth."], translation by Zoya Dashevskaya, accessed July 26, 2022, http://www.odinblago.ru/shpiller_propovedi_slova/6 [in Russian].

official structures. If one is speaking about ministries that presuppose women's participation in the celebration of the church mysteries (preparation for baptism, service in the context of the church assembly), then on what basis can a Christian woman be recommended for such a ministry, by whom, and by what means would it be attested and accepted into the life of the church? The act of consecration, in all likelihood, should presuppose election and various specific demands, but as is well understood, it is hardly true that all aspects of the church ministry of women today will fit neatly into the Byzantine rite of consecrating a deaconess that is well known to researchers of the *Euchologion Barberini gr. 336*. It seems likely that the consecration of deaconesses will be more closely linked with ministries relating to the field of catechesis, philanthropic/charitable work, and perhaps the services handled by junior clerics. The other aspects of women's ministry within the church, which in the church of the past perhaps fell under the services of women presbyters, widows and virgins, will be unlikely to 'fit' into the office of the deaconess.

But is it even necessary to institutionalize them? If it is worth doing, then what order of service should be used? If not, then how can one fully ascertain what these ministries are and identify those women who should be serving according to them? The questions of how particular people are recommended for consecration (i.e., the ancient order of testing), the type of gathering at which consecration should take place, and the reception of the service itself, are entirely separate. It seems that at present, outside of the context of community and brotherhood, it remains rather unclear how candidates for consecration to one or another ministry might be identified; how, if a candidate is consecrated, the full catholicity of her choice and consecration is made manifest; and even how the reception of her ministry (in each particular case) is made manifest. Is liturgical consecration needed in all cases or in only those cases where the ministry of specific Christian women is somehow related to the celebration of the church mysteries (baptism, the Eucharist)? Under such conditions, the ministry of church eldership falls outside the context of liturgical consecration. To what extent is this correct?

This is hardly a comprehensive list of questions if we, as Orthodox Christians, truly wish to attempt to bring various church initiatives aimed at the restoration of women's ministries to fruition. Many questions remain. But let not this point get in the way of researchers or those who in practice are searching to reveal the will of God. As Petros Vassiliadis noted quite wonderfully, "This doesn't have to do with what women (or men) want, but with what Jesus Christ wants for the Church in the twenty-first century for the Glory of God." This search must be led "in the light of a viable and respectable theological anthropology based on the authentic, though hidden, Holy Tradition of the church, and not only on historical tradition."[31]

---

31. Petros Vassiliadis, "The Roles of Women in the Church", 82.

Chapter Twelve

THE ORDER OF DEACONESSES ACCORDING TO THE 1917–18 SOBOR DISCUSSION

Alexander Mramornov

Since the moment that the Incarnation of God took place through the Virgin, the highest and most difficult ideal to achieve was established for women's social roles and behavioral strategies. In the era of early Christianity, the importance of women's ministry in the church was relatively clear. But the remainders of political and social discrimination toward women, so prevalent in the Middle Ages, survive in the Orthodox Church, especially in the Russian Church. However, the Great Moscow Council of 1917–1918 was that special moment when the episcopate, clergy, and laymen spoke out against such discrimination.

In this way, the expansion of ecclesiastical rights of women takes place in the Russian Church with the sanction of the higher ecclesiastical authority because the local council is still the highest level of such authority. To this day, it remains the most representative and legitimate council. Thus, the expansion of ecclesiastical rights of women was not "liberal," as official commentators and publicists of the Russian Church try sometimes to present it, but truly a Christian, evangelical act of the council.

In Christ, according to the word of the apostle, "there is neither male nor female" (Gal 3:28). These key New Testament words were quoted many times at the proceedings of the council in revolutionary Moscow.

The council studied seriously the issue of the restoration of deaconesses' order. The special department of the council ("Church Discipline") proposed the report for the council's approval with appendix, "the liturgical succession of the consecration of a deaconess." Unfortunately, sister of mercy Lyudmila Gerasimova from Petrograd and widow Olga Klyueva from Rostov-on-Don remained without their consecration: the council did not manage to pass the canon on deaconesses despite a consensus on this issue among the council members.

The era of persecution of the Russian Church (1920–1930s) often brought women to the forefront of spiritual life and to the frontline of parish opposition to the persecution of faith and the destruction of church property. But in bringing decisions like consecrating deaconesses to life, the church of the Soviet period was placed in a rigid framework. However, during the thirty-two years that have elapsed since the beginning in 1988 of the so-called 'church renaissance' in Russia, nothing has been really done on this issue. At the same time, as all Orthodox and non-Orthodox well know, deaconesses appeared in the Patriarchate of Alexandria in 2016.

The Great Moscow Council also created a broader basis for the restoration of the order of deaconesses, for example, in giving women the rights to participate in church governing bodies. For the first time in Russian Church history, women were present at the Council of 1988 and at the electoral local councils of 1990 and 2009 as full members. Was it precisely that way in which the members of the Council 1917–1918 saw female representation in the bodies of higher church administration? Did they have in their minds this current representation of the Legal Commission of the Moscow Patriarchate in Patriarch Cyril's Supreme Church Council when they wisely pondered the need of the church to have two types of women represented in such a council–"Mary" from female monasticism and "Martha" from women involved in education, catechesis, and mission?

CHAPTER TWELVE

The question of deaconesses and the role of women in the church continued to be actively pondered by the Metropolitan Vladimir (Bogoyavlensky) (1848–1918) in the last months of his life, just before his martyrdom in Kiev. His paper on deaconesses, which he had left in Moscow before his last departure for Kiev, was then read as part of the council proceedings as a tribute to his memory. This theoretical paper has been already published by Russian scholars E. V. Belyakova, N. A. Belyakova, and E. B. Yemchenko.[1]

But today it seems important to pay attention to the most relevant nuances of the council discussions, since the Russian Church over the past century has taken steps backwards in the development and enhancement of the vitality of its spiritual institutions. By the revolutionary time, the cleaning of the altar by girls and even their attendance at the divine services in the altar was a normal practice. Today there are no such examples in the Russian Church, and, for instance, when the Vicar of Patriarch Cyril, Archbishop of Vereya Amvrosij (Ermakov), uploaded a photo with an altar girl (from somewhere in Montenegro) to his Instagram account,[2] many Russian people discussed this as never unseen and completely impossible.

Or here is another example: the Council 1917–1918 pointed out already more than a hundred years ago the abnormality and inappropriateness of the prohibition against women participating in divine services and the Eucharist during menstruation. Hygienic practices were already advanced enough at the turn of the nineteenth and twentieth centuries to consider such a prohibition a relic of ancient times and irrelevant today. The twenty-first century has come, but the prohibition remains, giving a reason for the unintentional 'excommunication' of many women from participation in the Eucharist.

---

1. See their book E. V. Belyakova, N. A. Belyakova, E. B. Yemchenko, *Zhenshchina v pravoslavii: cerkovnoe pravo i rossijskaya praktika* [*Woman in Orthodoxy: Canon Law and Russian Practice*] (Moscow 2011).

2. Instagram Post, June 4, 2019, accessed July 15, 2022, https://www.instagram.com/p/ByS6GJYCKfY/.

Let me provide a reminder about the key moments of discussion of the role of the women on the council's 1917–1918 proceedings.[3] The question of the role of women in the church was raised at the All-Russian Local Council 1917–1918 in Archpriest Iakov Galakhov's speech during the discussion on the formation of the council's departments at the ninth plenary sitting, August 24, 1917. On September 3, the council's presidium received the statement from thirty-five members of the council; the first of them was Archpriest Galakhov's. They proposed "to put an end to the powerlessness of women." On September 12, after corrections, the statement was accepted and on the next day transferred to the Department for Church Discipline issues, which was formed by the council due to the fact that at that time, according to the chairman of the department, Metropolitan Vladimir (Bogoyavlensky) of Kiev, "Church discipline was in depression, and that stood in connection with the anarchy of the Church life."[4]

The question of "the position of women in church life" was raised in the council's Department for Church Discipline issues, on September 1, 1917, for the first time (its first sitting). Further, the Special Department's Commission for determining the limits of the department's jurisdiction, at its first meeting on September 6, included this issue in the department's agenda. At the second sitting, September 9, the commission combined the issues of "the position of women" and "the poisoning of the fetus" (abortion), and it was suggested that the issue of the position of women in the church was a matter of marital discipline.

At the third sitting on September 11th, it was discussed whether the question of women in the church means restoring the order of

---

3. Materials for the following discussions and resolutions of 1917–1918 on women's questions are published by E. V. Belyakova, N. A. Belyakova, and E. B. Emchenko, *Woman in Orthodoxy* and Alexander Mramornov, *Svyashchennyj Sobor Pravoslavnoj Rossijskoj Cerkvi 1917–1918 gg. o roli zhenshchin v Cerkvi, "Spasskoe delo"* [*The Holy Local Council of the Orthodox Russian Church 1917–1918 about the role of the women in the Church*] (Moscow: Spasskoe delo, 2020) [in Russian].

4. State archive of the Russian Federation. Fund R-3431. Inventory. 1. File 316. Sheets. 6–8.

deaconesses or was it broader and whether it should be generally discussed by the Department for Church Discipline issues as it is. At the seventh meeting, October 12th, Archpriest I. I. Galakhov presented his report on women. The department informed the council at the last plenary sitting of the first session, on December 9, 1917, about the results of its work during the session.

The report of the Department for Church Discipline issues "On the Participation of Women in the Life of the Church" was discussed by the council only during the third session, at the plenary sitting No. 133, July 11 (24), 1918. At meeting No. 138, July 21 (August 3), the report of the Editorial Department on this document was read. However, the Editorial Department presented two versions of the conciliar resolution, and, moreover, the issue of the right of the women to enter the altar was by that time not yet fundamentally resolved. Therefore, the project was returned to the Department for Church Discipline issues.

On the sittings of the Department No. 25 (August 6, 1918) and No. 26 (August 12, 1918), the "Project . . . on attracting women to active participation in various fields of church ministry" was examined for the second time. Further on, the council, on its plenary sitting No. 169, on September 19th, heard the additional report of the Department for Church Discipline and adopted a resolution on it. Finally, at the last plenary session of the council, on September 20th, the resolution of the Editorial Department "On attracting women to active participation in various fields of church ministry" was heard, adopted, and transmitted to the conference of bishops. At the bishops' meeting, at session No. 47, September 9th (22nd), the resolution was adopted. Nine bishops voted in favor and twenty-two against. According to the council's charter it was enough for the document to be absolutely accepted by the council.

A number of other important problems followed the question of the role of women in the church. Sometimes the discussion of such problems came from the discussion of a key topic and was embodied in separate outcome documents. Sometimes this discussion, often held in other departments of the council, then merged into a discussion of the role of women in the church in the Department for Church Discipline issues. These were the following: the right of women to enter the altar; the institution of deaconesses; the right of women to be members of the higher, diocesan, parish councils; and the right of women to be churchwardens.

The order of deaconesses was primarily discussed on the sittings of the Department No. 2, September 9, 1917. At meeting No. 7, on October 12th, the concrete question, the election of Ludmila Gerasimova (the writer and nurse from Rostov-on-Don) and her ordination to a deaconess, was discussed.[5]

At the plenary meeting No. 67, January 22, 1918, the transfer of files on this issue from the Holy Synod to the Conciliar Department was approved. At the plenary meeting No. 85, February 15 (28), the report on the restoration of the institution of deaconesses by Metropolitan Vladimir of Kiev (who had by that time been killed in Kiev) was included. This report was also mentioned at other meetings of the department. At sitting No. 25, July 24 (August 6), the department's report on the restoration of the order of deaconesses was read and discussed.

The question of the right of women to enter the altar was raised in the Department for Church Discipline issues on July 24 (August 6), 1918. The council discussed this issue on its plenary sitting No. 133, July 11 (24), 1918, during the debates on the report "On the Participation of Women in the Life of the Church," read by Archpriest P. A. Mirtov.

At the meeting of the Disciplinary Department No. 26, July 30 (August 12), the report of Professor I. M. Gromoglasov "On the right of women to enter the altar" was heard and discussed. At session No. 29, September 4 (17), the report to the council was approved. The Conciliar Presidium, at its meeting No. 124, September 6 (19), decided to transfer this report to the organs of higher church administration, the Holy Synod and the Supreme Church Council.

The reports "On the Right of Women to Enter the Altar" and "On the Restoration of the Order of Deaconesses" were not consid-

---

5. Her petition to be ordained is stored here: State archive of the Russian Federation. Fund R–3431. Inventory. 1. File 327. Sheet 8.

ered by the council at the time of the forced completion of its work. The question of the introduction of women into church administration was raised for the first time in the Department for Higher Church Administration, at meeting No. 23, November 6, 1917, when the question of the membership in the Supreme Church Council was discussed. Further, it was discussed at a meeting on March 16 (29), when analyzing the issue of the composition of church district councils, then at meeting No. 54, July 25 (August 8), when deciding on the issue of representation from convents at the Local Council.

At the plenary session of Council No. 49, November 23, 1917, the question of the introduction of women into the Supreme Church Council was discussed when considering article No. 7 of the report of the Department for Higher Church Administration, "On the bodies of Higher Church Administration." Supporters quoted the words of the Apostle Paul: "There is neither male nor female" (Gal. 3:28), while opponents pointed out that the collegial or corporate principle is unacceptable in the Orthodox Church.

The issue of the right of women to participate in deanery and parish councils was considered by the Department for Church Discipline at Session No. 25, July 24 (August 6), 1918. By that time, the council decided that women could not participate in judicial and administrative institutions. Therefore, since the deanery council has these kinds of functions, it was decided that women cannot become members.[6]

However, the council also decided positively on the question of the right of women to be churchwardens at the plenary meeting No. 125, April 4 (17), 1918, when discussing the statute on churchwardens.

The general problems of the role of women in the church can include a variety of discussions that are unrelated or almost unrelated to the development by the Department for Church Discipline of the decree "On the involvement of women in active participation in various fields of church ministry." These discussions took place

---

6. State archive of the Russian Federation. Fund R–3431. Inventory. 1. File 316. Sheets 272–274 reverse.

in different sections and at the plenary sessions of the council. The most important of these are questions about: admitting women to the work of preaching and teaching, opportunities for women to be members of the clergy and members of fraternities, participation of women in mission affairs, out-of-school education, and parish meetings. The council of 1917–1918 attempted to carry out the decision on each of these issues.

IV

ECUMENICAL PERSPECTIVES

Chapter Thirteen

WOMEN DEACONS IN THE ROMAN CATHOLIC CHURCH
Phyllis Zagano[1]

Introduction

Women deacons (deaconesses) have been in the Catholic consciousness since the restoration of the diaconate as a permanent vocation after the Second Vatican Council. There has never been any doubt that women deacons existed and ministered in various ways in multiple locations both East and West throughout the church's long history. However, within the Catholic Churches, and especially within the Roman Catholic Churches, the type and nature of the ministries of women deacons, as well as the nature of their ordinations, have been repeatedly analyzed and debated. Most recently, the question was addressed by the Pontifical Commission for the Study of the Diaconate of Women, which met several times in Rome from November 2016 to June 2018.

---

1. This paper reviews discussions about restoring women to the ordained diaconate in the Catholic Churches following the Second Vatican Council, from the academic debate between Roger Gryson and Aimé-Georges Martimort, through the work of the International Theological Commission during the last quarter of the twentieth century to the twenty-first century calls for women deacons from Synods and the International Union of Superiors General of women's institutes and orders, which resulted in the 2016 establishment of the Pontifical Commission for the Study of the Diaconate of Women, and concludes with comments about recent events.

CHAPTER THIRTEEN

Post-Conciliar Debate

There was some informal discussion about restoring the tradition of women deacons during the Second Vatican Council, but the council only recommended restoration of the male diaconate as a permanent office, which would be opened to celibate and to married men. However, the question of women deacons hovered in the rarified, postconciliar air.

In the early 1970s, the Belgian Professor, Roger Gryson, now Ordinary Professor Emeritus in the Faculty of Theology at the University of Louvain, published *The Ministry of Women in the Early Church*. Gryson found that women were ordained to the diaconate and performed diaconal ministries for many centuries. Although he presented their ministries as somewhat more limited than those of their male counterparts, Gryson found in the ordinations of women deacons "nothing distinguishing it formally from the ordination of their male colleagues."[2]

Coincidentally, in Rome, Paul VI asked the noted Eastern liturgist and International Theological Commission member, Cipriano Vagaggini, Camodolese Congregation of the Order of St. Benedict (OSB Cam.), about women deacons. In his dense essay, eventually published in *Orientalia christiana periodica*, Vagaggini concluded that women deacons belonged to the group of bishops, presbyters, and deacons, not to the lesser clergy, and that they received and can receive diaconal ordination equal to that of deacons. Vagaggini responded to the point of historical restrictions to the ministry of women by affirming that contemporary society accepts ministries once denied women, especially distributing Communion. He wrote, "It is noteworthy that today there are cases in which, by indult, women do almost everything that can be done by the clergy, except say Mass, hear confessions, and do the anointing of the sick." Vagaggini notes that this latter restriction, against anointing the sick, af-

---

2. Roger Gryson, *The Ministry of Women in the Early Church*, trans. J. Laporte and M. L. Hall (Collegeville, MN: Liturgical, 1976), 113. Translation of *Le ministère des femmes dans L'Église ancienne, Recherches et synthèses, section d'histoire* 4 (Gembloux: J. Duculot, 1972).

firms the Western idea of anointing regarding the remission of sin and relegates to a secondary status the intent of obtaining healing from God.³

Then, some years later and in an attempt to overtake the growing acceptance of women deacons in accordance with the restoration of the diaconate as a permanent ministry for men, French liturgist Aimé-Georges Martimort produced a book-length compilation of his essays and other writings refuting Gryson.⁴ Even so, Martimort concludes: "theologians must strictly guard against trying to prove a hypothesis dependent upon only a part of the documentation available" and "There exists a significant danger of distorting both the facts and the texts whenever one is dealing with them secondhand."⁵

The discussion about women in the diaconate seems to have been waylaid by growing calls for women to be ordained as priests during the last quarter of the twentieth century, which saw the publication of two documents affirming church teaching against the possibility of women priests: the International Theological Commission document, *Inter insigniores* (1976), and the Apostolic Exhortation of John Paul II, *Ordinatio sacerdotalis* (1994). Each document expressly eliminated any discussion of women deacons.

International Theological Commission

In 1992, the International Theological Commission (ITC) set out to settle the question of women deacons. By 1997, the nine-member, all-male subcommittee found no objection to women deacons and presented a numbered, printed document that the entire ITC voted

---

3. Cipriano Vagaggini, "The Ordination of Deaconesses in the Greek and Byzantine Tradition" in *Women Deacons? Essays with Answers*, ed. Phyllis Zagano (Liturgical Press, 2016), 142–43; Cipriano Vagaggini, "L'ordinazione delle diaconesse nella tradizione greca e bizantina," *Orientialia christiana periodica* 40 (1974): 146–89.

4. Aimé-Georges Martimort, *Deaconesses: An Historical Study*, trans. K. D. Whitehead (San Francisco: Ignatius, 1986); *Les Diaconesses: Essai Historique* (Rome: C.L.V.-Edizioni Liturgiche, 1982).

5. Martimort, *Les Diaconesses*, 249.

to affirm.[6] However, Cardinal Joseph Ratzinger, prefect of the Congregation for the Doctrine of the Faith (CDF) and ITC president, refused to promulgate the findings. Cardinal Ratzinger created a new subcommittee, named Rev. Henrique de Noronha Galvão (one of his former graduate students) as its chair, and promulgated a greatly expanded document. The document concludes that 1) men and women deacons did not perform exactly the same duties; 2) the diaconate is not the priesthood; 3) the matter of women deacons is something the ministry of discernment that the Lord has left his Church to decide.[7]

That is, the subcommittee did not say "no," it just did not say "yes."

The question of women deacons in the Catholic Churches then languished through two papacies. John Paul II, pope when the second ITC document appeared in 2002, did nothing before his death in 2005; Benedict XVI, who reigned until his resignation in 2013, also did nothing. However, in a footnote to his recent letter marking the fiftieth anniversary of the ITC, the retired pontiff stated that Eastern Catholic Churches were polled on the matter without result, apparently during his term at CDF.

Meanwhile, a few academics and other writers took up the discussion about Catholic women deacons from time to time. Both the Canon Law Society of America (in 1995) and the Catholic Theological Society of America (in 1997) considered women deacons.

My own work began to appear in 2000, assuming the proven history and focusing on questions related to sacramental theology

---

6. Mgr. Max Thurian chaired the subcommittee, which included the following members: H.E. Mgr. Christoph Schönborn OP, H.E. Mgr. Joseph Osei-Bonsu, Rev. Charles Acton, Mgr. Giuseppe Colombo, Mgr. Joseph Doré PSS, Prof. Gösta Hallonsten, Rev Father Stanislaw Nagy SCI, and Rev. Henrique de Noronha Galvão.

7. The second subcommittee was chaired by Rev. Henrique de Noronha Galvão and composed of Rev. Santiago del Cura Elena, Rev. Pierre Gaudette, Mgr. Roland Minnerath, Mgr. Gerhard Ludwig Müller, Mgr. Luis Antonio G. Tagle, and Rev. Ladislaus Vanyo, accessed July 27, 2022, https://www.vatican.va/roman_curia/congregations/cfaith/cti_documents/rc_con_cfaith_pro_05072004_diaconate_en.html.

and pastoral need. Subsequent writings arguing against the restoration of women to the ordained diaconate turned and continue to turn to Martimort, whose research was completed prior to 1982.

Synods and the International Union of Superiors General

The most intriguing entries into the recent discussion have come from official and semi-official quarters. At the October 2015 Synod of Bishops on the Family in Rome, Canadian Archbishop Paul-André Durocher presented a strong case on behalf of the dignity of women. Durocher presented strong proposals to the synod—first, that women be appointed to curial positions and, second, that the permanent diaconate be opened to women. Even so, resistance in Rome was deep. For example, the French-English Vatican spokesman did not mention Archbishop Durocher's comments on women deacons to the English-speaking media.

The question of women deacons languished in Rome until surfacing at the May 2016 meeting of the International Union of Superiors General (UISG), the worldwide membership organization for some 1500 women religious general superiors. In advance of their meeting, Pope Francis asked the organization's leadership to submit six questions. They included one about women deacons. Pointing out that women already served in diaconal ministries, the women religious asked, "What prevents the Church from including women among permanent deacons, as was the case in the primitive Church? Why not constitute an official commission to study the matter?" The Holy Father responded,

> It seems that the role of the deaconesses was to help in the baptism of women, with their immersion; for the sake of decorum they baptized them; and [they] also anointed the body of women, in baptism. And another curious fact: when there was a judgment on a marriage because a husband beat his wife and she went to the bishop to lay a complaint, deaconesses were responsible for inspecting the bruises left on the woman's body from her husband's blows, and for informing the bishop. . . . I would like to constitute an official

commission to study the question: I think it will be good for the Church to clarify this point; I agree, and I will speak [to the Congregation] in order to do something of this nature.[8]

Pope Francis's words were electrifying. He in essence agreed that women deacons had a place in sacramental ministry, that women were considered competent to testify, and that he would establish a commission.

As it happened, just a few weeks later, on August 2, 2016, Francis named twelve commission members, apparently chosen from among individuals nominated by CDF and the UISG. By late November 2016, the commission held the first of several meetings. The Pontifical Commission for the Study of the Diaconate of Women completed a document in June 2018, and eventually, CDF staff prepared and Cardinal Ladaria submitted documents to the pope.

In October 2018, the Synod of Bishops on Young People, Faith, and Vocational Discernment, also in Rome, produced a document that mentioned women thirty-one times, and included pointed commentary on the treatment of girls and women worldwide, using terms like "domination" and "discrimination." The final document noted that the synod participants called for greater recognition of women in society, the inclusion of women in ecclesial decision-making processes, and, specifically, as applied to women deacons, "the vocation to the permanent diaconate calls for greater attention, because the full potential of this resource has yet to be tapped" (para. 89).[9]

The Pontifical Commission for the Study of the Diaconate of Women

In May 2019, the Holy Father responded to the women religious' initial request, and gave what he termed a portion of the commission's work to the Sister-President of the UISG at their first Triennial

---

8. Pope Francis exchange at the UISG May 2016 meeting, accessed July 16, 2022, https://www.vatican.va/content/francesco/en/speeches/2016/may/documents/papa-francesco_20160512_uisg.html

9. "Final Document of the Synod of Bishops on Young People," http://secretariat.synod.va/content/synod2018/en/fede-discernimento-vocazione/final-document-of-the-synod-of-bishops-on-young-people--faith-an.html

Meeting since asking for the study. Pope Francis said he had more materials, which they could request.

Then, in October 2019, the Special Assembly of the Synod of Bishops on the Pan-Amazon region—the nine South American countries of the Amazon River Basin—met. The post-synodal apostolic exhortation from that synod is about to be promulgated, and the *Final Document* of the synod reported:

> In the many consultations carried out in the Amazon, the fundamental role of religious and lay women in the Church of the Amazon and its communities was recognized and emphasized, given the wealth of services they provide. In a large number of these consultations, the permanent diaconate for women was requested. This made it an important theme during the Synod. The Study Commission on the Diaconate of Women which Pope Francis created in 2016 has already arrived as a Commission at partial findings regarding the reality of the diaconate of women in the early centuries of the Church and its implications for today. We would therefore like to share our experiences and reflections with the Commission, and we await its results (para. 103).[10]

In his closing remarks to the Amazon Synod, Pope Francis said about the Pontifical Commission for the Study of the Diaconate of Women:

> I welcome the request to reconvene the Commission and perhaps expand it with new members in order to continue to study the permanent diaconate that existed in the early Church. You know [they] reached an agreement among [themselves], which however, is unclear.[11] I delivered this to the women religious, to the Union of [Superiors General] of Women Religious who asked me to conduct the research. I

---

10. "Final Document; Amazonia: New Paths for the Church and for an Internal Ecology," Amazon Synod, http://www.sinodoamazonico.va/content/sinodoamazonico/en/documents/final-document-of-the-amazon-synod.html.

11. The English on the Vatican website is less clear. " Words of His Holiness Pope Francis," delivered October 26, 2019, accessed July 16, 2022, http://www.vatican.va/content/francesco/en/speeches/2019/october/documents/papa-francesco_20191026_chiusura-sinodo.html

delivered it to them and now each of the theologians is seeking, is investigating. I will try to do it again with the Congregation for the Doctrine of the Faith and include new people in this Commission. I welcome the challenge that you have given me, "and that they may be heard." I accept the challenge [applause]. Some things emerged which should be reformed: the Church must always reform.¹²

There have been other indications that the commission will be recalled—it was mentioned at the synod's closing press briefing—but nothing official has been announced.

Reviewing the Argument

As individual research has continued, and as synods repeatedly ask for women to be restored to the ordained diaconate, a concerted effort has arisen to press two related points against women deacons.

First, current and former curial officials are known to have argued that the 1994 Apostolic Letter of John Paul II, *Ordinatio Sacerdotalis*, that outlaws women priests, applies as well to women deacons.

Second, the so-called "iconic argument" that states that a woman cannot image Christ, is given as the major reason women cannot be ordained as deacons.

As an example, most recently, Cardinal Robert Sarah, the 74-year-old Guinean prefect of the Congregation for Divine Worship and the Discipline of the Sacraments since November 2014,

---

12. "Discurso del Santo Padre Francisco": "Asumo el pedido de re-llamar a la comisión o quizas abrirla con nuevos miembros para seguir estudiando cómo existia en la Iglesia primitiva el diaconado permanente. Ustedes saben que llegaron a un acuerdo entre todos que no era claro. Yo entregué esto a las religiosas, a la Unión general de religiosas que fue la que me pidió hacer la investigación, se lo entregué, y ahora cada uno de los teólogos esta con su linea buscando, investigando en eso. Yo voy a procurar rehacer esto con la Congregación para la Doctrina de la Fe, y asumir nuevas personas en esta Comisión, y recojo el guante, que han puesto por alli: 'y que seamos escuchadas.' Recojo el guante [aplausos]. Aparecieron algunas cosas que hay que reformar: la Iglesia siempre tiene que ir reformándose." Delivered October 26, 2019, accessed July 16, 2022, https://www.vatican.va/content/francesco/es/speeches/2019/october/documents/papa-francesco_20191026_chiusura-sinodo.html

wrote connecting what he calls a "weakening of celibacy" with "questions about the possibility of women being ordained as priests or deacons." Sarah continues, "This question, nevertheless, was settled definitively by Saint John Paul II in the Apostolic Letter, Ordinatio Sacerdotalis."[13]

Early in his essay, Sarah writes of the "three-fold ministry" of deacons, priests, and bishops without accounting for the distinctive nature of each. Neither does he consider the medieval development of the *cursus honorum* (course of honor), which refused diaconal ordination to anyone not on the path to priesthood. Because women never entered the *cursus honorum* (tonsure, lector, porter, exorcist, acolyte, subdeacon, deacon, priest), the female diaconate died out in the West by the close of the twelfth century. But Sarah's argument, supported by a small chorus in Rome, supports a so-called "unicity of orders" that states that because women cannot be ordained as priests, they cannot be ordained as deacons.

Further, Sarah dismisses the documented histories of women deacons by stating (without support) that women "were not recipients of the sacrament of Holy Orders," that they were forbidden altar service, and that their "sole liturgical function in the region of Syria would have been to perform the pre-baptismal anointing of the entire body of women."[14] Sarah also asserts that "deaconesses were not ordained, but only blessed," citing one source.[15]

Sarah's overall perspective is that "cleverly orchestrated media campaigns are calling for the female diaconate" and he asks, "What is hidden behind these strange political demands?"[16]

---

13. Cardinal Robert Sarah, *From the Depths of Our Hearts*, trans. Michael J. Miller (San Francisco: Ignatius Press, 2020), 87–88; *Des Profondeur de nos coeurs* (Paris: Libraries Arthème Fayard, 2020). The book first appeared as co-authored by Benedict XVI, but his involvement beyond one of the book's essays has been denied.

14. Sarah, *From the Depths*, 92. It is interesting that he only cites Syria, although Pope Francis's cited examples come from that region as well.

15. Ibid., 94.

16. Ibid., 90.

Conclusions

Obviously, the requests for women deacons are not political requests. The fact that women deacons are historically documented, doctrinally possible, and pastorally necessary guides the positive discussion.

Proponents of the restoration of women to the ordained diaconate are perplexed by the resurgence of the argument that women cannot image Christ, the risen Lord, given that the whole church's constant teaching that all are made in the image and likeness of God. The reduction of the concept of ordained ministry to a naive physicalism is both embarrassing and wrong. It would seem that this effort to deny women their full humanity, combined with both the documented dismissal of women's intelligence and belief in superstitious blood taboos that evolved throughout Western history, are now relied upon to keep women away from the sacred. Yet the argument against women deacons is essentially an argument against women priests, even though the Catholic Church (officially at least) now understands the diaconate is not part of the priesthood. That is, the medieval Catholic practice of only ordaining as deacons men destined for priesthood has morphed into a reason not to ordain women deacons.

The Final Document of the Pan-Amazon Synod was the basis of the Post-Synodal Apostolic Exhortation, which may by now have been released. The doctrinal decision on the restoration of women to the ordained diaconate may still be recommended, but the church as a whole seems to want women to be recognized as full participants, and it does not want to wait any longer.

Editors' update: The Study Commission on the Diaconate of Women 2016 final report was inconclusive. On April 8, 2020, a new commission with all new members was appointed to again consider the ordination of women deacons.[17]

---

17. Hannah Brockhaus, "Pope Francis establishes new commision to study women deacons," accessed November 19, 2022, https://www.catholicnewsagency.com/news/44137/pope-francis-establishes-new-commission-to-study-women-deacons.

Chapter Fourteen

FEMALE DIACONAL SERVICE IN THE COPTIC ORTHODOX CHURCH: PAST AND PRESENT

Christine Chaillot

Introduction

In church history, deaconesses are mentioned in the New Testament and since the early church. The word "deaconess" comes from a Greek word, *diakonos* (διάκονος), for "deacon" meaning a servant or helper. The topic of deaconesses is currently under discussion in many churches. In some, a female diaconate has been recently organized, usually in a local and ad hoc manner. Nowadays, one can say that the most developed and active form of female diaconal service and the one with the largest number of women is best organized by the Coptic Orthodox Church with rules decided/organized by the Holy Synod, throughout Egypt and even abroad.

During an interview on Coptic deaconesses that I conducted in 1988 with the Patriarch Pope Shenuda (1971–2012), at that time head of the Coptic Orthodox Church in Egypt, His Holiness told me that the historic deaconesses who inspired the modern Coptic experience were Phoebe (Rom 16:1–2); Olympias, who worked with St. John Chrysostom; and Anastasia, who is named in the writings of St. Severus of Antioch. He also said that at that time (in 1988) there were more than 150 "consecrated women" (*mukarrasat* in

Arabic, singular *mukarrasa*) present in many dioceses.¹ In 2005, there were over 400, in 2013 about 500, and even more in 2019, but there are no exact statistics.² Deaconesses are to be found in most of the Egyptian dioceses. Whereas in some dioceses they are numerous; in others, there are only one or two as Bishop Dimitrios of Mallawi confirmed to me in 2013.³

In this article I shall concentrate on the question of female diaconal service in the Coptic Orthodox Church as it exists today, also including its history and organization. Let us note that in the Coptic Orthodox Church there are also a few male consecrated deacons, who do not marry and lead a dedicated life of service to the church similar to that of the deaconesses/sisters. This issue, however, falls outside the scope of this paper.⁴ Habib Girgis (1876–1951) is a well-known, unmarried deacon, who dedicated his whole life to the service of the Coptic Orthodox Church and organized the beginning of the Sunday school movement in his church.⁵

---

1. Interview with Pope Shenuda on February 20, 1988, in his residence in the Monastery of St. Bishoy, published in "Comment vit la femme copte aujourd'hui au sein de l'Eglise," *Le Monde Copte (LMC)* 16 (1989): 66–73, here at 70 and 69, henceforth cited as LMC 16.

2. Christine Chaillot, *The Coptic Orthodox Church* (Paris, 2005), 39. Interview with Metropolitan Pachomius in Damanhur in February 2013. In March 2019, some *mukarrasat*, whom I met in Egypt, told me that there were about 900 mukarrasat.

3. Interview with Bishop Dimitrios in February 2013. In that year there were twenty-six consecrated women in Mallawi.

4. Some deacons of the Coptic Orthodox Church have chosen to follow a similar consecrated life for serving the church at the spiritual and social levels. Some may become celibate priests in parishes. In 2004 there were at least thirty dedicated celibate deacons and priests in Egypt; Chaillot, *The Coptic Orthodox Church*, 39–40. This exists also in the diaspora, for example, in Los Angeles, California, where there is a house of male consecrated deacons, St. Paul's Brotherhood. This way of life began in the House of the Consecration (Bayt a-takris) opened by Fr. Matta al-Maskin in 1958. A majority became priests and monks. Those consecrated men who want to serve the church are called mukarrasin, cf. Ugo Zanetti, "La vita monastica nell'Egitto di oggi" in *Popoli, Religioni e Chiese lungo il corso del Nilo*, eds. C. Alzati and L. Vaccaro (Vatican City: Libreria Editrice Vaticana, 2015), 445, 447.

5. He was canonized in 2013. See Bishop Suriel, *Habib Girgis: Coptic Orthodox Educator and a Light in the Darkness* (Crestwood, NY: St. Vladimir's

CHAPTER FOURTEEN

Recent Historical Background[6]

During an interview on the topic of deaconesses and female diaconal service, Iris al Masri [Iris Habib Elmasry] (1904–1994),[7] a prominent Coptic historian, told me the following: under Pope Yousab (Joseph) II (1946–1956), there were already "deaconesses" (or rather some kind of women serving in the church) in 1953, but not officially. At the time of Pope Cyril VI (1959–1971), there were a few women living as consecrated women, also unofficially. For example, Fr. Salib Surial (d. 1994) of the Church of St. Mark in Giza (Cairo) seems to have had a house for women serving families and girls, who taught and held meetings of girls and young women.[8] They used to give a weekly report to the bishop, and were called "the eyes and ears of the bishop." In 1954 Fr. Bolos of the Church of St. George in Damanhur, Egypt, had a special room in the church courtyard for consecrated young women.[9]

In St. Mark's Cathedral in Cairo, then situated in Azbakeya (Klod Bey) near Ramses Railway Station, Pope Cyril supported a group of church women, whom he encouraged to serve and help the people. They used to meet once a week in St. Stephen's Church, ad-

---

Seminary Press, 2017).

6. As for the ancient history of the Coptic deaconesses, there currently exists no text to testify to it; see C. Chaillot, "Deaconesses in the Coptic Orthodox Church," *Ecclesia Orans,* 35/2 (2018): 307–25.

7. Interview with Iris al Masri on March 16, 1988. In 1932 Iris al Masri received her Bachelor of Arts, majoring in education from Maria Grey College, University of London. Between 1952 and 1954, she pursued her research at Dropsie College, Philadelphia. From 1955 to 1985 she continued to lecture in Coptic history at the Coptic Theological Seminary in Cairo and Alexandria and at the Institute of Coptic Studies. In 1979, she published her book, Women in the Church. See also Iris al Masri, *The Story of the Copts,* 10 vols. (Middle East Council of Churches, 1975).

8. There were then two women working with Fr. Bolos: Mother Zakia, a kind of "nun-in-the world," who served those with needs and Sister Aïda, who was responsible for girls in church meetings, home economy, needlework; she was married with five children and served the church all her life until she died.

9. Details about this period and these dates (1953 and 1954) need to be verified and recorded.

jacent to the cathedral. They lived in their own homes nearby.[10] This ecclesial service, offered to the church by women, was also followed in other places in Egypt. According to Iris al Masri: "The real work of deaconesses is not to chant but to take care of people: visiting families, reading the Bible and praying together." In 1956 Pope Cyril VI gave her a letter appointing her "general moderator/leader of the young women in the Coptic Church."[11]

Another type of female diaconal work in the Coptic Orthodox Church was that of the Daughters of Mary (Banat Maryam) in Beni Suef, which was begun in 1965 by the bishop of Beni Suef, Athanasios (1962–2000), who initiated the first women in 1970.[12] In fact, they called themselves "nuns" and had their own rules, recalling the Catholic way of active nuns,[13] which followed the model of female apostolic congregations in the Catholic Church.[14] In reality, their life, activities, and prayers were similar to those of

---

10. Interview with Iris al Masri on March 16, 1988. Iris al Masri also told me that Pope Cyril (the only pope to allow this) gave these women permission to clean the sanctuary (*haikal*), to wash all the priests' vestments as well as the altar coverings and the handkerchiefs used at the time of Coptic communion.

11. Interview with Iris al Masri. This was confirmed to me by email by her grandnephew Youhanna Elia (Cairo), who is now in charge of all her papers and documents.

12. Ugo Zanetti, "La vita monastica nell'Egitto di oggi" (see the section entitled "Altri tipi di vita religiosa femminile," 444–45); Pieternella Van Doorn-Harder, *Contemporary Coptic Nuns* (Columbia, SC: University of South Carolina Press, 1995).

13. Pope Shenuda also told me that deaconesses and "consecrated girls" in the Coptic Orthodox Church have the same functions as some active nuns in the Catholic Church. Certain Coptic Orthodox nuns may give help to needy people who come to their convents asking for it, *LMC* 16: 70.

14. In 2001 a Jesuit father living in Egypt, Jacques Masson, wrote that a new form of consecrated life for women was developing, with the foundation of the so-called "Banât Maryam," founded by the charismatic bishop of Beni Suef, Athanasios, on the model of the female apostolic congregations in the Catholic Church. Masson was also mentioning the "consecrated women" who lived in groups and dedicated themselves to the service of the church in the world. "They are gathered under the direction of a bishop, according to the eparchies. Their number does not cease to grow, although we are not able to determine precisely their number." Jacques Masson, "Les coptes entre tradition et modernité," *Proche-Orient Chrétien* 51 (2001): 127.

the Coptic consecrated women (*mukarrasat*). Since Bishop Athanasios' death in 2000, the new bishop Gabriel considers the newcomers as being like the other consecrated women (mukarrasat) of the Coptic Orthodox Church. The new *tasonis*[15] are blessed by a prayer as the other *tasonis* in Egypt; although not blessed as nuns, their lifestyle and prayers are similar.[16]

In a short article by Iris al Masri, translated into French as "Le service des diaconesses," she asks a question about deaconesses during a lecture by Pope Shenuda in London on January 28, 1979. His Holiness then answered that this question was in the mind of many people, but no decision could be taken about it by the Coptic Orthodox Church before a serious study was made. He outlined some relevant themes and asked her to write studies on this topic. She looked for some appropriate texts and prayers on deaconesses and gave them to Pope Shenuda.[17]

The First Sisters' House in Giza

Let us now turn to explaining how this female diaconia began in an organized way in Giza (Cairo). When I was preparing my book, *The Coptic Orthodox Church,* I went to the city and was told the following. The first group in Giza was *formally* set up in 1960 under the spiritual guidance of Fr. Salib Surial (d. 1994), the priest of the Church of St. Mark (in Giza), with two young women,[18] Fibi Ebeid

---

15. Coptic word meaning "sisters."
16. Interview with Sister Catherine in Cairo in February 2017. According to Sister Catherine, a mukarrasa of the community under Bishop Mousa and one of the organizers of the yearly meeting (organized by her group) for all the Coptic Orthodox mukarrasat/deaconesses in Egypt, the sisters of Beni Suef now come to these yearly conferences in al Agami Centre, 30 km west of Alexandria. Interview in Cairo with Fr. Polos Ramzi and a *taconi*, both from Beni Suef, March 24, 2019. In 2019 there still were some elderly nuns from the time of Bishop Athanasius in Beni Suef.
17. Iris al Masri, "Le service des diaconesses," *LMC* 8 (1979): 8–10. Iris al Masri told me that she searched in the British Library and other libraries for prayers and other texts about deaconesses. It would be useful to compile a bibliography of everything written by Iris al Masri on deaconesses/female diaconia. Nagla Hamdy Boutros (IFAO, Cairo) is preparing an article about Iris al Masri.
18. Fibi Ebeid who was then 26 years old.

and Jasmine;[19] they wanted to dedicate their whole life to God, not as enclosed monastics, but rather as serving people in the church in their daily life. In November 1959, together with Fr. Surial, they visited Pope Cyril, who gave them his blessing to lead such a life. They were consecrated on May 20, 1960 by the late metropolitan of Giza, Yoannes. In 2005, there were twenty-two sisters in Giza, and Sister Fibi was the superior.[20]

In February, 2017, when I revisited the sisters' house in Giza, Sister Fibi (Ebeid) had passed away (on November 23, 2010), and I met Sister Irini, one of the first deaconesses there who told me about Sister Fibi's life and gave me a booklet published in her memory, *The Wheat Seed*.[21] As her life is closely linked to the beginning of the history and organization of the modern work of the consecrated women in the Coptic Orthodox Church in Egypt, it is interesting to hear her story.

Sister Fibi Ebeid was born in 1934 in Asiut, where her father, Archdeacon Ebeid Mikhail, was well-known as a preacher, Bible teacher, and servant of the church. In 1947, Bishop Mikhail of Asiut chose their home to be a place for spiritual meetings with talks. It was at that time that Sister Ebeid began to think about how she might serve the church. After she finished high school, she went to study English literature in Cairo in 1953. At this time, she spoke about her call to serve the church to Fr. Salib Surial, her spiritual father, whom she met for the first time in 1953. Fr. Surial rented a flat in Giza for her and her friend Jasmine; they formed the first group (in Giza) in 1960. Both studied at Giza University in the faculty of literature and then taught English at school. They worked in the morning and served the church in the afternoon. Other young women joined them. In 1971, the then eight sisters all moved to a villa, 9 Ramzi Farag Street, opposite the Church of St. Demiana

---

19. The sisters in Giza cannot remember her family name.
20. Chaillot, *The Coptic Orthodox Church*, 38. Some of these servants of the church in Giza became nuns and some joined other groups, for example Mother Yuanna (d. 2000) became the head of the Convent of St. George in Old Cairo.
21. *The Wheat Seed*, published in 2010 by the Giza deaconesses' home in Cairo.

built in 1971. All followed a profession during the day and held their prayers and helped the sick and the poor in the evening. After 1981, they became full-time servants of the church.

After Bishop Yoannes died in 1963, his follower, Bishop Domatios (d. 2011), also followed the project; he suggested that Fr. Surial contact Bishop Antonios to establish some schedules and a way of life for the sisters. Before becoming patriarch in 1971, Bishop Antonios had been a 'general' bishop living in Cairo and responsible for Christian education at all levels since 1962. He became the spiritual father of this group of women in Giza from 1963 to 1971. The number of sisters in Giza grew with time. In 2005, there were twenty-two sisters; and in 2017, thirty sisters in the community working in Giza and related places.[22]

Similar stories may be told of other places in Egypt, concerning bishops who were spiritual fathers of other young women who also wished to serve in the church. One may name, for example, Metropolitan Pachomius in Damanhur (Delta), Bishop Bimen (d. 1986) in Mallawi, Bishop Tadros in Port Said, Bishop Yohannes (d. 1987) in Tanta (Delta), and Bishop Benjamin in Shibin al Kom (Delta). They had a great interest in service (*khidma* in Arabic) in the church. Some had been active servants in the church before being appointed as bishops. For example, the late Bishop Bimen of Mallawi, as a celibate deacon, had previously worked closely with women in his ten years as a church servant in Giza; he could very well understand their diaconal aspiration and help them to become organized when he became the bishop responsible for diaconical work in his own diocese.[23] As for Bishop Moussa (Moses), the administrator of the Bishopric for Youth Affairs with responsibility for all youth activities in

---

22. Interview with Sister Irini in Giza in February 2017. See also Chaillot, *The Coptic Orthodox Church*, 38.

23. Bishop Bimen was one of the most outstanding personalities in the Coptic Orthodox Church, a pioneer in the field of socio-economic development and the emancipation of women, trying to emancipate the women of the villages of his diocese and carve out a role for women in church service. He sent some of his consecrated women (mukarrasat) to study abroad in S.S. Hasan, *Christians versus Muslims in Modern Egypt* (New York: Oxford University Press, 2003), 155.

Egypt and abroad since 1980, was orginally trained as a lay Sunday school teacher in the Church of the Virgin in Faggala (Cairo), had studied medicine, and also served the church as a celibate deacon, helping for medical and spiritual care in rural areas, especially with youth with Bishop Athanasius in Beni Suef.[24] Today, a large group of sisters (mukarrasat), thirty-five in 2017, help him in his task.

At the time of Pope Cyril VI (1959–1971) only a few women lived as consecrated women, but they were not consecrated deaconesses. It was in 1981 under Pope Shenuda (1971–2012) that female diaconal work began to be organized at the official level. On Pentecost 1981, Pope Shenuda III consecrated a group of twenty-eight elderly women as "deaconesses" in the Cathedral of St. Mark in Cairo during the liturgy in the presence of many bishops. These women, most of them widows, had already served in the church and continued to do so as deaconesses. But it soon became obvious that their age hindered their ability to be active as most of them were fifty years of age or more. It was therefore decided to accept young women for this diaconal work. They performed the same service as the elderly deaconesses; they also received a blessing through a prayer. It was at this time that the name consecrated women (mukarrasat) began to be used officially.[25]

In 1985, Pope Shenuda gathered a group of bishops who had consecrated women under their supervision. They drafted a by-law for their regulations. In 1988, Pope Shenuda felt that the time had come for the consecrated women to become deaconesses gradually, advancing through several steps: consecrated woman (mukarrasa), sub-deaconess, and deaconess.

From an interview in Cairo in March 1988 with Sister Esther who was a mukarrasa under Bishop Bimen: Amba Bimen had tasted the fruit of social work when he was himself a celibate deacon. He prepared the congregations and the priests to accept the new order of deaconesses. He saw the necessity of helping and working for people in need and the necessity of doing it with love.

24. Chaillot, *The Coptic Orthodox Church*, 70–71.

25. During my interview in English with Pope Shenuda in Cairo in 1988, he called them "consecrated girls" which I render in this article as "consecrated women."

At the time of my interview on February 20, 1988, some proposals had already been drafted and were going to be discussed by the Holy Synod meeting at Pentecost 1988.[26] In the course of the following years, the Holy Synod continued to study and discuss the matter in order to establish certain rites and conditions pertaining to the order of consecration for the consecrated deaconess.[27]

The final texts, with a view to adjusting their status as well as their consecration vows and prayers, were printed in Arabic in a booklet published in September 2013 by the Bishopric of Youth in Cairo: "The Regulations for consecrated women approved by the Holy Synod with other matters concerning consecrated women. Ritual of Consecration of the consecrated woman—of the subdeaconess—of the deaconess" ("*Lâ'iha al-mukarrasât allatî aqarra-hâ al-majma' al-muqaddas ma'a bâqî shu'ûn al-mukarrasât. Taqs takrîs al-mukarrasa—musâ'idat al-shammâsa—al-shammâsa*"), with prefaces by Metropolitan Bishoy (d. 2018) and Bishop Moussa, the two bishops responsible for the section of the deaconesses at the level of the Holy Synod. From this booklet, one understands that the Holy Synod approved several texts on the rules and prayers—on May 25, 1991, for the status and consecration of the consecrated woman or mukarrasa, on June 5, 1993, on the sub-deaconess, and on June 6, 1998, about the deaconess.[28] These stipulations are recorded in the Book of Canons of the Holy Synod. Copts call them *tasoni* (my sister) in Coptic. I use the terminology from the aforecited booklet, supplemented with the informal term, tasoni/sister, in this article.

---

26. *LMC* 16: 66.

27. "The Sacrament of Priesthood," accessed February 27, 2021, http://www.copticchurch.net/topics/thecopticchurch/sacraments/7_priesthood.html.

28. See the booklet by Bishop Mettaous, *Deacons and Deaconesses* (St. Mina Monastery Press, 2005), 40–44. This is expanded on in Bishop Mettaous, *The Sacraments of Church,* no. 7, *Priesthood* with the section on "Deaconesses in Church" from 49, with the vow and prayer for the consecrated women and deaconesses, 53–70, accessed February 27, 2021, https://stnoufer.files.wordpress.com/2015/01/the-sacrament-of-church-priesthood-bishop-mettaous.pdf. See also the section "consecrated sisters" (sisters, consecration, becoming consecrated, life of service, misconceptions) on the official website of the Coptic Orthodox Diocese of the Southern United States, accessed February 27, 2021, https://suscopts.org/coptic-reader/.

CHAPTER FOURTEEN

Organization

1. Activities

In parishes and elsewhere, the sisters serve mostly among women and young girls; they may also serve male children and aged men. They are entrusted with educational Christian work among young girls and children in Sunday schools and with religious meetings in church with women of all ages. Some take care of orphans and the handicapped (physically and mentally). They supervise student hostels for girls, kindergartens and childcare centers, nursing homes, homes for aged women, retreat houses, and sometimes church administrative departments (such as the Bishopric for Youth). The sisters visit and help young girls and women at home, widows, the poor, the sick, and the elderly. They help Christian families in poor villages and run-down quarters. A few work for medical care, including in dentistry. Some are secretaries, selling spiritual books and other items in church bookstores (for example, in the Bishopric for Youth). A couple of deaconesses have studied theology and may teach this or other subjects.[29]

Their work is also adapted to the local context. For example, in 2013, in Samalut, where the bishop built a large hospital, of the thirteen sisters some were nurses and worked in the hospital; others worked with poor people in the villages, giving spiritual service and also some medical help; and yet others helped with the administrative work of the diocese. In Giza, the sisters serve the sick in the nearby hospital of St. Demiana, take care of a kindergarten and several orphanages in four places in Cairo, and look after women students in special hostels. Some sisters (eleven in 2013) work in the retreat house of Anafora, 75 kilometers from

---

29. In 2017 no sister was teaching English or theology in the Coptic Orthodox theological seminary or in the Institute of Coptic Studies in Cairo, but one (under Bishop Mousa) was professor of English at the American University in Cairo (AUC).

Cairo on the desert road to Alexandria, a place that is visited especially by many young Copts.[30]

The consecrated women can help in counseling services for spiritual care and guidance. Their work is social, educational, pastoral, but above all spiritual.[31] They assist the priest and bishop in this service. Their activities have diversified. The service of women by consecrated sisters is described on several websites of the Coptic Orthodox Church.[32]

2. Female Diaconal Service in the Diaspora

In countries outside Egypt, one also finds some consecrated women in the United States of America, Australia, and Africa. In the USA, sisters are found in the two dioceses of Los Angeles and of the Southern United States. In 2017, one sister was working under Bishop David at the St Mary Christian Center and Coptic Orthodox Church of Staten Island, New York. Since 2003, there have been two consecrated young women under Archbishop Serapion in Los Angeles. These women serve Sunday school children and youth and care for individuals; their service is mainly for women and children.[33] In 1993, the Diocese of the Southern United States became the first Coptic Orthodox diocese established in the United States, serving eleven southern states with its seat in Dallas (Texas) under Bishop Youssef. There have been consecrated sisters in the diocese since 2006, with six sisters living across the South as of 2018—two in Dallas, two in Orlando, one in Nashville, and one in Atlanta. They serve the women and female youth, working in a retreat center, caring for the sick, and providing counseling services.[34]

---

30. In 2013 two sisters were working in the house called Anamnesa to receive the groups and other visitors.

31. *LMC* 16: 68; Chaillot, *The Coptic Orthodox Church*, 39.

32. For example see the section "the service of consecrated sisters" on the website of the diocese of the Southern United States, accessed February 27, 2021, http://sisters.suscopts.org/life-of-service/

33. Metropolitan Serapion, email, July 8, 2016.

34. Bishop Youssef, email, April 28, 2018. On the website of the Coptic Orthodox Diocese of the Southern United States you can find one section

In Australia, there has been a House for Consecrated Sisters in Sydney since November 2002, with two sisters in 2018. It was the first mukarrasat/sisters' house to be established outside of Egypt.[35] In 2013, they moved into a campus built specifically for them in the parish of Archangel Michael and St. Bishoy in Mount Druitt, on the top floor of the Coptic school on site. Apart from their prayer life, they serve in Sunday school, Bible study, spiritual meetings, retreats for girls, and conferences. They also help newly arrived Coptic immigrants adjust to their new environment and make sure the needs of families struggling financially are being met.[36] The house has its own constitution/rules.[37] The sisters are under the direct responsibility of the Bishop of Sydney, Daniel, though the person who looks after the sisters' needs day to day is Fr. Botros Morkos, who is a priest in the parish.[38]

In Africa, under Bishop Antonios Marcos—from 1976–1998, bishop for African Services with seat in Nairobi and then since 1998 based in Johannesburg—two sisters were sent from Egypt. When I visited Kenya, I met the two sisters. Sister Esther studied medicine in Egypt and was then sent to England for further social studies by Bishop Bimen of Mallawi before her service in Kenya. A local convert, Sister Naomi of the Kamba tribe was then working in Kisumu near Lake Victoria with girls and women in the field of social and spiritual life and vocational training.[39]

---

dedicated to consecrated sisters (The St. Mary and St. Phoebe consecrated sisters), accessed February 27, 2021, http://sisters.suscopts.org/

35. Sister Mary Kamel, email, November 28, 2002.

36. Tasoni Mary is also the coordinator of a charity called Solace of the Lord that aims to get as many people as possible serving others with a focus both within the Coptic community and in the wider Australian community. As such, groups visit prisons and help disadvantaged indigenous and refugee children with their studies.

37. It was based on the constitution from St. Demiana's House in Damietta under Metropolitan Bishoy, but was adapted for Australian conditions.

38. Fr. Antonios Kaldas, email, November 27, 2017.

39. Interview with Pope Shenuda, *LMC* 16: 68. C. Chaillot, "Activités missionnaires de l'Eglise copte en Afrique," *LMC* 20 (1992): 99–103.

In 2017, under Bishop Boulos, Bishop of Mission Affairs for East Africa (with his seat in Nairobi), there were four consecrated sisters—two in Kenya, one in Tanzania, and one in Zambia doing service mainly with children and young women; they also helped with conferences and family meetings.[40] As of 2018, however, there were no sisters under Bishop Antonios Marcos in South Africa.[41]

3. Life Before the Consecration of the *Mukarrasat*

Before they are consecrated, the young women are asked to have some years of experience in practical work for the church. They should also be recommended as suitable for such diaconal work. In Egypt, there are two main places for their training, which lasts for three years—a house[42] next to the monastery of St. Demiana in Belkas founded by the late Metropolitan Bishoy of Damietta (Delta) and the house of the sisters under Bishop Mousa in Deir al Malak (Cairo). They may also be trained directly in the bishopric, where they wish to live and work. After their consecration, they are sent to the bishopric of their choice or to any bishopric in need of sisters.

There are several stages (as mentioned above),—a preparatory trial time as novice, then as consecrated sister (mukarrasa), then as sub-deaconess, and, lastly, as deaconess.[43] One must be over forty to become a deaconess. The time for passing from one stage to another is not systematic, with at least five years between the stages. In fact, most of the sisters remain consecrated women (mukarrasat) and only a few become deaconesses. Most of the candidates are young.[44]

---

40. Bishop Paul, email, November 27, 2017.

41. Bishop Antonios Marcos, email, May 1, 2018.

42. In March, 2019 I was told by a nun from St. Demiana's that about 130 young women were being trained to become consecrated sisters.

43. "Becoming Consecrated," St. Mary and St. Phoebe Consecrated Sisters, accessed February 27, 2021, http://sisters.suscopts.org/becoming-consecrated/.

44. Most of them are about 23–25 years old when they begin to live their vocation, according to Pope Shenuda in 1988, *LMC* 16: 69.

With regard to the educational background of the sisters, many have completed university studies in different fields such as medicine/dentistry, pharmacy, psychology, law, commerce, mathematics, engineering, agriculture, languages, psychology, and philosophy.[45]

4. The Consecration

The consecration (*takris*) is usually performed by the bishop in the diocese where the sister will serve. The prayer of consecration[46] with the vow takes place before the morning raising of the incense prayer, i.e., just before the beginning of the liturgy, outside the altar, in front of it. It is done without the laying on of hands as this practice is only for deacons and priests in the Coptic Orthodox Church. At the time of consecration, the young women are given new names and receive new garments (a special dress and a small veil for the head), which are blessed during the consecration and which they put on in the church after the prayer said by the bishop. The sister also reads a pledge of commitment. At the end of the liturgy the sisters receive communion together with other women.[47] After the consecration, they wear their habit every day with a cross on the chest and a small veil/scarf on their head.

5. The Vows

Consecrated women make four vows, the three vows like those of nuns (poverty, celibacy, and obedience) and a fourth vow of service (*khidma*).[48] A mukarrasa must be totally involved in the service for the church. She must be a virgin and her age should be more than twenty-five.[49] The sisters make a lifelong vow of celibacy and cannot marry after being consecrated. But elderly widows may be accepted

---

45. *LMC* 16: 69.

46. See the prayer for consecrated women (mukarrasa) in the appendix to this chapter.

47. *LMC* 16: 67. See the prayer in the appendix.

48. The St. Mary and St. Phoebe Consecrated Sisters, accessed February 27, 2021, http://sisters.suscopts.org/.

49. The regulations to become consecrated women approved by the Holy Synod (booklet published in 2013), 11.

as deaconesses if they are more than fifty years of age and widowed for at least five years.[50]

6. Daily Life

After the official revival of the order of deaconess in 1981 by Pope Shenouda III, the first deaconesses, in 1981, were permitted to live at home, rather than in a communal setting, but today the consecrated women live together in one place, in groups, in houses or flats set aside for them, with an organized life, and meals and prayers in common. In this way, they can share their daily experiences and have their own rules for community life and prayer. Rules are necessary to answer all questions/events in the life of the deaconesses/sisters.[51] Their timetable and prayer rules may slightly differ from one diocese to another and also according to their work.[52] For their livelihood, they receive whatever they need from the churches/parishes where they serve. They obey the priest or bishop with whom they work.[53] The sisters have fixed visits with their families on certain occasions and by permission. A sister may be transferred from one place to another one according to the decision of the bishop.

7. Prayer life

Apart from their daily prayers, the sisters have periodic retreats. For example, a sister might spend one week in a monastery. Other spiritual meetings are also organized for them. In church, during the liturgy, the sisters/mukarrasat keep discipline among female parishioners, for instance, organizing the women receiving communion by

---

50. If the widow has lost her husband for five years or more, and if she is less than fifty. *LMC* 16: interview at 68. Chaillot, *The Coptic Orthodox Church*, 39. See also "Service of Deaconesses in the Church," accessed May 9, 2019, http://www.copticchurch.net/topics/thecopticchurch/sacraments/7_priesthood.html; Chaillot, *Orthodox Outlook*, vol. 4, no. 3, 1990, 15.

51. Rules include questions/problems that may arise after the consecration of the consecrated women/deaconesses about any vow they have made. If the life of the sisters is well organized and well guarded by the bishop and clergy, this also reassures the parents about the safety of their daughters in a society, in Egypt, where women rarely live by themselves, *LMC* 16: 70.

52. Chaillot, *The Coptic Orthodox Church*, 79.

53. *LMC* 16: 69.

checking that each woman covers her head and holds a linen veil in her hand to be put in front of her mouth after receiving communion (as is the custom in the Coptic Orthodox Church).[54] The sisters also sing together with the other women.

At the time of the baptism and chrismation of adult women (although nowadays this practice rarely occurs), the sisters may help before and after baptism; but they do not assist the priest directly as this is the duty of the priesthood. In any case, the consecrated women/deaconess will not and cannot do any work of the priest in the liturgy and the sacramental life, or perform any function of the deacons and sub-deacons in serving at the altar.[55] No woman may enter the sanctuary.[56] Consecrated women/deaconesses are not regarded as clergy. They cannot read during the liturgy or even at public meetings, but only at special meetings for women.[57]

Conclusion

Coptic consecrated women function similarly to certain active nuns in the Catholic Church. But in the Coptic Orthodox Church, nuns are devoted only to the life of prayer and contemplation in the monasteries in solitude and apart from the world. For Copts, service (*khidma*) of the church is important. As Pope Shenuda underlined, the service of the Coptic consecrated women/deaconesses is a real dedicated life and a vivid experience. This experience of organizing a female diaconia in the Coptic Church is unique and successful. During my interview in 1988, Pope Shenuda told me that the service

---

54. "The Sacrament of Priesthood," accessed February 27, 2021.

55. Deaconesses/consecrated women have no part in the service of the altar; they do not serve at the altar or for the sacraments. During our interview, Pope Shenuda insisted on these points and the fact that the deaconess/consecrated woman cannot exercise any function of the priest, *LMC* 16: 68.

56. See "Supervising the cleaning of the church and organizing its furniture, except for the sanctuary," accessed February 27, 2021, http://www.copticchurch.net/topics/thecopticchurch/sacraments/7_priesthood.html under "Deaconesses in the Church."

57. *LMC* 16: 68. See also "Helping the priest during the Baptism of elderly adult women," accessed February 27, 2021, http://www.copticchurch.net/topics/thecopticchurch/sacraments/7_priesthood.html and "Helping the priest during the Baptism of adult women," http://sisters.suscopts.org/life-of-service/.

of mukarrasat/deaconesses was already well accepted and respected by the laity, who understand that it is needed. Many parishes were at that time asking him to have some consecrated women for their social projects. Currently, as the parishes need these women serving the church, and *at the same time* these young women want to devote themselves entirely to the service of the church, this proves to be a very fitting and fruitful combination. The deaconesses are assigned to services that are needed for the church today. Their work is recognized as an official work of the church.[58] They mediate between the women and the clergy. As teachers of the spiritual life, they can also play the role of spiritual mothers, a role that is highly important in the Coptic Orthodox tradition, which highlights spirituality and, as in all the Oriental Churches, emphasizes the attainment of holiness during one's life in this world.[59]

This modern female diaconal service in the Coptic Orthodox Church is worthy of a detailed and fully documented history. However, this requires that all the information given in this presentation be developed not only for Giza, but also for all the groups around Egypt, with correct names and dates. This information needs to be sought in Coptic publications, which are mostly in Arabic, and, furthermore, through recording interviews with witnesses before their generational knowledge is lost through the inevitable passage of time.

APPENDIX

The Prayer of Consecration for Consecrated Women

After the doxology for Matins (but before Matins itself), the woman coming forward to be consecrated reads the appropriate pledge, which is one of three forms of pledge. She stands before the sanctuary, contritely and with bowed head.

---

58. *LMC* 16: 70, 71.
59. Kyriaki Karidoyanes FitzGerald, *Women Deacons in the Orthodox Church: Called to Holiness and Ministry* (Brookline, MA: Holy Cross Orthodox Press, 1998), 185.

CHAPTER FOURTEEN

The Consecrated Woman's Pledge

I, the weak *N.*, who seek to be admitted to the way of consecration in the Coptic Orthodox Church, pledge myself before God's altar and before our father His Holiness Pope Tawadros II[60]/His Grace the Metropolitan or Bishop Father *N.*, to keep the commandments of the Bible, to adhere to the Coptic Orthodox beliefs, to go to confession and receive communion and to engage in the combat of the spiritual life. I also pledge myself to be faithful in responsibilities, to conduct myself well towards others and to obey the ecclesiastical authorities represented by His Holiness Pope Tawadros II/His Grace the Metropolitan or Bishop Father *N.*

And, as I receive the blessing of putting on the habit of . . . on this day, [date in AD and AM], I pledge that my continued wearing of this habit is conditional upon my keeping to the way of consecration until the end, by the grace of God.

I beseech you to pray for me. Accept my prostration. Grant me absolution and bless me, my master, Your Holiness the Pope and Your Grace the Metropolitan/ Bishop.

The Lord's Prayer follows and the Pope (if present) or Metropolitan/Bishop then recites the Prayer of Thanksgiving.

Then the Bishop recites over her the following prayers:

- O Lord wise in counsel, who created mankind in His image and likeness, male and female He created them in His image and likeness, granting them blessing; we ask You, O Lord, hear us and have mercy on us. (Response: *Lord, have mercy*).
- O Lord, You, who granted prophecy to Miriam, the sister of Moses and Aaron, to Deborah, Hulda and Anna, the daughter of Phanuel, and who granted Philip the Apostle to have virgin daughters who prophesied; we ask You, O Lord, hear us and have mercy on us (Response: *Lord, have mercy*).

---

60. Rarely referred to by the English form of his name, Theodore.

CHAPTER FOURTEEN

- O You who poured out the grace of Your Holy Spirit upon men and women alike, according them the gifts of the Spirit, we ask You, O Lord, hear us and have mercy on us (Response: *Lord, have mercy*).
- O Lord, You, who granted Mary Magdalene to be sent to announce Your Resurrection to Your holy apostles and granted Phoebe to be appointed a deaconess in Your holy Church, we ask You, O Lord, hear us and have mercy on us (Response: *Lord, have mercy*).
- As You granted in the past, O Lord, grant now in Your presence to *NN*, to share in Your service, and make us worthy to accomplish this service without incurring condemnation before You, and pour out the grace of your Holy Spirit upon them, through grace and compassion, we ask You, O Lord, hear us and have mercy on us (Response: *Lord, have mercy*).
- O Lord God, You who do not reject the women who offer themselves, in accordance with Your divine will, with a pure intention to accomplish Your service, but have granted that they should be called Your handmaids, grant the grace of the Holy Spirit to these Your handmaids, who desire to offer themselves to You that they may accomplish Your service; as You entrusted the grace of this service to Your handmaid Phoebe whom You had called to work in Your Church and who became a helper to Your servant the Apostle Paul, pour out on them Your holy gifts, through grace and compassion, we ask You, O Lord, hear us and have mercy on us (Response: *Lord, have mercy*).
- O Eternal Lord, Father of our Lord Jesus Christ, look now upon these Your handmaids, who have been called to the service of consecration, grant them the grace of the Holy Spirit. Purify them from every defilement of body and soul, that they may worthily accomplish the work which You have entrusted to them. Yours is the glory and worship together with Your only begotten Son and the Holy Spirit, to the ages of ages. Amen.
- O Lord God, Holy and Almighty, who sanctified women through the birth of Your only begotten Son of the holy Virgin Mary according to the flesh, we ask You, O Lord, hear us and have mercy on us (Response: *Lord, have mercy*).

- O You who gave the grace of the Holy Spirit not only to men but also to women, look down now, O Lord, on these Your handmaids, call them to Your service, send down, O Lord, on them the gift of Your Holy Spirit, preserve them in the Orthodox faith, that they may always accomplish Your service without blame, according to Your good pleasure. For to You are due all glory, honor and worship, Father, Son and Holy Spirit. We ask You, O Lord, hear us and have mercy on us (Response: *Lord, have mercy*).

- O Holy God, You who are most high and who look down upon the humble women, You who have chosen both weak and strong and honored the lowly, send down the grace of Your Holy Spirit on these Your handmaids. Affirm them in Your righteousness, so that when they follow your commandments and serve in the house of Your holiness, they may be honored vessels to glorify You. We ask You, O Lord, hear us and have mercy on us (Response: *Lord, have mercy*).

- Grant them, O Lord, strength to walk joyfully in the way of Your teachings which You have set forth as a precept for their service. Grant them, O Lord, the spirit of humility, strength, praise, endurance, and patience, so that, bearing Your yoke with joy and persevering in combat, they may earn crowns of service. We ask You, O Lord, hear us and have mercy on us (Response: *Lord, have mercy*).

- Yes, O Lord, You, who know our weakness, make Your handmaids perfect, so that they may carry out the service of women, visiting sick women and those absent from church, caring for women who are poor and needy, assisting adult women on the day of their baptism, instructing women catechumens, and keeping order among the women in church. Give them strength to edify and set a good example, sanctify them, enlighten them, give them wisdom. For You are blessed and glorified, O Father, Son and Holy Spirit. We ask You, O Lord, hear us and have mercy on us (Response: *Lord, have mercy*).

- Hear our prayers, O Lord, and send down on them blessing from the Holy Spirit, that they may accomplish Your service without occurring condemnation and offer an ideal of sanctified life. Bless them, O Lord, these women whom You have purchased with Your precious blood. We ask You, O Lord, hear us and have mercy on us (Response: *Lord, have mercy*). The deacon says: *We ask of the Lord.*

The bishop completes the prayer, saying:

- For the peace of the Holy, Catholic and Apostolic Church, we ask of the Lord (Response: *Lord, have mercy*)
- For the service of women in the Church, for the poor and sick women and for the women who are catechumens, we ask of the Lord (Response: *Lord, have mercy*)
- For those coming forward to the service of consecration, recommended by those who have put them forward, that the Lord may grant them grace and strength and bless their service, as He blessed the service of Phoebe of old, we ask of the Lord (Response: *Lord, have mercy*)

And finally, make us worthy to say with thanksgiving: Our Father, who art in Heaven . . .

After that the Bishop makes the sign of the cross over the women being consecrated three times, as is customary (without laying his hand on them), saying each time:

N. is consecrated in the Holy Coptic Orthodox Church of God, in the name of the Father, and the Son, and the Holy Spirit . . .

Then he blesses the habits set aside for the consecrated women, making the sign of the cross over them three times, before they are put them on.

The following exhortation is then read:

The Special Exhortation for the Consecrated Woman

You should know, blessed daughter, that the Lord has chosen you for service as a consecrated woman in the Holy Church. Observe the commandments, take care to be without blame, preserve the garment of consecration from shame. Fill your mouth with the praise of God, remain always in fullness of grace through participation in the Holy Mysteries. Walk in obedience to your Father the Bishop and those who guide you in the path of God. Remain faithful to the doctrine and to the service which has been entrusted to you by the Church. And may the Lord grant you strength through His Grace and count you among the Wise Virgins, the blessed brides of Christ.

The service ends in the customary manner ("Amen. Alleluia . . ."), followed by the "Our Father" and blessing. The consecrated women then attend the Divine Liturgy and receive the Holy Mysteries.[61]

---

61. Source: The Coptic Orthodox Patriarchate, *Lā'iḥat al-mukarrasāt allatī aqarrahā al-majmaʿ al-muqaddas maʿa bāqī shuʾūn al-mukarrasāt* [*Ordinance for consecrated women passed by the Holy Synod together with the other matters concerning consecrated women*], trans. Hilary Kilpatrick (Cairo: Maktabat usqufiyat al-shabāb, 2013), 28–36.

Chapter Fifteen

A NEARLY FORGOTTEN HISTORY: WOMEN DEACONS IN THE ARMENIAN CHURCH
Knarik O. Meneshian

Introduction

Before most Armenians converted to Christianity, "[they] were initially nature worshipers. They worshiped eagles, lions, the sun, and heaven. They called themselves *Arevortik* (Children of the Sun). The sun god was called AR (*Arev,* meaning sun in Armenian). Later nature worship was replaced with national gods, among them Vanatur, the supreme god of the Armenian pantheon" and later Zoroastrianism.[1] After Armenia accepted Christianity as the state religion in 301, magnificent things began to take place in the country. Churches were built, some over the ruins of pagan temples. Tatev Vank (Tatev Monastery), for example, was built atop a pagan ruin and Holy Etchmiadzin Cathedral over a Zoroastrian temple. Following the invention of the Armenian alphabet by Mesrob Mashtots in 405, the Bible was translated into Armenian, and the arts, scholarship, and literature flourished. Significant books were written, including Yeghishe's *The History of Vartanank*, Khorenatsi's *The History of Armenia*, and, later, Narekatsi's *The Book of Prayers*.

The scribe, Susan, copied Yeghishe's and Khorenatsi's books, and the scribe Goharine copied Narekatsi's book. *Sharagans* (hymns or

---

1. Knarik O. Meneshian, "The Remnants of Armenia's Paga Past," *The Armenian Weekly*, November 27, 2019.

psalms) were written, some by women, notably Sahagadoukht, a poetess and composer, who wrote some of the sharagans for the Armenian Apostolic Church (known simply as the Armenian Church) and taught men while she was seated behind a canopy. It is believed that some of the ancient pagan tunes were used to sing the hymns.

An Ordained Ministry

Women deacons or deaconesses, an ordained ministry, have served the Armenian Church for centuries. In the *Haykazian Dictionary*, based on evidence from the fifth-century Armenian translations, the word deaconess is defined as a "female worshiper or virgin servant active in the church and superior or head of a nunnery."[2] Other pertinent references to women deacons in the Armenian Church are included in the "Mastoc [Mashtots] Matenadaran [Mesrop Mashtots Institute of Ancient Manuscripts, or the Matendaran, in Yerevan, Armenia] collection [that] contains at least seven manuscripts from the period between the fall of the Cilicia [1375] and the end of the 16th century which contain the ordination rite for women deacons."[3]

The diaconate is one of the major orders (deacon, priest, bishop) in the Armenian Church. The word deacon means "to serve with humility" and "to assist." The Armenian deaconess historically has been called *sargavak* or deacon, deaconess sister, or deaconess nun and is sacramentally ordained: after the candidate is called, the bishop lays his hand upon the candidate in order to confirm the calling and then to confer the rank. The following words are spoken, "the Divine and Heavenly Grace . . . calls (name of candidate) to the Diaconate." The people confirm by saying in Armenian, "*Arjanee eh*. He/She is worthy."[4] The rights and privileges are the same for each gender:

---

2. *Haykazian Dictionary* (Yerevan, Armenia: Yerevan University Publication, 1979).

3. Roberta R. Ervine, "The Armenian Church's Women Deacons," *St. Nersess Theological Review* 12 (2007): 29, https://stnersess.edu/wp-content/uploads/2022/05/SNTR-XII.pdf.

4. Classical Armenian is genderless. Therefore, *Arjanee eh* refers to male or female, and the bishop ordains the candidate in the same service for both male and female. Description of sacrament and 930 date for oldest surviving manuscript from Rev. Dr. George Leylegian, Archdeacon in the Prelacy of the Arme-

CHAPTER FIFTEEN 253

both may read the holy gospel and perform the *veraberoom* (offertory). Although the diaconate is one of the major orders, the deacon is not anointed, a ritual reserved for priests and bishops. Little is known about women deacons in Armenia before the ninth century, but by the tenth they were being ordained. The oldest surviving manuscript of the ordination of a woman deacon in the Armenian tradition dates from the year 930.

The deaconesses, like the bishops and monks, are celibate. Their convents are usually described as *anabad*, meaning, in this case, not a desert as the Armenian word implies, but rather an isolated location where monastics live away from populated areas. Anabads differ from monasteries in their totally secluded lifestyle. In convents and monasteries, Armenian women serve as nuns, scribes, subdeacons, deacons, and archdeacons, not only giving of themselves, but also enriching and contributing much to the Armenian nation and church. In the seventeenth century, for example, the scribe and deaconess Hustianeh, wrote "a devotional collection of prayers and lives of the fathers . . . [and a manuscript titled] 'Book of Hours . . . dated to 1653."[5]

The following illustrates the length of time it took a candidate to become an ordained deaconess: the Deacon Hripsime Sasunian, born in Damascus, Syria, in 1928, entered the Kalfayan Sisterhood

---

nian Apostolic Church, in conversations with Knarik Meneshian. In an email dated September 26, 2021, he states, "Unfortunately, the complete text for the Ordination of a Deacon has never been fully translated into English." However, he cited two sources: "Sargavak Ordination Mashdots [Ritual], 1876," transcribed and edited by George Leylegian, and a book, "which contains only the prayers recited by the bishop during the service" by Frederick Cornwallis Conybeare, *Rituale Armenorum: Being the Administration of the Sacraments and the Breviary Rites of the Armenian Church together with the Greek Rites of Baptism and Epiphany*, (Oxford, 1905). The book includes *The East Syrian Epiphany Rites*, trans. A. J. Maclean, accessed October 1, 2021, https://archive.org/details/ConyRitualeArmenorum.

5. Ervine, "The Armenian Church's Women Deacons," 38.

Convent in Istanbul, Turkey, at the age of 25. At age 38, she was ordained sub-deacon, and at age 54, deacon in 1982.[6]

On the importance of the role of the deaconess in the church, Father Abel Oghlukian writes, "If the bishop represents God the Father and the priest Christ, then the deaconess, by her calling, symbolizes the presence of the Holy Spirit, in consequence of which one should accord her fitting respect."[7]

Armenian Deaconesses from the Fourth Through the Sixteenth Centuries

The development of the office of deaconess in the Armenian Church can be divided into four historical periods: 1.) Greater Armenia in the fourth to eighth centuries . . . 2.) Eastern and Cilician Armenia in the ninth to eleventh centuries. There the term deaconess is employed in the ritual texts (*mastoc*) of ordination. 3.) From the twelfth century there are literary references and rites for the ordination of deaconesses in liturgical texts, first in Cilicia and then eastern Armenia. 4.) The renewal of the female diaconate in the seventeenth century.[8]

Roberta Ervine's paper, "The Armenian Church's Women Deacons," includes many photos of deaconesses and the names, ordinations, various activities, and contributions to the church of twenty-three women deacons.[9]

Over the centuries, in some instances, the mission of the Armenian deaconesses was educating, caring for orphans and the elderly, assisting the indigent, comforting the bereaved, and ad-

---

6. For images, see figs. 4–7 in Ervine, "The Armenian Church's Women Deacons," 35.

7. Abel Oghlukian, *The Deaconess in the Armenian Church —A Brief Survey*, trans. S. Peter Cowe (New Rochelle, NY: St. Nersess Armenian Seminary Press, 1994), 6, accessed July 16, 2022, https://orthodoxdeaconess.org/wp-content/uploads/2020/07/FrAbel_The_Deaconess_in_the_Armenian_Church_1994.pdf.

8. Ibid., 12–13.

9. A list of the names of the women deacons can be found in Ervine, "The Armenian Church's Women Deacons," 18. For photos, see Ervine, 41–56.

dressing women's issues. They served in convents, cathedrals, and local parishes.

Though there were those who approved of women in the diaconate, certain church fathers did not, including the bishops, Boghos Taronatsi (1050?–1123) and Nerses Lambronatsi (1153–1198), whose great uncle was Nerses Shnorhali.[10] Instead, these hierarchs wanted to close the diaconate to women. Interestingly, when Lambronatsi "was around 37 years old (in 1190, just 8 years before his very early death), his mother Sahanduxt and his two sisters, Susan and Talita, entered the Lambron convent as founding members of that congregation."[11]

Mkhitar Gosh (1130–1213), however, who was a priest, public figure, scholar, thinker, and writer, "defended the practice of ordaining women to the diaconate," Ervine writes, also adding that, in his law book titled *On Clerical Orders and the Royal Family*, Gosh describes women deacons and their specific usefulness in the following words:

> There are also women ordained as deacons, called deaconesses, for the sake of preaching to women and reading the Gospel. This makes it unnecessary for a man to enter [the convent], or for [a nun] to leave it.
>
> When priests perform baptism [of mature women], the deaconesses approach the font to wash the women with the water of atonement behind the curtain.
>
> Their vestments are exactly like those of nuns, except that on their forehead they have a cross; their stole hangs from over the right shoulder.

---

10. Nerses Shnorhali was catholicos from 1166 to 1173. The name Shnorhali in Armenian means "filled with Grace." Nerses Shnorhali was a hymn composer, poet, writer, theologian, and saint in the Armenian Church. The Armenian Church has two catholicoi. They are the Supreme Patriarch and Catholicos of All Armenians (currently, His Holiness Karekin II (Holy See: Vagharshapat, Armenia), and the Catholicos of the Great House of Cilicia, (currently, His Holiness Aram I (Holy See: Antelias, Lebanon).

11. Ervine, "The Armenian Church's Women Deacons," 21, n.11.

Do not consider this new and unprecedented, as we learn it from the tradition of the holy apostles: for Paul says, "I entrust to you our sister Phoebe, who is a deacon of the church." [Rom 16:1].[12]

Smbat Sparabet (1208–1276) was the brother of King Hetoum and an important figure in Cilicia.[13] He was a diplomat, judge, military officer, translator (especially of legal codes), and writer. In his book, *Datastanagirk* [Law Book], he, like Gosh, also mentions women deacons, but places them "under the authority of priests, rather than of male deacons."[14]

In his book, *The History of the Province of Syunik*, the historian and bishop of Syunik, Stepanos Orbelian (1260?–1304), also wrote about women deacons. He, like Mkhitar Gosh and Smbat Sparabet, approved of women deacons and believed that it was a laudable institution. In her paper, Ervine explains that Stepanos "places the deaconess in the role [*sic*] of preacher and reader" and denotes her status "of office as a stole [*oorar*] on the right side." Later, the women deacons would wear the *oorar* on the left side, like the male deacons. She summarizes a passage from his book on Sisakan (Syunik): "The woman deacon served on the altar, as did her male counterpart—and the bishop did not limit her liturgical service to convent churches only—albeit she stood apart from male deacon(s), presumably for the avoidance of any perceived impropriety . . . she does not touch the sacred Elements."[15]

Armenian Deaconesses in the Modern Era: Seventeenth Century to Present Day

In the seventeenth century, a great reform movement, begun by Movses Tatevatsi (1578–1632) took place in Etchmiadzin. When

---

12. Ibid., 22–3.
13. In ancient Armenia, Sparabet was the hereditary title of the military commander-in-chief.
14. Ervine, "The Armenian Church's Women Deacons," 26.
15. Ervine, "The Armenian Church's Women Deacons," 27. Summary of Stepanos Orbelian's description of deaconesses who serve in nunneries in K. Sahnazareanc, ed., *History of the Province of Sisakan*, vol. 1 (Paris: 1860), 153.

Tatevatsi became catholicos (patriarch) in 1629, he "sparked a spiritual and cultural revival not only in the Armenian homeland, but also in communities as far away as Jerusalem."[16] He was a great believer in the education of women and encouraged them; as a result, the number of women deacons in the church increased.

Among the progressive and inspiring changes Tatevatsi made before his election to catholicos was the construction of a convent next to St. Hovhannes Church in Nor Julfa (New Julfa, Iran) in 1623. The convent complex, which included a church for monastic women, was called Nor Julfaee Sourp Kadareenyan Anabad [St. Catherine's Convent of New Julfa] after a fourth-century martyr named Saint Catherine and was dedicated to education. Sisters Uruksana, Taguhi, and Hripsime were the founding members of St. Catherine Convent,[17] which remained in existence for 331 years. The convent ran two schools and an orphanage and oversaw a factory.[18] In its early years, the convent had many sisters. Throughout the convent's history, some of the monastic women were ordained as deaconesses, while others "were satisfied with receiving the four minor clerical orders."[19]

By 1839, the number of women at St. Catherine had decreased to sixteen. The last abbess, Elisabet Israelian "had been ordained a deacon by Abp. Nerses Meligtangian, 'prelate of Atrpatakan.'"[20] Eventually, the number of monastic women at the convent decreased even further, and in 1954, the doors of St. Catherine were closed.[21]

Around this period, approximately a thousand miles north of New Julfa, in the city of Shushi in Artsakh (Nagorno Karabakh),

---

16. Ibid., 30.
17. Ervine, "The Armenian Church's Women Deacons," also cites them as founding members, but not deaconesses, 31.
18. Ervine, "The Armenian Church's Women Deacons," 31, 32.
19. Oghlukian, *The Deaconess in the Armenian Church*, 29–30.
20. Ervine, "The Armenian Church's Women Deacons," 32, n. 44 explains that the ordination information is from a biography about Archbishop Taddeos Begnazarian published in *Sion*, a periodical of the Armenian Patriarchate of Jerusalem.
21. For the opening and closing of St. Catherine Convent, see Oghlukian, *The Deaconess in the Armenian Church*, 29.

there was a small convent whose members never grew beyond five. In the village of Avedaranots, southeast of Shushi, there was another convent. In the northern part of Artsakh, in the Mardagerd region, there was once a monastery for monastic women in the village of Koosabad known as Koosanats Anabad [Convent of the Virgins]. Upon the ruins of the monastery a church was built.

The women's monastic community of Sourp Stepanos Vank [Convent of St. Stepanos Monastery] was established in Tiflis (Tiblisi), Georgia in 1725. The mission at St. Stepanos was the training of women deacons. As at St. Catherine's, many of the sisters at St. Stepanos were ordained deaconesses. "In 1933, the community comprised eighteen members, twelve of whom were ordained deacons."[22]

The *abaouhi* (abbess) of the convent was always an archdeaconess. She wore a ring on her finger and two crosses that hung down her chest. St. Stepanos's last abbess, Archdeaconess Hripsime Tahiriants (fig. 1), who was a woman of authority and influence, came from a prominent family.[23] During a trip to Jerusalem, she served at the altar of the Cathedral of Saint James in Jerusalem. The deaconesses of St. Stepanos were noted for their musical abilities and, as a result, they were frequently asked to perform at functions, including funerals. These engagements helped support their religious community. When women entered convents, they brought funds with them to help support themselves. If, however, someone came from an indigent family, then the abbess provided for her needs. Upon the death of a deaconess, whatever money remained after funeral expenses was kept by the convent. If, however, she had not yet attained the rank of deaconess, half of the money that the deceased monastic had brought with her to the convent was returned to the family after funeral expenses.[24]

It is interesting to note that the finely carved wooden doors of Holy Etchmiadzin are a gift from Archdeaconess Tahiriants. The inscription on the doors reads: *"Heeshadak Avak-Sarkavakoohi Hrip-*

---

22. Ervine, "The Armenian Church's Women Deacons," 33.
23. Note that the term 'Tayireane' is a variation of 'Tahiriants.'
24. Ervine, "The Armenian Church's Women Deacons," 33.

sime Aghek Tahiriants, 1889," which translates to "In Memory of Archdeaconess Hripsime Aghek Tahiriants, 1889."[25]

In 1892, Archdeaconess Tahiriants traveled to Etchmiadzin for the consecration of Khrimian Hayrik—a revered Armenian church leader, teacher, and publisher—to the rank of catholicos, and there she presented him with a gold and silver embroidered likeness of the Cathedral of Etchmiadzin. It was on this occasion that she gave H.F.B. Lynch, the author of *Armenia: Travels and Studies*, her photo, which the author used in his book, and is on the cover of Fr. Oghlukian's book as well as in Ervine's paper.[26]

Although St. Stepanos's women's community was not in existence in 1939, Nicolas Zernov (1898–1980), a Russian theology professor at Oxford, wrote then how impressed he had been in the St. Stepanos Armenian Church in Tiflis, "where a woman deacon fully vested brought forward the chalice for the communion of the people."[27] In 1988, the Georgian government took ownership of the fourteenth-century Armenian church. From 1990 through 1991, all Armenian inscriptions were either removed or destroyed, and burial vaults where the Armenian deaconesses were laid to rest were demolished. (Koosanats) Sourp Stepanos Vank is now a Georgian Orthodox church.[28]

The Kalfayan Sisterhood of Istanbul, responsible for the care and education of orphans, was established in 1866. Patriarch Mesrop Naroyan ordained the sisterhood's first member, Aghavni Keoseian, to the diaconate in 1932. See Figures 2 and 3 for photos of the ordi-

---

25. Holy Etchmiadzin Cathedral, located in Vagharshapat, Armenia, is the mother church of the Armenian Apostolic Church. Photos of the doors at Ervine, "The Armenian Church's Women Deacons," 45–46.

26. Ervine, "The Armenian Church's Women Deacons," 33–34, n. 49 and 50. H. F. B. Lynch, *Armenia—Travels and Studies, I, The Russian Provinces*, originally published in London: 1901, 252. Oghlukian, *The Deaconesses in the Armenian Church*, 30.

27. Yedvard Gulbekian, "Women in the Armenian Church," *Hye Sharzhoom* (April, 1982): 14, accessed June 17, 2022, https://hyesharzhoom.com/wp-content/uploads/2014/03/011-HS-Vol-04-No-3-April-1982.pdf.

28. For information and photos, see monograph by Levon Chooaszian, *Arshag Fetvajkian* (Yerevan: Printinfo, 2011).

nation of Deaconess Mother Mariam in 1955. Patriarch Snork Galustian ordained the last deaconess, Hripsime Sasunian, in 1982.[29]

Ervine writes that Deaconess Hripsime Sasunian "visited the Western Diocese of America in 1986, where she served the liturgy in a different parish of the diocese on each Sunday of her visit. At one time she had functioned as head of the Kalfayan Orphanage, and in the year of her American visit she was serving the Patriarchate as an accountant, in addition to serving the Sunday liturgy in various parishes in the capital."[30] See figures 4–7 for photos of Deaconess Sasunian serving at a liturgy. Patriarch Galustian used the canon for a male deacon on the occasion of the ordination of Deaconess Hripsime Sasunian.[31]

Deaconess Sasunian was invited to Lebanon in 1990 by His Holiness Catholicos Karekin II to found a new sisterhood. Called the Sisterhood of the Followers of St. Gayane, it was established next to the Bird's Nest Orphanage in Byblos, Lebanon. As a result, the monastic veil was awarded to the sisterhood's first candidate, Knarik Gaypakyan, in the Cathedral at Antelias in Lebanon, on June 2, 1991. At the present time, three women deacons serve the Bird's Nest Orphanage under the jurisdiction of the Catholicosate of the Great House of Cilicia.[32]

In a press release from the Armenian Prelacy of Azerbaijan (Aderbadagan), Iran, it was announced that on June 24, 2013, the Very

---

29. Ervine, "The Armenian Church's Women Deacons," 34–35.
30. Ibid., 35.
31. Ibid., 35, n. 58: Patriarch Galustian stated this in a letter to M.K. Arat in M.K. Arat, "The Deaconess in the Armenian Church," in *Voices of Armenian Women: Papers presented at the 1997 international conference of the Armenian International Women's Association*, eds. B. J. Merguerian and J. Renjilian-Burgy (Belmont, MA: Armenian International Women's Association, 2000), 179, n. 320.
32. Information from 2014 email exchanges between author and Father Krikor Chiftjian who had served from 2009 to 2011 as the "spiritual advisor and dean of the Gayanayant Sisterhood and the spiritual director of the Bird's Nest Orphanage." See also Knarik Meneshian, "Women Deacons in the Armenian Apostolic Church Revisited," *The Armenian Weekly*, April 13, 2014. https://armenianweekly.com/2014/04/13/women-deacons-in-the-armenian-apostolic-church-revisited/.

Reverend Father Krikor Chiftjian (now archbishop of the Armenian Prelacy of Azerbaijan, Iran), attended a meeting regarding church matters at the Catholicosate in Antelias. He also visited the Bird's Nest Orphanage and met with Sisters Knarik Gaypakian, Shnorhig Boyadjian, and Gayane Badakian to discuss how to attract more women to the sisterhood.[33]

Women's religious communities also existed in Astrakhan, Russia; Bursa, Turkey; and Jazlowiec, Poland. In Astrakhan, two deaconesses, sisters Hrpsime and Anna Mnatsaganyan, served the community. Two similarly inscribed diaconal stoles were donated by Anna in memory of her sister to the Cathedral of Etchmiadzin: "This stole is a memorial for the soul of Hripsime Mnacakanian, Deaconess nun at the Cathedral of the Holy Theotokos in Astrakhan, 1837."[34] In the 1800's, in Turkey's Bursa region, Deaconess Nazeni Geoziumian ran a school for girls, along with her religious duties.[35] In Jazlowiec Hripsime Spendowski was ordained deaconess. She was the daughter of Stepan Spendowski, an Armenian who had immigrated to Jazlowiec in 1648. The town had a sizeable Armenian population, and the Armenian Prelacy was established there in 1250. Because of Spendowski's heroism and distinguished military service fighting the Tatars and Turks, who had invaded the town, the King of Poland honored him with noble rank and bestowed upon him the title of "mayor for life" of Jazlowiec.[36]

In 2002, Archbishop Kisak Mouradian, Primate of Argentina performed a sacramental ordination of Maria Ozkul to the diaconate.[37] For the first time in history, on September 25, 2017, Ani-Kristi Manvelian, who was a lay person and not a nun or a member of a convent, was ordained parish deacon at St. Sarkis Mother Church (Prelacy Church), Tehran, Iran, by the Prelate Archbishop

---

33. Press release in "Ardaz Monthly," a monthly electronic newsletter from the Armenian Prelacy in Iran. Date not available.
34. Ervine, "The Armenian Church's Women Deacons," 37. Photos of stoles at 47–48.
35. Ibid., 37.
36. Ibid., 38.
37. Ibid., 39.

Sebouh Sarkissian under the jurisdiction of the Catholicosate of Cilicia, which is based in Antelias, Lebanon.[38] See Figures 8–9 for photos of ordination. Currently, there is a small number of nuns serving the Armenian Apostolic Church in Armenia. Established in the early part of the twenty-first century, their order is known as the Sourp Hripsimyants Order. They reside in Etchmiadzin at the *vanadoon* (monastery) at Sourp Hripsime Church built in 618 and now part of the UNESCO World Heritage List "Cathedral and Churches of Echmiatsin [Etchmiadzin]" for its historical and architectural significance.[39]

I conclude this paper with a quote from Armenian poet, Bishop Karekin Servantzdiantz (1840–1892): "Patriotism is a measureless and sublime virtue, and the real root of genuine goodness. It is a kind of virtue that prepares a man to become the most eager defender of the land, water, and traditions of the fatherland."[40]

The women deacons of the Armenian Apostolic Church, who through the centuries have reverently and humbly served their church and nation, are shining examples of the most eager defenders of the land, water, and traditions of the fatherland.

> Lord benevolent and compassionate, who made everything by the word of your command and who through the bodily incarnation of your only son rendered male and female equal through holiness.
>
> —Prayer for the ordination of a women deacon, the year 1216.[41]

---

38. Hratch Tchilingirian, "Historic Ordination: Tehran Prelacy of the Armenian Church Ordains Deaconess," *The Armenian Weekly*, January 16, 2018, 7, accessed October 1, 2021, https://armenianweekly.com/2018/01/16/historic-ordination-tehran-diocese-armenian-church-ordains-deaconess/.

39. The Holy Etchmiadzin Cathedral is near Sourp Hripsime Church and part of the same World Heritage List, https://whc.unesco.org/en/list/1011.

40. Karekin Servantzdiantz in *The Pillars of the Armenian Church*, comp. and ed. Dickran H. Boyajian (Watertown, MA: Baikar Press, 1962), 322.

41. Ervine, "The Armenian Church's Women Deacons," 25, n. 25.

CHAPTER FIFTEEN

The divine and heavenly Grace which always fills the needs of service in the apostolic church calls (name) out of the rank of Acolyte and into the rank of Deacon, into service in the holy church; according to the testimony of himself and of all of the people he is worthy.

—Prayer during the ordination of a deacon/deaconess.[42]

Photos used with permission of *St. Nersess Theological Review* and the Tehran Prelacy.

The author would like to express her appreciation to Archbishop Krikor Chiftjian, Prelate of the Armenian Prelacy of Azerbaijan (Aderbadagan), Iran, and Rev. Dr. George A. Leylegian for graciously responding to her inquiries regarding the ordination of women deacons in the Armenian Church and for providing material.

---

42. Prayer transcribed and edited by George A. Leylegian.

Archdeaconess Hripsime Tahiriants

Figure 1. Archdeaconess Hripsime Tahiriants of the Convent of St. Stepanos Monastery in Tiflis (Tiblisi), Georgia in 1892. Source: H.F.B Lynch, *Armenia: Travels and Studies*, vol. 1, 252, in Ervine, "The Armenian Church's Women Deacons," 44.

Ordination to the Diaconate of Mother Mariam

Figure 2. Ordination to the diaconate of Mother Mariam, Kalfayan Sisterhood Convent in Istanbul, Turkey, 1955. Source: Ervine, "The Armenian Church's Women Deacons," 50.

Figure 3. Ordination of Mother Mariam, Kalfayan Sisterhood Convent in Istanbul, Turkey, 1955. Source: Ervine, "The Armenian Church's Women Deacons," 51.

Deaconess Hripsime Sasunian Serving at Divine Liturgy

Figure 4. Deaconess Hripsime Sasunian serving at a Divine Liturgy, Kalfayan Sisterhood Convent, Istanbul, Turkey, 1984. Source: Ervine, "The Armenian Church's Women Deacons," 51.

Figures 5 and 6. Deaconess Hripsime Sasunian at the altar, Divine Liturgy, Kalfayan Sisterhood Convent, Istanbul, Turkey, 1984. Source: Ervine, "The Armenian Church's Women Deacons," 52.

Figure 7. Deaconess Hripsime Sasunian reading the Gospel, Divine Liturgy, Kalfayan Sisterhood Convent, Istanbul, Turkey, 1984. Source: Ervine, "The Armenian Church's Women Deacons," 53.

The Ordination of Deaconess Ani-Kristi Manvelian and Deacon Mayis Mateosian

Figures 8 and 9. The ordination of Deaconess Ani-Kristi Manvelian and Deacon Mayis Mateosian by the Prelate Archbishop Sebouh Sarkissianat St. Sarkis Mother Church, Tehran, Iran, September 25, 2017. Source: Iman Hamikhan, MEHR News Agency.

Chapter 16

THE DISTINCTIVE DIACONATE CASE IN THE ANGLICAN CHURCH: AN ORTHODOX APPROACH

Spyridoula-Eleni Mantziou

Introduction

To begin with, I would like to state that this topic was chosen before my emigration to the United Kingdom; and it resulted, while trying to find resources for my thesis, in my employment at the Church of England Diocese of Exeter, where I was given material and support for my work.

The Ordination of Deaconesses in the Anglican Communion

The order of deaconesses is distinct from the later ordination of women as priests and bishops into the Anglican Communion. This *sui generis* order, as characterized by the Lambeth Council in 1930 and differing from male deacons, is associated with the ancient order of deaconesses. This is why it should be examined separately from the other degrees of priesthood. The order of deaconesses was revived by Protestant Moravians, initially in Holland. From there, the Lutheran pastor, Theodore Fliedner, took the initiative; and a training institution for deaconesses was founded in Germany in 1836.[1]

---

1. A. N. Papathanasiou, *Γυναίκες στον δρόμο της ιεραποστολής: Η γυναίκα ως θύμα, ως ύποπτη, ως ευαγγελίστρια* [*Women in the Road to Mission. Woman as Victim, as Suspicious, as Evangelist*] (Athens: En Plo, 2019), 127.

The order of deaconesses began in England in 1861 with the establishment of St. Andrew's Deaconess Community. It was then that Elizabeth Catherine Ferard, after having visited the newly established movement of deaconesses in Germany, was influenced; and upon her return, she started living with two other women, who had the same ideas of following a common way of life dedicated to worship and service. The following year, Ferard became the first deaconess of the Church of England. Thus, the deaconess community began to expand and evolve.[2] At first, Ferard received an episcopal 'dedication' from the bishop of London; (the modern form of ordination followed later). Initially, there was some debate as to whether what was revived was an order of ministry or a religious community. At that time, it was women devoted to Christ's life, who, despite facing disbelief and the belittling title of "these ladies," showed bravery during difficult times, such as epidemics and cholera.[3] The concern was whether the order of deaconesses was related to the degree of deacons and what this female order's role would be. In 1920, the Lambeth Council decided that women would participate in councils on an equal level to men,[4] and that the order of the deaconesses would be formally and canonically revived and recognized by the entire Anglican Communion. In addition, the council decided that the order of the deacons belonged to the holy orders as well as the deaconesses who dedicate their lives to lifelong ministry.[5] Decision 48 from that council declared that "the order

---

2. J. Sister, "The Deaconess Community of St. Andrew," *The Journal of Ecclesiastical History* 12, no. 2 (1961): 215–30.

3. "Women and Holy Orders, Being the Report of a Commission appointed by the Archbishops of Canterbury and York, Chapter 8," accessed November 26, 2018, http://www.womenpriests.org/related/arch_08.asp.

4. "Resolution 46—The Position of Women in the Councils and Ministrations of," accessed November 26, 2018,

https://www.anglicancommunion.org/resources/document-library/lambeth-conference/1920/resolution-46-the-position-of-women-in-the-councils-and-ministrations-of?author=lambeth+conference&year=1920

5. "Resolution 47—The Position of Women in the Councils and Ministrations of," accessed November 26, 2018, https://www.anglicancommunion.org/resources/document-library/lambeth-conference/1920/resolution-47-the-position-of-women-in-the-councils-and-ministrations-of.aspx

of deaconesses is for women the one and only order of the ministry which has the stamp of apostolic approval."⁶ They also described the role of the deaconesses, distinguishing it from the male deacons. Part of the deaconesses' duties was to prepare candidates for baptism and to help during the administration of the rite of holy baptism. Other duties included standing by and praying for women who suffer difficulties and, on some occasions, with the approval of the bishop and the priest, reading morning and evening prayer and the litany (apart for the portions that are only for the priest) and "to lead in prayer and under the license of the bishop to instruct and exhort the congregation."⁷

In 1987, about 700 female deacons were ordained without the prospect, at least without the immediate prospect, of being ordained priests; this created the need to discuss a separate form of ministry involving men and women. In the 1990s, there were many social changes in the ecumenical theological movement, and within them emerged a new form of ministry in England involving men and women. Nowadays, following the ordination of women in all degrees of priesthood, there are no deaconesses in the Church of England, since they are ordained deacons.

The Ordination of Women in the Three Degrees of Priesthood

The decision of women's ordination in the Anglican Church was not taken overnight, and was not an easily accepted decision. Even today, the issue that the Anglican community has appointed women priests in all degrees of priesthood is still causing debate among the Anglicans and also difficulties in the Anglican community's relationship with the other Christian churches. The reasoning behind the

---

6. "Resolution 48—The Position of Women in the Councils and Ministrations of," accessed November 26, 2018, https://www.anglicancommunion.org/resources/document-library/lambeth-conference/1920/resolution-48-the-position-of-women-in-the-councils-and-ministrations-of.aspx

7. "Resolution 52—The Position of Women in the Councils and Ministrations of," accessed November 26, 2018, https://www.anglicancommunion.org/resources/document-library/lambeth-conference/1920/resolution-52-the-position-of-women-in-the-councils-and-ministrations-of.aspx

decision has many parameters and varies historically, depending on the era and the degree of priesthood. Generally speaking, the issue began for practical reasons because of the wars in the twentieth century and the lack of men (as they were taking part on the battlefields), which caused an issue in the congregation and in performing the sacraments. This gap was filled by the first female priest, Tim-Oi, in 1944 in Hong-Kong; in this particular case, the theological evidence behind that specific ordination remains unidentified. It was probably a solution of necessity, but it launched developments in the following years. Women bishops, after a long debate, started being appointed in 2015.

Practical Issues Caused by Women's Ordination

The Anglican Church is made up of various groups that function as part of one main body, but also individually, and deal with various theological issues in different ways. Some groups are considered more conservative, some more progressive.

The General Synod needed to find a way for women-bishops to fulfill their duties and at the same time respect the position of dissenters. A practical solution was the introduction of provincial episcopal visitors, popularly known as "flying bishops." Parishes that did not accept female priests receive the pastoral oversight of these flying bishops, who have jurisdiction over specific parishes, rather than geographical areas.[8] This system is called Alternative Episcopal Oversight (AEO), and there has been opposition to it. In 2011, Women and the Church (WATCH) reacted to the Archbishop of Canterbury's appointment of two flying bishops to meet the needs of parishes that did not accept female priests, claiming that this downgraded the validity of women priests and described it as "deeply disappointing."[9]

---

8. "Flying bishops › The Glossary: Church of England Companion," accessed March 24, 2019, https://www.churchofenglandglossary.co.uk/dictionary/definition/flying_bishops.

9. R. Butt religious affairs correspondent, "Archbishop of Canterbury Appoints Flying Bishops," *The Guardian* 5 May 2011, World News, ac-

It is worth noting that the House of Lords includes twenty-six bishops. The archbishops of Canterbury and York and the bishops of London, Durham, and Winchester traditionally have a place. When there is a vacancy, it is filled by the senior diocesan bishop without a seat; and the vacated seat is placed at the foot of the list of those awaiting seats. Following the recent Lord's Spiritual (Women) Act 2015, whenever a vacancy arises during the ten years following the act, the position must be filled by a female bishop, if one is eligible.[10]

The Distinctive Diaconate Case

The Church of England realized the need to support the diaconate and initiated a separate diaconate with permanent deacons with no prospect of becoming priests: the distinctive deacons. There are two types of deacons in the Church of England. The first kind become priests after their training, and the second remain deacons. The latter are also called vocational deacons, who may also have secular professions. The report to the General Synod of the Church of England in 2001 entitled "For Such a Time as This: A Renewed Diaconate in the Church of England" was intended to strengthen the ministry of deacons in the Church of England. The report's authors justified their initiative by suggesting that the diaconate, as it was, needed to be taken more seriously in the Church of England and not taken for granted or to be considered a transitional stage.

This report was conducted by the "Membership of the Renewed Diaconate Working Party" committee, which was set up by the General Synod in November 1988 and chaired by Barry Rogerson, Bishop of Bristol.[11] The basic argument in their attempt to initiate

---

cessed March 24, 2019, https://www.theguardian.com/world/2011/may/05/archbishop-canterbury-flying-bishops.

10. "Bishops in the House of Lords," accessed September 21, 2019, https://www.crockford.org.uk/bishops-in-the-house-of-lords.

11. Church of England Renewed Diaconate Working Party, *For Such a Time as This: A Renewed Diaconate in the Church of England: A Report to the General Synod of the Church of England of a Working Party of the House of Bishops* (Church House Publishing, 2013), vii.

changes in the ministry of the deacons was that the diaconate is the foundation of all Christian ministries, and as such should be rejuvenated in the life of the church. The working party was convinced that "the diaconate can be rediscovered as a distinctive, permanent ministry for some ordained ministers."[12] Nevertheless, the report failed to make clear what role these new distinctive deacons would have; and some argued that, for example, the reader's role would be undermined.

A second report was conducted by the Diocese of Salisbury in 2003 that clarified these points. It distinguishes between *caritas* (charity work), which can be freely and voluntarily carried out from lay people, and *diakonia*, which is part of the role of the ordained diaconate and is ecclesiological. In their arguments, they cite Christos Yannaras, who states that the deacon's "chief role is to provide and care for those in need. They have need of a separate ordination in order to carry out this work, need of a distinct spiritual gift by the lifegiving intervention of the Holy Spirit because in the church caring activity is a manifestation of truth and the actualization of life, not altruism and utilitarian love for one another."[13]

The distinctive deacons differ from deacons intended to become priests, as they have a different calling and do not have the same training. They are self-supporting ministers, who may have secular jobs, and are considered community-minded ministers, who serve the church by being 'out and about,' building relationships, and identifying the needs of the congregation. Distinctive deacons serve under the bishop's authority and, alongside the parish priest, have a recognized role in church services, reflecting the hallmarks of their ministry, such as reading the Gospel, encouraging prayer and sending the congregation out at the end of the service. The Right Reverend Nick McKinnel, Bishop of Plymouth, comments on the importance of distinctive deacons in the

---

12. Ibid., 1.

13. Diocese of Salisbury, *The Distinctive Diaconate: A Report to the Board of Ministry, the Diocese of Salisbury* (Salisbury: Sarum College Press, 2003). Cf. C. Yannaras, *Elements of Faith: An Introduction to Orthodox Theology* (Edinburgh: T & T Clark, 1991), 138–39.

Church of England: "Distinctive deacons add to the richness of ministry in the Diocese by their concern for those on the margins of Church and Society, and in reminding us of the One who came not to be served, but to serve and to give His life as a ransom for many."[14]

Possibility of Reviving the Order of Deaconesses and Reflections

The issue of the revival of the order of deaconesses is not something new; it has been a discussion topic for many years. University of Athens Professor Evangelos Theodorou's work played an important role in these discussions among the Orthodox with his book, *Heroines of Love: Deaconesses through the Ages*, and his efforts for the revival of the deaconesses. Thus, some theologians, taking all these into account, expressed their reservations about the revival of the order of deaconesses, but also expressed the view that there is no longer any reason for its revival.

The main argument against the ordination of women was Tradition, but in this argument many modern theologians raise the question of the dynamic rather than the static nature of Tradition as well as the change of the social situation from the time of Apostle Paul and the fathers. For Eleni Kasselouri, Tradition is important, but she gives two important parameters to be taken into account: first that church fathers have always been open to dialogue, and second that respect for Tradition does not mean "mechanistic transfer of shapes or structures of the past to the present," but adaptation to it.[15] Valerie Karras suggests that the Orthodox Church distinguishes traditions, like practices that have been adopted in a particular time

---

14. "Exploring the Ordained Ministry of Deacon," Diocese of Exeter, accessed January 5, 2020, https://exeter.anglican.org/ministry/vocations/diocesan-deacons/.

15. Eleni Kasselouri, "Η Γυναίκα στην Ορθόδοξη Παράδοση και Λατρεία. Προβληματισμοί στο πλαίσιο των σύγχρονων θεολογικών αναζητήσεων για τον παράγοντα «φύλο»" ["Woman in Orthodox Tradition and Worship"], in *Φύλο και Θρησκεία: Η θέση της γυναίκας στην Εκκλησία* [*Gender and Religion: The Place of Women in the Church*], eds. P. Kalaitzidis and N. Dodos (Indiktos: Athens 2004), 337–52.

to cover practical needs, and Tradition, the theology and spirituality of the Orthodox Church, which remains unchanged over time and is not affected by space or time.[16] For others, however, the issue remains unacceptable, since revival of the order of deaconesses is considered an attempt to infiltrate a social issue into the ecclesiastical class rather than a theological concern.

Any reservations about the order's revival have to do with using it as a means of women entering the priesthood, but what is needed in Orthodox Christianity is to revise the degree of deacons in general. Kyriaki Fitzgerald in *The Deacon's Ministry* indicates that the ministry is on the verge of revival in the Orthodox Church, and expresses the belief that Orthodox theology provides the foundation for this. The new form of ministry is to be expressed locally, must be based on Tradition, and must depend on the response of the local churches to the varied needs of their priests. The future development of the ministry seems to be at a crossroads today.[17]

Father John Chryssavgis comments that "the diaconate resembles a kind of sub-priesthood" and is not considered a permanent office but the first step towards progressing to other degrees of priesthood. This can be overcome by elevating deacons and by separating the role of the deacon from the first stage of simply being promoted to the higher degrees of priesthood. He suggests that "matters of pastoral care, practical administration, financial concern and even theological education can be delegated to deacons' and men and women, deacons and deaconesses can offer their service."[18]

---

16. Valerie Karras, "Orthodox Theologies of Women and Ordained Ministry," *Thinking through Faith: New Perspectives from Orthodox Christian Scholars*, eds. Aristotle Papanikolaou and Elizabeth H. Prodromou, The Zacchaeus Venture Series, vol. 1 (Crestwood, NY: SVS Press, 2008), 119.

17. Kyriaki Karidoyanes Fitzgerald, in *The Deacon's Ministry*, ed. Christine Hall (Leominster, UK: Gracewing, 2001), 147–57.

18. John Chryssavgis, "'In the Service of Christ' Reflections on the Diaconate in the Orthodox Church," in *Deaconesses, the Ordination of Women and Orthodox Theology*, eds. P. Vassiliadis, N. Papageorgiou, and H. Kasselouri (Newcastle upon Tyne, UK: Cambridge Scholars Publishing, 2017), 62–64.

My question is: is it possible to support the first order of ordained ministry in the Orthodox Church by adding a branch like the distinctive diaconate, adjusted to the Orthodox Tradition and including women to serve as well as men? This will allow women to commit themselves to lifelong serving as deacons without moving forward to becoming priests.

V

SPIRITUAL PERSPECTIVES

Chapter Seventeen

THE INSTITUTION OF DEACONESSES IN THE LIGHT OF THE MODERN MISSION OF THE ORTHODOX CHURCH

Evi Voulgaraki-Pissina

Introduction

Before delving into the important subject of the deaconess in an African context, I think it necessary to note that the following piece is not only based in academic study, but also in firsthand experience working in the mission field. This article thus presents strongly held understandings on the subject based on my extensive personal knowledge of the dire situation in Africa. Therefore, I hope the reader will indulge my candid and colloquial tone, which is an integral part of illustrating the writings of conscience that my statements represent.

Theology within the African Context

Developments in African theology move quickly on the ecumenical level. Among important trends within the broader frame of what one could call African theologies of liberation, such as the black theology of South Africa or African theology of reconstruction,[1]

---

1. Julius Mutugi Gathogo, "A Survey on an African Theology of Reconstruction (ATOR)," *Swedish Missiological Themes* 95, 2 (2007): 123–48. J.N.K. Mugambi, *From Liberation to Reconstruction: African Christian theology after the Cold War* (Nairobi: East African Educational Publishers, 1995). For a broader view of African theology today, cf. Dr. Humphrey Mwangi Waweru, "African Theol-

African women's theology is an integral and vital part.² Women, such as Mercy Amba Oduyoye,³ have marked African theology with their thought and settings of priorities, priorities that are down to earth but still do include vision or theoretical and contemplative quality. The impact of this theological production out of Africa has been small, and has hardly reached any of the Orthodox, who are traditionally preoccupied with their Byzantine or Russian heritage and their need to engage with the West. However, beyond the issue of perception there is a deeper issue concerning the production of genuine Orthodox theology by native African theologians. Among the few scholarly works that contribute significantly to the self-awareness of the African Orthodox, there is not one African Orthodox woman to my knowledge. This is partly due to the fact that church-based education is tightly linked with the need to equip future priests. A gender imbalance in higher education is thus a striking by-product of the church's policies.

Without wishing to become technocratic, one can say that both the quality and quantity of theological output are indicators of the vitality and well-being of a church. The vitality of a church is the vitality of its theology. This would also apply to Orthodox churches beyond Europe, the Western world, and the traditionally Orthodox areas of the Middle East. The new local churches that have emerged

---

ogy in the 21st Century: Mapping Out Critical Priorities," *European Scientific Journal* 14, 8 (March 2018): 213–26, accessed July 19, 2022, Doi: 10.19044/esj.2018.v14n8p213, in which he introduces his idea of African Christian theology of responsibility.

2. Tinyiko Sam Maluleke, Professor in Pretoria, a highly influential author, found that "African women's theology has been by far the most prolific and challenging in the past decade and half": "The Rediscovery of the Agency of Africans: An Emerging Paradigm of Post-Cold war and Post-apartheid Black and African Theology," *Journal of Theology for Southern Africa* 108 (November 2000): 19–37, 19.

3. Mercy Amba Oduyoye was leading a group of women theologians since 1989 and emphasised the diversity of people's experiences. Among her books are: *Hearing and Knowing: Theological Reflections on Christianity in Africa* (Maryknoll, NY: Orbis Books,1986); *African Women's Theologies, Spirituality, and Healing: Theological Perspectives from the Circle of Concerned African Women Theologians* (New York: Paulist Press, 2019) and *Introducing African Women's Theology, Introductions in Feminist Theology* (Sheffield, UK: Academic Press, 2001).

(mainly) in Africa, sometimes called, in a contested usage, 'missionary churches' will herein be discussed. One will find very little theory produced by Orthodox Africans and literally nothing by Orthodox African women. On the contrary, there is a lot of talk *about* them. Most of it is colored by paternalism and is addressed to an audience far away with a view towards fundraising. The African voice as to what women indeed need and want and what they consider liberating is largely missing. Theology here is not at its best, and one should not forget that theology is liberation in all things, as God is ultimate freedom and infinite love.

Discussions about enculturation, adaptation, incarnation, and other favorite topics in the field of mission remain an empty letter, degraded to minimal folk customs. Only a native sense of self-consciousness can adequately address these issues. A consciousness of the reality of the church at the local level in connection with the ecumenical and the universal, a living theological tradition, remains to be developed.

These introductory remarks are tightly linked with the issue of deaconesses and the broader issue of the presence of women in the ecclesial life of the Orthodox churches in Africa. I find that the range, variety, and quantity of theological writing by women among heterodox Christians is a high indicator of the vitality of their own ecclesial life, regardless of the fact that one might be critical of the content. In the Orthodox Church there seems to be a great reserve towards lay people with a variety of talents and gifts. Far from valuing lay talent, there seems to be a love for wielding authority, disconnected from a spirit of service, and a highly controlling hierarchical mentality. To be narrow-minded is sometimes a resolution of convenience, but at the end of the day it will not bear fruit. These are burning issues in relation to the Orthodox churches in Africa, but they are certainly no less dramatic for the old churches in countries that provide missionary support.

The Nature and Identity of Orthodox Mission

In mission, missionaries not only convey the message verbally; but, by example, convey the totality of our being. This is what Christian witness is all about. It is therefore important that a reasonable critical reflection constantly evaluates action and practice, with the aim of continuous improvement and self-correction. We need to repeatedly ask ourselves the following: is it probable that by example we convey not only the authenticity of tradition, but also practices that have become sedimentary in the body of the church and theology? Does our speech unintentionally become a language of fall, subjugation, transmission of passions, and decay, instead of opening up to resurrection and liberation from evil and death?

All human passions and practices that falsify the integrity of church tradition, are magnified in the relentless light of Africa, as they are carried unfiltered and invested with the authority of someone from outside, the missionary, who is sometimes perceived as sponsor and arbiter of faith and truth. All this can contribute to an extreme dependence on the outside world, instead of supporting the spiritual growth of the local church.

The presence of Orthodoxy in Africa was strongly associated with the anti-colonial struggle.[4] This historical conjuncture, in harmony with Christian theology and tradition, is a matter of true pride—as long as it does not translate into complacency.

Unfortunately, it can be observed and noted as a tragic irony that there is a contemporary tendency to repeat former mistakes in the field of mission that others—heterodox Christians—have made in times past and with the direct influence and manipulation of their

---

4. Elekiah Andago Kihali, *Challenges Facing the Orthodox Church Movements in East Africa: A Historical and Canonical Survey* (Sheridan, WY: Eastern Light Publishing, 2019). Idem., *The Orthodox Christian Witness in East Africa: Historical, Ecclesiological and Theological Approach* (Sheridan, WY: Eastern Light Publishing, 2020). John Ngige Njoroge, "Χριστιανική Μαρτυρία και Ορθόδοξη Πνευματικότητα στην Αφρική: Η Δυναμική της Ορθόδοξης Πνευματικότητας ως Ιεραποστολικό "Παράδειγμα" της Ορθόδοξης Μαρτυρίας στην Κένυα ["Christian Witness and Orthodox Spirituality in Africa: The Dynamics of Orthodox Spirituality as a Missiological "Paradigm" of Orthodox Witness in Kenya"] (Doctoral Dissertation), (Thessaloniki, CEMES publications, 2011). Joseph William Black, "Offended Christians, Anti-Mission Churches and Colonial Politics: One Man's Story of the Messy Birth of the African Orthodox Church in Kenya," *Journal of Religion in Africa* 43 (2013): 261–96. Evi Voulgaraki-Pissina, "Orthodoxy in East Africa beyond Decolonisation," in *Salt: Crossroads for Religion and Culture* (forthcoming).

countries of origin. We do this, without pressure or need, as if we have nothing to learn from the experience or even the mistakes of others. At the same time, we hide the actual reality behind loud declarations of our presumed infallibility as Orthodox. Orthodoxy, however, may express the fullness of the truth in a theological understanding of the church, especially as regards its inseparable relationship with Jesus Christ, but this on its own is not sufficient to prevent the failures that we, as fallible members of the body of Christ commit daily, individually, or collectively.

"All Inclusive" Orthodoxy in the Countries of the Mission

Those who embark on the journey of believing and belonging to the Orthodox Church in Africa, converted, catechised, newly baptized, or older faithful (even of a second or third generation) have no room for exploration, leisure, initiative, or contemplation. It looks like an "all-inclusive" travel package, as if all people have to rush together from one scheduled stop to the next. This situation is associated with a particularly strong sense of ownership on the part of the missionaries, who do not seem to bestow on newcomers full and equal rights; it is as if they grant converts only a conditional leasehold, while maintaining the freehold for themselves.

The bearers of the missionary message are not the bishops exclusively or some priests within the limits of their own parishes. Different kinds of associations, companies, or even individuals step in, operating on their own initiative and often in highly individualistic ways, opposed to ecclesial and communal feeling. The level of passion, energy, and emotional charge of such players is inversely proportional to their level of knowledge. The unawareness of their own ignorance breeds unforgivable arrogance and a tendency to determine things on the basis of biased preconceptions, often combined with a pietistic, puritanical, or even fundamentalist predispositions. Unfortunately, missionary workers in Africa (or for Africa) have little to no knowledge of the continent, except for a few stereotypical understandings. This lack of knowledge reflects the lack of seriousness with which Orthodox Christians prepare for missionary work. Therefore, the only way to cover such gross ignorance is to underestimate the recipient of the missionary message. By refusing to recognize others as equal counterparts, Orthodox Christians fail to acknowledge the same image of God and the same measure of his freedom and judgment. In this way we betray our traditional understanding of mission as witness and dialogue.

One of the greatest mistakes is to consider people in Africa uncivilized, easy to manipulate from above, or even as a tabula rasa. This approach represents a reversion to the darkest pages of the nineteenth century, and devastates the work being done in the mission field. Nevertheless, the grace of God may work despite our mistakes or our incapacity. Yet, one has to admit that there exist exceedingly few guiding figures who can lead the way, with an adequate sense of responsibility, knowledge, and sensitivity. One has to study the needs of the times and the deep, real needs of Orthodoxy in Africa.

Developments on the Issue of the Institution of Deaconesses

It is to such wise people that we owe the dynamic developments that took place recently in the Patriarchate of Alexandria, with regard to the female diaconate. I shall confine my remarks here only to the well-grounded proposal of Metropolitan Gregory (Stergiou) of Cameroon (2009 and 2016).[5] (That proposal led to an official synodal decision and its implementation by His Beatitude Patriarch Theodoros in February 2017 as well as much regrettable hesitation later on.) In his presentation to the hierarchy on the afternoon of October 7, 2009, Metropolitan Gregory stressed particularly that the ordination of a deaconess is completely analogous to that of a deacon, and suggested a full analogy of roles. He developed his pro-

---

5. "Ἐπαναφορὰ τοῦ θεσμοῦ τῶν διακονισσῶν εἰς τὴν Ὀρθόδοξον ἱεραποστολήν" ["The Reestablishment of the Institution of Deaconesses in Orthodox Mission"], Σύναξη [Synaxis] 118 (2011), 25–41. First presented before the Holy Synod on October 7, 2009, accessed July 19, 2022, https://www.patriarchateofalexandria.com/index.php?module=news3&action=details&id=8, and again on November 16, 2016 http://www.patriarchateofalexandria.com/index.php?module=news&action=details&id=1207.

posal in relation to the customs and traditions of Africa, perceptions of the relationship between men and women, and other particularities such as matters of taboo that make communication between the sexes—and hence of a priest with his flock in some cases—completely impossible. We must deeply understand how impossible it is for men (priests or even bishops) to have access to women for pastoral work in some African environments and the absolute necessity of reinstituting and widely implementing the order of deaconesses. One such example is access to prisons. The pastoral work of the church among prisoners is usually addressed to men only, while the women and children are almost abandoned unless a network of lay women undertakes the work of pastoral care among them, within the confines of their limited possibilities.

It is, therefore, of paramount importance to reestablish the female diaconate, utilizing its full potential, as was proposed by Metropolitan Gregory. In many cases in Africa, women's access to the sacraments of the church must necessarily pass through the ministry of other women.

The negative reaction that erupted after Patriarch Theodoros consecrated five deaconesses in February 2017 came partly from within the African Church, from a few African priests as a reflection of their own limitations and fears; but, most importantly, it came from outside unethical means and a most unethical and unchristian prejudice—white male supremacy. This is not a good sign, and is deeply damaging to ecclesial order as well as to the whole of Christian anthropology.

Unfortunately, these external interventions do not concern only the specific issue of the ordination of deaconesses, where they have found greatest expression. These interventions are constant, and concern most of the issues that hinder the development of the new churches and impede the incarnation of faith in the cultural and social context of Africa and beyond.

How many untimely and harmful discussions on Byzantine hagiography or music have been instigated in other parts of the world by Greek critics? How much insistence there has been on mimicking Byzantine or modern Athonite artistic patterns in other parts of the world, in a failure to embrace the culture of every people among whom the gospel is preached?

It must therefore be emphasised that such outrageous interventions from afar are not only detrimental to the case of the ordination of deaconesses, but are also harmful to missionary activities as a whole. These interventions nullify any notion of Orthodox ecclesiology and give rise to a sense of helplessness and frustration on the part of those solely responsible for running a local church, namely the local bishops and the synod.

In missiological scholarship, there is already sufficient and recent documentation of the dangers arising from the financial dependence of a local church on overseas funding. Among the Orthodox, there also exists recent scholarship on financial dependence as a deterrent to the progress of mission and much discussion about self-sustainability.[6] In this particular case, the institution of deaconesses, is it legitimate for sponsors from overseas to lobby to determine the life of a local church in direct opposition to the decisions of the patriarchal synod? Every person of goodwill understands how much damage is done to the church and missionary work by practices of this sort.

After all, the success of such practices is by its nature self-defeating. The attempt to liquidate the life of a local church in a deal with foreign agents will not last in the long run. But if there is no timely and lively resistance, the body of this church will be led to decay or even death.

---

6. Evangelos Thiani, "African Churches, Financial Stability and Self-Reliance," in *Anthology of African Christianity, Regnum Studies in Global Christianity*, eds. Isabel Apawo Phiri and Dietrich Werner (Oxford: Regnum, 2016), 1097–1106. Joseph William Black, "Dependency, Harambees and the Struggle for Christian Stewardship in the Orthodox Churches of Kenya," *Pharos Journal of Theology* 98 (2017): 1–11, accessed July 19, 2022, http://www.pharosjot.com/uploads/7/1/6/3/7163688/article_17_vol_98_2017.pdf. As an example of the ecumenical discussion, see Jonathan Bonk, *Missions and Money: Affluence as a Missionary Problem*, American Society of Missiology Series 15, 2nd ed. (Maryknoll, NY: Orbis Books, 1991).

CHAPTER SEVENTEEN

Diakonia in the Field of Mission

Here a wider issue is raised, that of the needs arising from the inseparable connection of missionary witness with social ministry (diakonia). Poverty in Africa undoubtedly concerns the church. We need to take care of both the souls and the bodies of the Christian community and in the wider community beyond, to the best of our ability. There is no doubt that there is nothing more Christian than to care for the poor, the sick, the prisoner, and the needy African brother and sister, in accordance with the criteria of the last judgment (Matt 25:31–46). It is self-evident that Christian love is the main motivation for sharing spiritual and material goods indiscriminately with the aim of healing injustice and building real brotherhood and unity. The work of Christian witness (*martyria*) is indeed inextricably linked with diakonia.

The sense of solidarity and responsibility for sharing coupled with the inner guilt that results from the inability to actually address inequalities leads to a relentless struggle to collect and redistribute donations. Charity from the top down may be a temporary relief, but it is certainly not a cure. One should rather consider taking important and courageous steps in the direction of actual healing, creating indigenous structures and resources, and building self-sustainability instead of dependence (economic or otherwise). This approach would lead to a lively local church, perhaps poorer at first, but with a developed self-consciousness. The members of the church, instead of receiving handouts, could take on a more active role towards a lively community. Thus, the bonds of brotherhood and solidarity would increase, as was the case in the early church and also within the traditional structures in Africa, before the encounter with the modern, so-called 'developed' world.

And yet, in addressing social inequalities, one should be attentive. First, it is not the sole or the main responsibility of the church. Second, as emphasised earlier, philanthropic work may generate new forms of dependence, while leaving intact both the capitalist and exploitative structure of the economy and the high level of corruption in countries with weak institutions, which is yet another aspect of underdevelopment.

Should one demonstrate that poverty in Africa is neither a metaphysical nor a natural phenomenon, and name and denounce its specific causes? Following the Holy and Great Council, Metropolitan Alexander (Yanniris) of Nigeria, in a public interview, condemned the multinational corporations that hold the wealth of Africa.[7] Metropolitan Panteleimon (Arathymos) of Congo Brazzaville expressed concern about the extent of charitable work that is expected and always welcomed by government agencies, yet carries the risk of replacing the welfare state.[8] In addition, there is a risk that the recipient may become passive and develop an almost childish attitude, expecting care from someone else but not taking responsibility.

A Broader Vision and Roadmap for Mission

Given the importance of the social work of the church, we come now to the drawing up of a roadmap for the sort of work that can primarily be implemented by deaconesses. The social dimension of their work is closely linked to their mission and role in worship. With these elements inextricably interwoven, I then wish to develop an important proposal for social and ecclesial work in Africa.

There is no way out of poverty on the African continent without developing the self-awareness of women. Women are often an important pillar of social and economic life in Africa, coping with extremely difficult circumstances in their private and family lives. There is no chance for the development of the African continent unless child marriage, childbearing by girls, and polygamy are com-

---

7. George Konstas, "Βολές κατά του Νεοφιλελευθερισμού στη Μεγάλη Σύνοδο της Ορθοδοξίας" ["Criticisms directed against Neoliberalism at the Great Council of Orthodoxy"], *Χανιώτικα Νέα*, May 21, 2016.

8. This was raised by Metropolitan Panteleimon, among other issues, in the framework of my postgraduate course "Orthodoxy in Africa," at the Department of Social Theology and Religious Studies, National and Kapodistrian University of Athens, on November 30, 2019. A similar concern has been expressed during the debt crisis in Greece, when the church stepped in, while the state largely withdrew from social care. See Evi Voulgaraki-Pissina, "The Mission of the Church amidst European Social and Economic Crisis: The Case of Greece," in *Mission and Money: Christian Mission in the Context of Global Inequalities*, eds. Mari-Anna Auvinen-Pöntinen and Jonas Adelin Jørgensen (Leiden and Boston: Brill, 2016), 101–28.

bated and stopped. In these matters the Orthodox Church must seek alliances with other more experienced organizations, such as the UN, whose program includes the fight against polygamy.[9] This struggle cannot be led with moral appeals and invocations, and centuries-old habits cannot be uprooted from the top down or from the outside. Nevertheless, it would be unthinkable to give in to this habit because polygamy (no matter what circumstances might have led to it originally) has enormous implications that touch on the core of Christian anthropology. Therefore, polygamy must not be taken for granted, as it sometimes is in a pseudo-liberal understanding or some false eagerness for adaptability, although existing particularities of human lives can be treated in a spirit of theological economy.

This problem will be solved and further social well-being and prosperity will be established in Africa through the education of women, obviously in parallel and not in contrast to that of men. I would point out, however, that the rise of the educational level of men alone will not bring about any major changes because it is not necessarily diffused to all, but usually remains a privilege of the few. Educating women, on the other hand, will move marriage to a more mature stage, allow women some financial independence by expanding their opportunities to find a way to make a living, change attitudes, boost their self-confidence and self-esteem, and strike a crucial blow against polygamy.

Growth and social well-being and prosperity in Africa can only be feminist.[10] Feminism currently has various tendencies and versions, but in a framework of such injustice, it proves a necessary condition for the restoration of that Christian anthropology, which we boast of in anniversary volumes on the legacy and social contribution of Christianity, the abolition of slavery and the (so-called) "elevation"

---

9. "Monogamy is encouraged as the preferred form of marriage and that the rights of women in marriage and family, including in polygamous marital relationships are promoted and protected." "Protocol to the African Charter on Human and Peoples' Rights on the Rights of Women in Africa," Article 6, 8–9, accessed July 19, 2022, https://www.un.org/shestandsforpeace/content/protocol-african-charter-human-and-peoples-rights-rights-women-africa.

10. Cf. Hazel Barrett, "Women in Africa: The Neglected Dimension in Development," *Geography* 80, 3 (1995): 215–24.

of women. Improvement in women's positions is improvement in society as a whole, having a direct impact on the position of children and the elderly, as well as all those who belong to the economically inactive population and are highly dependent on female care.

But such a development requires a high level of leadership in the local churches and well-developed theological and leadership skills. The active presence of women as lay or diaconal leaders of church communities, with appropriate training and authorization, could make a difference and a significant contribution to social progress and justice for all. I consider the ordination of deaconesses to be a central factor in the unfolding of a roadmap that will fully benefit Orthodox mission as well as African society. What argument can be raised against it other than prejudice or misogyny? Mission, like the church in all its authenticity, can only be a field of unfolding ministries and *charismata*.

A missional church can only be as the late theologian, Panagiotis Nellas, envisioned:

> So, each member of the Church has his own ministry, his charisma, his special function. All members are lay people or priests—the terms are equivalent—but their functions are different. One is a bishop, the other an elder, the third a deacon or a deaconess, another a teacher, a prophet, a layman or a monk, married or unmarried, an apostle or a preacher, a theologian, simply a man who prays. These functions are different, but they are all in essence hieratic, all necessary and complementary. Because only when all the members perform their functions does the Body remain healthy, and the Church can manifest itself fully and truly perform its work.[11]

---

11. Panagiotis Nellas, "Βασίλειον Ιεράτευμα: Μελέτη επί του Προβλήματος του Λαϊκού Στοιχείου" ["Royal Priesthood: A Study on the Issue of Laity"], Σύναξη [Synaxis] 83 (2002): 48–60.

Chapter Eighteen

THE SCHOOL OF DEACONESSES AND THE OPPOSITION IN THE CHURCH OF GREECE

Vasiliki Stathokosta

Introduction

Women's presence in Greece, both in the life of the country in general and of the church in particular, was acutely felt during the post-war period. World War II highlighted in various ways the need to utilize women's abilities in public life, and, in fact, necessitated their active participation in every aspect of it. Women, mostly volunteers, ministered to the sick, the wounded, the hungry, and the poor among decimated families, battle-ravaged men, widows, orphans, the helpless, and the needy. Similarly, education, as well as the charitable and catechistic work of the church, could not have happened without the ministry of women.

It soon became clear that women could contribute much to society and the church, paving the way for the education and training of women in many fields. One of these was social welfare for three primary reasons: the great need to organize and to provide assistance to vulnerable groups within the population; the prevailing mentality and stereotypical roles for the sexes, i.e., that social concern befits women's nature; and the enlightened vision by some luminaries in the Church of Greece of the need for church renewal and a vivification of its life through ministry. These things were made possible through women's increased participation.[1]

The field of social welfare (or social work, as it later became known) developed in a systematic way particularly in the United States and Great Britain, where women's abilities were utilized. But in Greece and in the Orthodox Church, the tradition of Christianity's first centuries—and the social teaching of the fathers about ministering to those in need—continued. A necessary condition, however, was the education and training of women, which the Church of Greece was obliged to provide them for their development in order to respond to the new demands placed upon them.

The first decisive factor in the rise of women's education was the Church of Greece's renewed interest in social welfare as a result of its contact with the non-Orthodox churches and denominations in Western Europe. Recognizing the methods these Western denominations had developed within the field of social work, as well as the opportunities that these developments provided to Western societies, the Church of Greece hastened to combine the ecclesiastical experience of women's ministry to those in need with women's education and utilization. In this way, social welfare in Greece sprang from the initiative and planning of the church.[2] The second decisive factor was the Church of Greece's participation in the World Council of Churches (WCC). The WCC leveraged its member churches' know-how and experience in social welfare to build a collaborative infrastructure for the benefit of all. Significant here was the establishment of the Inter-Church Aid Service, through which the member churches were provided with everything that was required for their work.

---

1. Cf. V. Stathokostas, *The relationship between the church of Greece with the World Council of Churches 1948–1961, Based on the Archives of the World Council of Churches*, PhD Dissertation [in Greek], (Thessaloniki, 1999), accessed July 19, 2022, https://www.didaktorika.gr/eadd/handle/10442/24771. Dissertation includes description of the archival material on which this study is based.

2. Anait Mertzanidou's dissertation provides some useful (although not always accurate) information that supports the above conclusions. See A. Mertzanidou, *Social Work Education in Greece: Its Historical Development and Modern Reality* [in Greek] (Democritus University of Thrace, 2017), 64–93.

CHAPTER EIGHTEEN

The School of Deaconesses

Thus, in the postwar period, various programs were developed with the support of the WCC. Their goal was to bolster the church's social and pastoral work. From the Orthodox perspective, these programs were part of the vision and general demand of the time for church revival and for the promotion of the Church of Greece and theology among major players in Greek society.

One of these programs was the School of Deaconesses. The project was developed under the aegis of Apostoliki Diakonia of the Church of Greece. It was an ambitious, groundbreaking project, with its beginnings deeply rooted and theologically substantiated in the ecclesiastical life of the church, which was focused on the moral and spiritual reconstruction of the country.[3]

The Church of Greece's need for such a school was articulated by Archbishop Spyridon of Athens and All Greece on November 25, 1949, when he submitted a list of the Church of Greece's needs and asked the other churches to provide for them.[4] The hope for this project was that it would contribute to the social ministry of the Church of Greece, addressing both the spiritual and material needs of its faithful (providing education to children, job opportunities for the unemployed, and so on). Fortunately, the endeavor was warmly received by the WCC, as it was something completely new for the Church of Greece, which promised to further develop both its ministerial work[5] and ecumenical cooperation with

---

3. See Apostoliki Diakonia's informational booklet on the Venerable Educational Institutions of St. Barbara's, which includes material outlining their history, Gr & Cyp Dossier 280 (495) A, 2/5. This is the name of the dossier at the library of the World Council of Churches in Geneva where the documents referred to in my dissertation and this chapter are located. The numbers are my own. See Stathokosta, *Relationship*.

4. November 25, 1949: Archbishop Spyridon to R. Zigler (Executive Secretary for the Brethren Service Commission): Greece I, 7/9, Stathokosta, *Relationship*.

5. A. G. Elmendorf, "The World Council helps Greek Churches," Dossier 280 (495) A, 1/2, 4, Stathokosta, *Relationship*. See also A. Alivazatos, "Review and Perspective," in *O. S.* [*Orthodoxos Skepsis*], no. 1, (January 14, 1958): 1–5, (2–3) [in Greek].

women from other churches, especially the Anglican Communion and other Orthodox.[6]

It is no mere happenstance that the school was not listed in the same category with the rest of the proposals for the reconstruction of ecclesiastical and educational buildings, which was submitted to the WCC for funding. Rather, the Inter-Church Aid Service described the project as the highest priority of all the proposals.[7] The project included a complex of buildings to house the School of Deaconesses as well as a "female student dormitory" for the housing primarily of young women from the villages who came to Athens for studies.[8] The female student dormitory would be "the twin brother of Petraki Monastery's dormitory for students of theology," according to the general secretary of Apostoliki Diakonia, Vasillios Vellas, in his remarks at the dedication of the buildings at St. Barbara [one of the largest pilgrimage churches in Athens].[9] In a similar vein, Amilkas Alivizatos, a professor and one of the visionaries for the building up of the church's work, believed that the female student dormitory would inspire young women from the villages to come study, offering them the security necessary in a large city such as Athens. The complex also included the Charter School for Girls, which planned to undertake the education of some 400 female students.[10] Of course, this was a project that required high levels of funding, but those involved believed that,

---

6. April 6, 1959: Elizabeth C. Beath, (Associate Secretary, Church Missions Houses. National Council, Protestant Episcopal Church, in New York): Gr. & Cyp., 2/32.

7. This was Tillman's view after his visit to Greece in March 1954. See March 11, 1954: R. B. Tillman to R. Maxwell: Gr. & Cyp., 2/58.

8. For more information, see "Female Student Dormitory" in *E* [*Ecclesia*], no. 21, (1957): 431–32 [in Greek].

9. See "Report of His Beatitude Archbishop Spyridon of Athens and all Greece to the Holy Synod of the Hierarchy of the Church of Greece" (Athens, 1952), 28 [in Greek].

10. Ibid.

once the building was operational, the necessary financial means would soon be provided for its completion.[11]

These buildings were located next to St. Barbara, and the foundation was laid on November 26, 1950, in an official ceremony attended by King Paul and Archbishop Spyridon, who, among other remarks, expressed his gratitude to the WCC and its member churches, characterizing the WCC as a "bond of love between Christian churches."[12]

As preparation for the School of Deaconesses, Apostoliki Diakonia organized a series of classes during the academic years 1951–1952 and 1952–1953. Participants included female students from the School of Theology at the University of Athens, as well as other women who had related interests. The head of the school was Fr. Barnabas Tzortzatos, who later became Metropolitan of Kitros. The late Provost of the University of Athens and professor at the School of Theology, Evangelos Theodorou, and his wife Harikleia Theodorou,

---

11. Throughout R. B. Tillman's visit to Greece in March 1954, Vellas, King, and Tillman agreed that once the building began operating, it would be easy to find the financial resources for its completion. See March 11, 1954: Robert B. Tillman to Ray Maxwell (cc to Dr. Mackie): Gr. & Cyp., 2/58. For more on foreign churches' contribution of both money and material goods to the construction and operation of this project, see the detailed annual reports that A. Alivizatos provided to the WCC, in *E*. Also informative is the WCC's rich archival material that revealed the pioneers' anxious efforts to build the School of Deaconesses, as well as the later process to secure the necessary financial assistance. See, for example, the incident in which R. E. Maxwell, upon returning to Geneva from his visit to Greece and his audience with the Archbishop of Athens on October 31, 1958, was informed that the General Division of Women's Work of the Protestant Episcopal Church in the United States had donated $27,000 to complete the School of Deaconesses (see November 12, 1958: R. Maxwell to Archbishop Theoklitos: Orth. 22, 5/37). "Orth" is the name of another WCC dossier; see Stathokosta, *Relationship*. More specifically, the $27,000 was for the completion and furnishing of two additional floors. This doubled its capacity from fifty to 100; see Chr. King, (W.C.C. S.R., Senior Field Representative in Greece), "St. Barbara School—Tradition meets today's needs," in "World Council of Churches Information," F/1–59, February 6, 1959: Gr. & Cyp., 2/8.

12. See "Foundation stone laid for St. Barbara Center for the training and education of women and girls. Archbishop of Athens expresses his gratitude to World Council": Orth. 26, 11/16.

among others, also taught there.¹³ This initiative encouraged discussion about the institution of deaconesses, which Apostoliki Diakonia of the Church of Greece seemed to support. This climate developed in large part due to Apostoliki Diakonia's publication of Evangelos Theodorou's work, *Heroines of Christian Love: Deaconesses through the Centuries* (Athens 1949), as well as from the aforementioned courses. It is noteworthy that the participants in these courses formed the nucleus for the establishment of the Association of Friends of the Institution of Deaconesses (1952).¹⁴ It seems that there was an intense desire in the postwar period to restore the institution of deaconesses in particular and to utilize women's abilities in the church's work in general, but without attempting to equate or even correlate the institution of deaconesses with the increase in female participation and ministry in the church.

The whole project was supported by the Church of Greece. Even after Spyridon, his successor to the archepiscopal throne showed a keen interest in its completion. Specifically, Archbishop Theoklitos, as president of the council of Apostoliki Diakonia, expected that graduates of the School of Deaconesses would participate in the social work of the church. To this end, in addressing the WCC to request its aid in completing the project, the archbishop noted, "Hence, we resolved to ask your Council if it would be willing once again to come to our aid and help us complete this school, many of whose graduates will become Deaconesses to conduct the social work of our Church."¹⁵ Archbishop Theoklitos was not indisposed toward Western Christians or ecumenical dialogue; on the contrary, he was well aware of the possibilities and prospects of inter-Christian cooperation and the many benefits it could bring as a "manifestation of Christian love and solidarity." Not only that, but Theoklitos also regarded Christian love and solidarity as the indispensable founda-

---

13. E. Theodorou, *The Office of Deaconesses in the Orthodox Church and the Possibility of its Revival* [in Greek], accessed July 28, 2022, http://www.myriobiblos.gr/texts/greek/theodorou_diakonisses7.html.

14. Ibid. The decision was made on May 21, 1952.

15. See June 18, 1958: "The president of the Central Committee of Apostoliki Diakonia, Archbishop Theoklitos to the WCC," Geneva: Gr. & Cyp., 2/48.

tions for building a better future—a future for which "Christians around the world have an obligation to work together."[16]

But what specific role would the graduates of the School of Deaconesses fill? In order to avoid misunderstandings, the Church of Greece took care at that time to make it clear that the office of deaconess is not a "degree of Priesthood, as in the case of the Deacon." On this point, the church referred to the *Apostolic Constitutions*, which state that the work of the deaconesses "is not liturgical, ritual, like that of the Deacons, but merely auxiliary."[17] Furthermore, the church stipulated that the character of the deaconesses' role in the modern age was to offer their services as assistants to the priests in the exercise of their pastoral work in the family and according to the Orthodox conception of society. The deaconesses would report to the priests and assist them.

The construction of the building complex was completed in 1955, but two years passed before both the school and the female student dormitory began to operate.[18] Finally, the Central Council of Apostoliki Diakonia of the Church of Greece officially approved the opening of the "School of Social Welfare/Deaconesses" for the training of deaconesses and post-graduate social workers during their meeting on September 20, 1957, and the school opened its doors on November 21, 1957.[19]

---

16. As described in the letter from June 24, 1959: "The president of the Central Committee of Apostoliki Diakonia, Archbishop Theoklitos to the WCC," Geneva: Gr. & Cyp., no. 2884: Gr. & Cyp., 2/7.

17. Apostoliki Diakonia of the Church of Greece, *The Deaconess and Her Work* (Athens, 1958) [in Greek]. See Gr. & Cyp., 2/57.

18. It is interesting to note A. Alivizatos's optimism, declaring that the school would start as early as October 1954. Cf. R. Maxwell, D.I.C.A.S.R., Administrative Committee, July 24, 1954, I.C.A. Greece, Mid-year 1954: Orth. 25, 8/1.

19. The school began operating on November 21, 1957. The information above was drawn from material generously provided to me by Sophia Mourouka, director of the School of Social Welfare-Deaconesses and later Professor Emeritus at the Technological Educational Institute of Athens. I owe her my heartfelt thanks for the valuable assistance and time she dedicated to me. I dedicate this paper to her memory: Sofia Mourouka (+2013).

Reactions

Obviously, this two-year delay raises questions, and it is clear that this delay stands in stark contrast to the "anxious efforts" that were made to complete construction and despite the fact that intensive work[20] had been done for the "enlightenment of the Holy Synod concerning its purpose and usefulness." The eventual opening was surely aided by Archbishop Theoklitos' determination and support.[21] Specifically, the archbishop not only attended the graduation ceremony of the first ten graduates of the school on June 20, 1958;[22] but, in order to set a good example, recruited them to an equal number of parishes in Athens and Piraeus.[23]

The program was welcomed by those who supported the Church of Greece's participation in the ecumenical movement. They believed that this effort would strengthen the work of the parish, as the parish would cease to be only a center of worship and would come to include, with the help of deaconesses, a center of social welfare and social solidarity, as a practical expression of the teaching of the gospel. Thus, the church would not only teach Christ's love for humanity on a theoretical level, but would also apply it in practice, demonstrating lived Christianity to the fullness of Christ's people.

Nevertheless, dark clouds began to gather as opponents of the ecumenical movement hastened to criticize the work of the School of Deaconesses as dangerous, misguided, and even scandalous. In fact, they deemed it unacceptable to invest millions in the education of women and not men. Typical of this reaction was a publication

---

20. Since this was an enormous and unprecedented undertaking for Greek society, Apostoliki Diakonia published an informational booklet on the history of deaconesses and the work of today's deaconesses in the Church of Greece. See Apostoliki Diakonia of the Church of Greece, *The Deaconess and Her Work*. See Gr. & Cyp., 2/57.

21. Apostoliki Diakonia of the Church of Greece, *The Deaconess and Her Work*.

22. Ibid. The first ten deaconesses were all graduates of the School of Theology of the University of Athens.

23. Ibid.

that censured the beginning of the school's operations, saying, characteristically, "Zafeiritsa [girl's name] had everything; only her hat was missing,"[24] and thus resorting to ridicule in the absence of better arguments.

It is clear that the young women's high level of theological and pastoral education created tension with the majority of priests, who lacked even basic education.[25] It should be emphasized that the school was taught at the postgraduate level, meaning that the candidates were university graduates, preferably from the theological schools of the Universities of Athens and Thessaloniki, who were accepted only after successful examinations. The curriculum of the School of Deaconesses included courses on the history of the office of deaconesses, parish organization, contemporary social problems, social welfare, criminal law, first aid, psychiatry, home economics, sociology, hygiene, etc.

The polemic against the school continued throughout its operation. Perhaps the biggest obstacle was the Church of Greece's inability to understand the significance and purpose of its social work, as well as women's participation and contribution in this particular area. One of the project's visionaries, the late Amilkas Alivizatos, bitterly remarked that the effort "was essentially butchered by base personal motives and an inability to understand this great project."[26] Similar was the experience of Apostoliki Diakonia, which was in danger of being dissolved precisely because of the hierarchs' inability to understand its work. Thus, history once again confirmed that although the tradition of the church is quite rich, it is not always well understood by some believers, who participate in the church as if it were an ideological group or a political party, and who like to hear their own voices more than the voice of the living church of Christ.

---

24. Φωνή της Εκκλησίας, Athens, November 10, 1957.

25. Apostoliki Diakonia of the Church of Greece, St. Barbara's Deaconess School, Dafni, Time Table, Academic Year 1961–62'. Gr. & Cyp., 2/4 [in Greek].

26. A. Alivizatos, "Review and Perspective," in *O. S.*, no. 1 (January 15, 1958): 1–5 (2–3).

Assessment

It is worth noting that, as it turns out, the church's social and broader pastoral work was strengthened during the postwar era, and this was directly connected with the ecumenical movement not only because it was encouraged and subsidized by it, but also for another important reason. This project's development was seen by opponents of the ecumenical movement as Protestantism's negative influence on Orthodoxy, i.e., as an undesirable change to the Orthodox way of thinking and the Orthodox ecclesiastical life. For this reason, they also disapproved of the establishment of the School of Deaconesses, a classic example of the church's self-proclaimed supporters abandoning the tradition of the church—a tradition that they are supposedly defending. Unfortunately, this practice of distorting the truth without evidence, instead maligning the opposing view as supposedly Protestant or heretical, has been, and continues to be, a standard tactic for those opposed to the ecumenical movement.

Nevertheless, the School of Deaconesses reflected a dynamic ecclesiological view, according to which the church's witness to the world is amplified through efforts to renovate and revitalize church life—based always, of course, on the ancient traditions of the church. The two great visionaries for this School of Deaconesses were Amilkas Alivizatos and Vassilios Vellas, professors who sought ways to better utilize the church's spiritual power to provide Greek society with a stronger witness to the faith. Thus, they sought to enhance church life and ministry by increasing women's participation.

The importance of the School of Deaconesses was undoubtedly significant for a number of reasons. First, it signaled the Church of Greece's decision to breathe life into a desolate and unused ecclesiastical treasure. Second, it was pioneering, as it represented a breakthrough not only in the education of women, but also in the way women participated in the church, since it officially confirmed their contribution to the work of social welfare, catechism, evangelism, and pastoral care. Third, the School of Deaconesses was an outstanding example of the spiritual renaissance in postwar Greece and the Church of Greece's desire to help by utilizing all of its potential.

Finally, the School of Deaconesses operated for about twenty years, until the early 1980s, when it was incorporated into the Centers for Higher Technical and Vocational Education and then the Technological Educational Institute of Athens.[27] The three-story building where the School of Deaconesses operated was abandoned for years and finally renovated at the initiative of the late Archbishop Christodoulos of Athens and All Greece, with the aim of relocating the Student Dormitory to accommodate 120 students from the Faculty of Theology at the University of Athens.

Ultimately, the great effort to educate and train women for the church encountered enormous obstacles. When one speaks of the School of Social Welfare/Deaconesses of Apostoliki Diakonia of the Church of Greece, one is speaking of deaconesses in the broadest sense—serving others—and not of deaconesses as "ordained" or even "tonsured" women in the Church. If the title of this symposium poses the question of whether the deaconess has a past, present, and future, then the only safe answer is that, yes, there is a past. The present and the future of deaconesses remain open. In any case, the School of Social Welfare/Deaconesses did operate, and it can certainly be argued that it was an example of the spiritual renaissance that took place in postwar Greece. It can also be recorded in history as a brave effort on the part of the Church of Greece to incorporate women's abilities, utilizing all its members, free from social prejudices and stereotypes foreign to the teaching of the gospel.

May this major step taken in the 1950s be a source of inspiration as well as a reflection on the possibility of reviving the institution of deaconesses in the Orthodox Church, as well as other forms that can utilize women's abilities in the life of the church, especially today when a large percentage of graduates of the theological schools in Greece are women.

---

27. The name of the institute in Greek is Κέντρα Ανώτερης Τεχνικής Επαγγελματικής Εκπαιδεύσεως, often abbreviated as ΚΑΤΕΕ.

Chapter Nineteen

ST. NEKTARIOS AND THE DEACONESSES
Evanthia Adamtziloglou

One hundred years after his righteous repose, the Holy Synod of the Church of Greece decided to dedicate the year of grace, 2020, to St. Nektarios, Metropolitan of Pentapolis in Egypt, who was Director of the Rizareios Seminary in Athens and founder of the Sacred Convent of the Holy Trinity on the island of Aegina.

For this occasion, the Apostoliki Diakonia (Apostolic Ministry) of the Church of Greece published in both Greek and English an academic study in two volumes written by His Eminence Metropolitan Cleopas Strongylis of Sweden and All Scandinavia entitled *St. Nektarios Kefalas, Metropolitan of Pentapolis*.[1] This study is based on unpublished archival sources and covers the entire history of the saint's life from his birth (October 1, 1846) until his repose (November 8, 1920).

St. Nektarios was not an ordinary man. His writings and other published works are impressive. I will not present all of these in detail, but will refer to just three of them as representative of his studies.

1. St. Nektarios published *The Divine Liturgy of the Holy and Glorious Apostle Mark*,[2] which he transcribed on June 1, 1890

---

1. Cleopas Strongylis, *Saint Nektarios Kefalas, Metropolitan of Pentapolis, A Historical Study Based on Archival Sources* [in Greek] (Athens: Apostoliki Diakonia of the Church of Greece, 1919), vol. 1, 7.

2. Ibid., 143–45.

from manuscript codices of the Patriarchate of Alexandria. His signature, "Nektarios of Pentapolis," appears at the end of the text. According to his preface, the liturgy of St. Mark was housed in a library of the Alexandrian throne in Cairo under the manuscript code number thirty-five. This liturgy was composed in the fifth century and derived from the ancient Egyptian liturgy, which was based on prayers of the sacramentary of St. Serapion, Bishop of Thmuis—a contemporary of St. Athanasios the Great. This work points to St. Nektarios' great respect for the liturgical tradition of the church, which he studied from the manuscripts.

2. The saint's publication, "*On the Holy Councils*,"[3] is another important work of his. It was published in Alexandria in 1888 and focuses on the necessity, importance, and utility of the ancient church's synodal system of governance. The disregard for Byzantium and the Eastern Orthodox Church exhibited by many European historians during the late nineteenth century along with the uncertainty and confusion regarding the necessity of the ecumenical councils led St. Nektarios to study this subject and undertake the very difficult and challenging task of refuting scholars' prevailing views concerning the ecumenical councils while restoring the standing of the unjustly scorned Byzantine Empire.

3. The third book that portrays his distinctive personality is his lengthy two-volume work, *A Historical Study on the Causes of the Schism, on its Perpetuation, and the Possibility or Impossibility of the Unification of the two Churches, of the East and West*.[4] This study was written in 1895, as the hierarch mentions in his prologue, but was published in 1911 and 1912, when he was serving at the convent of the Holy Trinity on Aegina.

The saint used to send his publications as complimentary copies to the Christians of other denominations—to Roman Catholics,

---

3. Ibid., 103–05.
4. Cleopas Strongylis, *Saint Nectarios Kefalas*, vol. 2, 202–3.

CHAPTER NINETEEN

Old Catholics, and Anglicans—with whom he maintained correspondence. In this way, he sought to promote relations between the Eastern Orthodox Church and other Christian denominations.[5]

The hierarch maintained correspondence with Roman Catholics in particular and presented the Orthodox viewpoint in his letters. One result of the research that was conducted by the Metropolitan of Sweden was the discovery of six letters[6] exchanged between St. Nektarios of Pentapolis and the Brotherhood of the Assumption Monastery of Grottaferrata in Rome. In his letter of 1910, the saint wrote:[7]

> Of course, the time has come for reconciliation and unification and joint actions against all sorts of enemies of the One, Holy, Catholic and Apostolic Church. However, I believe that for the accomplishment of the desired goal, communication should be cultivated not through correspondence but through dialogue with the Ecumenical Patriarchate, with which you may establish the guidelines through which discussions on the issue of the unification of the Churches should take place.[8]

Despite the fact that the saint belonged to the Patriarchate of Alexandria, he had deep respect for the Ecumenical Patriarchate of Constantinople and recognized its primacy, maintaining regular correspondence with all the patriarchs[9] who served during his time but especially with Ecumenical Patriarch Joachim III.[10]

I have relayed all this in an attempt to sketch the brilliant life of St. Nektarios and his importance for the church at the end of the nineteenth and the beginning of the twentieth centuries. This is the saint who ordained deaconesses at the Holy Trinity Convent in Aegina, thus reviving this forgotten institution of the church.

---

5. Cleopas Strongylis, *Saint Nectarios Kefalas,* vol. 2, 208.
6. Ibid., 208–9.
7. Ibid., 211.
8. Ibid., 218.
9. Ibid., 211.
10. Ibid., 40.

It thus appears that the saint had an excellent knowledge of church tradition regarding this institution. In addition, he bore the name of Patriarch Nektarios of Constantinople[11] (381–397), who succeeded St. Gregory the Theologian as patriarch. It was this Nektarios who ordained the deaconess Olympia[12] in Constantinople. According to the historian Palladius, she was the patriarch's counselor and collaborator.[13] Olympia frequently voiced her ideas for the solution of ecclesiastical problems. Later on, she became abbess of the convent near the Church of Holy Wisdom and worked with Patriarch John Chrysostom. Chrysostom also ordained many deaconesses in this convent. Among them were three relatives of Olympia—Elissanthia, Martyria, and Palladia.[14] Research indicates that forty deaconesses served there. There were many other known deaconesses[15] in Armenia, Palestine, Egypt, and in the West as well (such as Tatiana in Rome).

Following this tradition, St. Nektarios revived this forgotten institution of deaconesses in the twentieth century at the Holy Trinity Convent on Aegina. He "ordained" as deaconesses the nuns Elisabeth Roka and Magdalene Moustaka.[16] According to existing information, the saint ordained these deaconesses in front of the holy altar inside the holy sanctuary, and they wore the deacon's crossed stole.[17]

It is interesting to see how St. Nektarios chose nuns from his convent to serve as deaconesses. The blessed nun Nektaria (secular name Zenovia Lalaouni), spent her childhood years on Aegina near St. Nektarios. In one discussion, she spoke of the method by

---

11. Sophocles G. Demetrakopoulos, *Saint Nektarios of Pentapolis. The First Saint of our Century* [in Greek] (Athens, 2000), 48, n.15.

12. Sozomen, "Ecclesiastical History," VIII, 9, PG 67:1537. Evangelos Theodorou, "Olympias" [in Greek)], ΘΗΕ [*Religious and Ethical Encyclopedia*], 12 vols. (1962–1968), 9:890. P. G. Nikolopoulou, "Nectarios, Patriarch of Constantinople," (381–397 AD) [in Greek], ΘΗΕ 9:395.

13. Palladios, *Historical Dialogue on the Life of John Chrysostom*, PG 47:61–2.

14. Evangelos Theodorou, "Olympias" [in Greek], ΘΗΕ, 9:891–895.

15. Evangelos Theodorou, "Deaconess" [in Greek], ΘΗΕ 4:1149–50.

16. Cleopas Strongylis, *Saint Nectarios Kefalas*, vol. 2, 17, n. 1458.

17. Sophocles G. Demetrakopoulos, *Saint Nectarios of Pentapolis*, 270, n. 25.

which the saint chose nuns from his convent to officially appoint as subdeaconesses:[18]

> When he came out during the Small and the Great Entrances, he had two nuns with him serving as subdeaconesses and wearing the deacon's crossed orarion. When he was to officially lay hands on a subdeaconess, he would pray for God to reveal to him who was worthy of this position. He would ask God to give him a "sign" to show him who was worthy of assuming this service. And so, he would "see" one or two nuns in the church "wearing" the stole, without, of course, him having given it to them. He would immediately call them and put the orarion on them.[19]

This testimony refers, of course, to subdeaconesses, but St. Nektarios also ordained deaconesses, which, according to the church's tradition, belong to the upper and not the lower clergy. The saint ordained them inside the holy sanctuary and not outside it.[20]

Before undertaking such actions, St. Nektarios would have been fully aware of the order of the deaconesses in the church. He would have known, too, that the place of deaconesses in the church is analogous to that of deacons. Deaconesses do not have the rights of the priests, but those of the deacons.[21] He certainly would have known Justinian's Sixth Novel,[22] with the descriptive title "how bishops, presbyters, and deacons, male and female, must be ordained." He would also have known Justinian's Third Novel,[23] that describes the number of clergy in Hagia Sophia. According to this work, the full

---

18. Cleopas Strongylis, *Saint Nectarios Kefalas*, vol. 2, 171, n. 1458.

19. M. Melinos, *I Have Spoken with Saint Nektarios* [in Greek], vol. 1, 252, 254.

20. Evangelos Theodorou, "The Institution of Deaconesses according to Saint Nectarios," *Female Monasticism: Proceedings of the Pan-Orthodox Monastic Conference* [in Greek] (Athens: The Convent of Holy Trinity, Aegina, 1998), 222.

21. Evangelos Theodorou, "The Deaconesses in the History of the Church," in *Sex and Religion. The Place of Women in the Church* [in Greek], Holy Metropolis of Demetrias (Athens: Indiktos, 2004), 190–95.

22. Evangelos Theodorou, "Deaconess" [in Greek)], ΘΗΕ 4:1148.

23. Ibid.

complement of servers there would be sixty priests and 100 deacons, forty deaconesses, ninety subdeaconesses, 110 readers, and twenty-five chanters.

Generally speaking, the deaconesses were classified between the male deacons and subdeacons—between the upper and lower clergy.[24]

It is worth underlining that deaconesses enjoyed great respect among the people. Clear proof of the respect and the honor of this female dignity in the Eastern Church is the fact that many women from the official and eminent families in Byzantine Constantinople took it as a great honor and gift from God to be ordained deaconess of the church.[25] Usually, deaconesses were wives of bishops, according to Canon 48 of the Council in Trullo.[26]

At the conference organized in September 1996 by the Holy Convent of the Holy Trinity and St. Nektarios on Aegina for the 150-year anniversary of the saint's birth, there was a lengthy discussion on the subject of deaconesses.[27] One question that arose was why the saint, although he had followed the ancient tradition of the church for ordaining deaconesses in the holy sanctuary, felt it necessary to write an apology about subdeaconesses when he was pressured by his ecclesiastical superiors. Theodorou did not go into this question in great depth. For him, it sufficed to observe that "Since the Church recognizes the ordination of deaconesses, who belong to the order of the upper clergy, what would prevent the Church from using the combination of ordaining deaconesses and laying hands on subdeaconesses? Since the greater form of the order exists, why not allow for the lesser to exist as well?"[28]

---

24. Ibid.
25. Ibid., 4:1148.
26. Ibid., 4:1144–45.
27. Sophocles G. Demetrakopoulos, *Saint Nectarios of Pentapolis*, 265.
28. Evangelos Theodorou, "The Institution of Deaconesses according to Saint Nektarios," *Female Monasticism: Proceedings of the Pan-Orthodox Monastic Conference* [in Greek] (Athens: The Convent of Holy Trinity, Aegina, 1998), 224.

CHAPTER NINETEEN

Allow me to delve further, to determine the motivations of those who pressured St. Nektarios and asked him to apologize for ordaining deaconesses.[29]

It is important to note that the issue of deaconesses at the Convent of the Holy Trinity on Aegina was closely related to the issue of the official recognition of the convent by the Metropolitan of Athens at that time, Theokletos (Minopoulos).

In 1904, St. Nektarios received Metropolitan Theokletos's oral consent to construct the convent on Aegina.[30] Moreover, the metropolitan had visited the monastery in 1907 and had the best impression of the work that was taking place there, as well as the convent's spiritual atmosphere.[31] When, however, St. Nektarios prepared the papers for the recognition of the convent in 1914, Metropolitan Theokletos changed his mind[32] and expressed antipathy. The metropolitan argued that the construction of this convent had been undertaken without his consent; he posed eight questions on points for which the saint ought to apologize. Among these was why nuns dressed in holy vestments to participate in the holy services held in the convent.[33]

Sending a new letter to Metropolitan Theokletos, St. Nektarios reminded him that the convent was built with his approval and that he had received the holy myrrh used in the consecration of its church from *his* metropolis. In this letter, St. Nektarios also addressed the other questions raised by the metropolitan. With regards to the issues of deaconesses, St. Nektarios wrote:[34]

> Regarding the subdeaconesses, I inform you that they are primarily the sacristans of the sanctuary. Their dress was adopted according to the manner that the readers who are in the churches of the cities wear their holy vestments. Maniples (cuffs) were allowed for the following reasons.

---

29. The proceedings of the Holy Synod of June 4, 1918, ibid., 223.
30. Cleopas Strongylis, *Saint Nectarios Kefalas,* vol. 2, 251.
31. Ibid.
32. Ibid., 168–69.
33. Ibid., 169.
34. Ibid., 170, n. 1458.

Since there are no deacons in the Convent, and there is no priest in the Aegina Convent and I am neither able to attend to the cleanliness of the church, nor to constantly remain in the church serving as a sacristan, and as the sanctuary has an absolute need to appoint persons to clean the holy vessels, change the covers and cloths of the Holy Altar, move the holy Artophorion (Tabernacle) and perform every other duty of a sacristan in the sanctuary, I thought to appoint two, so that they could alternate performing duties in the sanctuary. In an absolute necessity, they bring the holy Eucharist to very sick sisters in a small Chalice designed for this purpose. Aside from this exception of necessity, they are sacristans in all their other duties.

St. Nektarios writes in this letter about the deaconesses, but refers to them as subdeaconesses. The late Theodorou had met the elderly and very venerable deaconess, Magdalene Moustaka, when she served as abbess in the Convent of the Dormition (Panagia Chryssoleontissa) on Aegina. She told him that her ordination took place on the day of Pentecost in 1911, *"inside the holy sanctuary during the Divine Liturgy through the laying on of hands and the prayers recited during the ordination of a deacon."*[35]

Theodorou explained[36] (tactfully) that because some people considered this "laying on of the hands" improper and had been scandalized, St. Nektarios' explanation to then Archbishop Theokletos stressed that the work that he assigned them resembled more that of a subdeacon and was a necessity to the convent, especially during the absence of a priest.

Did the Metropolitan of Athens change his mind because some had been scandalized by the ordination of deaconesses—or was there some other reason? Based on the course of political and ecclesiastical matters at the time, one can think of other explanations for

---

35. Cleopas Strongylis, *Saint Nectarios Kefalas*, vol. 2, 174–75, n. 1471. Evangelos Theodorou, *"Ordination" or "Laying of Hands" for Deaconesses* (Athens, 1959), 95–96.

36. Cleopas Strongylis, *Saint Nectarios Kefalas*, 175, n. 1471. Evangelos Theodorou, "Ordination" or "Laying of Hands," 95–96.

why St. Nektarios might have received pressure from Metropolitan Theokletos.

Two years later, on December 12, 1916, the "National Defense" movement formed in Thessaloniki, spearheaded by former prime minister of Greece, Eleftherios Venizelos. The political division between the royalists and Venizelists negatively impacted the official church as well. It appears that Metropolitan Theokletos of Athens, a royalist, had been pressured to excommunicate Eleftherios Venizelos, the Cretan politician. Up to the last minute, Metropolitan Theokletos insisted that he would not excommunicate Venizelos, but the next morning Theokletos, as a royalist, signed the anathema against Venizelos—seemingly under great pressure. According to the records of the Holy Synod, Metropolitan Theokletos pressured the clergy to take part in the anathema as well. "The most Reverend President has declared that he will call the holy clergy in order to be present at the anathema gathering," according to document 30/11–12-1916.

Following Venizelos' victory, Theokletos was deposed, and the Cretan, Meletios Metaxakis, took Theokletos' place as Metropolitan of Athens.

These incidents suggest that Metropolitan Theokletos was being pressured by powerful forces inside and outside of Greece. These forces were surely unaware of the noble tradition of the saints in Byzantium. And not only were they ignorant, but they actually dismissed it in principle because they wanted to impose their own tradition.[37] It is worth noting that the church of Christ does not rely on male seminaries but on Christian families, from which the next generation springs up in the *koinonia* of love.

The newly consecrated Metropolitan Meletios Metaxakis adopted the perspective of his predecessor and thus looked unfavorably upon St. Nektarios. It is sad to note that there are statements in the records of the Holy Synod of the Church of Greece in 1918

---

37. Barbara Ch. Yiannakopoulou, "Monasticism's crisis in the second half of the 19th century and the beginning of the 20th century, and St. Nektarios" in *Female Monasticism, Proceedings of the Pan-Orthodox Monastic Conference* (Athens: The Convent of Holy Trinity, Aegina, 1998), 113–28.

that clearly indicate that St. Nektarios was called to "apologize for ordaining deaconesses" (records of July 14, 1918). It goes without saying that St. Nektarios would almost certainly have provided the necessary justification.

Metropolitan Meletios once visited Elder Nektarios' convent, but maintained a dissatisfied attitude throughout his visit. His querulous demeanor grieved the convent's founder and damaged his popularity with the people of Aegina in general. The convent's founder wished to see the convent recognized by the official Church of Greece in his lifetime, but it never came to pass. The matter was not finally settled until four years after the repose of the blessed elder, when Chrysostomos Papadopoulos, a wise professor at the University of Athens, ascended to the throne of the Archdiocese of Athens.

As St. Nektarios' successor at Rizareios, Chrysostomos came to admire his predecessor and the work he left behind. He accepted his revival of the institution of deaconesses in the church as well. Only a few years after the saint's repose, Chrysostomos laid hands on other nuns in the Holy Trinity Convent, pronouncing them subdeaconesses on two occasions. On the first occasion, the nuns appointed to this position were Christofora, Kyriaki, Evniki and Paraskevi, and on the second were the nuns Efrosini, Theoktisti, and Haritini.

Archbishop Christodoulos ordained deaconesses as well, following St. Nektarios' example. He ordained Abbess-Deaconess Abbess Efthimia of the Holy Convent of St. Spyridon in Promyriou. He largely used the typikon of the Byzantine Sacramentary, but changed it slightly by inserting the prayers of the deacon's ordination. So the appointing ceremony was a combination of "laying on of hands" and the deacon's ordination, served outside the Holy Altar.

According to Theodorou, the archbishop mainly took this action in order for the abbess-deaconess to be able to bring the presanctified gifts of the Holy Eucharist to the nuns when a priest was unable to reach the convent due to the area's inaccessibility.

In this presentation, I have described the Greek context of the institution of deaconesses and the various efforts by St. Nektarios and others following him to revive it. In the meantime, God has revealed to us St. Nektarios' holiness and at the same time granted us assurance of his saintly actions.

A film about the life of St. Nektarios is in production at the time of the writing of this presentation. I hope that it will portray the historical reality of his life without myths and legends and will be able to be seen on the big screen. Just as the saint's repose has spread the fragrance of the Holy Spirit all around us, so may this film and this conference also cultivate respect for the institution of deaconesses in the noble tradition of the one church united throughout the oikoumene.

Editors' update: The film, titled "Man of God," produced by Yelena Popovic, and starring Aris Servetalis and Mickey Rourke, was released in the summer of 2021. However, it did not include the matter of deaconesses.

Chapter Twenty

THE ROLE OF WOMEN IN THE LIFE OF THE CHURCH ACCORDING TO ST. AMPHILOCHIOS OF PATMOS

Nikolaos G. Tsirevelos

Introduction

Jesus Christ gave a clear command to his disciples: "Go therefore and make disciples of all the nations" (Matt 28:19). Throughout the ages, his disciples, obeying this command of the risen Jesus, proclaimed the coming of God's new world, a world that promises victory over humanity's last enemy, death (1 Cor 15:26). It is especially worth noting that many women have worked and continue to work in spreading the message of the gospel, as well as in social and pastoral ministry.[1] The question that arises, however, is whether this activity can acquire a special institutional character, such as through reinstituting the female diaconate and then organizing a response to the needs of the modern age while also creating the conditions for an effective witness by women.

While there have been some brave, necessary theological reflections on this question,[2] I personally have the sense that history—

---

1. See Θαν. Παπαθανασίου, *Γυναίκες στο δρόμο της ιεραποστολής. Η γυναίκα ως θύμα, ως ύποπτη, ως ευαγγελίστρια*, εκδ. Εν πλω, Αθήνα 2019, σελ. 37 κ.ε. [Thanasis Papathanassiou, *Women on the Road to Mission: The Woman as Victim, Suspect, and Evangelist* (Athens: En Plo, 2019), 37, et seq. (in Greek)].

2. See Ευαγ. Θεοδώρου, *Ἡρωΐδες τῆς χριστιανικῆς ἀγάπης – Αἱ διακόνισσαι διὰ τῶν αἰώνων*, ἐν Ἀθήναις 1949, σ. 29–30 [Evangelos Theodorou, *Heroines of*

specifically contemporary ecclesiastical history—can shed much-needed light on the issue. The church of Christ is a community that has marched through the centuries under the guidance of the Holy Spirit.³ The saints—both male and female—are the ones who have grafted twenty centuries of ecclesiastical tradition onto the demands of each time and place, infusing meaning into the present.

A contemporary saint, who was attuned to today's needs and faithful to the Christian tradition, while also highlighting the role of women, was St. Amphilochios Makris.⁴ Both his ecclesiastical life and his theological discourse worked at formulating a role for women in the context of the life of the contemporary church.

The goal of this work is twofold, first, to capture the special significance that St. Amphilochios gave to active ecclesiastical ministry of women and, second, to highlight a previously unknown incident related to the *cheirothesia*⁵ of deaconesses. I believe that this incident has the ability to some extent to provide a framework for the

---

Christian Agape: Deaconesses through the Ages (Athens, 1949), 29–30]. *Also see,* «Ἡ χειροτονία» ἢ «χειροθεσία» τῶν διακονισσῶν, ἐν Ἀθήναις 1954. *Also see,* «Ο θεσμός των διακονισσών εν τη Ορθοδόξω Εκκλησία», διαθέσιμο στο, accessed July 22, 2022, https://www.imaik.gr/?p=6665. Ν. Ματσούκα, Οἰκουμενική Θεολογία, εκδ. Π. Πουρναράς, Θεσσαλονίκη 2005, σελ. 274–281 [N. Matsoukas, *Ecumenical Theology* (Thessaloniki: P. Pournara), 274–81 (in Greek)]. Κ. Γιοκαρίνη, Η ιεροσύνη των γυναικών στο πλαίσιο της οικουμενικής κίνησης, εκδ. Επέκταση, Κατερίνη 1995, σελ. 97–142 [K. Giokarini, *The Priesthood of Women in the Context of the Ecumenical Movement* (Katerini: Epektasi), 97–142 [in Greek]]. Π. Βασιλειάδη, Διακόνισσες, χειροτονία των γυναικών και ορθόδοξη θεολογία, εκδ. Επίκεντρο, Θεσσαλονίκη 2017, σ. 512 [P. Vassiliadis, *Deaconesses, Ordination of Women, and Orthodox Theology* (Thessaloniki: Epikentro), 512 (in Greek)].

3. Ν. Ματσούκας, Δογματική και Συμβολική Θεολογία Β΄, εκδ. Π. Πουρναράς, Θεσσαλονίκη 1999, σελ. 373 κ.ε. [N. Matsoukas, *Dogmatic and Creedal Theology*, vol. 2 (Thessaloniki: P. Pournara), 373, et seq. [in Greek].

4. For the life of St. Amphilochios Makris, see the study by Ἰγνατίου (Τριάντη) Μητροπολίτου Βερατίου, Αυλώνος και Κανίνης, Ο Γέροντας της Πάτμου Αμφιλόχιος Μακρής (1889–1970). Βίος - Ὑποθῆκαι - Μαρτυρίαι, Ἐκδ. Ι. Μ. «Εὐαγγελισμός» Μ.Η., Πάτμος 1997 [Ignatios (Triantis), Metropolitan of Berat, Vlorë, and Kanina, *The Elder of Patmos: Amphilochios Makris (1889–1970): Life, Maxims, Testimonies* (Patmos: Holy Monastery of the Annunciation, 1997) (in Greek)].

5. The term, which literally means "a laying-on of hands," can signify either or both ordination or tonsure.

church's decisions in the modern age. This new information surfaced during recent research on the life and missionary activity of St. Amphilochios of Patmos (1889–1970).

St. Amphilochios and His Missionary Activity

St. Amphilochios was born and lived in Patmos.[6] He was well known for his pioneering philanthropic endeavors,[7] his peaceful, patriotic resistance to the Italian conquerors of the Dodecanese, and his trailblazing efforts to raise Christian environmental awareness in a time before widespread ecological concern. Moreover, like a new St. Kosmas the Aetolian, he visited many areas of Greece with a missionary ethos aimed at re-evangelizing the Orthodox.[8]

Glowing reports of his spiritual work and missionary zeal exceeded the narrow confines of Greece. Even though he did not travel abroad, word of his holiness drew people from all over the world to Patmos. Additionally, St. Amphilochios inspired contemporary spiritual leaders such as Ecumenical Patriarch Bartholomew, the missionary-minded Archbishop Anastasios of Albania, as well as Metropolitan Kallistos (Ware) of Diokleia, Metropolitan Amphilochios (Tsoukos) of Ganos and Chora (formerly of New Zealand), Gerontissa Gavrielia, Gerontissa Efstochia in the Dodecanese, and many others.[9]

Utilizing Women in Mission and Ministry

In his multidimensional missionary, pastoral, and ministerial work, St. Amphilochios had many women as collaborators. These women—married, widows, unmarried, and nuns—witnessed for Christ in the Dodecanese and cared for the relief of those who were suffering.

---

6. *The Elder of Patmos*, 18.

7. Ibid., 14.

8. Ν. Τσιρέβελου, Ένας Πρόδρομος της Ορθόδοξης μαρτυρίας στα έθνη. Άγιος Αμφιλόχιος Πάτμου, εκδ. Ostracon Publ., Θεσσαλονίκη 2019, σελ. 48–53 [N. Tsirevelos, *A Forerunner of Orthodox Witness to the Nations: St. Amphilochios of Patmos* (Thessaloniki: Ostracon, 2019), 48–53 (in Greek)].

9. Ibid., 57–62.

As early as the late 1920s, his monastic virtues and self-sacrificial ministry prompted some young Kalymnians, first of whom was the teacher Kalliopi Gounari (later nun Efstochia), to work with him.[10] During the Asia Minor Catastrophe of 1922, when the islands of Kalymnos and Kos received a large number of refugees from Smyrna, Bodrum (Halicarnassus), and other Greek cities, as well as during the occupation by the Italians and the Germans during the Second World War,[11] St. Amphilochios used his spiritual renown to call Christians—men and women, young and old—to provide practical and moral support for the refugees' pain, suffering, and hunger. In order to deal more quickly and effectively with the refugees' problems and poverty, he set up rehabilitation committees for their impoverished brothers and sisters. Women were almost always in charge of these committees, and the committees found accommodations for the refugees in private homes and monasteries.[12]

St. Amphilochios believed that monasticism should play a leading role in this social work. Thus, when St. Amphilochios was abbot and patriarchal exarch, he founded the Convent of the Annunciation on Patmos. The sisterhood of nuns—in addition to the ideals of monasticism and the asceticism it cultivated—worked to spread the Orthodox tradition and develop important charitable works. They thus lived the monastic life within the framework of St. Basil the Great's Rule,[13] i.e., "as an expression of monastic love for God and neighbor, emphasizing the importance of communal life."[14] Specifically, they founded and taught Sunday schools throughout the Dodecanese,[15]

---

10. Ibid., 32–3 and 139.
11. Ibid., 37.
12. See Ν. Τσιρέβελου, Ένας Πρόδρομος, ό.π., σελ. 139–40 [N. Tsirevelos, *A Forerunner*, 139–40 (in Greek)].
13. See St. Basil the Great, *The Longer Rules and The Shorter Rules*, PG 31.
14. See Γ. Μαντζαρίδη, Κοινωνιολογία του Χριστιανισμού, εκδ. Π. Πουρναράς, Θεσσαλονίκη 1999, σελ. 120 [G. Mantzaridis, *Sociology of Christianity* (Thessaloniki: P. Pournara, 1999), 120 [in Greek]].
15. Ελ. Κουλοπούλου, Η μακαριστή Γερόντισσα Ευστοχία, ό.π., σελ. 24–29 [El. Koulopoulou, *The Blessed Gerontissa Efstochia*, 24–29 (in Greek)].

held religious events focusing on women and children, supported patriotic activities, and helped organize a unique solidarity network.

After World War II, St. Amphilochios and the nuns founded the charitable fund of St. Xeni. This philanthropic group organized soup kitchens, cared for the needy, nursed the sick, and comforted marginalized people.[16]

This activity culminated in the nuns' ministry at the Rhodes Orphanage. The holy elder encouraged the nuns of Annunciation Convent to assume care for the infants and education of the orphanage's children. One group of nuns, led by Gerontissa Efstochia, accepted this high calling,[17] offering their services to the orphanage, which at the time numbered 150 orphans and approximately thirty infants.[18] The nuns taught at the orphanage's elementary school as well as at the workshops on housekeeping, sewing, woodburning, and traditional embroidery. St. Amphilochios often visited the orphanage, celebrating the divine liturgy in the Church of St. Irene and sitting with the orphans as a loving father.[19]

In his advice to the nuns, he asked each of them personally "to be a mother to the orphans, a teacher of the children, a nurse to the sick, a social worker." Through this social activity, he wanted mo-

---

16. Ibid., 24 and 128.

17. For more information, as well as a rich photograph collection, see ibid., 73–116.

18. Nuns from the Holy Monastery of the Annunciation continue to this day to serve at the Rhodes Orphanage, which was honored with an Award of the Academy of Athens in 1952. The nuns base their selfless ministry on the example and advice of St. Amphilochios. For more, see Ν. Τσιρέβελου, Ένας Πρόδρομος, ό.π., σελ. 142 [N. Tsirevelos, *A Forerunner*, 142, in Greek only]. The importance of the nuns' ministry to this day at the Rhodes Orphanage was recognized even by St. Porphyrios the Kapsokalyvite in *Ο Όσιος Πορφύριος (Μαρτυρίες – Διηγήσεις – Νουθεσίες), εκδ. Ενωμένη Ρωμιοσύνη, Θεσσαλονίκη* 2017, σελ. 51 [*St. Porphyrios: Testimonies, Narratives, Instructions* (Thessaloniki: Enomeni Romiosyni, 2017), 51 (in Greek)].

19. Ιγνατίου Μητροπολίτη Βερατίου, *Ο Γέροντας της Πάτμου*, ό.π., σελ. 83 [Ignatios, Metropolitan of Berat, *The Elder of Patmos*, 83 (in Greek)].

nasticism in general and particularly his nuns "to gain the respect, appreciation, and trust of the people."[20]

In addition, he wanted women, and especially nuns, to take the lead in the work of re-evangelizing the Orthodox and bearing Christian witness to the nations.[21] The holy elder continually emphasized that "we need missionary-minded nuns as well as monks."[22] On these grounds, he urged Gerontissa Gavrielia to work as a missionary in India and other women to mission in Europe and Africa.[23]

St. Amphilochios promoted the role of women in the life of the church at a time when this was anything but self-evident. In this

---

20. Αρχιμ. Π. Νικηταρά, *Ο Γέροντας Αμφιλόχιος Μακρής*, ό.π., σελ. 42 [Archim. P. Nikitara, *Elder Amphilochios Makris*, 42 (Greek only)].

21. On women's contribution to mission, cf. the following articles for an entirely suggestive introduction to the issue: Γ. Πατρώνου, «Οι 'μικροί' και 'άσημοι' της ιεραποστολής», *Πάντα τα Έθνη*, τεύχ. 10 (1984), σελ. 6–7. Ηλ. Βουλγαράκη, «Γυναίκες και ιεραποστολή στους πρώτους ιεραποστολικούς χρόνους», *Πάντα τα Έθνη*, τεύχ. 38 (1991), σελ. 35–37. *Also see* «Η Πρίσκιλλα», *Πάντα τα Έθνη*, τεύχ. 40 (1991), σελ. 107–109. Regarding women's missionary responsibilities, see Εύης Βουλγαράκη Πισίνα, *Η προσέγγιση των εθνικών κατά τον άγιο Ιωάννη τον Χρυσόστομο*, εκδ. Μαΐστρος, Αθήνα 2016, σελ. 322 κ.ε. [Evi Voulgaraki Pissina, *Approaching the Gentiles According to Saint John Chrysostom* (Athens: Maistros, 2016), 322, et seq., (in Greek)]. On women's role in the church, see Ελ. Κασσελούρη-Χατζηβασιλειάδη, «Ο ρόλος των γυναικών στη ζωή της Εκκλησίας. Από τις μαρτυρίες της Καινής Διαθήκης στο σύγχρονο οικουμενικό διάλογο», *Δελτίο Βιβλικών Μελετών* 24 (2006), σελ. 123–136 and Θαν. Παπαθανασίου, *Γυναίκες στο δρόμο της ιεραποστολής. Η γυναίκα ως θύμα, ως ύποπτη, ως ευαγγελίστρια*, εκδ. Εν πλω, Αθήνα 2019, σσ. 168 [Evi Voulgaraki Pissina, Approaching the Gentiles According to Saint John Chrysostom (Athens: Maistros, 2016), 322, et seq. (in Greek)] and Θαν. Παπαθανασίου, *Γυναίκες στο δρόμο της ιεραποστολής. Η γυναίκα ως θύμα, ως ύποπτη, ως ευαγγελίστρια*, εκδ. Εν πλω, Αθήνα 2019, σ. 168 [Thanasis Papathanassiou, *Women on the Road to Mission: Woman as Victim, Suspect, and Evangelist*, 168 (in Greek)].

22. Ν. Τσιρέβελου, *Ένας Πρόδρομος*, ό.π., σελ. 92 [N. Tsirevelos, *A Forerunner* 92, in Greek only]. Ιγνατίου Μητροπολίτη Βερατίου, *Ο Γέροντας της Πάτμου*, ό.π., σελ. 193 και 196 αντίστοιχα [Ignatios, Metropolitan of Berat, *The Elder of Patmos*, 193 and 196, respectively (in Greek)]. In fact, he believed that "the nuns are the dedicated [. . .] who must hold well the lamp of divine light, in order to shine in the darkness of the present wandering age and to give light to the many others who are running away from the precipice of sin, destruction and annihilation."

23. Ν. Τσιρέβελου, *Ένας Πρόδρομος*, ό.π., σελ. 95 [N. Tsirevelos, *A Forerunner*, 95 (in Greek)].

context, he likened the nuns to the myrrhbearers. He perceptively observed that the Lord revealed his resurrection first to the myrrhbearers, while elsewhere he noted, referring to nuns, that "Christ uplifted women; that's why you [nuns] should love Him all the more fervently.... That is also why the Apostle Paul chose the Greek woman Lydia to be the first missionary in Europe."[24]

A Previously Unknown Incident Related to the Cheirothesia of Women.

Based on all the above, it should be clear that St. Amphilochios wanted women to play a leading role in the church and in public. In fact, he wanted women's mission to be more dynamic and to be able to offer more through the institutional diaconate of women. This understanding is fully confirmed by an incident discovered during my research. More specifically, Eleni Koulopoulou, in a book about Gerontissa Efstochia (born Kalliopi Gounari), one of St. Amphilochios' first co-workers, has preserved an otherwise unknown incident. This incident occurred in the wake of the Dodecanese's liberation from the Italian fascist and German Nazi occupation. The material and spiritual needs in the eastern islands of the South Aegean were particularly acute. The saint thus engaged many women in support of other women, children, and the elderly.

At that time, the Exarch of the Ecumenical Patriarchate in the now-free Dodecanese was Metropolitan Panteleimon (Papageorgiou) of Edessa and Pella.[25] According to sources, in light of these unprecedented historical conditions[26] as well as the unique spiritual

---

24. See Ιγνατίου Μητροπολίτη Βερατίου, *Ο Γέροντας της Πάτμου*, ό.π., σελ. 194 και 238 αντίστοιχα [Ignatios, Metropolitan of Berat, *The Elder of Patmos*, 194 and 238 (in Greek)].

25. Π. Βασιλειάδη (επιμ), *Μνήμη Μητροπολίτου Παντελεήμονος Παπαγεωργίου. Αναμνήσεις από τη ζωή, το έργο και τη μαρτυρία του*, Πρακτικά Επιστημονικής Διημερίδας, εκδ. ΙΜ Εδέσσης, Έδεσσα 2012, σ. 336 [P. Vassiliadis, ed., *In Memory of Metropolitan Panteleimon Papageorgiou* (Edessa: Holy Metropolis of Edessa, 2012), 336 (in Greek)].

26. Χρ. Παπαχριστοδούλου, *Ιστορία της Ρόδου*, Αθήναι 1972, εκδ. Στέγη Τεχνών και Γραμμάτων Δωδεκανήσου, σελ. 178 [Chr. Papachristodoulou, *History of Rhodes* (Athens: Stegi Technon and Grammaton Dodecanesou, 1972), 178 (in Greek)].

needs, St. Amphilochios asked Metropolitan Panteleimon to "lay his hands on" Gerontissa Efstochia as a deaconess, so that she would be able, "in an hour of need, to distribute Holy Communion to sick and dying nuns."²⁷ Metropolitan Panteleimon "laid his hands" on her on September 24, 1946. Efstochia, a deaconess and abbess to the nuns of the Holy Convent of the Annunciation of the Theotokos on Patmos, continued to minister to the nuns and to the public, following the instructions of her saintly elder. In this way, in response to the urgent needs of the church, the holy elder proposed a solution that stemmed from the church's historical experience and essentially recognized the ministry of women in the life of the church.

Conclusions

St. Amphilochios's proposal to Metropolitan Panteleimon was in accordance with the church's ancient tradition regarding the office of deaconesses.²⁸ It seems that the holy elder was influenced by St. Nektarios, Metropolitan of Pentapolis,²⁹ with whom he had been spiritually connected from a young age. St. Nektarios was the first to revive this institution after many centuries.³⁰

---

27. Ελ. Κουλοπούλου, *Η μακαριστή Γερόντισσα Ευστοχία*, ό.π., σελ. 67 [El. Koulopoulou, *The Blessed Gerontissa Efstochia*, 67 (in Greek)]. Of course, the sources consulted did not indicate whether she was ordained according to the Typikon for the ordination of deaconesses or whether she received a special blessing for the distribution of Holy Communion.

28. For more on this issue, see Ευαγ. Θεοδώρου, *Ο θεσμός των Διακονισσών εν τη Ορθοδόξω Εκκλησία και η δυνατότης αναβιώσεως αυτού*, Αθήνα 1954, σ. 112 [Evangelos Theodorou, *The Office of Deaconesses in the Orthodox Church and the Possibility of Its Restoration* (Athens, 1954), 112 (in Greek)]. Ν. Ματσούκα, *Οικουμενική θεολογία*, εκδ. Π. Πουρναρά, Θεσσαλονίκη 2005, σελ. 276–281 [N. Matsoukas, *Ecumenical Theology* (Thessaloniki: P. Pournara), 276–281) (in Greek)]. Π. Βασιλειάδη (επιμ.), *Διακόνισσες, χειροτονία των γυναικών και ορθόδοξη θεολογία*, εκδ. Επίκεντρο, Θεσσαλονίκη 2017, σσ. 512 [P. Vassiliadis, *Deaconesses, Ordination of Women, and Orthodox Theology*, 512 (in Greek)].

29. Π Βασιλειάδης, *Ρινίσματα καθημερινότητας: Θεολογικά και κοινωνικά*, Θεσσαλονίκη 2019, σελ. 158 [P. Vassiliadis, *Reflections on Everyday Life: Theological and Social* (Thessaloniki, 2019), 158 (in Greek)].

30. Patriarch and Pope of Alexandria Theodoros "laid his hands on" deaconesses to minister to the African Church. Accessed May 1, 2020, https://

How is one to understand the church's position on this issue in the face of the challenges posed by postmodernity?³¹ In the secularized public sphere, important steps have been taken to institutionalize the equality of women, such as the Universal Declaration of Human Rights and the European Charter for Gender Equality in Local Communities.³² With regard to the church's position, Petros Vassiliadis' observation is apt:

> When society was dominated by a patriarchal worldview, the Church had women apostles, equals-to-the-apostles, and deaconesses, who belonged—I hasten to note—to the upper clergy. Today, when society either has or is seeking full equality, participation, and democracy, unfortunately the Church behaves in an un-Orthodox, anti-Christian, anti-social and, ultimately, anti-democratic way.³³

Thus, on the one hand, the fact that women played a multifaceted role in the life of the church is indisputable, while, on the other, it is clear that this is a major concern for the modern age.

However, one should not forget that, "no dogmatic ruling precludes the priesthood of women, but rather only canonical prohibition and social concerns."³⁴ Furthermore, since it is not a dogmatic issue, any changes enacted by the local Orthodox churches are valid.³⁵ For example, *mutatis mutandis*, the charter of the Auto-

---

ierapostoli.wordpress.com/2017/02/18/historic-day-for-the-patriarchate-of-alexandria-the-institution-of-deaconesses-women/.

31. See the reflections by Petros Vassiliadis, in *Ρινίσματα καθημερινότητας*, ό.π., σελ. 70–76 και 133 [*Reflections on Everyday Life: Theological and Social*, 70–76 and 133 (in Greek)].

32. "Universal Declaration of Human Rights (Preamble)," accessed July 22, 2022, https://www.ohchr.org/en/human-rights/universal-declaration/translations/english. Cf., "European Charter for Gender Equality in Local Communities," accessed July 22, 2022, https://www.ccre.org/docs/charte_egalite_en.pdf.

33. Π. Βασιλειάδη, *Ρινίσματα καθημερινότητας*, ό.π., σελ. 195 [Petros Vassiliadis, *Reflections on Everyday Life: Theological and Social*, 195 (in Greek)].

34. Ν. Ματσούκα, «Η Εύα της θεολογίας και η γυναίκα της ιστορίας», *Σύναξη* 36 (1990), σελ. 15.

35. Π. Βασιλειάδη, *Ρινίσματα καθημερινότητας*, ό.π., σελ. 159 [Petros Vassiliadis, *Reflections on Everyday Life: Theological and Social*, 159 (in Greek)]: "In general terms, it must be said that only dogmatic impediments and commonly

cephalous Orthodox Church of Albania, calls from the very beginning for a balanced representation of clergy and laity in all mixed councils. This quota ensures the participation of the laity as well as equal participation of men and women.[36]

Based on all these considerations, is it fair to wonder whether the institutional restriction of women is ultimately linked to outdated social perceptions and cultural conditions, which have "assumed the prestige of unchanging tradition"[37] and thus ultimately hindered the mission of the church?

If today one lists women's activities in the church, one will find that they are largely continuing the activity of the deaconesses of the fourth century AD—i.e., teaching, catechism, and charitable work—but also general participation in the events of the local church according to the needs and possibilities of each time and place.

However, at this point, another question arises. Is it not enough to highlight the importance of women through the contributions of the presvytera (priest's wife) or the nun or even the women who are active co-workers in the life of the local parish? I believe that the

---

accepted, valid precedents can prevent an autocephalous Orthodox Church from instituting liturgical reforms within its jurisdiction. Liturgical and canonical issues that have consequences beyond the boundaries of local churches are generally resolved with the consensus of all the autocephalous churches. With the restoration of the order of deaconesses, however, neither dogmatic issues nor canonical precedents are at stake. It is refreshing that a local church has faced the challenge, carefully studied the subject, and proposed measures to implement an important adjustment—the restoration of the order of the deaconesses—through a carefully planned program."

36. See Αναστασίου Αρχιεπισκόπου Τιράνων, Δυρραχίου και πάσης Αλβανίας, Η ανασύσταση της Ορθοδόξου Αυτοκεφάλου Εκκλησίας της Αλβανίας, 1991–2012. (Συνοπτική αναφορά). Β΄ επαυξημένη έκδοση, Ορθόδοξος Αυτοκέφαλος Εκκλησία της Αλβανίας, Τίρανα 2013 [Archbishop Anastasios of Tirana, Durrës, and all Albania, *The Reconstitution of the Autocephalous Orthodox Church of Albania, 1991–2012. (Summary report).* 2nd ed. (Tirana: Orthodox Autocephalous Church of Albania, 2013) (in Greek)].

37. Δημ. Κούκουρα, Η θέση της γυναίκας στην Ορθόδοξη Εκκλησία και μελετήματα οικουμενικού προβληματισμού, εκδ. Σφακιανάκη Κορνηλία, Θεσσαλονίκη 2006, σελ. 118 [D. Koukoura, *The Role of Women in the Orthodox Church and Essays of Ecumenical Reflection* (Thessaloniki: Sfakianaki Kornilia, 2006), 118 (in Greek)].

answer to this question lies in the tradition of the church and the needs of contemporary society.

If one truly desires to ground oneself in the authentic eucharistic experience that leads to the "liturgy after the Liturgy,"[38] witness to the nations, and the re-evangelization of Christians, then the Orthodox Church needs to seriously examine the advantages of restoring the office of deaconess in the contemporary life of the church, especially in light of today's challenges. In this process, theology must be an aide. According to the late Nikos Matsoukas, "theology must dialogue with the problems that emerge in each era and offer its conclusions in service of the Church, which can then implement them when needed. The Church knows that 'when.' It may be never."[39]

In other words, the restoration of the office of deaconesses could contribute—under certain conditions—to the church's more effective missionary witness and pastoral ministry to the world. It could gain the trust of society and especially women in light of the challenges of postmodernity. It would officially recognize women's contribution to the life of the church. At the same time, however, it would encourage the more active involvement and reception of the church's women in the public sphere, and, consequently, their ministry and offering on the "altar of society."[40]

---

38. This important concept first began to be developed in a talk by then lay theologian Anastasios Giannoulatos to the members of the Christian Union of Academics during the Second Sunday of Lent (Feast of St. Gregory of Palamas) in 1963 in Athens. The term "liturgy after the Liturgy" was first used at the missionary conference on "Confessing Christ through the Liturgical Life of the Church Today" at Etchmiadzin in Armenia in 1975. Archbishop Albania of Tirana, Durres and All Albania, *Mission in Christ's Footsteps* (Boston: Holy Cross Orthodox Press, 2010). See also Ν. Τσιρέβελου, Θεολογική θεμελίωση της Ορθόδοξης μαρτυρίας. Σπουδή στο έργο του Αρχιεπισκόπου Αλβανίας Αναστασίου, εκδ. Ostracon Publ., Θεσσαλονίκη 2015, σελ. 101–07 [N. Tsirevelos, *The Theological Foundation of Orthodox Witness*, 1991–2012 (Thessaloniki: Ostracon, 2015) (in Greek)].

39. Cited in Δημ. Κούκουρα, *Η θέση της γυναίκας*, ό.π., σελ 118, υποσ. 23-4 [D. Koukoura, *The Role of Women*, 118, n. 23-4) (in Greek)].

40. Ibid., 119.

Ultimately, it is worth noting that the church journeys through history utilizing its praxis and experience to respond in a therapeutic way to the problems of each age. This praxis is always trailblazing and resists unhealthy ideologies, stereotypes, and fundamentalist preconceptions. This work is carried out by the saints, who graft the tradition of the spirit of the fathers into every time and place. One such act is St. Amphilochios's utilization of women, both lay woman and nuns, in the life of the local churches of the Dodecanese. The culmination of this praxis was the *cheirothesia* of Abbess Efstochia as a deaconess.

Such actions provide a framework for the church's present and future witness to the world. They also highlight women's ministry to contemporary needs and demonstrate that in the church, the Body of Christ, there are no distinctions between male and female (Gal 3:28), but rather different spiritual gifts, kinds of ministries, and a variety of activities (1 Cor 12:4–6), which God generously bestows on both men and women. Through courageous decisions and actions, in accord with the spirit of the patristic tradition, the church can offer its witness to the challenges of the twenty-first century at both the local and global levels, proclaiming in practice that the Orthodox eagerly await "new heavens and a new earth" (2 Pt 3:13).

APPENDIX

(i) IN MEMORIAM

MARIA SPYROPOULOU: THE SEMI-TRANSPARENT DEACONESS[1]

Athanasios N. Papathanasiou

On January 17, 2022, the feast day of St. Anthony, a deaconess of the Orthodox Church was transferred to the jurisdiction of the Church Triumphant. Maria Spyropoulou, deaconess of the missionary Church of Korea, fell asleep after an 89-year journey on earth.

Her Background

A short biography, which the deaconess herself prepared on a typewriter, provides us with some details about her life before missionary work: Born February 6, 1933 in Meligalas, Messinia, Greece, she studied at the Maraslio Pedagogical Academy of Athens (1952–54) and worked as a teacher in private (1954–56) and public (1958–61) schools. She studied theology and journalism in France (1963–66) and collaborated with the magazine *Contacts* of the Orthodox Theological Institute of Saint Sergius in Paris. She then went to Bucharest (1968–70), where she attended courses on the Romanian language and theology, as well as the ecclesiastical life of the country.

---

1. Published in the quarterly *Panta ta Ethni* 161 (2022): 14–21 [in Greek]. Translated by Rev. Dr. Gregory Edwards. A condensed version of the English appeared in "Public Orthodoxy" on June 24, 2022, accessed July 4, 2022, https://publicorthodoxy.org/2022/06/24/maria-spyropoulou-the-semi-transparent-deaconess/.

Returning to Greece, the Archdiocese of Athens placed her in charge of the spiritual center "Bethlehem" (1970–71) and, starting in November 1972, she worked on the Standing Synodal Committee, from which she resigned in July 1973. In November of the same year, she began work at the Inter-Orthodox Center of Athens, responsible for relations with the Church of Romania.

Ultimately, however, the European context played a small role for Maria Spyropoulou, who already felt that mission was (as she told us) "a madness"—a stretching forth of the wings to the ends of the earth!

In the Land of the Morning Calm

On December 1, 1975, the Very Rev. Archimandrite Sotirios Trambas (who later became Metropolitan of Korea and is now Metropolitan of Pisidia[2]) left the parish of Holy Protection (Agia Skepi), Papagos, Athens, to embark on a surprising missionary endeavor at the Orthodox church of St. Nicholas in Seoul, South Korea. Maria Spyropoulou was one of his collaborators in the Athenian rearguard who supported the missionary resumption in Korea that the Orthodox communities founded at the dawn of the twentieth century by the missionary work of the Church of Russia, which had become essentially extinct. Shortly thereafter, Maria Spyropoulou moved to Seoul and began a multi-faceted missionary endeavor that lasted nearly twenty-five years—until July 13, 2000, when she returned to Greece for health reasons. Even this, however, did nothing to slow her missionary work, which she continued through publications and any other way she could.

Maria Spyropoulou was a motherly apostolic presence in the newly formed Korean Church. She learned only a little Korean, but her preeminent contribution was her heartfelt communication with

---

2. Cf. Hye Won (Eleni) Cho, *The Orthodox Message in Korea: Transmission and Reception* (doctoral dissertation in the Department of Theology, Aristotle University of Thessaloniki), Thessaloniki 2021, 75–76 [in Greek]. Cf. also Andreas S. Heliotis, *Orthodoxy in Korea: A Brief History of the Mission of the Orthodox Church in Korea* (Athens: Patriarchal Foundation for Orthodox Mission in the Far East, 2005), 238 [in Greek].

the Korean faithful, both women and men. She has related[3] how the Korean women asked her to mediate for them in a very special way with their confessor Fr. Sotirios: they wanted her to be present and to hold their hands tightly! Their need (which one suddenly realizes on the ground in the missionary field, if one is truly open to cultural diversity) stems from the traditional Korean sense of respect and hierarchy—a pyramidal social structure, influenced especially by Confucianism. Maria Spyropoulou's presence, I believe, helped bring about a special incarnation of the gospel. The local culture was adopted, but at the same time it was engrafted with a new perspective: Women were called to a new candor with their male shepherd, made possible by the dynamic female example set by Maria Spyropoulou, who played a mystagogical role. In my reading, from the perspective of the field of missiology, Maria Spyropoulou's impact corresponded to the impact made by female missionaries in societies with various class and gender barriers, which male missionaries struggled to broach.[4]

Maria Spyropoulou prepared teaching material, taught religious education, contributed to translations, edited publications, assisted in worship and the celebration of the sacraments, and penned articles for *Panta ta Ethni* (a quarterly publication from the Office for Mission of the Church of Greece)[5] and elsewhere. The springboard for all this activity was her firm conviction that what was needed was a new incarnation of the gospel, and not simply an export of Greek or Byzantine culture. Indicative of this was her openness to the possibility of using something other than wheat bread and wine in the celebration of the Eucharist, if these materials were not part of the local culture. Conversations with her were always in-depth and

---

3. From her talk (recorded but unpublished) at an event at the Holy Church of St. Philip (Theseion, Athens), organized by Fr. Demetrios Maroulis, on June 17, 2019.

4. Cf. Athanasios N. Papathanasiou, "From Women of the Bible to Women with the Bible," in *Women on the Road to Mission: The Woman as Victim, Suspect, Evangelist* (Athens: En Plo, 2019), 105–11 [in Greek].

5. The title of this publication, *Panta ta Ethni* (literally, "all the nations") is taken from Matt 28:19: "Go therefore and make disciples of all the nations."

wide-ranging, but she committed few of them to paper. Her activities and views are currently to a large extent unrecorded, since she herself was the one who edited the publications in which these would normally be found. In fact, she often destroyed her notes, which she thought might upset some people. Her modesty and sensitivity thus demanded that she leave herself out of stories and photographs, even though people close to her insisted that respectful reporting does not equal personal promotion, but rather is something necessary for the church body and its arduous course through history.

In 2005, Fr. Sotirios Trambas, then Metropolitan of Korea, highlighted her contribution in the introduction to the two-volume publication commemorating the centennial of the Orthodox Church in Korea:

> This publication would not have been possible if not for the invaluable contribution over thirty of years of the Deaconess and teacher of the Korean Orthodox Mission, Maria Spyropoulou, who took care to record, throughout her years of service to the Church of Korea, what she heard from the older Korean faithful, as well as what she herself lived and experienced in the land of our Church. Additionally, she diligently collected everything that was written about Orthodoxy in Korea in various publications. For her sacrificial offering to the Korean Mission as well as these additional efforts, she justly deserves the Church's praise, and we, from our position, warmly thank her.[6]

However, the crown of Maria Spyropoulou's efforts is something that deserves special attention: the institutional role given to her by the church, for the life of the church itself!

"Something Has Now Changed!"

On Sunday, September 24, 1978, the Cathedral Church of St. Nicholas in Seoul was consecrated by then Metropolitan of New Zea-

---

6. *The Orthodox Church of Korea:* vol. 1, *In Progress* (Athens: Tinos, 2005), 9–10.

land and Exarch of Korea, Dionysios Psiachas (1916–2008).[7] During the service, Metropolitan Dionysios tonsured Maria Spyropoulou a deaconess. The idea came from the metropolitan himself, who was spiritually and theologically grounded, and who—from what we can tell—had already tonsured other deaconesses in his diocese. The metropolitan, along with Fr. Sotirios and Maria, were well aware that in the tradition of the church deaconesses were ordained (χειροτονία) and not simply tonsured (χειροθεσία), as Professor Evangelos Theodorou had demonstrated beginning in 1949.[8] Nevertheless, it seems that ordination was seen as a bridge too far for the ecclesiastical milieu of the time, with its well-known proclivity to replace the church's robust and dynamic tradition with a feeble traditionalism. And, unfortunately, history has witnessed to the staying power of this ailment. I will return to this after first quoting the prayer read during (and for) her tonsure. The prayer was composed by the late Metropolitan Dionysios in Greek, and I publish it in full here below[9] (the deaconess had preserved the typewritten text in her personal archives):

> O great, wonderful, and eternal God, Who through the inexpressible descent of Your only-begotten Son and the visitation of Your Holy Spirit established Your Holy Church, Who through Your ineffable foreknowledge also called this Your servant to the deaconate in Your Holy Church—we beg and entreat You, this same Master, to send your grace from on high down upon your servant Maria and make her a Dea-

---

7. The construction of the church began in 1967. The *thyranoixia* (ceremony for the opening of the doors) occurred in 1968, but the consecration had been left hanging. Cf. Cho, *The Orthodox Message in Korea*, 73; Heliotis, *Orthodoxy in Korea*, 129–30.

8. Evangelos D. Theodorou, *Heroines of Christian Love: Deaconesses Through the Centuries* (Athens: Apostoliki Diakonia, 1949 [in Greek]. Theodorou, *The "Ordination" or "Tonsure" of Deaconesses* (doctoral dissertation) (Athens, 1954) [in Greek].

9. Most of the prayer by Archimandrite Sotirios Trampas was published in *The Orthodox Church of Korea:* vol. 2, *Testimonies*, ed. Maria Spyropoulou (Athens: Tinos, 2007), 62. His text was first published in the journal *Fos Ethnon*, 193.

coness of Your One, Holy, Catholic and Apostolic Church. Sanctify her with an imperishable blessing. Strengthen her so that she may blamelessly serve in Your Church for the salvation of souls and to the honor and glory of Your Holy Name and for a share in the portion of Your Elect in Your Kingdom, through the intercessions of the Most-Holy Theotokos and ever-virgin Mary, the holy Deaconesses Phoebe and Olympia, and all Your saints. For You are our God Who rests in Your saints and to You we offer up glory, to the Father and to the Son, and to the Holy Spirit, now and ever and unto ages of ages. Amen.

The Certificate of Tonsure, which the Metropolitan signed on the Holy Altar and gave to the deaconess (and which she also preserved in her archives), is typewritten in Greek on Metropolis letterhead, which reads "The Greek Orthodox Archdiocese of New Zealand, Exarchate of India, Korea & Japan," followed by the postal address and the name of the metropolitan. It reads as follows:

> According to the episcopal authority given to Our Humility by the Holy Apostles for the administration of the Holy Church of Christ, during the consecration of the Holy Church of St. Nicholas in Seoul, Korea, on Sunday, September 24 of the year 1978, the most devout Maria Spyropoulou, a teacher, catechist, and coworker of the Orthodox Mission of Korea, was appointed a Deaconess of the One, Holy, Catholic, and Apostolic Church. I bestowed this blessing to serve the holy Church, to care for the propriety of the holy churches and the proper order of women in the sacred rites, to lead works of charity and the catechism of women, offering to women being baptized every possible aid, ministering to the work of the Orthodox mission with all her might and, ultimately, performing all the ministry belonging to the Deaconesses, according to the Sacred Tradition of our Holy Orthodox Church. Whence, and to this end was the present Certificate of Tonsure composed by Our Humility and given to the most devout Deaconess Maria for proof thereof. Given on September 25, 1978, in the Cathedral Church of

St. Nicholas of Seoul, Korea. The Metropolitan of New Zealand and Exarch of Korea, Dionysios.

Two years after her tonsure, Maria Spyropoulou's name and office appeared (as was fitting) in the official "Ecclesiastical Register" of the Church of Greece, which was later renamed "Diptychs." This is the annual publication in which the structure and staff of the Church of Greece and other local Orthodox Churches are recorded.[10] In the volume for 1981, we find the inscription: "Deaconess-Teacher Maria Spyropoulou." This entry is also found in the publications over the next six years, through 1987 (namely, for seven straight years). It then disappears! Which means that the Greek ecclesiastical obduracy tolerated this beautiful and deserving witness for just seven years, and then extinguished it for the next thirteen years of the deaconess' Korean ministry, and the next thirty-three years of her life! Maria knew full well that this miserly move would harm the whole case for women's ministry, but she kept silent, sharing it only with a few people close to her. Just a few years before her repose, she began to mention it publicly, but always at the urging of her persistent friends. In short, Deaconess Maria was a person both seen and unseen, visible and invisible, semi-transparent![11]

At any rate, the Korean Orthodox communities embraced their deaconess with insightful joy. They sensed, in other words, that the dark blue garment, with the dark blue headdress, which the deaconess wore from then on (and with which she aided in worship, held the Communion cloth during the Eucharist, collaborated in the performance of the sacraments, catechized, etc.) signaled something essential: the church's desire for apostolic motherhood's struc-

---

10. Beginning in 1954, the Church of Greece published the "Ecclesiastical Register" as a continuation of the "Handbook of the Ecclesiastical Register" (1924–1953) by Emmanuel Farlekas. In 1989, the "Register" was renamed the "Diptychs of the Church of Greece." Cf. Dionysios Anatolikiotis, "The Diptychs of the Church of Greece: Ninety Years of History," *Ephemerios* 62.3 (2013): 23–24 [in Greek].

11. I chose this term to illustrate: 1) Deaconess Maria's effort to become a transparent vessel for Christ's light to shine through, as well as, 2) the relative obscurity in which she toiled.

tural (and not simply incidental) integration into its body. Maria told us of the Koreans' joy, that "something has now changed," and she particularly recalled the words of the elderly man Pavel,[12] who enjoyed everyone's respect: "You are the same, but you are different. Something changed." Indeed, the Spirit had blown where it wished!

The following illustrates the deaconess' ethos and her unceasing withdrawal from the spotlight (and also speaks to the importance of thorough study of the history of the mission): in 2001, the Church of Korea published a 246-page photo retrospective on the centennial anniversary of Orthodoxy in Korea.[13] One must search with a microscope to locate Maria Spyropoulou in a single photograph from 1977, holding a lighted candle among the newly illumined Christians from a group baptism (46). Among the photos from the consecration of St. Nicholas (48–52), there is not a single one of her tonsure, nor is there any reference to it in the section on "Ordinations and Tonsures," where we find photos even from the awarding of patriarchal *offikia* (awards) to various members of the community (203). The diligent reader will finally find information about the tonsure in the "Chronology of Events in the Orthodox Church of Korea," at the end of the album (260 and 263). Similarly, in a chronicle that Maria herself wrote about the consecration for the missionary Greek journal *Fos Ethnon* ("Light to the Nations"), she completely neglected her own tonsure![14] Fortunately, however, it was

---

12. From Deaconess Maria's talk at the Holy Church of St. Philip Theseiou, *op. cit.*, n. 3. Cp. the interview with Pavel Kim in: *The Orthodox Church of Korea:* vol 1., *In Progress*, 51–56.

13. *100 Years of Orthodoxy in Korea: Commemorative Album, 1900–2000*, ed. Fr. Antonios Woo; photographs, captions, and timelines by Deaconess Maria Spyropoulou, published by Bishop Sotirios of Zelon and Archimandrite Dr. Ambrosios Zografos (Seoul: Orthodox Editions, 2001). The volume is trilingual, in Korean, Greek, and English.

14. *The Orthodox Church of Korea:* vol. 1. *In Progress*, 39–41. (The text was first published in the journal *Fos Ethnon*, 155). It is worth noting that, although a deaconess is a rare and remarkable phenomenon in today's Orthodox Church, Deaconess Maria was usually overlooked also in the travel accounts published by visitors to the Church in Seoul!

included by Archimandrite Sotirios Trambas in another account of the consecration, which he wrote himself.[15]

Twenty-two years after her tonsure, the day of Deaconess Maria's final departure from Korea came. It was July 13, 2000. The Korean community of St. Nicholas in Seoul said goodbye to her as she was: a deaconess. As a token of their love, they offered her a crystal vase, on the base of which, under a red cross, the following was engraved in Korean: "May this serve as a token of our appreciation for the Rev. Deaconess Maria's tireless material and spiritual contribution and sacrificial efforts for the mission of the Korean Orthodox Church over 25 years. Together with our best wishes and prayers, may you always enjoy the abundant grace of our Lord."[16]

I don't believe that this gesture on the part of the Korean faithful was simply a formality, nor only an expression of love. I take it also as a request: welling up from the bowels of the missionary community, their voice cries out to those who boast about Orthodoxy, and we would do well to pay attention. There is a reason, after all, that we have ears and not just mouths: "He who has an ear, let him hear what the Spirit says to the churches" (Rev 3:6).[17] I thus take it as the faithful's plea for the church to constitute itself in a way that allows it to fulfill its divine mission. The charismata (spiritual gifts) are to take flesh and blood in ministries with real content, far from vain and empty titles. The revival of the order of deaconesses—of apostolic motherhood—as a practical function of the Body, hangs in the balance.

---

15. *The Orthodox Church of Korea:* vol. 1, *Testimonies*, 62 (the text was first published in the journal *Fos Ethnon*, 193).

16. I am grateful to Fr. Daniel (Chang Kyu) Na, pastor of the Holy Church of the Apostle Paul in Incheon, South Korea, who provided an English translation at my request.

17. Cp. the brilliant remarks of the current Metropolitan of Korea (then Archimandrite) Ambrosios Zografos: "The missionary who trusts no one but himself, on the grounds that the 'others' are still 'spiritually immature,' [. . .] will find it impossible to properly inspire and train his coworkers." Archimandrite Ambrosios Zografos, "Educational Presuppositions and Theoretical Emphases for the Development of Mission," *Synaxis* 78 (2001): 37 [in Greek].

Deaconess Maria Spyropoulou, who bore many children, thus journeyed from the open skies of the historical incarnation of the gospel to the eternal heaven of the triune God. She supported, encouraged, loved, taught, cared, and became—as she noted with joy—"grandmother Maria" for the children of her spiritual children. She always strived to be transparent so that the light of Christ, which she preached in both word and action, could pass unhindered through her.

(ii) THE STATEMENT OF SUPPORT BY ORTHODOX LITURGISTS FOR THE REVIVAL OF THE ORDER OF DEACONESS BY THE PATRIARCHATE OF ALEXANDRIA

It has come to our attention that the venerable Patriarchate of Alexandria, after due consideration, has decided to reinstitute the ancient order of deaconess, in order to better serve the pastoral needs of the ever-increasing number of missionary parishes within the Patriarchate, which serves the entire continent of Africa. The validity of this decision, however, has been questioned by some.

We, the undersigned, active and emeriti professors of liturgics and liturgical theology at various theological schools and seminaries in Greece and the United States of America, wish to express respectfully our support for His Beatitude Patriarch Theodoros and the Holy Synod of the Patriarchate of Alexandria in their efforts to restore, in a timely fashion, the order of deaconess within the borders of the Patriarchate.

The historical, theological, canonical, and liturgical validity of the order of deaconess has been attested to time and again in recent years by Orthodox scholars and theologians. Although the order of deaconess gradually fell into decline by the end of the fifteenth century, it survived among the Oriental Orthodox Churches and in some monastic communities. The Russian Orthodox Church before the 1917 Revolution and again in more recent times has considered restoring it. Likewise, St. Nektarios and other contemporary Greek bishops have ordained deaconesses. In fact, the Church of Greece established a School of Deaconesses, which ultimately developed into a school for social workers.

The reinstitution of the female diaconate does not constitute an innovation, as some would have us believe, but the revitalization of a once functional, vibrant, and effectual ministry in order to provide the opportunity for qualified women to offer in our era their unique and specific gifts in the service of God's people as publicly commissioned and authorized educators, evangelists, preachers, counselors, social workers, etc.

Initially, the liturgical role of the female diaconate, according to the sources, appears to have been limited. These same sources provide us with the rite of ordination of a female deacon, which is strikingly similar to that of the male deacon. Significantly, the liturgical vestments are the same as those of the male deacon's. The decision as to whether or not women deacons will perform added liturgical functions in our times, as one theologian puts it, "remains exclusively the prerogative of bishops in synod."

Indeed, the very process of restoring the female diaconate requires careful consideration of several other factors as well, including the adequate preparation and education of the people who will be called upon to receive, honor, and respect the deaconesses assigned to their parishes. Also crucial to the process of restoration is to carefully articulate the qualities and qualifications of the candidates for the office. St. Paul, in his Pastoral Epistles, provides guidance as to the qualities required of candidates. The canons tell us of some qualifications, such as the minimum age. However, nothing is said of other qualifications, such as education and marital status. These and other matters, including the public attire, remuneration, and the method of assignment and removal of the deaconess, must also be addressed. Above all, the process requires that the role and functions of the deaconess be identified, properly defined, and clearly stated.

Talk of the restoration of the order of female deacons has been with us for several decades. In fact, one of the conclusions (VIII) of the Inter-Orthodox Symposium, "The Place of the Woman in the Orthodox Church," which was held on the Island of Rhodes in 1988, addressed this very issue. It bears repeating parts of the conclusion: "The apostolic order of deaconesses should be revived . . . The revival of this ancient order should be envisaged on the basis of the ancient prototypes testified in many sources . . . Such a revival would represent a positive response to many of the needs and demands of the contemporary world in many spheres . . . and in response to the increasing specific needs of our time . . . The revival of women deacons in the Orthodox Church would emphasize in a special way the dignity of woman and give recognition to her contribution to the work of the Church as a whole."

Generally speaking, it is safe to say that only doctrinal impediments and commonly accepted authoritative precedents would preclude an autocephalous Church from enacting liturgical reforms within its borders. Liturgical and canonical issues that have implications beyond the local church are generally resolved through a consensus of the autocephalous churches. The restoration of the female diaconate is such that neither doctrinal issues nor authoritative precedents are at stake. It is refreshing to know that a local Church has taken up the challenge, has studied the matter carefully, and is proposing measures for the implementation of a significant reform, the restoration of the order of deaconess, through a prudently conceived program.

In light of these positive developments, we respectfully support the decision of the Patriarchate of Alexandria to restore the female diaconate, thus giving practical application to an idea that has been discussed and studied by pastors and theologians for decades.

With deep reverence and respect,

Evangelos Theodorou,
Emer. Professor of the Theological School of the University of Athens
Alkiviadis Calivas,
Emer. Professor of the Holy Cross Greek Orthodox School of Theology
Paul Meyendorff,
Emer. Professor of St. Vladimir's Orthodox Theological Seminary
George Filias,
Professor of the Theological School of the University of Athens
Panagiotis Skaltsis,
Professor of Theological School of the University of Thessaloniki
Stylianos S. Muksuris,
Professor of the Byzantine Catholic Seminary
Nicholas Denysenko,
Jochum Professor and Chair of Valparaiso University
Phillip Zymaris,
Professor of the Holy Cross Greek Orthodox School of Theology

John Klentos,
Professor of Graduate Theological Union

October 25, 2017

(iii) RESOURCES

St. Phoebe Center for the Deaconess

The St. Phoebe Center for the Deaconess is a non-profit, private organization established in 2013 in the United States to "educate and prayerfully advocate for the revival of the ordained female diaconate to help serve the ministerial needs of the Orthodox Church and the world today." It sponsors conferences and webinars, encourages networking, and provides guidance for hosting an educational event. In addition, "[it] is the largest online resource on the female diaconate and its revival" in the following categories at www.orthodoxdeaconess.org/resources/:

- Frequently Asked Questions
- Videos and Webinars
- Scholarship on the Female Diaconate
- Prayers for the Ordination of a Deaconess
- Canons
- From the *Didascalia*
- Websites
- Appeals for the Restoration of the Female Diaconate
- Publications
- Books
- Radio Interviews
- Excerpts from Publications
- Articles and Letters

CONTRIBUTORS

His All-Holiness Ecumenical Patriarch **Bartholomew** is Archbishop of Constantinople-New Rome.

Dr. Evanthia **Adamtziloglou** (now Sr. Theologia in the Convent at Panorama) taught biblical studies at the University of Thessaloniki.

Dr. Eirini **Artemi** is Lecturer at the Institute of Biblical Studies at the Hebrew University of Jerusalem and at the Open Hellenic University in Athens.

Rev. Dr. Leonide **Beka Ebralidze,** a Georgian Orthodox theologian, completed his doctorate at the Pontifical Oriental Institute of Rome.

Christine **Chaillot** is the author of books on Oriental Orthodox Churches and the dialogue between Eastern and Oriental Orthodoxy.

Rev. Dr. John **Chryssavgis** is Archdeacon of the Ecumenical Patriarchate and Honorary Professor at the Sydney College of Divinity.

Dr. Zoya **Dashevskaya** is Dean of St. Philaret Christian Orthodox Institute of Moscow.

Dr. Aikaterini **Drosia** studied at the Theological School of the University of Thessaloniki and teaches religious education in Crete.

Dr. Valerie **Karras** holds doctorates in patristic theology from the Aristotelian University of Thessaloniki and church history from the Catholic University of America.

Dr. Ally **Kateusz** is Research Associate at the University of Missouri (USA) and Fellow at Wijngaards Institute of Catholic Research (UK).

Spyridoula-Eleni **Mantziou** holds a masters in theology from the Open Hellenic University.

Knarik O. **Meneshian** is an Armenian journalist and author on the Armenian religious and cultural tradition.

Rev. Alexander **Mramornov** is Associate Professor and Director of the Cultural Institute "Spasskoe Delo."

Dr. Niki **Papageorgiou** is Professor of Sociology of Religion in the School of Theology at the Aristotle University of Thessaloniki.

Dr. Athanasios **Papathanasiou** is Associate Professor of Missiology, Intercultural Christian Witness and Dialogue, at the Supreme Ecclesiastical Academy of Athens.

Dr. Dimitrios **Passakos** is Associate Professor of Social and Cultural Anthropology at the Higher Ecclesiastical Academy of Athens.

Dr. Teva **Regule** is Adjunct Professor at Boston College and President of the Orthodox Theological Society in America.

Marilyn **Rouvelas** has published and edited books on Orthodox Christianity and spirituality for adults and children.

Dr. Vassiliki **Stathokosta** is Associate Professor of Theology at the Theological School of the University of Athens.

Dr. Nikolaos G. **Tsirevelos** studied theology in Thessaloniki, lectured at the "Logos" University (Albania), and teaches at the Volos Academy for Theological Studies.

Professor Emeritus Petros **Vassiliadis** is Honorary President of CEMES and Director of the Theological Graduate Program at the International Hellenic University.

Dr. Evi **Voulgaraki-Pissina** is Associate Professor of Missiology at the Theological School of University of Athens.

Dr. Phyllis **Zagano**, American author and academic, was a member of the Papal Commission for the Study of the Diaconate of Women (2016–2018).

www.ingramcontent.com/pod-product-compliance
Lightning Source LLC
Chambersburg PA
CBHW050200240426
43671CB00013B/2191